THE MESSAGE IN OUR TIME

Other Books by Pir Vilayat Inayat Khan

TOWARD THE ONE

THE SUFI MASTERS

NEW AGE MEDITATIONS

Published in San Francisco by

HARPER & ROW, PUBLISHERS

New York, Hagerstown, San Francisco, London

THE MESSAGE IN OUR TIME

the life and teaching of the Sufi Master

Pir-O-Murshid Inayat Khan

by

PIR VILAYAT INAYAT KHAN

Many of the quotations in this book are from unpublished sources; about this material Hazrat Inayat Khan wrote:

No doubt a time will come when these Gathas will be given to a larger population. But just now this privilege my mureeds will appreciate.

To express my ideas fully my own words are necessary. When they are interpreted they seem clothed in clothes that do not belong to them.

Do not change my word, form or phrase unless it is most necessary. Even so, most carefully avoid all changes which can be avoided; otherwise you might lose the sense of my teaching, which is essential to the Message as the perfume in the rose. If the form in which I give my teaching seems to you not as correct as it ought to be from a literary point of view, do not mind, let it be my own language. There will come a time when there will be a search for my own words. Just now, if my words are not accepted as the current coin, they will always be valued as the antique.

Hazrat Inayat Khan makes clear his wish that those of his teachings that were restricted to the perusal of initiates of various degrees would one day be made public. I have aimed at respecting the original phrasing, but have taken the liberty to edit wherever necessary, as implied in the text above, since most of the quotations in this book are borrowed from verbatim reports of lectures and not written by Hazrat Inayat Khan's pen.

FIRST EDITION

Designed by Patricia Girvin Dunbar

Library of Congress Cataloging in Publication Data

Inayat Khan, Pir Vilayat.
 The message in our time.

 Includes index.
 1. Inayat Khan, 1882–1926. 2. Sufism—Biography.
I. Title.
BP80.I55I52   1979   297'.4'0924 [B]   78-4751

ISBN 0-06-064237-8

---

78 79 80 81 82 52 10 9 8 7 6 5 4 3 2 1

Acknowledgments

The author extends his heartfelt thanks to all those who have helped in editing and typing the manuscript and checking the references, in particular Mr. Richard Morley, Mr. Guy Phillips, Mr. Munir Graham, Ms. Siddiqi Kiss-Kirsch, and Ms. Wahaba Broede.

Dedicated to all the masters, saints, and prophets who form the ranks of the hierarchies of the spiritual government of the world.

My deep sigh rises above as a cry of the earth, and an answer comes from within as a message.—Pir-O-Murshid Inayat Khan (Gayan, 72)

List of Illustrations

Contents

x

There is a race of half-gods that persists upon the earth. We look upon them for a while calling them men, but they are of an immortal stuff somewhat more deific than ourselves, and only insofar as their seraphic vision shakes us in the innermost of our being, only insomuch as we receive and comprehend their utterance, do we partake in brief and finite measure of their godlikeness.

When we write of these persistent half-gods let us dip our quill in light, not ink. Let us write of them with passion, not with platitude. Better still, let us sit at their feet and hearken to them, writing only when the marvel and the magic of their power and wisdom strike fire from the fagots of our silent heart, and when our writing shall be a flame upon the surrounding night.
—Kahlil Gibran

Preamble

When we strove to understand why things happen the way they do, Hazrat Pir-O-Murshid Inayat Khan pointed out how one-sided our private point of view must necessarily be in comparison with the divine outlook, whose vision we restrict through the limitation of our understandings. And when we struggled to unfold pent-up potentialities, he showed us how the vastness of the universe knocking at the door of our personality suffers from our little faith in the divine perfection vested in us. When we strained to see into the souls of others, he carried us to a pinnacle from which we could see them in ourselves, and ourselves in them. When we coveted joy, he led us into the dance of the soul, defying the gravity pull of the ego, moving away in freedom from the staleness of our fossilized assumptions, so that we danced ourselves out of ourselves into cosmic ecstasy. And when we yearned to grasp the purpose of our lives, he beckoned us to dedicate ourselves to an overall purpose in the service of divine guidance—a challenge worth living and dying for.

As we penetrate into Hazrat Inayat Khan's thinking, feeling, and experiencing, communing with him by his presence in his teaching, rather than trying to interpret it in our limitation, he comes right into our thinking, placing us in the perspective that we had failed to see because of our egocentrism. He reattunes us to the divine emotion that we had so long forsaken, owing to the impression of the earth. When our self-confidence has grown weary, he edges into our conscience, rededicating us to the truth we had inadvertently betrayed and which was beckoning to us all the time under the scepter of our highest ideal.

When approaching this thinking, or rather the place from which it encompasses us, we realize how vain it is to hope to know, when knowing would shatter our minds; or to see, if getting close will burn our eyes; or to love, when our heart would agonize by love's wounds; or to peer into secrets whose betrayal would flood the world; or to wield a power that would turn the tables on us!

First achieve, says the Master, before you endeavor to unfold potentialities—in fact, in order to unfold, as a preliminary to realization. Attain realization that you may become on earth what you are and always have been in your eternal self, then resurrect by letting all that you have become be transmuted into an essence that survives the dissolution inherent in the process of becoming.

THE MESSAGE IN OUR TIME

Part I

THE WAY OF THE
ASCETIC

CHAPTER 1

Master, Saint, or Prophet?

I am a tide in the sea of life, bearing toward the shore all who come within my enfoldment.—Gayan, 72

Many children used to play in the field opposite Fazal Manzil, the house of Hazrat Pir-O-Murshid Inayat Khan at Suresnes, near Paris—our house. Dutch children, French children, English, German, Swedish, Italian. Yes, I was among them. We spoke the language that children of all lands know so well to make themselves readily understood, peering through the high grass at that mighty figure descending the front steps of Fazal Manzil, opening the gate, crossing the road and wending his way along the narrow path leading to the lecture hall, walking with such majesty that we hid in the grass in wonderment! He could not possibly be my daddy or that of my brothers or sisters! No, he was the father of us all, young or old, the grand patriarch around whom our lives and beings revolved. Later it became clear that he had made a little spot on earth a paradise by his presence.

It was 1926, the annual Summer School. The *mureeds* (pupils), from all walks of life, were gathered from all corners of the planet and congregated in that prosaic hall covered with ivy at the end of the field. They had been waiting in silence and awe, and each heart stirred as his mystical atmosphere was already felt behind their backs as he advanced up the aisle leading to the pulpit. When his figure emerged before their eyes, he filled the hall by his presence, calm, radiant, exalted. It was a communion with a being so sacred that he seemed to walk out of the Old or New Testament. He looked at them with a glance that flashed from some distant vastness, searching their souls. What were the thoughts that beset their minds in those timeless moments? Today, as we read their memoirs, we catch a hint of the awe and reverence and sheer enchantment, for this was the most important thing that could happen to a person.

4

Thoughts flashed back to the past; the prophets, magi, rishis, dervishes, and heroes we had relegated to a bygone past were stepping right out of our scriptures and legends and continuing to live, for we had the evidence right in front of our eyes.

The fishermen among whom Jesus Christ walked were incapable of knowing the greatness of the Master, and not ready to understand the Message He had brought. And yet they used to stand spellbound in the presence of the Master.

Indeed, we were experiencing the enchantment of that wonderful personality, the wanderer from the East who had come into our lives to stay.

The personality of the prophet is the divine net in which God captures the souls drifting in the world.

When he ascended the steps to the platform, many felt this was someone they had always known. He looked right into our souls with a luminous glance that made many aware for the first time of the very existence of their souls, which, so far, had seemed just a theory. After the communion in silence, when he attuned all present to a high pitch, his voice started suffusing the atmosphere, slowly and gently at first, filling the hall with vibrations that seemed to pour in from another world. The personal communication with his presence was so impelling and fulfilling that there was no room in people's minds to follow the intricacies of his teaching, except in snatches. They knew that it was being transcribed and consequently they would be able to go through it at their leisure, but here before their eyes was the rarest and most inspiring spectacle they had ever come across and they wished to take in every iota of it.

When we now read Murshid's teaching in print, we are partaking of only one dimension of an originally multidimensional reality, unless we make the effort to penetrate into his consciousness retrospectively. Since the teaching was formulated from the vantage point of a consciousness raised above the usual personal focus, it makes sense in proportion to the level to which we can raise our consciousness while reading it. In fact, the Master helped people to understand the issue behind their problems by modulating their consciousness under the spell of his own attunement. At those moments pupils were able to see the cause behind the cause of their problems. Meanwhile he was picking up each thought of each person and answering it. An obsessing thought outshone every other: Who is this being? How incredibly privileged I am to be able to meet such a being! What meaning does he have in my life?

"He must be a master!" thought the Theosophists who had heard so much of the masters in the Far East from Blavatsky. Murshid himself had talked highly of the masters, so that it was easier for the pupils to see their greatness in the descriptions he was giving than to recognize the real thing in front of them, camouflaged by his humility.

Some directly asked me if I was a master! It made me speechless. What could I have said? The truth or a lie? Could I have claimed and have become one amongst the various false claimants, as there are so many in this world? Even so I was reluctant in saying no. If ever I said anything, it was, "If you wish to think of me as your father, or your brother, or your friend, or your servant, it is all right."

If I were to tell you that I am so and so and so and so, that would not give you anything, and if I told you that I am this or I am that then it would be a taught belief, a belief which I have taught you to believe. I would rather not do it. Besides, truth is its own evidence. What is true will sound itself in every heart, sooner or later. Whether the heart is not ready yet, or little ready, or fully ready, as the sound will re-echo through a gong, so the truth will echo through hearts. The Message of God is the Truth, that must echo sooner or later through the heart, and no claims, no proclamations, no recommendations, no pleadings will make anything true which is not true. And what is true cannot be spoiled or denied, or stopped by anybody. What is true will prove to be true to the end. That is our situation. You learn the path [of realization] of God, the path of philosophy without any claim on my part. Let your heart tell you about the Message, about your Murshid. On the part of Murshid there is no attempt to make you feel or know what Murshid is. Besides, is it not enough to know that Murshid is your friend, your father, your counsellor, someone who understands you, someone who stands by you in your struggles, in sorrows, in joys? That is enough. We shall work together, we shall stand hand in hand to do the service to humanity. We do not want any claims, we do not want to say I am this or I am that.

The greater a person is in spiritual advancement, the more unassuming he becomes.[1]

The Master had already encountered the same blindness in someone who did not see the greatness of his own *murshid* (*guru*, or teacher).

Once I met a learned man, a doctor of philosophy with a great many degrees. We spoke about the deeper side of life. And he became very interested in what I said and told me that he thought very highly of me; so I thought that if I were to tell him about my teacher how much more interesting it would be for him. I told him, "There is a wonderful man in this city; he has no comparison in the whole world." "Are there such people?" he asked, "I would very much like to see him. Where does he live?" And I told him in such and such a part of the city. He said, "I live there also, where is his house? I know all the people there. What is his name?" So I told him. He said, "For twenty years I have known this man and now you are telling me about him!" I thought to myself, "In a hundred years you would not have been able to know him." He was not ready to know him.

Once I asked my spiritual teacher how we can recognize the godly man. And my teacher replied, "It is not what he says and it is not what he seems to be, but it is the atmosphere that his presence creates. That is the proof, for no one can create an atmosphere which does not belong to his spirit."[2]

Of course, they had become Hazrat Pir-O-Murshid Inayat Khan's disciples because they recognized him, though he told one close disciple that he had to screen himself, or rather screen people from himself, when he found that the power coming through him was overwhelming beyond what people could bear. There is a story told by the Sufi Farid-ud-Din Attar of a king whose splendor and beauty were so great that his subjects fainted as he rode by in his chariot, so he had to wear a veil to protect people from his radiance. When one witnessed that power, and the way Murshid was transforming people and circumstances all around, it became obvious that he fitted perfectly with the description of a master to be found in his teaching. By setting the example he was giving encouragement to those gifted with the propensities of following the path of mastery.

It is a path of accomplishment. All that the master takes up, he accomplishes. The path of the master requires self-discipline and will-power to make headway through life. He conquers himself; he battles with life; he is at war with destiny; he crusades against all that seems to him wrong; he finds the key to the secrets unknown to him; he moulds as he likes the personalities that come in touch with him; he tunes personalities to the tone which will suit his orchestration.[3]

The work of the master is to protect individuals and to safeguard the world, to keep away all disasters that might be caused by the inharmony of the nature, both of individuals and of the collectivity.[4]

Sixteen years before this gathering, while on the ship on the way from India to America, he had foreseen the monumental dimensions of his mission, which would have seemed like an impossible dream if it had not been for his implicit power to overcome all personal misgivings. Here he was at the peak of its fulfillment by dint of that indomitable will, persevering yet so gentle, which he ascribed to the Divine Will. By what means he accomplished his task will never be entirely known. What a taskmaster he was to himself! How he had sat up meditating for the best part of the night for years while on his constant travels, after crowded days counseling disciples; how he had faced starvation, giving food to guests, while he kept none for himself; how he had sat serenely in meditation in the middle of air raids in London when everyone else ran for shelter; how he had faced incredible pain unflinchingly, and often masked pain while lecturing. This discipline Murshid demonstrated consistently throughout his life. Murshid underwent an operation on his gums, all the teeth being extracted and an incision cut the length of his gum, without any anesthetic, and he did not show the slightest sign of the agony he was going through, to the utter amazement of the surgeon. He practiced more than he preached, and he used the power he gained by concentration to help people.

Another time Murshid showed this power by opening the mind of a mureed traveling on the train with him, enabling her to see a scene she had to see:

The journey is from Holland to Paris, and the way taken is through part of the country then known as the *Devastated Area*. The train is approaching Mons, that name which no English heart can hear without the tremor of an anguished pride and pain, that spot sacred through all future generations as the Calvary of an unspoilt youth of a Nation. The Master feels the quickened pulse of the disciple's heart, and with His unfailing response to need He answers it. Turning to another pupil, who is not English, He asks to be left alone with the disciple; and, when the door into the corridor is shut, He looks steadily out of the window for a moment or two, and then closes His eyes. The disciple followed His example; and then, with His Power staying and supporting through endless vistas and red-hot mists of agony and pain, sees as it was—the *War*. No words can paint those scenes—though many pens have tried; seen as it is now by the disciple in one complete whole (and not, as by those who took part in it, in separate sections and fractions of sections), to see the War is to see into the cauldron of Hell itself—a cauldron from which arise, as from some vast abyss in the bowels of the earth on which we live, the fumes of a poison deadlier than death, brewed from the lusts and hates of men. Red skies and murky clouds of pitch, the stench of dissolution and decay, the foulness of the tainted air and breath of human life!; all this and more have many seen, and told it in the quiet days of peace; but not to them might it be given to see the Picture that God saw and *lived*, lived as we men have marvelled He could do, unmoved and silent while an Age passed out beneath His Feet. Not theirs to see the life that leapt immortal from the festering clay, not theirs to note the white souls trooping up to God. The soldiers saw the angel hosts at Mons, for once the enshrouding horror broke and let them through; but only once the glory flamed from out the Pit, and all the time those heavenly forms were there, and pain was drenched with dew from out their hearts, and dim eyes glazing saw their light and closed to wake with God.[5]

Another story illustrates Murshid's masterful power, together with his gentle concern in restraining it should it interfere with human freedom:

One day a young man came to him, a son of a mureed, and said his mother had sent him, for he was in a great despair, thinking that Murshid would give him some advice; and Murshid asked him what was the reason of his despair. He answered he had loved a girl who first showed him a great love, but now she was beginning to get detached, because she seemed to be getting interested in some other young man. Murshid seemed amused at hearing this from quite a young man. He said, "Then what do you wish to do?" The young man said, "I want her to love me or else life has no interest for me any longer." Murshid laughed and said, "O, life is always interesting. If not in one object, in another object, one finds interest. It is perhaps your momentary spell that makes you so depressed. Let her alone, if she loves someone else, you go and love somebody else too." The young man made a face of disappointment and looked at Murshid, who asked, "What do you want?" "I want her to love me." Murshid said, "Go just now and she will be all right." He went immediately from there to her and found her to his great surprise entirely changed, as amiable, sympathetic and agreeable as ever. The young man was so pleased that he left a note of thanks at the house of the Murshid. When next day he went, she was quite indifferent and did not care for him and he again was very unhappy. For two or three days he was too depressed and then came again to Murshid and said, "The time when you sent me she was loving and good, but after that she has been treating me in the same manner as before. Now I do not know what to do." But Murshid said, "What do you want?" He said, "I want her to be good to me." Murshid said, "Go just now, she will be good to you," and when he went there she was very kind to him, very loving, but only that day; next day she again turned. He came again home and was very disappointed and came to Murshid to give the report of her behavior. Murshid was very amused and said to him, "Now look here, my son, I showed you what power is latent in man. But at the same time this power is not to destroy anybody's freedom. As you wish your freedom in life, so she must have her freedom to choose whom she must love."

The Master's main work was accomplished on the inner planes, communing with people at a high level, and helping them to unfold.

My smallest work in the inner plane is worth more than all I do in the outer world.

By mastering himself, the master unleashes a cosmic law of action and reaction, which confers upon him a power that implements the divine creativity.

Whatever arises in his mind becomes a reality.

Yes, he must be a master. But others noticed a note of gentleness in his being. Once a mureed came to see him in a rage, fully decided to quit because he had been badly treated by a fellow mureed. After a few minutes of conversation, the pupil was completely transformed. "What is it that you have done to me to have changed my mind so completely?" he asked. "What is it about you? You've completely disarmed me," Murshid replied. "It is because I have disarmed myself." Murshid described this as the crucifixion of that part of man's being which he has created in himself, and which is not his real self, although on the way it always appears that he has crucified his own self.

On seeing this graciousness in Murshid, some thought he fit his own description of the saint:

The work of the saint is to console the wretched, to take under the wings of mercy and compassion those left alone in life, to bless the souls that he meets on his path.[6]

His work is to help all those who may be disappointed at the results of all the little expectations they had, of their love and devotion. The saintly soul accepts all insults as a purifying process. He is therefore resigned to every loss, for there is no loss without some gain, and there is no gain without any loss. Renunciation is not difficult for that soul, for in renunciation it finds its freedom. No sacrifice is too great for the saintly soul, for it gives it happiness. It need not learn generosity, for this is its nature, its character. Modesty, humility, tolerance and forgiveness are part of the saint's being; he cannot do otherwise for he knows no other way.[7]

Had he not given up everything that life had offered him, particularly his music—if one only knew what that sacrifice meant—in order to help those assembled at the Summer School, and many others throughout the world, who valued what he had to give.

His being was paradoxically perplexing, no doubt because of the rare blend of an overwhelming divine power such as one would expect to find in Moses, together with a disarming gentleness; or the deportment and disposition of a sage, while he would clad his wisdom in the most simple terms, sometimes almost with the simple and endearing innocence of a child; or again, a strange combination of a winning joy with a desolate sadness beyond description. No doubt sensitivity enhances one's awareness of all the suffering in the world, the starving millions, the ailing in hospitals, victims of war or natural catastrophes, the anguish of a person dying of cancer, people abandoned by those they love, parents of a retarded child, the mental confusion of the victims of the psychological violence of our time. Murshid was tuning into the Divine Awareness of what is happening to us. At times he would express an inconsolable sadness when he was picking up a strain of suffering in the distant reaches, although everything seemed to be smooth in the immediate environment. One time he had to interrupt a lecture because of the urgency of the calls upon his attention from a distance; when asked what happened, he said there had been a terrible catastrophe in the Far East and thousands were calling for help. The next day the papers reported the great 1924 earthquake in Japan.

Murshida Saintsbury-Green witnessed another scene when Murshid's heart bled in communion with abject human suffering:

The disciple awaits the Master in the dim building; alone as it would seem, when suddenly a movement is felt rather than heard in one of the darkest corners and two figures move from the shadows. They approach the disciple, who sees that one is that of a woman, and that she leads by the hand a man, whose head and face are covered almost entirely with white wrappings, falling loosely as if just undone. In broken words the woman speaks, "The great Saint! Last night I heard Him speak and this evening I have brought—no! do not look!—but would He, could He help!" It is too late, sick and shuddering the pupil involuntarily recoils; for in that instant it was visible! a face—human once—but now so marred and ravaged by the foulest of all diseases that but half of it remains. So awful is the sight that even its piteousness is powerless to prevent the horror too instinctive to be kept back. The woman draws the merciful folds of the enswathing bandage into place; but all the time she is repeating her half-articulate request, "Would He—will He?—"

Ah! yes, he is there, standing at the door of the vestry and beckoning them in; it closes behind the trailing forms and once more the dim silence enfolds the waiting disciple. They do not again enter the Church, but go out by another door, and after a long interval the Master comes. No word is spoken on that homeward walk, but ever and again, with a deep sigh, the Master lifts his head and looks up at the dark blue sky of night, in which there is no light except the stars. And then, as a cry from a Heart overburdened and borne down by the sins of the World, there came all at once the low, intensely uttered words, "I would rather be known as the Great Consoler than as the Great Teacher." Unconscious of any human presence He walks on in a deeper silence; and the pupil, following, knows that the veil has been for an instant lifted to show the features of a Saint of God.[8]

Another story illustrates this dedication, this time in healing. Murshid was about to give a lecture, when a frenzied lady implored him to help: Her friend's baby was dying. Murshid delayed the lecture, drove to the home of the mother, and, instead of laying hands on the baby, blessed the mother and left. The next morning the doctor called, having fully expected a call from the mother the evening before to say that the baby had breathed his last breath. She said the baby was smiling and kicking. Amazed, the doctor came to the child's bedside and declared that this was medically impossible. The maid said she had seen in the dark the evening before a Christ-figure mounting the stairs and leaving a few moments later, serene and majestic.

Some gurus or murshids rule over their disciples by inspiring awe, exacting blind obedience and formal deference. With Murshid the relationship was founded upon the genuine holiness of being and a trust gained through sharing in service of a cause. In contrast to many gurus and murshids who sit on high thrones and expect people to bow at their feet, he would open the door to the Oriental Room himself and say "Come in" to casual visitors as to long-lost friends, and bid them sit down next to him on a sofa. This touching gesture put them at their ease; however, facing the whole impact of his being, they could not but be overwhelmed with reverence for what he was.

Many remained silent during interviews. But Murshid had the art of putting a shy person immediately at ease by his unruffled calm and peaceful atmosphere, and inspired the most utter confidence as a spiritual father to whom one could confide everything and trust unto death. Mureeds would find that their burning questions, sometimes carefully prepared weeks before the long-awaited five or ten minutes with the Master, would fall aside as superfluous when they entered into his serene presence in the Oriental Room. He was their living answer. He would never give a ready-made solution to an anguished personal problem, for he knew the problem was an opportunity to teach the mureed by bringing him to the point of seeing the solution himself. The will of the mureed was not to be alienated; he was taught to stand upon his own feet, though Murshid helped him by lifting his consciousness. He would know at a distance when a mureed was in difficulty, sometimes even dispatching another mureed with a message.

For the relationship between guru and *chela* (pupil) to be real, it cannot be a formal one; it must be based upon mutual trust, as alpinists attached to the same cord grow to trust each other's reliability. And what does trust mean, if not that the Murshid opens the most secret of his innermost heart to his disciples, "entrusting himself into their hands as a fragile glass, precariously," as Murshid says. But sometimes, not understanding the Murshid's intention and pressing to exert his own will, the disciple says, "If you do not do what I wish, I will break it."

Had he not continued to love those who had betrayed him? Once a woman came to Murshid disconsolate. "Will you ever pardon me? I now realize that I have done a dreadful thing to you!" "I have already forgiven you a long time ago," replied Murshid, "and you are always in my prayers." This was the woman who, after she had incurred Murshid's displeasure for acting insolently toward some of her fellow-mureeds, went to the landlord of the Gordon Square property where Murshid lived in London, and persuaded him to ask Murshid to leave. This accounted for Murshid's sudden departure from London for the Continent. When one realizes that this had been a slur on Murshid's honor and what that meant to his kingly disposition, as he had always been so upright, it is the more evident how the Master had overcome his feelings out of compassion. This same woman had even shared an occasional meal at the Master's house, probably never knowing that to make this hospitality possible the family had had to miss a few meals.

The path of the saint is a constant battle with the self, for there is no end to the world's demands; in this world no one can be too good or too kind. The better one is, the more good is asked of one; the kinder one is, the more kindness is expected from one; and so it goes on through life. The happiness a saintly soul finds, through all the continual sacrifices that he makes as he goes through life, lies in the fact that his will is gradually becoming harmonized with the will of God, so that God's will and his will in time become one. And no one can imagine the happiness that comes except the souls who have experienced the feeling of resignation to all the crosses that one has to bear in life.

The spirit of a saint at last becomes attuned to that of the whole universe. He is in tune with all climates, with the weather, with nature, with the animals and birds; he becomes in tune with the trees and plants, in tune with all atmospheres. with all human beings of various natures, because he becomes the keynote of the whole universe. All harmonize with him: the virtuous souls, the wicked souls, angels and devils, all become in tune. He is in harmony with every object, with every element; he is in tune with those who have passed from this earth, with those in other spheres, as well as with those who live on earth. The moral of a saint is very difficult, but the spirit of the saint is a benediction to himself and a blessing to others.[9]

Yes, when seeing him, one felt indeed how much in harmony he was within himself and with all beings. In all those years there had never been a harsh word from him, and all the people coming from such different walks of life managed to tolerate and even love one another because of his harmonizing influence. What struck a disciple who remembers meeting him when still a lad of fifteen was his prepossessing joviality and contagious humor; little did the disciple realize at the time what a heavy cross the Master was carrying. It was so obvious that Murshid was describing in his teaching precisely how he felt and behaved: he must be a saint!

However, there was yet another dimension of Murshid's being, beyond the master or the saint, that struck his disciples. In the East, most gurus exact of their pupils to concentrate on their picture and contemplate upon their personality; some teach their followers to meditate on their eternal being rather than their personality. As a consequence, many disciples begin to think and feel and act like their teacher. Seeing one's inherent qualities in another who presumably is better able to manifest the very bounty that one feels deeply stored in oneself helps one to believe in oneself and bring one's potentialities to blossom. According to the tradition, the teacher is supposed to proceed thus with his guru, and the guru in turn with his guru. Thus the eternal prototype of man in his perfected form, evidencing the divine attributes, is carried through from the beginning of time by the masters, saints, and prophets succeeding one another. These form, according to the Sufi tradition, the hierarchies of ranks of the spiritual government of the world.

Have you seen the pictures of the Prophets, of Christ, of Zoroaster, of Moses, and of the other Prophets? You will say: "They are made from imagination." I could show you in India the pictures of our murshids, of the Order to which we belong, from Khwaja Muin-ud-din Chishti; the picture of ten or twelve murshids and their mureeds are all alike.

If a person has an expression twenty times a day, a certain impression caused by a certain thought, then in twenty days a person's face is formed according to the thought, and in this way the thought makes the countenance.

Obviously, the greater the being, the greater the scope of his consciousness, for the greater his capacity to encompass and therefore incorporate the attributes evidenced in the vast universe. It is a matter of continually stretching one's consciousness to embrace an ever greater perfection. But who was this guru who, instead of inviting his pupils just to concentrate on himself, beckoned upon them to attune to *all* masters, saints, and prophets?

As he started his lectures, after invoking the One, he would unite in thought with "all the illuminated souls who form the embodiment of the Master, the Spirit of Guidance." In the joint prayer worship he gave, including all religions, called the Universal Worship, the officiant says, lighting the last candle, that it represents "all those who, whether known or unknown to the world, have held aloft the light of truth amidst the darkness of human ignorance." The prophets are named personally in one of the prayers:

Allow us to recognize Thee in all Thy holy Names and Forms; as Rama, as Krishna, as Shiva, as Buddha. Let us know Thee as Abraham, as Solomon, as Zarathustra, as Moses, as Jesus, as Mohammad, and in many other names and forms, known and unknown to the world.

It became obvious that Murshid was not simply promoting an esoteric school among many others, the Sufi Order, but opening the consciousness of people to the Message of our time, the Message of all Masters.

This was precisely the feeling that the pupils experienced in the presence of Murshid: vastness, the vastness of a being staggering in its magnitude, like the vastness of the sky. Thus he spurred his pupils to become less personal and more cosmic. He quoted Sri Krishna:

When Dharma is hindered, then I am born.[10]

He often spoke of Christ, whom he called the Murshid of Murshids:

Some object to Christ being called divine; but if divinity is not sought in man, then in what shall we seek God? . . . One who is conscious of his earthly origin is an earthly man; one who is conscious of his heavenly origin is the son of God.[11]

Those who do not want Christ to be a man drag down the greatness and sacredness of the human being by their argument. . . . But there is nothing wrong in calling Christ God or divine. It is in man that the divine perfection is to be seen. . . . He identified himself with that spirit of which he was conscious . . . with that spirit of perfection which lived before Jesus, and will continue to live till the end of the world, for eternity.[12]

To awaken the awareness of the unity of religions, it was necessary for the consciousness of man in our era to see the Ariadnean thread running through the diversity of personalities of the prophets, as handed down through history.

In what way are the Messengers different from any other human beings? Are we not all humans in respect of God? If each being is like a cell in that body that is the universe, then the Messenger, Christ, or Rasul is like the seed cell. As we know, the gene contains all the characteristics of the plant and more. In that, it differs from other cells which may well contain many potentialities but not all the inheritance of the being.

In the same way, the Christ spirit is perpetuated in humanity, and periodically reappears in various forms. As the seed cell is distinguished from the ordinary cell, though the essence of the other cells is perpetuated through the seed, so the Christ or Rasul thought, always inherent in humanity, may undergo an eclipse and then reappear as another personality. Similarly, humanity is represented in its Messenger.

As Murshid was making us feel the Ariadnean thread running through the diversity of the prophets, a disciple thought: He makes us aware of the divine presence manifested by the prophets we have read about; here we have before us the very embodiment of the sacredness he is talking about. He remembered Murshid saying, speaking of the prophets, that the tour de force of the prophet is his ability to combine the sacredness of the divine with the human touch, more so than any other human being. It is indeed because they rise above their own personalities (however fascinating to their followers), thus becoming impersonal, that prophets become the embodiment of a single being with many facets (if one can use the word *being* to denote the saving grace of humanity which Murshid calls the Spirit of Guidance). This is the reason the followers of Buddha called him the *Tathagata*, the "one who has thus become," never *Gautama* or *Siddhartha*. Traditionally Christians are supposed to say *Christ* or *Jesus Christ*, not *Jesus* alone, and Muslims say the *Prophet Mohammed*. There was a time when Jews would never say *Moses*, but the *Blessed One*. This is the meaning of the Avatar, who is considered to be the continuation of the impersonal reality that can assume several names and forms.

When Jesus Christ is represented as saying, "I am Alpha and Omega, the beginning and the end," it is not meant that either the name or the visible person of Jesus Christ is the Alpha and Omega, but the Masterspirit within. It was this spirit which proclaimed this, moved by its realization of past, present and future life, confident of its eternity. It is the same spirit which spoke through Krishna, saying, "We appear on earth when Dharma is corrupted," which was long before the coming of Christ. During his divine absorption Mohammed said, "I existed even before this creation and shall remain after its assimilation."[13]

It is said in the Qur'an that Abraham, the father of the nations and the fountain from which such streams as Moses, Jesus, and Mohammed came, had offered a prayer when leaving his son Ishmael in the barren desert of Arabia. His heart was broken, and there came forth from it a prayer, "O Lord, bless this land, that it may become a centre of attraction to the whole world." And so it happened in the course of time that the Word of God was born again among the descendants of Ishmael, Mohammed who glorified the name of the Lord of Abraham aloud; this was heard from the depths of the earth to the summit of heaven, and re-echoed from the North to the South Pole; it shook the nations and stirred up races.[14]

An irate woman had once objected to such a broad vision of the Messenger, saying: "Now I believe that Jesus Christ was the Son of God, and our redeemer. And I hear that you consider all the Prophets equal." Murshid answered, "I have never said that all Prophets are equal. I only say that I do not feel equal to judge them." Each prophet was specifically unique in his way, answering the need of his time. This accounts for the need for the differences, which together form a continuity.

When wealth was esteemed, the message was delivered by King Solomon; when beauty was worshipped, Joseph, the most handsome, gave the message; when music was regarded as celestial, David gave his message in song; when there was curiosity about miracles, Moses brought his message; when sacrifice was highly esteemed, Abraham gave the message; when heredity was recognized, Christ gave his message as the Son of God; and when democracy was necessary, Mohammed gave his message as the Servant of God, one like all and among all.[15]

Some felt like adding: When unity was valued, this sacred being came in our midst opening up our perspectives to the continuity of divine guidance and its present renascence. "If only I know whether he is a prophet!" thought one of the mureeds, as Murshid spoke of the prophets of the Old Testament, of the Hindu Avatars, of Buddha, of Christ, of Mohammed. He was answering the question they were asking him in their hearts, "Who are you?" But Murshid made no claim. He taught his mureeds the Islamic adage according to which the Prophet Mohammed was the last prophet in the cycle of what Muslims call *Beni-Israel*, including the prophets mentioned in the Qur'an. This was obviously a way of guarding against all the spurious claims of phoney prophets or avatars we come across. *Khatam ar Rasul il'llah* means the seal of prophethood.

This means that, exactly as the seal protects the contents of a letter, and when the seal is broken, the matter which one wants to read is disclosed, so it is with the words of the prophet. The seal is not a letter, it is only a seal; and so are the prophet's words . . . and when the seal is opened, then everything is disclosed, just as in an open letter.[16]

There is no seal that cannot be opened, though it must not be opened by everyone, but only by the one who has the right to open it. The last one left a warning for the one who would come after him, which was that the prophecy was sealed. It was a clue for his successor that since the claim was now sealed, in the future, the Message should be given without a claim, and it would be the work that was done that would prove its genuineness instead of a claim.[17]

Some realized that he was talking of the very wonder that filled our eyes, something too real to be relegated to a memory of the past. Yet while including and embodying the past, he was extending it into our living spaces. He was preparing for the new age, breaking into new horizons, pointing the way to a liberated spirituality, emancipated from dogmas. Some of the overzealous whispered to each other, "He must be a prophet," for he had merged his personality into the current of prophethood so completely as to identify himself with them. Indeed, there was a dimension there that could not be pigeonholed under the category of master or saint. How can one recognize a prophet?

The Message is the proof of the Messenger.

In the life of the prophet, there is a balance of the power of attainment and the patience to be resigned to the will of God. So the Prophet is at the same time a warrior and a peacemaker. He acts as a warner, a healer, a reformer, a lawyer, a teacher, a priest and as a preacher. Such service keeps the Prophet away from what his soul always craves for: the solitude of the wilderness. The very soul who constantly yearns to flee from the crowd because of his mission, is put right in the midst of the crowd. He must be in the world and yet not of the world. His life's mission is to serve humanity in time of need.[18]

He comes into the lives of those who are meant to be guided along the spiritual path. He is sent to nations when they are meant to change their conditions. . . .
Rasul is the world-messenger, who comes for all people at the time of the world's need . . . answering the cry of humanity.[19]

The prophet opens to you the vantage point enjoyed by the prophets looking upon the destiny of mankind in its overall sweep and surge toward fulfillment, and jolts it with a new impulse.

He is an ambassador of the spiritual hierarchy.[20]
The prophetic soul must of necessity rise so high that it can hear the voice of God, yet at the same time it must bend so low that it can hear every little whisper of human beings.[21]
The branch has bent and the fruit has touched the earth, but it has not lost connection with the stem.[22]
The life of the prophet is . . . the imperfect self journeying towards perfection and at the same time bearing the burden of numberless souls, many of whom have not yet learnt to walk even upon the earth.

Murshid was answering questions that would have never occurred to them to ask, while many felt embarrassed at asking the personal questions they had entertained for years, for they seemed suddenly so irrelevant and unimportant. He had a different way of answering questions than the usual metaphysical dialectics most people expect of a philosopher, whose theorectical inferences may weave vicious circles, binding the mind.

Even the presence of the prophet is the answer to every question.[23]

Most people, faced with something of great significance, failed to find the words or concepts to express their question.

How difficult it is to translate fully the poetry of one language into the poetry of another. How much more difficult, then, it must be to translate or to interpret the ideas of the divine world to the human world!

The prophet's mission is to sound the celestial note, to present the divine point of view.

God speaks to the prophet in His divine tongue, and the prophet in his turn interprets it in the language of man.[24]

The task of the prophet is a most difficult one; it is trying to present to the world the whole ocean in a bottle.[25]

As such, it is his mission to make the point of view of the masters, saints, and prophets who govern the world intelligible to people who cannot possibly imagine how all beings and situations look from Olympian heights. He has to fathom the limitations of human thinking while keeping a hold of the divine vantage point, and express the divine point of view in terms of human concepts and vocabulary. In order to answer people's questions, prophets cannot use the human tongue, but have to use the human mind, in comparison with which their thinking is like infinity. There are no human words, there is no human logic to convey their realization. It can only be given in approximations. Imagine—the breadth of cosmic insight has to be passed into a limited frame, like a three-dimensional scene in a two-dimensional photograph. Better still, imagine that one sees a scene simultaneously from an infinite number of vantage points, and tries to describe it to someone who has seen and imagined things from only one vantage point.

The prophet can never tell the ultimate truth, which only his soul knows and no words can explain. His mission is, therefore, to design and paint and picture the truth in words that may be intelligible to mankind.[26]

But if Murshid heard of any speculations about his status, he would always say, "If you like to consider me as your brother, or father, or friend, or servant, it is all right, you may do so. But offer your allegiance to the divine message throughout history." Yet some said, "How can we discount what we are witnessing?"

He who appeals to the human intellect will knock at the gate of the human brain; he is a speaker. He who appeals to the human emotions will enter into the hearts of men; he is a preacher. But he who penetrates the spirit of his hearers is a prophet, who will abide in their souls forever.[27]

Why, if he is a prophet, thought some, are there so few people in this hall? And others: Why are the masses so blind as to fail to take this unique opportunity of grasping a being like this with both hands? The master explained why in describing a play:

It shows how people are drawn by a real sage, and at the same time how dissatisfied they remain. They are drawn because it is a living magnet, and yet they are dissatisfied because they cannot understand his language. And no sooner the man of the ordinary evolution comes and he talks to them than they can at once understand and follow him. When there is a false one that comes there, he wants to take them away; he can take them away in a moment's time, because his mentality belongs to them and their understanding belongs to him.

It was clearly to avoid false claims by charalatans that the Islamic *Khatam an Nabbiya* (Seal of the Prophets) or *ar Rasul il'Ilah* (of the Messengers of God) was formulated.

The seers and saints, who live a life of seclusion, are happy when compared with the prophet, whose life's work is in the midst of the crowd. The prophet, representing God and His message, is tested and tried and examined by every soul; a thousand searchlights are thrown upon him; and he is not judged by one judge but by numberless judges; every soul is a judge and has its own law to judge him with.

Here were these beings, gathered together, bemused by the magic of a holy man; but what relevance could this have for the world? We know how he longed for solitude, yet his appearance in the streets of New York had caused a traffic jam, and his meeting with Henry Ford had been hailed by the press as a historic event of the meeting of East and West. People were beginning to test each other's broadmindedness gingerly by saying there is some good in all religions. To say that all religions were one was going a little bit too far, but the Master's Message was wending its way surely if subtly, spurring conversations, tuning consciousness to something people thought was fascinating, though strange and unknown. Yes, he had already foreseen his message sixteen years earlier, when he first traveled to the West:

Will people be favourable or unfavourable to the Message which I am taking from one end of the world to the other? One constant voice I always heard coming from within: Thou art sent on a service, and it is we who will make thy way clear.

And here he was in the lecture hall, filling it with his presence, lost in cosmic consciousness, yet speaking to his followers of their problems that they might understand the spiritual implications from where they were.

A further reason there were not more people in the hall was the bigotry of those whom Murshid called the followers of the followers, contrasted with the followers of Christ or the other prophets. But for this bigotry, they would have recognized their own prophet's reflection in one who was so attuned.

If the same one came in another form, in a garb adapted to another age, would they know him or accept him? No, they would not even recognize him.[28]

Therefore the people of that part of the world who have acknowledged the Hebrew prophets do not for instance recognize Avatars such as Rama and Krishna, or Vishnu and Shiva, simply because they cannot find these names in their scriptures. The same thing occurs in the other part of humanity, which does not count Abraham, Moses or Jesus among its Devatas, as it does not find those names written in the legends with which it is familiar.[29]

Murshid illustrates the problem of the Messenger who is not recognized because people fail to see in him the continuation of the one they are attached to, by the story of the man who renounced his family life and went into retirement to Mount Sinai, taking his eldest son with him. After many years he sent his eldest son home, but the younger children did not recognize him, as "his smooth face had become bearded, and his cheerful look had given way to a serious expression." As he had no proof of his heritage and their mother had died, the guardians were so bold as to attempt to kill him. So it is with the prophet.

They waited while Jesus Christ came and went and they still wait and will wait for ever.[30]

"I am Alpha and Omega, I am the first and the last." Can that mean, "I came only for a time, and then I was called Jesus, and only then did I give a message; I spoke neither before nor after that time."[31]

All the teachers who came before taught for whatever community or group of people they were born, and prophesied the coming of the next Teacher, foreseeing the possibility and the necessity of the continuation of the Message until its fulfillment.[32]

To some that great ideal has appeared and they have called it Jesus Christ. In other parts of the world, among other races and in other times, this same manifestation which human beings felt to be divine was called Buddha or Moses or Mohammed.

And now they were looking at him at close quarters. How could people be so blind as to stick to their prejudices, they thought, when faced with the living evidence of all that they believed in? His being was more than an ordinary consciousness could possibly assess, because people felt that they had become part of his being, or that he incorporated the essence of all beings. At times it dawned upon a mureed that not only was this because he was a composite being, in whom the characteristics of so many prophets of the past had been imprinted, but because each found in him the quality he most cherished: divine power, sovereignty, majesty, nobility, truth, love, compassion, kindness, gentleness, self-sacrifice, intelligence, creativity, wit, luminosity, radiance, purity. No doubt the divine perfection is distributed throughout the universe and all beings display some of the facets of his many-splendored face, thought the mureed; but Murshid was like the heart of the totality of beings, and as the heart, he contained them all.

The Rasul is the soul through which God Himself has attained that which is the purpose of creation, in other words, the Rasul is the one who represents God's perfection through human limitation . . . who is behind the picture which history or tradition makes of him.[33]

Yes, the prophet brings a religion, but that is not all: What he really brings to earth is the living God. . . . In point of fact, God Himself is the messenger. . . . He is seen by all, and yet not really seen . . . Warning of danger and consoling the broken-hearted . . . Master of life within and without, yet the servant of all. Such is the being of the Master. He is man in the sight of man, but God in the Being of God.[34]

This became clear to the mureeds in its extreme magnitude on Saturday evenings. Murshid had started to meditate in the early morning, probably five o'clock, and went on meditating the whole day until evening, when he was literally carried to the hall. As he sat behind the screen, each mureed tiptoed up to sit in his presence for a second. He was peering into existence from his *samadhi*, looking right into their soul.

There comes a time in the life of the prophet or of anyone who contemplates, when whatever object he casts his glance upon opens up and reveals to him what it has in its heart.

Yes, he was revealing the mureeds to themselves, but in their cosmic dimension; more, he was revealing God to them, in a manner that outrides all the teaching ever given in words, because he was revealing the very raison d'être of life. At those moments our personal problems were falling out of focus because he was flashing so great a purpose before our understanding that in comparison any personal purpose seemed hideously selfish and trivial.

Here was his purpose: to make us conscious of the great need of humanity, to make us prophets of the new age. He did not come to the West as a missionary to expand the Sufi Order to the West. No, the Order had grown beyond its origin.

Dare you dedicate yourselves to the purpose of purposes, work for the forward advance of humanity by elevating the consciousness of beings, serving the spiritual government of the world? The path of the prophets is for the strong, the staunch spirits, the dedicated.

There were moments when some still greater dimensions broke through: The miracle of the very happening of life would sweep across one's soul before one had a chance of grasping it, and when one realized it, one was back into consciousness again; try as one might, one could never reiterate or recall it. It was a sense of reality raised to the power of infinity, but flashed into an instant of time and compressed beyond belief in a point of space. Maybe it had to do with that secret of the secrets of life, of which the crucified Sufi Al Hallaj speaks when he says *"ana'l Haqq,* I am the truth!" It was no doubt referring to him that Murshid said:

The soul on its journey reaches a plane where it exclaims, "I am the truth."

The whole accent of the Message which Murshid incorporated was "Make God a reality," and then the miracle happens, "God makes you the truth." Imagine you are gazing upon a master, and suddenly the created aspect of his being only makes sense in terms of what is coming through, and you realize that the reason for this is that his whole being has become the truth! Yes, what struck one continually in his presence was his complete authenticity: He incorporated truth. Why is this so, particularly in this being? Because:

While to many God is imagination, to him God is a reality.[35]

CHAPTER 2

Reconquer Your Inheritance

THE ASCETICS OF INDIA

If I may not dance, what shall I do?—XII, 114

At the time of the birth of Hazrat Inayat Khan in 1882, the clouds of discouragement attendant upon the Indian Mutiny had lifted and a new India was awakening to reforms, social progress, and a happier future. Of all states Baroda was one that seemed to take the lead under the enlightened guidance of Maharajah Sayaji Rao Gaekwar, who encouraged reforms in agriculture and education, so that soon scholars, educators, and artists were drawn to this promising state.

Inayat's family history was steeped with the wonderful foresight and influence of sages and ascetics in whose proximity he grew up, and to whom he was irresistibly drawn. A Sufi wandering ascetic of the Chishti Order foresaw and perhaps promoted the outstanding success and fame of Inayat's grandfather Chole Khan, when the latter was but fifteen. "My soul longs for music," the Sufi said, "pray will you sing for me?" Chole Khan protested that he had no talent for singing, but made a good attempt, whereupon the ascetic said: "Though a poor man, I have power to give you a treasure; I baptize you with the name Moula Bakhsh [God-gifted], and this name shall be known throughout this land of India, and your music will make it famous."

Three years passed, and the young Moula Bakhsh was in search of a teacher. This was no easy matter those days when teachers transmitted their learning as a closely guarded secret, sometimes, if they were sufficiently gifted, to a beloved pupil who had to serve his teacher in his household. Moula Bakhsh heard of a famous singer called Ghasit Khan who had never allowed anyone to know the secret of his art. He traveled to the village, singled out the house where Ghasit was staying, and sat dumbfounded in the garden when he heard his voice. The

25

master used to practice every night between midnight and early morning. The lad befriended the old gatekeeper, keeping him amused with his stories. Sodden with opium from his hukkah, the old man would be glad to have someone to watch for him and would doze off. The young boy would then study and memorize everything he had heard and practice it the next day. The master, passing by the door of Moula Bakhsh's house one day and recognizing his own song, a recent one which he had never sung before anybody, entered the house and asked Moula Bakhsh who was his teacher. "My teacher is great truly," he answered, "but if I reveal his name to you, then indeed any hope of progressing further under his guidance must be given up." Thereupon the Ustad admitted Moula Bakhsh as his pupil.

Moula Bakhsh's masterly exposition of the music of the North of India was a revelation at Mysore. However, the Karnatic style peculiar to the Brahmins of the South, which had remained unadulterated in its almost scientific classicism of tone and rhythm, steeped in Hindu mythology, had a powerful ascendancy upon his soul. But this music was jealously reserved for Brahmins only, and he was told that if he wished to acquire its practice, he must be born again as a Brahmin. Ruffled in his pride, this heir to a Zamindari family established at Sambrial (in Kashmir), whose great-grandfather had been a Brahmin Vyas, left the Court to which he had now become attached, vowing only to return should he have mastered this highly stylized and intricate Brahmin art. He so won the friendship of a venerable Brahmin musician of Malabar called Shubramani Ayar who, despite his orthodoxy (to the point of taking a bath every time the mere shadow of a non-Brahmin fell upon him), taught him all he knew. Now suddenly the Hindus recognized Moula Bakhsh as the reincarnation of their cherished singer Tyagaraja.

Fortified by recognition of his outstanding proficiency in this highly traditional art, Moula Bakhsh returned to Mysore to face a contest with all the musicians of repute of the South—all Brahmins—which lasted ten months, until he was acknowledged by all to have surpassed all the others. Thereupon the Maharajah bestowed upon him a kind of peerage; according to tradition, the insignia thereof consisted of a *kalaggai*, or gold ringlet; the *sarpich*, a chaplet of pearls for the turban; the *chhatra*, or gold canopy held over the head by a foot servant; the *chamar*, or scepter of honor which a servant carries in front; and the *mashal*, a torch that is carried in front and lighted at night. A marriage was then arranged with Kasim Bey, a granddaughter of Tippu Sultan, the ruler of the previous Muslim dynasty, who had for years held out against the British. Accompanied by two retainers of the ancient household, Sultan Khan Sherif and Pir Khan Sherif, she had been living in hiding under the generous protection of the new Hindu ruler, Maharajah Krishna Rajo. Fearing political persecution, the family never referred to her ancestry by name, but she was trained in noble bearing. Invited to the kingdoms of several ruling princes, Moula Bakhsh decided to establish himself in the state of Baroda. In the highly stratified society of the time, musicians were not considered equal with the noble gentry of the court. One can imagine their dismay when Moula Bakhsh displayed himself ceremoniously, according to the standing conferred upon him. Maharajah Khanderao sent an ironic note: "If you wear crown and scepter, what will rajas wear?" Not wishing to stand on distinctions, but on merit, he replied by quoting a Sanscrit verse: "The King is honored in his country, a chief in his district, a fool in his home; but a genius is honored everywhere." The Maharajah hoped to humiliate him by calling a contest of famous musicians. Moula Bakhsh surpassed all the others and, when acknowledged the winner, he departed. Realizing his unique position of being the only musician who mastered both Northern Indian music, with its Persian, Arabic, and even Greek overtones and charm, and the Southern Karnatic style, with its rigor and power, and his contribution to the progress of Indian music nationally by melding both, he found in the highly cultured city of Hyderabad a good outlet for his genius. Accepting Sir Salar Jung's invitation to the court of the Nizam of Hyderabad, he invented the first real system of Indian musical notation, combining the systems of notes adopted in both the North and the South. Despite the reluctance of musicians bent on improvisations, the system nevertheless soon gained recognition throughout India. As Indian music is performed chiefly by way of extemporizations on standardized ragas, the innovation of a system of notation was bound to prove irksome to most musicians who considered it a straight jacket, limiting them in the spontaneous flow of their inspiration; also, it could never cover all the niceties of the complex themes and rhythms with its quarter tones. Referring to it many years later, Inayat wrote:

The Indian musician is recognized chiefly for the inspirational beauty he expresses by his improvisation; therefore our composers are much less known, because their compositions are performed by each artist differently; only the foundation and poetry remain the same. The artist is supposed to be a composer himself before he can become an artist. Even if he sings one song, it will be different each time. Therefore, notation did not become universal in India until of late, when Moula Bux [sic], the great composer, invented a system of notation for beginners and founded a school on modern principles in the state of Maharajah Gaekwar of Baroda. Notation would hamper the musician, and not leave him free to sing and play what his soul speaks. But Indian music is so complicated that no notation can render it exactly.

After the death of Maharajah Khanderao, Moula Bakhsh returned to Baroda for a short episode trying to support the new young maharajah, whose manners inevitably led to his deposal by the British, causing Moula Bakhsh once more to leave Baroda temporarily. Thereupon he visited Calcutta as a guest of Maharajah Jotindra Mohan Tagore, and later sang at the *durbar* of the British viceroy in Delhi.

Now Baroda was spurred to a fresh impulse by the young and promising Maharajah Sayaji Rao Gaekwar, under whose patronage Moula Bakhsh founded the Gayan Shala, or Royal Academy of Music of Baroda. Under Moula Bakhsh's powerful drive and unique proficiency in both northern and southern music, it fast became India's leading school of music, drawing musicians from all parts of the country. Whereas Indian music previously had been confined to the few and transmitted by heredity, Moula Bakhsh gave access to the school to all and encouraged introducing music as a basic item in the curriculum of schools, which triggered a wave of renewed enthusiasm for music throughout India. Rapt in his art, Moula Bakhsh used to sing and practice his *rudr veen* (the ancestor of the *vina*, producing deeper tones) into the early hours of the morning.

It was often seen that as he played or sang or listened to others, that he would be caught up by some feeling or thought of exquisite emotion and tears would fall from his eyes.

Moula Bakhsh used to hold a court at his house in the Yaqudpura quarter at Baroda, where he received not only famous musicians but poets, artists, philosophers, and holy men from all walks of life and various religions. But he never lost the human touch. The story is told of how the servant who had helped him down from his elephant after a long concert at the court of Hyderabad had asked him what was the instrument he was carrying—the rudr veen—and how it produced sound, and the great Moula Bakhsh, though weary, took hours of his time answering the questions. It was this spirit of recognition of the dignity of the human being, and the sense of the sacredness of music, art, and poetry as an expression of spiritual life, contrasting with the formalism of the courts, that animated these receptions at Moula Bakhsh Durbar where, sitting in a corner of his grandfather's seat, Inayat Khan, still a boy, received his first impressions of life, and where he learned music.

Inayat's father, Rahmat Khan, belonged to a family said to have originated in Afghanistan and settled near Sialkot in Kashmir. Descending from the chieftains of Turkish tribal clans, his ancestors were believed to have broken through the Khyber Pass with the early Moghul invasions, and bore a martial reputation of bravery and pride. A brother of his grandfather was renowned and revered in Punjab as a saintly dervish: Juma Shah, whose grave is a place of pilgrimage. Some of these dervishes, when in the state *Madhzubiyat* (God-intoxication), inadvertently perform great wonders that attract to them popular awe and respect.

Rahmat Khan trained as a singer under the tutorship of a Sufi sage, called Saint Alias, who was a great musician. Living by the rules of those who have given up the world, he tolerated only five things in his hut: a mat, a brick as a pillow, an earthenware bowl, a walking stick, and a broom, and he never kept anything for the morrow. If there were no means, he would starve in all simplicity, and when the Maharajah of Kashmir left a fair sum, he had to invite the entire neighborhood in order to keep to his rule of consuming the token the same day, thus avoiding substituting provision to reliance on God.

Rahmat's departure from home hastened his mother's death, causing him a guilt that obsessed him throughout his life. He had left, desperately in search of his destiny, not knowing whither. On his way, he came across a fakir who had subjected himself to a gruelling austerity: standing for years on the same spot under scorching sun and rain to the point that the government had built a roof over him. Rahmat Kahn asked the ascetic where he should go, whereupon he pointed in a direction which led Rahmat's wandering steps to Baroda. Moula Bakhsh invited him to the Academy, where he excelled as an exponent of the highly refined *dhurpad* style. And, appreciating his upright and steadfast nature and endearing gentleness, he offered him his eldest daughter in marriage, and, when she died, her sister Khatidja Bibi.

Inayat's mother, Khatidja Bibi, had a great longing for learning that could be availed of in seclusion, outside household chores. She was well versed in the Arabic, Persian, and Urdu literature of the ancient Sufis. When expecting Inayat, she dreamed that Christ came to heal her, and found herself under the protection of the saints and prophets:

As though they were taking care of her, or receiving her, or were waiting for something coming, or preparing for a time which they had foreknown.

She confided in her grandmother Bima, who told her it was a good tiding for the soul that was coming.

At the time of Inayat's birth on Wednesday, July 5, 1882, at 11:35 P.M., his aunt was about to die. "He is born with the ideal for which I am dying," she said when she heard the news: "Call him by my name, Inayat, which means benignity or divine grace."

The child showed signs of unusual intuition. One night he was asleep when his father brought sweets for him. When he awoke, he asked for them. His mother, not knowing about them, said there weren't any, whereupon he insisted and even pointed out where they were.

He showed generosity by never failing to share sweets with his friends, and he tried sparing them distress. For example, when he was bitten by a scorpion, he told his father it didn't hurt much; and gladly swallowed bitter medicines if that meant being brave; or taught himself to swim in a deep river; or mounted dangerously spirited horses before he knew how to ride; and learned from his father never to do anything that would result in making one feel humiliated. Later he was to teach mastery, overcoming fear, disciplining oneself, enduring all manner of unpleasantness, braving the challenge of life's hardships with a valiant heart.

He revealed himself as a little leader of his playmates. He once stopped his Muslim comrades from slinging stones at Hindu idols, and severely reprimanded a boy for being insolent to his mother. He was the organizer of his playmates' games, making each play the part of an animal in a circus, or even improvised plays for them to enact, like the story of King Haris Chandra.[1] Later he founded a speaker's association, in which he himself excelled. At school he was dreamy and not much interested in mathematics, though he distinguished himself in his essays. His propensity for drawing or writing poetry on his slate, or simply wandering off, was not much appreciated. When he witnessed people suffering, he would slip away in a quiet place, ascetic fashion, and ponder for hours.

He saw in life more pain than pleasure and more falsehood than truth.

Though not particularly partial to the tedium of the school routine of his time, driven by the cane he excelled in literature, and a teacher with foresight saw in him a teacher rather than a pupil.

Rahmat Khan, a conservative, became worried about his son's excessive predisposition for poetry and mysticism, for he wished him to grow up a practical man, capable of playing his role in active life.

Rahmat Khan proved himself throughout his life self-sacrificing, diligent, utterly devoted. He was by temperament austere, strict, expecting others to be as he; with his children, he was strict to the point of severity, although most loving and kind, always granting their wishes at whatever sacrifice. He was unassuming, honest and sincere, and it is no exaggeration to say that he never told a lie in his life. He was a philosopher with little love of booklearning. Kind actions and courtesy he held to be the chief thing in life, and he took pains and care to spare the feelings of others. If one of the children hurt himself, tears would come into his eyes, and the child had to comfort the father.

Hazrat Inayat Khan's entire life and thinking was steeped in and interwoven with the lives and spirit of sages, ascetics, and prophets, ever present behind every word or emotion and undertaking; in fact, they were the very expression of his soul, and in turn he increasingly became their embodiment in the world at large.

Moula Bakhsh, his grandfather, who no doubt had a great influence on Inayat's upbringing, noticing his spiritual leaning, often took this obviously gifted child (nicknamed Buddhi Arwah, old soul) on his visits to hermits, fakirs, and holy men of all denominations, including Jinsi Wali, a Sufi *pir* (elder).

When eleven years old, Inayat was taken by his uncle Ustad Murtza Khan (Moula Bakhsh's eldest son and later his successor) to Pattan, to the home of Bartiji, where sages of many different orders met; this left an indelible impression upon him.

A fakir, Narsiji, noted for his uncanny insight, presaged: "You have no idea of the inheritance with which he is entrusted." Did the veils of oblivion separating past from present and present from future lift before the eyes of this seer at that instant, so that he was able to grasp the eternal soul of that great being, now encased in a child's body, fulfilling his mission while growing to the full stature of his calling by ever greater realization? Did he have the insight to grasp in that flicker of a moment in time how the portentous hand attributed to destiny was planning these encounters with the realized beings of his time, with a view to preparing him already at the budding of his life for the task that he was predestined to fulfill in the Message to come?

Inayat's uncle retells how, at an age children are interested in kites or playing ball, Inayat used to sit in the company of sages and longed to be a recluse. It is something that is inherited by the race. He had it in his very blood.

Not only have the sages made their impression on the race, but the race has been impressed by sagehood itself. The people have the greatest respect for a sage. It is as if such a desire has been carried on for thousands of years.[2]

The land of India is impregnated with the spirit of the sage. It is a tradition in India that when men or women having a yearning for the spiritual life and a basic knowledge of religion have completed their *dharma* (duty), have a grown son, and have made a success of their job or of cultivating their land, they may renounce the world and live as a mendicant and later a recluse. They must first seek a guide, a guru, practice assiduously for years, begging for their teacher and themselves "without soliciting."

The house of any Buddhist is open to a sage.[3]

After having been tested by his guru and initiated accordingly, such a person may become a wandering *sadhu* without an abode, or may find himself a cave or build himself a rudimentary hut in the jungle. Should he develop *siddhis,* his reputation can spread far and wide by the word of anyone passing by, if he is at all within reach. Most of the greater souls, called *rishis,* so shun the world that they are well concealed in a mountain fastness "where angels fear to tread," living alone off roots, herbs, and odd fruit.

The background of Indian thinking, ever present as an idyll, hardly believable these days when so much abuse has been poured on this calling, suddenly springs into evidence once every twelve years, at the time of the Kumbh Mela at Hardwar or Allahabad, where, for a few hours, by some mysterious signal, based on the position of Jupiter in Aquarius, *sadhus, rishis,* and *burhais* from the most distant outposts converge upon the *ghats* of the Ganges for holy communion with the drops of the divine ambrosia said to be sprinkled by Shiva while rescuing the chalice from the demons for the Gods.

No doubt the secret of the serenity of these spiritual beings is to be found in their way of life. The principles they follow arise out of a life cloistered away from the egotism that most frequently develops when men are striving to compete in social intercourse and business. Many years later, speaking of the tradition of the *sanyasins* (wandering Hindu recluses), Murshid said it represents a certain emotion called *vairagya* in Sanskrit, "a feeling quite different from all other ways of looking at life, an outlook which brings one into an entirely different world of thought. The values of things and conditions seem to change completely."[4]

The whole world seems changed, the same world in which one has lived and suffered and enjoyed and learned and unlearned—everything appears to change once renunciation is learned.[5]

Those undergoing this internal state become very sensitive, are wounded by the brashness, selfishness, and cruelty of people and the sham of the world. They long for the peace of the snow-capped mountain tops, or the crystal-clear streams, immaculate and glistening in the dapple luster of dawn, or the etheric aloofness of the deer in the forest, or the silent gliding of the hawk as it hovers in space, or the presence of a being who has become completely selfless and serene.

The life of the Vairagi is very surprising, very extraordinary, and it is a great puzzle to those who meet him. One might be quite afraid of a man who was lying down with ashes rubbed all over his face and body, or perhaps sitting almost in a fire. His very appearance is so strange. He may be living in a graveyard outside the city, and going into the city only to obtain food for himself and his friends, who are Vairagis like himself. At other times he goes off into the wilderness and lives there. He spends most of his time in meditation and in striving after the mastery of the self. . . . It is through . . . the path of abstinence, that the Vairagi endeavours to develop his spiritual life. In following this path, practices may be carried out which seem hideous, or at least very strange, to those who do not understand the underlying philosophy or ideal. Whatever he does, the object is to reach the spirit by killing everything that hides the spirit from his sight. . . . To perform a miracle all he has to do is to flick his hand. His whole life seems to stand before him as his obedient servant. . . . He is master of life. . . . The self is that which makes our life limited, so when we master it we master life . . . in proportion to the degree to which we have attained self-mastery. Such a person is master even of plants and trees, or any living being; he has mastered everything. We cannot easily appreciate this, for it is quite unintelligible until one has oneself developed that mastery in one's own life.[6]

When one is in the presence of a Vairagi everything seems faded and pale, as if nothing in life had any value; it seems as if one had risen above all weakness and above all earthly goods. One receives a feeling of kingliness, as if one were above everything; it seems as if all else was just a hindrance. That is the feeling one gets.[7]

The first feeling of the Vairagi is to turn away from everything. He shows the nature of the deer, which runs away at the flutter of a leaf; for he becomes sensitive and convinced of the disappointing results that come from the limitation and changeableness of life in the world. Hurt within, he becomes sensitive, and the first thing that occurs to his mind is to fly, to hide somewhere, to go into a cave in the mountains, or into the forest where he will meet no one.[8]

As he progresses, says the Master, the sanyasin becomes wise like the snake, and later, strong and fearless like the lion. This is the time one can face life again.

With a brave spirit he stands in the crowd in the world . . . strengthened in truth and clear of conscience. What is called the Master or Saint or Prophet or Sage is the developed Vairagi. It is this soul that brings the divine Message, whenever the Message comes, to a community, a nation, or to the world.[9]

The dervishes belong to a different tradition, against the background of Islamic thought. You will find them in a gap of the crumbling wall of an old city, or standing on the roof of some dilapidated house overlooking the tomb of a Sufi saint, uttering the most paradoxical truths, surveying the crowd as though they were conducting an orchestra. If you get closer to them, you will notice that they have the manner and bearing of some great king or magus of old, and display the same courtesy, although they may be clad in an old mattress cover or threadbare rags. In Iran, the birthplace of the dervish tradition, the genuine dervishes have fled the unholiness of materialism by taking refuge in remote and forbidding villages. You will be lucky to pass one on the desert roads. But the old photos of dervishes of the beginning of this century inside the tomb Baba Kuli of Shiraz show convincingly what greatness a human being can attain by following this path. Such was the power that Hazrat Inayat represented, and in fact he brought the essence of this way of thinking and experiencing to the West as a yeast that developed new richness for the new age.

In the years of Hazrat Inayat Khan's childhood and youth, people did not like to discriminate among Hindu or Muslim or Buddhist holy men; this came later, with the growing political strife. The only differences Murshid outlines are differences of temperament:

The Sadhu controls and masters things; the Saint is resigned and contented in all circumstances of life. He chooses a life of retirement and resignation.

I would say that neither is superior nor inferior. . . . In the West, people have the idea that a sage must be kind, retiring, and renouncing, or perhaps even a wonder-worker. . . . To gain a deep understanding of what the saintly life means, and to form a reasonable opinion about the sages in the East, much patience and tolerance are required.[10]

The Sufis strive to bring spirituality into life, yet some become so intoxicated by the miracle of their interaction with that which is behind the scene of life that it is difficult to see how they fit into life. Hence, one distinguishes the *salik* and the *rind*:

The salik is a worldly man, with the responsibility of a home or profession or business or trade, and yet when he has attained to that height he can be made a murshid; he can be a teacher. It is not necessary to renounce the world and become a monk; he can be a murshid even though he is still working in the world.[11]

The salik carries his sense of honor to the extreme limit. Though in the world, he will never allow himself to be caught up in a situation in which he might feel ashamed or humiliated, or be prevented from acting according to his highest ideals. For example, he would give his guest a luxurious meal and starve for days rather than show that he is in financial straits. He does not show that he is suffering either in mind or in body.

He may give up his life, but not his pride, not his honour.

He is that person who will screen the faults of another and guard another's pride.

The rind is the other type of holy man, who veils his holiness by putting on a disconcerting appearance and exposes himself to reproval or contempt.

The way of the rind is that nothing matters, that, "I don't care," that, "I am nothing," that, "All else is nothing. Nothing I need, nothing I want, nothing I desire, nothing I long for, nothing is important, nothing I adore. God alone exists, none exists save He."

It is this detachment from worldly things that frees the rind's energy for intuition:

The Jelali among them, with their great psychic power, can prophesy, and cast out devils, and heal, and control the world and heavens, according to their development. They are mostly among dervishes and fakirs; and sometimes they are called rind, when they are under a guise which deludes the pious, keeping them from going near them. Jemali are the ones who are with God throughout the day and night; who love and repent, and bless and serve, and glorify the name of their Lord, and guide their followers through all difficulties in the spiritual path, and draw people to God from the struggles of life; their way is that of the saints of the past.

Following the way of the rind, the Sufi mystic poets, such as Shems-i Tabriz, Jami, Hafiz, and Omar Khayyam, deliberately "incurred the displeasure of people in general," referring to wine and intoxication in a Muslim country. Hence also the whirling dervishes:

If those pious ones of long robes listen to my song, they will immediately begin to get up and dance.[12]

If I may not dance, what shall I do?[13]

Forgive me, O pious ones, for I am drunk just now.[14]

One may jump to the conclusion that they are libertines, until one looks deeper into their beings.

Among them you will find some who have taken the vow of poverty and chastity. If you wished to see a living example of Christ's life you could see it among the dervishes.[15]

The *madhzub* (meaning one lost in God-consciousness) might be described as an exceptional kind of dervish. The action of the madhzub is always traumatic and unpredictable.

He is the cosmos in a human body ... the work of the madhzub is the command of God. He works with the elements, fire, water. He can cause instantly a great disaster: floods, earthquakes, volcanic eruptions, thunderstorms.

No doubt one of these was Shems-i Tabriz. The impact of this stormy fakir with eyes like the sun upon the erstwhile scholar Moulana Jelal-ud-Din Rumi was so overwhelming that he became practically over-night one of the greatest murshids the Sufis have ever known. Hearsay has it that, accosting the scholar riding his donkey in the precincts of the *medarsa* (academy), surrounded by his disciples, Shems snatched his manuscript out of his hand and threw it down a well. He then asked Rumi: "Would you like me to take it out of the well? It will be dry." The befuddled professor, took a deep breath to pull himself together, then replied: "No!" This was the "no" that transformed his life, by reaching beyond the mind epitomized by the book. It was this "no" that cast the die that made him one of the greatest of Persian poets.

In the East, on the roads, in trains, on buses, in the most unlikely places, you brush shoulders with a sanyasin in ochre cloth or half naked, holding his beggar's bowl; or a dervish in tattered clothes, endowed with the most incredibly bright eyes, murmurs some cryptic riddle to you. His pride not content with a penny, he will extol what seems a preposterous sum: a king's ransom—"My kingdom for a ... word that will transform you life!" Is it not worth the heartache? Or the deflated purse? With what measuring rod do you plot values? If you lose your chance, he will go on his way, keeping the secret intended for you forever buried in oblivion; and if you live up to the challenge, will you be any the poorer? Who knows, he may open up for you the wealth of the world, if that is what you want. But there is a need of the soul you cannot quench with the treasures of Solomon.

Murshid told the story of the beggar who challenged Alexander the Great to fill up his bowl. However much he put in, it always remained empty, like a bottomless well. Perhaps the dervish is testing you in whether your heart is on earth or in heaven. And if you tear out your heart and give it to him, what will he do with it? He might scatter it in the streets to beggar children, or bury it so that it may multiply, or buy the king's stolen jewels with it so that he may have access to the palace to warn the king against his courtiers. That dervish is playing the game of life with you. Are you game? Life is a great lottery, a gamble! Dare you give up your treasure for a greater treasure and run the risk of losing the lot, plus yourself? You are as great as your courage.

CHAPTER 3

The Musician
of the Soul

MUSIC, THE SHIVA TRADITION

Someday music will be the means of expressing universal religion. Time is wanted for this, but there will come a day, when music and its philosophy will become the religion of humanity.

Naturally, the soul of Inayat, recognizing its kin in that of the ascetics and hermits, was brooding an irresistible longing for solitude. One day when he was twelve years old, the nostalgia gripping his soul burst into a fateful decision: He left home, intent upon devoting his life to contemplation, leaving his dear brother Maheboob Khan as sole custodian of his secret. However, when searchers told him of the panic he had created at home, his heart ached with compassion for those to whom he had caused so much suffering, and he returned home. Rahmat Khan, seeing here the outcome of a tendency he had always tried to curb, attempted to bring home to Inayat the value of a life of mutual responsibility for one's fellow man rather than the selfish pursuit of one's inner longings in retirement.

Recognizing the high motives of his father's attitude to life, Inayat now resolved to serve his ideal by promoting music as a means of tuning the soul to its highest realization. This meant upholding the role of music and restoring it to its pristine function amid the decadence that had set in. He spoke on this subject at the High School of Baroda and wrote a textbook to facilitate the study of music, especially for girls, who were still so much handicapped from taking lessons by being held in the background; and he was most assiduous in his teaching at the Gayan Shala, his grandfather's music school.

Moula Bakhsh took a special interest in his education and every morning used to wake him up. Inayat would then spend the morning with him learning music, reading the papers to him, and discussing philosophical subjects.

Inayat wrote a dialogue on fate and free will, which Moula Bakhsh took to a friend, the lawyer Govind Vishnu Dev, who was very impressed with its purport. Moula Bakhsh had delayed a long time writing his autobiography, required by the magazine *Mahajan Mandal;* Inayat, still a child, wrote it to their satisfaction and amazement. Although brought up a Muslim, Inayat was keen on Hindu mystics like Dayanda Saraswati, Kabir, Nanak, Badu and Sundar, Ram Das and Tukaram, whose ideals were so close to those of the Sufis. He spoke the local Hindu tongue so well that Brahmins called him by a Hindu name, Vinayak. His style in poetry was perfected under the tutorship of a great Hindustani poet, Kavi Ratnakar.

In the prevailing musical environment Inayat soon became a proficient musician, singing all ragas by heart, distinguishing himself in improvising and picking up any musical instrument with surprising skill. He surprised musicians by being able to reproduce their songs, some most complex, faultlessly upon the first hearing. Later he wrote a music textbook that represented a step forward in pedagogy in his time. He was granted a scholarship by the Maharajah of Baroda for his rendering of a hymn to Ganesh, the God of luck, in the raga *Hansa Dhwani,* composed by Dikshitar.

After speaking on the importance of musical education at the Gayan Shala, Inayat was invited to speak at Narsiji's temple, illustrating the talk by examples of different types of music, and stressing the urgency of giving women a chance to study music in their confinement. The talk was hailed by the press and was a landmark in Inayat's mission in rehabilitating the classical tradition of India and using it to promote spiritual values.

From early childhood Inayat had manifested a desire to travel to Europe, and great was his excitement when his uncle Ustad Allaodin Khan (Moula Bakhsh's youngest son) was planning to go to London to obtain his doctor's degree in western music. However, his entreaties to go with him were of no avail, much to his disappointment. Inayat's longing for the West flared up once more when there was talk of Moula Bakhsh's representing music at the Chicago Exhibition in 1893, for he longed to accompany him, but it was felt that the great veteran was too old to travel.

When Dr. Allaodin returned after having qualified at the London College of Music, and at Leipzig, and having made a wonderful and successful tour of France, Germany, and Italy, the tone of the family life was suddenly altered under the spell of a European influence, and Inayat's presentiment of a destiny in the West led him in a new direction. He started wearing European clothes, setting a new pace among his young friends who were emerging out of the traditional background.

Dr. Allaodin Khan was now given the charge of founding a Western section of the Royal Academy of Music of Baroda; he formed an orchestra with woodwinds and strings, probably the first in Indian history, and a musical band. He was making history: introducing Western music into India. Only a few years later his nephews were to be the first to introduce Eastern music to the West.

Inayat's brother Maheboob Khan studied European harmony and musical theory under his uncle. He was a very fine and gentle young boy, most attached to Inayat, and loved by all. He was nicknamed Pyaromia, meaning beloved. "He was wise, thoughtful and retiring," writes Hazrat Inayat. He had a wonderful gift of improvisation and was born with a yet more beautiful voice than that of Moula Bakhsh, in Inayat's opinion; but he was too shy to sing when anyone was present.

Ali Khan, a grandson of Moula Bakhsh's sister, was considered as a brother to Inayat and Maheboob and Musheraff (the youngest brother). The friendship was sealed since babyhood. When he was brought back to Baroda, after having been separated from his cousins for nine years, he became most attached to Inayat, and used to follow him wherever he went. As this was generally to visit a sage or fakir, it must have been boring at times for such a young child, bubbling over with the joy of life and with physical energy, to sit still listening or just keeping silence; yet when he was with his beloved cousin everything was fine. Ali Khan learned from his uncle the use of all brass instruments and the bagpipes and soon became the right hand of Dr. Allaodin in the formation of a new band constituted on the model of English brass bands, and later in setting up the Department of Western Music of the Academy of Baroda. He coached many youths in the most varied instruments, helping the deserving needy out of his own hard-earned remuneration, often to the point of his own privation. He trained later under a remarkable personality in Baroda: a famous wrestler and also a great healer who, recognizing Ali Khan's gift, taught him the old secrets in healing. This all prepared him to become "an iron wall" to stand in support of Inayat against many opposing influences. He showed a great religious spirit and a loving heart and was kind, serviceable, and most devoted.

The death of Moula Bakhsh in 1896 came as a great shock to Inayat, who had grown under his eminent and loving care. Now thoughts about the mystery of life and death beseiged his mind. Fortunately, the door of a great experience opened before him: The Maharajah Bhim Shamsher of Nepal had called an assembly of all the musicians of the land. Rahmat Khan was invited, and he took the young Inayat with him. On the way they paid their respects to the tomb of Tansen, India's most famous singer, at Gwalior, a great musical center. Little could it have occurred to Inayat that in less than a decade he would be awarded as a title the name of this legendary figure.

The story goes that one day when Emperor Akbar was particularly impressed with the singing of the court musician, Tansen, he asked who was his teacher. Tansen answered that it was a rishi living in a cave of the Himalayas. "Ask him to come and sing to me," commanded the Emperor. "He would never comply," was the reply. "But it is an order!" "He still would not comply!" "And if I threatened to have him beheaded if he did not obey my command?" "He still would not comply." "Supposing I went to visit him in his cave, would he not sing to me?" "No." "How then could I hear him?" "Well," said Tansen, "if you dressed as my servant, he might." At the cave, Tansen feigned to ask for advice regarding a raga he purposely sang wrongly, enticing the rishi to sing. Once started, the rishi sang on and on until both Akbar and Tansen were lost in ecstasy. When they came to, the rishi had disappeared. Akbar asked Tansen: "Why is it that you cannot sing as he does?" The answer was: "Because I sing to you, but he sings to God."

Next Benares. Inayat walked spellbound along the ghats on the shores of the Ganges and visited the shrines of the Hindus with the reverence of a Hindu. Here he felt at home. Here near the ghats was the hut of the king, Haris Chandra, whose story he had enacted with his schoolboy comrades just a few years before.

His encounter with the sanyasin awakened familiar nostalgia in his heart; had he not always yearned for the no-man's land of the renunciate? Here were men who had followed the call of that very restlessness for a beyond which pulsed deep within himself. Here was a way of life away from the world that opened up unending perspectives and struck him with its imponderable significance so intimately—a living confirmation of a certain way of looking at life which he felt in the higher reaches of his consciousness, acquired through aeons of time, and dawning upon his youthful spirit.

Presently started the great trek across the thick jungle foothills of the giant Himalayas. The rare travelers in those desolate parts usually travel in a kind of palanquin called *dandi*, carried by four *Sherpas* (hardy mountain tribesmen). Inayat refused this form of transport using human beings as beasts of burden, and enjoyed immensely walking freely in nature, communing with God in this sublime manifestation of his presence. The branches of the trees appeared to him as God's arms in blessing, or lifted in prayer; he said he was exhilarated by the furtive play of hide-and-seek of wild animals, tigers and leopards, bears and rhinoceroces, and dangerous monkeys. Then came the most wondrous scene of all: the Maharajah Dhiraja of Nepal, hunting tigers with five hundred elephants, which formed a united front against attack. Then the capture of wild elephants: A tame elephant, earmarked for his outstanding personality, is sent out to befriend the wild one; then another is delegated to join in, and the newcomer is conducted between the two, gripped between their massive bodies as in a vise.

Beyond Mount Akdanta, the ascent becomes steep and in parts dangerous. Inayat slipped and rolled several hundred feet down the slope and was saved by a shepherd who, by a miraculous chance, just happened to be there placing his cane in line with the circuit that the body was tracing on the slope. That night, Inayat's mother dreamed that her son had been wounded in the knee.

Now the fabulous spectacle of musicians opened itself to Inayat's view. It was wonderful, remarked Hazrat Inayat, to see how the art of each had molded each personality, so that their being was an expression of their music. But his premonition of the imperative need to restore music to its real status was abundantly confirmed when he saw so many musicians kowtowing to rajahs and flattering them, thus degrading themselves to the rank of entertainers. (The early *Moguls* used to call their musical staff "the company of pleasure.") However, he learned some new ragas and found counsel in an old Sufi from Punjab, actually the spiritual guide to the Maharajah Bhim Shamsher. "His presence was mercy and compassion itself," Inayat said.

One being in the course of this journey seems to have left an indelible impression upon Inayat for the rest of his life. One day as he was wandering on horseback among the hills surrounding Katmandu, he felt a magnetic presence from a distance. As he scanned the area, he spotted a *mahatma* (great soul) sitting in a nearly inaccessible position, in silent meditation. He approached the mahatma:

He seemed to have filled the whole environment with an atmosphere of peace and exaltation beyond expression. Untouched by earthly contact, ambitions or environment, he seemed to be the happiest man in all the world.

One can hardly imagine what it meant to him: Here was the very epitome of all that he had been searching for all this time—a being who touched upon the deepest springs of his being, rapt in ecstasy, and uplifting his soul. Every leaf of the trees was permeated by his presence, and his atmosphere radiated into great expanses.

It seemed as though the everblowing wind was hushed under the reign of perfect stillness, caused by the peace of his soul.

Inayat frequently returned to the spot, and sang to the mahatma, accompanied on his vina. Several times later in his life the Master was recalled to that moment that shaped his life. Though he was playing music, he said he learned the higher dimensions of music through the silence of the *mahatma*. Here, in the rapt solitude, the silent mahatma communicated a special *darshan* (spiritual blessing) to the youth; in the meeting of the glances, Inayat was filled with a feeling of exaltation.

Souls unite at the meeting of a glance.[1]

The transmission then received no doubt played a decisive role in designing the course of Inayat's life.

After Inayat's mother died in 1902, he started wandering throughout India, singing and lecturing on the sacred role of music. Everywhere he was received with appreciation and regard. After a great success at Madras, however, he found himself seated on a station platform hungry and worrying where he would get his next meal. A Brahmin, reading his thoughts, brought him impromptu a plate of *bhajias*, saying: "Do not worry, you will be received at the court of the Maharajah of Mysore as a royal guest." And so it happened. At Mysore, the land of his ancestors, Inayat was for his hearers the reincorporation of the genius they loved and honored through him: Moula Bakhsh, whom they had never forgotten.

In Bombay Inayat was appalled by the low level to which music had been relegated. The pseudo-Europeanized young men would talk, giggle, and smoke during performances, more interested in a contest between two musicians—for the sport of it—than in the real value of the music of which they had not the faintest notion.

Referring to this episode, which epitomized the downward trend, Inayat said:

No doubt the music of India has changed much during the last century. That which the Indians call classical music, or music with weight and substance, is not patronized any more, because of the ignorance of most of the princes and potentates of the country, and therefore the best music is no longer understood. The people have taken to smoking and talking while listening to music, and music was not made for that. It seems that the spirit of the great musicians is dead; for a great vina player, who considered his instrument sacred and who worshipped it before taking it in his hand, practicing and playing it for perhaps ten hours a day, regarded music as his religion.

Now a new music has come to India which is called theatrical music. It is neither Eastern nor Western; it is a very peculiar music. The themes of march and galop [sic] and polka, and airs which no one wants to hear any more in the Western world, are imitated, and an Indian twist is given to them. Thus they are spoilt for the ears of the Western listener and also for good Eastern ears. Since the masses have not been educated in the best music and for them there is only one source of entertainment, the theatre, they are becoming as fond of this music as they are of jazz in America.[2]

Murshid deplored, perhaps more than any other ill, the degeneration of Indian music in his time. Devoted as he was to upholding the sacred nature of music, he was alarmed about what this signifies in terms of civilization in the world, and its far-reaching consequence, which he expressed in a paean of agony:

Allah! if our people had lost their wealth and power, it would not have been so grievous to bear, since these temporal things are always changing hands in the mazes of Maya, but the inheritance of our race, the music of the Divine, is also leaving us through our own negligence, and that is a loss that my heart cannot sustain![3]

He was used to a quite different measuring rod.

I will say that such singers as I have heard sing in India when I was a boy, I never heard since in the next generation.

The singers of the ancient times, sang the same Raga, the same song, hundreds of times, thousands of times, a million times. It is by repetition of one thing, by association that we can produce in ourselves the creative power. To have acquired a great store of knowledge, so many songs, so many Ragas is nothing, it is the power of producing from within oneself, of creating that is great.

Murshid reveals an interest in the music of all nations and races.

There is a Chinese legend which says that the first music was played on little pieces of reed. . . . From this came the scale of five tones: one note was the original note produced by the reed, and the four other notes were made by placing the fingers on the holes. Afterwards many other scales were developed.[4]

During the time of the Chaldeans, Arabs, Greeks and Romans, different religious ideals were brought to humanity. To the few music was brought, to the many only a note.[5]

When Persian music, with its artistry and beauty, was brought to India, it was wedded to Indian music; and there resulted a most wonderful art.[6]

The Greeks had certain scales like the ragas in India, which also resembled the Persian scales.[7]

Pope Gregory I, after whom the Gregorian scales are named, co-ordinated those beautiful melodies which had come from ancient Greece via Byzantium to form the religious music of the Church.[8]

In the early days, it was music's sacred character that maintained its standard. But gradually it became desanctified, letting in lower emotions.

In the Golden Age there was the music of the soul, a music that appealed to the soul itself and that raised it to cosmic consciousness, the music of the angels. . . . And the music of the Silver Age was the music . . . which appealed to the depths of the heart, creating sympathy and love of nature. . . . The music of the Copper Age appealed to the mind. . . . The Iron Age has an influence on the physical body; it helps the soldiers to march and moves people to dance.[9]

There are five different aspects of the art of music: popular, that which induces motion of the body; technical, that which satisfies the intellect; artistic, that which has beauty and grace; appealing, that which pierces the heart; uplifting, that in which the soul hears the music of the spheres.

The effect of music depends not only on the proficiency, but also upon the evolution of the performer. Its effect upon the listener is in accordance with his knowledge and evolution; for this reason the value of music differs with each individual. For a self-satisfied person there is no chance of progress, because he clings contentedly to his taste according to his state of evolution, refusing to advance a step higher than his present level. He who gradually progresses along the path of music, in the end attains to the highest perfection. No other art can inspire and sweeten the personality like music; the lover of music attains sooner or later to the most sublime field of thought.[10]

It all depends upon what one is seeking, which of course is a gauge of one's state of evolution. No doubt then, humanity has reached the Iron Age since, apparently, the majority enjoys music that induces body movement:

How does the great success of jazz come about? . . . It touches the physical body. It gives it a renewed strength by the continuation of a particular rhythm and a particular sound; that gives people—I mean the generality—a greater strength and vigour and interest than music which strains the mind. [It attracts] those who do not wish to be spiritually elevated.[11]

The master attributes the magic of the mood induced not only to the rhythm but also to the life power in the drums made of skin.

The breath is the life-current or Prana; and this life-current exists also in such things as the gut string or the skin of drums. There is a part of life in these things too, and it is to the extent that their life-current becomes audible, that it touches the life-current of the living creatures and gives it an added life. It is for this reason that primitive tribes, who have only a drum or a simple instrument to blow, get into such a condition by the continual playing of these instruments that they enjoy the state of ecstasy.[12]

One's taste in music is so much an indication of one's aspirations in life.

The singing of the more refined people was quite different from that of the peasants; the song of the temple was altogether different from the song of the stage.[13]

When grown-up man enjoys and appreciates music in accordance with his grade of evolution, and with the surroundings in which he has been born and brought up, the man of the wilderness sings his wild lays, and the man of the city his popular song. The more refined man becomes, the finer the music he enjoys. The character in every man creates a tendency for music akin to it; in other words the gay man enjoys light music, while the serious-minded person prefers classical; the intellectual man takes delight in technique, while the simpleton is satisfied with his drum.[14]

For instance, the children in the streets are very pleased by beating the time, because that rhythm has a certain effect upon them; but as a person evolves, he longs for a finer harmony. Why people like or dislike each other is owing to their different stages of evolution. So it is in religion: Some stick to certain beliefs, and do not wish to evolve further. It is possible that the lover of music may be tempted to keep to a certain sort of music, and will not rise further. The true way of progressing through music is to evolve freely, to go forward, not caring what others think; and in this way, together with one's development in music, harmonizing one's soul life, one's surroundings and one's affairs.

However, the Master sensed that the sophistication of a lot of classical music hurt modern people in their sense of authenticity. And he noted a trend in our time from artificiality of the sophisticated life, to the less ornate, or rather rugged and uncouth bluntness that has emerged in our time, which has opened perspectives in art and music which his contemporaries would have never believed possible. Often in the history of music, a renascence has been triggered by a sounding into the pulse beat of folklore.

The modern revival of folk-music is an effort in the right direction.[15]

If the world feels a greater need for a better kind of music, then it will come; but if people mostly enjoy jazz, and if that is sufficient for them, then naturally it will only come slowly, because so few want anything better.[16]

In fact, Murshid's predictions are materializing; more Westerners than

Easterners are today studying Indian music, besides rock adepts seeking in Ravi Shankar a lead for a future style of music that would ally East and West.

Those who tuned their hearts, who raised their souls high enough, heard this divine music; but those who played with their rattle, their single note, would have refused a violin; they were not ready for it and they would not have known how to use it.[17]

There is music which makes one feel like jumping and dancing; there is music which makes one feel like laughing and smiling; and then there is music which makes one feel like shedding tears. If one were to ask a thoughtful person which he preferred, no doubt he would say, "The last, the music which brings tears." Why does the soul want sad music? Because that is the only time when the soul is touched. The other music, the music which reaches no further than the surface of one's being, remains only on the surface. It is the music that reaches to the depths of one's being which touches the soul. The deeper the music reaches, the more contented is the soul. No doubt a person who is very cheerful and has had dinner and a glass of wine could be quite happy with some dance music. But then he need not have serious music, for him jazz will be quite sufficient.[18]

Yet in his time, as things proved later, Murshid's music was yet premature. "It was like bringing old coins to a currency bank."

Maybe one day the Western world will waken to India's music as now the West is wakening to the poetry of the East, and beginning to appreciate such works as Rabindranath Tagore. There will come a time when they will ask for music of that kind too, and then it will not be found, it will be too late. But there is no doubt, that if that music which is magic, and which is built on psychological basis, is introduced in the West, it will root out all such things as jazz. People seem to spoil their senses; this music is destroying their delicacy of sense. Thousands every day are dancing to Jazz-music and they forget the effect it has upon their spirit, upon their mind, upon their delicate senses. There was a prince of Rampur who wanted to study music from a great teacher. And the teacher said: "I do not want you to hear any musician who is not an accomplished artist, because your sense of music must not be destroyed; it must be preserved for delicate music, it must be able to appreciate its fine intricacies."[19]

Now that so many Western ears have been trained to the intricacies of Indian *ragas* and *talas*, and value them, one wonders how much popular Indian musicians are able to retrieve of the treasures of the past. Since music cannot be appropriately notated, much must necessarily get lost, especially in those cases where a great teacher did not find a sufficiently skilled successor. However, Indian music presents a rare attraction and challenge for those looking for "something else," and particularly to those who are seeking a freer expression in music: improvisation, spontaneity.

It is just as well that I gave up my music when in the West, for if I had kept it up I would have never been fully satisfied with it, although the sacrifice of music for me was not a small one.

The characteristic of Indian music is that it depends upon the creative talent of the musician in improvisation. An outline is given by the composer.

Some Westerners have proven surprisingly proficient in it, and folk musicians have adopted and adapted Eastern themes willy-nilly into a Western context. It is all part of the extraordinary convergence of civilizations of our time into the cauldron of the new age yet to be sampled. However, there are items in the handover that open exciting perspectives, if music in the future is to free itself from expression of social clichés and glean something of the nature of the harmony of the universe. Since Indian music is traditionally derived from the spiritual discoveries of the rishis in the Himalayas, it incorporates dimensions that are related to the cosmic harmony, the planets, the sounds of animals, the moods of humans, *mantrams,* the psychological effect of sound, the nature of vibrations. One has a feeling that to progress, music has to get down to basics, in a new understanding of meaningfulness of the human in its relevance to the cosmos: space age music. Music as a science was known by them to have a great deal to do with the influence of the planets.

In the Sanskrit tradition of ancient times there were verses to be found having relation to certain planets.... Humanity in all periods has arranged its life according to the planetary influences.[20]

The very scales and melodic modes grew out of the moods inspired by awareness of the cosmic harmony.

The ragas are derived from five different sources: the mathematical law of variety, the inspiration of the mystics, the imagination of the musicians, the natural lays peculiar to the people residing in different parts of the land, and the idealization of the poets; these made a world of ragas, calling one *rag,* the male, another *ragini,* the female, and others *putra,* sons, and *bharja,* daughters-in-law.

Indian music grew out of nature. Of the way the art developed among the ancient people, references are to be found even now in the East. The idea was that they attached different themes of music to different seasons, and different strains of music to different times of the day and night. There was a logical reason for attributing certain melodies to certain times. If it had been only a poetic fancy it would have lasted for a short period and would have influenced only a limited circle. But it has lasted for ages, up till now, and has influenced the whole country.

Mahadeva found that at every time of the day and night a particular effect was made upon the human body and spirit and that a rhythm akin to that particular time must be prescribed psychologically and mystically in order to elevate the soul. And therefore a psychological science of music was made by Mahadeva, a science which was called "Raga," which means "emotion."[21]

Several Ragas are usually sung before dawn. In India, before dawn everyone goes to his work or to his devotions and there he finds himself very much helped by the stillness of the hour, by finer vibrations. At midday the noise from all around is much greater and stronger notes are needed. The Ragas for midday are made with natural notes. The Ragas of the night are with odd notes. The Ragas of the early morning are made with flat notes.

And the one who tunes himself not only to the external, but to the inner being and to the essence of all things, gets an insight into the essence of the whole being; and therefore he can to the same extent find and enjoy even in the seed the fragrance and beauty which delights him in the rose.

Raga is called the male theme because of its creative and positive nature; ragini is called the female theme on account of its responsive and fine quality. Putras are such themes as are derived from the mingling of ragas and raginis; in them can be found a likeness to the raga and the ragini from which they are derived. Bharja is the theme which responds to the putra. There are six ragas and thirty-six raginis, six belonging to each raga; and forty-eight putras and forty-eight bharjas which constitute this family.

Each raga has an administration of its own, including a chief, Makhya, the key-note; a king, Wadi, a principal note; Samwadi, a minister, the subordinate note; Anuwadi, a servant, an assonant note; Vivadi, an enemy, a dissonant note....

The poets have depicted the images of ragas.... The ancient gods and goddesses were simply images of the different aspects of life, and in order to teach the worship of the immanence of God in nature these various images were placed in the temples, in order that God in His every aspect of manifestation might be worshipped. The same idea has been worked out in the images of ragas, which create with delicate imagination the type, form, figure, action, expression and effect of the idea.[22]

The musician does not execute a composer's prefigured pattern, but gets himself into a given mood and explores the endless modalities within the main trend, capturing, as it were, cosmic conditions.

The musician sings first the key-note. Then he repeats over and over again so as to put himself so much in union with his instrument that his voice and the tone of the instrument may be one. Then he goes a little further and returns to the key-note.

The musician may take one Raga and play that for hours, or he may go from one Raga to another. But the more he plays one Raga, the more he indulges in that, the more he impresses his soul with it, the more he will find in that.

The Ragas have sometimes been understood as scales, they are not scales but patterns of notes within the octave. There are four different sorts of Ragas, Ragas of six notes, Ragas of seven notes, Ragas of odd notes, and Ragas of even notes, ascending and descending.

I have seen myself that in playing the Veena and singing the Raga Jogia in the early morning, when people were going to the temple and to the mosque, sometimes they would stop to listen and be wrapt in the music, at other times with the same Raga I did not even impress myself according as the mood was.

Certainly the great achievement of Indian music is the isochronism of a melody sung or played on an instrument and a rhythm fingered by a *tabla* or *bahia*, sometimes of amazing dexterity and skill. But the disadvantage of improvisation is that it does not allow of many instruments improvising simultaneously; that would soon prove a cacophony. This difference from Western music is no doubt due to the fact that Indian music was never intended for a concert, nor for great social occasions requiring pomp before large numbers of people; it arose in meditation and fosters internalization. The *sitar* developed later as more of a concert instrument, and so did the bugbear of all genuine musicians, the harmonium, or *juti bos*. The *sarod* is more adapted to Western-style concerts.

In the West, the music is made brilliant, impressive, lively by the chords. We make it so by the melody alone. When music is played before a thousand or ten thousand people, then, of course, many instruments are needed. When music is played before a few listeners only, then three or four instruments only are needed, or only one. When it is used for concentration, then one instrument, one voice is quite enough.

But of all instruments, the most traditional and spiritually inspiring is the vina, because it embodies the whole original impulse given to music by meditation. This was why this had to be the instrument of both Moula Bakhsh and the young Ustad Inayat Khan, and in which both excelled.

This instrument was invented by the Lord of Yogis, Shiva, whose name is also Mahadeva, who gave to the world his life-long experiences in the practice of Yoga, and who is worshipped in India as a godhead. His literature is considered as Holy Scriptures. He was a great master of breathing and an ascetic. He lived in the mountains where he sat and breathed the free air of the wide horizons of the East and practiced mantras, words and phrases which changed the whole being of man. There he wanted to make some instrument to be used for higher exaltation by help of music. In the forest, what he could do was to cut a piece of bamboo. He took two pumpkins, made them hollow and tied them around the bamboo. Gut strings he got from animals and these gut strings he tied upon it. In this way he made his first vina. And he practiced on it in the solitude. There is a quotation that when the deer in the forest used to hear him play the vina, they used to say "make the strings of my own veins and put them on your vina; but as long as I live, continue to play."[23]

When Parvati saw this instrument [Parvati was Mahadeva's consort], she said: "I must invent my Vina." So she took half the part of the pumpkins and produced another kind of Vina, the Saraswati Vina. So there are two Vinas: one is played by men, the other by women. On this instrument not only sharp and flat notes are produced, but also semi-tones. And in this way the music becomes rich. But to develop to the science of semi-tones is so difficult that it takes a life long time.[24]

Afterwards this instrument was improved and made more refined and now steel strings are mostly used; but the reason why gut string is appealing to the human soul, is that it comes from a living body, and even after being separated from the body it still calls out, "I am alive!"[25]

The effect of different substances used to make the instruments, whether guts, wire, bamboo or wood, were tested on different animals.

Wind-instruments, instruments with gut or steel strings, and instruments of percussion, such as drums and cymbals, have each a distinct, different and particular effect on the physical body. There was a time when thinkers knew this and used sound for healing and for spiritual purposes. It was on that principle that the music of India was based. . . .

Snakes of any kind are attracted on hearing the sound of the *pungi*. First they come out of the hole in which they live; and then there is a certain effect on their nervous system which draws them closer and closer to the sound of the pungi. They forget that instinct which is seen in every creature of protecting itself from the attack of man or of other creatures; at that time they absolutely forget, they do not see anyone or anything. They are then aroused to ecstasy; the cobra begins to raise its head and move it right and left; and as long as this instrument is played the cobra continues to move in ecstasy. This shows us that, as well as the psychical effect and the spiritual effect that sound has on man, there is also a physical effect.[26]

The snakes too are easily attracted by the Indian flute, a piece of bamboo, or by the vina, if they hear it. But the vina players are serious people, and would rather charm human beings than the snakes. A special raga is used for charming snakes. I have made experiments with cows, and found that they liked very much to listen to music. There was one old ox, in particular, which, when it heard an instrument played, would leave its fodder and come to listen.

The birds are very fond of music. I have seen that a peacock, when music was played before it, would listen and spread out its wings and begin to dance, and then it would follow the player; each day it would come a little nearer. It took such a delight in the music that it danced and quite forgot everything else. When I stopped playing it would come and tap the vina with its beak to get me to come back and play again.

The end effect of the music produced ensues both from the kind of substance that is set into vibration, either by the touch of the finger tips or the breath, and from the realization of the player.

The effect of instrumental music also depends upon the evolution of man, who expresses with the tips of his fingers upon the instrument his grade of evolution; in other words his soul speaks through the instrument. Man's state of mind can be read by his touch upon any instrument; for however great an expert he may be, he cannot produce by mere skill, without a developed feeling within himself, the grace and beauty which appeal to the heart.

Wind instruments, like the flute and the algosa especially, express the heart quality; for they are played with the breath, which is the very life; therefore they kindle the heart's fire.

Instruments stringed with gut have a living effect, for they come from a living creature which once had a heart; those stringed with wire have a thrilling effect; and the instruments of percussion such as the drum have a stimulating and animating effect upon man.[27]

However, music teacher Inayat Khan still preferred the voice, which he rated above any instrument because the instrument is the very flesh of the musician that responds far more readily than any extraneous substance to the slightest emotion, roused within.

The voice is not only indicative of man's character, but it is the expression of his spirit. The voice is not only audible, but also visible, to those who can see it; the voice makes impressions on the ethereal spheres, impressions which can be called audible but are visible at the same time.... No sound can be more living. Knowing this, the Hindus of ancient times said that singing was the first art, playing the second art and dancing the third art.... The Hindus discovered that the shortest way to attain to spiritual heights is by singing. Therefore the greatest prophets of the Hindus were singers, like Narada and Tumbara.[28]

This, of course, applies equally to the spoken voice, which may also manifest a cosmic quality; to wit, the Master's spoken voice when he later taught.

There are five qualities of the voice which are connected with the particular character of a person. The earth quality of the voice is hope-giving, encouraging, tempting; the water quality is intoxicating, soothing, healing, uplifting; the fire quality is impressive, arousing, exciting, horrifying, and at the same time awakening. Very often warning is given in the voice of the fire quality. The "tongues of flame" spoken of in the New Testament tell of that voice and the word which was the warning of coming dangers; it was alarming for the people to awaken from their sleep, to awaken to a greater, higher consciousness. Then there is the air quality of the voice, which is uplifting, taking one far away from the plane of the earth. The ether quality of the voice is inspiring, healing, peace-giving, harmonizing, convincing, appealing, and at the same time most intoxicating. Every Jelal voice, Jemal voice or Kemal voice has one or another of these five qualities predominant in it, and according to the quality it creates effect.[29]

That is why in ancient times the greatest of the prophets were great musicians. For instance, among the Hindu prophets one finds Narada, the prophet who was a musician at the same time, and Shiva, a God-like prophet, who was the inventor of the sacred Vina. Krishna is always pictured with a flute.

There is also a well-known legend of the life of Moses, which says that Moses heard a divine command on Mount Sinai in the words: Muse ke, Moses hark; and the revelation that thus came to him was of tone and rhythm, and he called it by the same name, Musik; and the words such as Music and Musike have come from that word. David's song and verse have been known for ages; his message was given in the form of music. Orpheus of the Greek legends, the knower of the mystery of tone and rhythm, had by this knowledge power over the hidden forces of nature. The Hindu goddess of beauty, of knowledge, whose name is Sarasvati, is always pictured with the Vina. And what does it suggest? It suggests that all harmony has its essence in music.[30]

Now we understand why the Master had to start as a musician. Music is a way of grasping the structure of a cosmic harmony within the soul in a manner that the mind could never clasp, and communicating one's insight into that harmony to others without passing through the mind and incurring its limitations.

What we call music in our everyday language is only a miniature, which our intelligence has grasped from that music or harmony of the whole universe which is working behind everything, and which is the source and origin of nature. It is because of this that the wise of all ages have considered music to be a sacred art. For in music the seer can see the picture of the whole universe; and the wise can interpret the secret and the nature of the working of the whole universe in the realm of music.

All the religions have taught that the origin of the whole of creation is sound. No doubt the way in which this word is used in our everyday language is a limitation of that sound which is suggested by the scriptures. Language deals with comparative objects, but that which cannot be compared has no name. Truth is that which can never be spoken; and what the wise of all ages have spoken is what they have tried their best to express, little as they were able to do so.[31]

When we pay attention to nature's music, we find that everything on the earth contributes to its harmony. The trees joyously wave their branches in rhythm with the wind; the sound of the sea, the murmuring of the breeze, the whistling of the wind through rocks, hills, and mountains; the flash of the lightning, and the crash of the thunder, the harmony of the sun and moon, the movements of the stars and planets, the blooming of the flower, the fading of the leaf, the regular alternation of morning, evening, noon, and night, all reveal to the seer the music of nature.[32]

All forms of nature, the flowers so perfectly formed and colored, the planets and stars, the earth, all give the idea of harmony, of music. And then the whole nature is breathing.[33]

The music of the universe is the background of the small picture which we call music. Our sense of music, our attraction to music, shows that there is music in the depth of our being. Music is behind the working of the whole universe. Music is not only life's greatest object, but it is life itself.[34]

The structures that life assumes in flowing in a stream, or crystallizing in snowflakes, or blossoming in a flower, or in the patterns in the sand of the desert written upon by the wind, or in the granulations in the texture of a tree trunk, or in the circumvolutions of the brain, flow, unfurl, and crystallize themselves into the patterns of musical master-

pieces, such as passages of Bach's Brandenberg Concertos or Preludes.
The whole of nature is singing its choir and playing its symphony of
glorification, if one could only hear the music of the spheres, and of
the earth.

*The insects have their concerts and ballets, and the choirs of birds chant in
unison their hymns of praise. Dogs and cats have their orgies, foxes and wolves
have their soireés musicales in the forest, while tigers and lions hold their
operas in the wilderness. Music is the only means of understanding among
birds and beasts. This may be seen by the gradation of pitch and the volume of
tone, the manner of tune, the number of repetitions, and the duration of their
various sounds; these convey to their fellow creatures the time for joining the
flock, the warning of coming danger, the declaration of war, the feeling of love,
and the sense of sympathy, displeasure, passion, anger, fear, and jealousy,
making a language of itself.*

*In man breath is a constant tone, and the beat of the heart, pulse, and head
keeps the rhythm continuously. An infant responds to music before it has learnt
how to speak; it moves its hands and feet in time, and expresses its pleasure and
pain in different tones.*[35]

Murshid sees the music of the spheres as the primal vibrations that
crystalized into the matter of the stars and planets, whose motion in
space now causes sound by friction; the same is true of that fragmentation of the earth that coalesces into the bodies of creatures.

Vibrations can be understood both as cause and as effect. Vibration causes
movement, rotation, circulation, but on the other hand it is the rotation of the
planets and circulation in the blood which cause vibration. Thus the cause as
well as the effect of all that exists is vibration.[36]

Murshid was so conversant with vibrations, whether in what is com-
monly known as music or the vibrations of beings and phenomena,
that he was a master of sound. Having mastered music, Murshid gave it
up in order to apply his knowledge of vibration to the unfoldment of
beings.

For the Master, music is our sense of harmony in our relationship
with the universe, our consonance with the pulse of life beating in all
beings at synchronic rates, our resonance in harmonic response to
vibrations of life everywhere, and therefore our way of experiencing
the one being behind all beings, the one we really love beyond all
those in whom we seek our highest aspiration.

It is because music is the picture of our Beloved that we love music. Our
Beloved is that which is our Source and our Goal. And what we see of our

Beloved before our natural eyes is the beauty which is before us. And that part of our Beloved which is not manifested to our eyes is that inner form of beauty of which our Beloved speaks to us. If only we will listen to the voice of all the beauty that attracts us in any form, we shall find that in every aspect it tells us that behind all manifestation is the perfect Spirit, the Spirit of Wisdom.

It is owing to our limitations that we cannot see the Whole Being of God, but all that we love in colour, line, form, or personality, all that is beloved by us, belongs to the real Beauty, Who is the Beloved of All.[37]

Now, if we trace in this beauty that we see in all forms, what attracts us, we shall find that it is the movement of beauty, the music.

It is a kind of sensitivity to the inherent order of things. It is experiencing inside that which is happening outside.

To me architecture is music, gardening is music, farming is music, poetry is music. All the occupations of life where beauty has inspired, where the divine Wine has been outpoured, there is music. But among all the different arts, the art of music has been especially considered divine, because it is the exact miniature of the law, working in the whole universe. . . . The sound is continually audible, the sound without and the sound within oneself, and that is music.[38]

As music can convey what words or images, symbols or religious ceremonies, cannot impart of the nature of the divine Beloved, Murshid considers it as the ultimate expression of religion. It is no doubt for this reason that the early church fathers, Catholic and Orthodox, knew the value of the sung mass; that Hindu and Buddhist priests and ascetics chant and recite mantrams; in fact, that the rituals of all religions are celebrated in the language of music, and that the dervishes reach spiritual realization in the *sama*, or musical recitations of Sufi lore. Religious fervor has inspired musical talent to reach its most sublime expression in the masses of J. S. Bach, Monteverdi, Victoria, and Charpentier, for example. This is particularly so in the traditional spiritual music of India, in which the Master was reared and which he inherited. Of all means of expressing and promoting spiritual realization and religious glorification, music is called upon for the role assigned to it by the "musician of the soul" no doubt because it transcends conceptual thought, which has so often harmed religion. It lends itself to convey the formless God, which is what happens to an emancipated realization of the meaning of religion.

Music is called a divine or celestial art, not only because of its use in religion and devotion, and because it is in itself a universal religion, but because of its fineness in comparison with all other arts and sciences. Every sacred scripture, holy picture or spoken word produces the impression of its identity upon the mirror of the soul; but music stands before the soul without producing any impression of this objective world, in either name or form, thus preparing the soul to realize the Infinite.[39]

Art no doubt is most elevating, but at the same time contains form; poetry has words, names suggestive of form; it is only music which has beauty, power, charm and at the same time can raise the soul beyond form.

The Sufis use music to lift consciousness to higher states in meditation.

What the art of painting cannot clearly suggest, poetry explains in words; but that which even a poet finds difficult to express in poetry is expressed in music. By this I do not only mean that music is superior to art and poetry, but in point of fact music excels religion; for music raises the soul of man even higher than the so-called external forms of religion.

By this it must not be understood that music can take the place of religion; for every soul is not necessarily tuned to that pitch where it can really benefit by music, nor is every music necessarily so high that it will exalt a person who hears it more than religion will do. However, for those who follow the path of the inner cult, music is essential for their spiritual development. The reason is that the soul who is seeking for that is in search of the formless God.[40]

During my travels throughout the world, I have heard the music of many different places, and always I have felt that intimate friendship and brotherhood existing in music; and I always had a great respect for music and for the devotee of music. And one thing I believe, and, when in India, was convinced of it time after time, in meeting those who have touched some perfection in music, that not only in their music, but in their life one can feel the harmony which is the real test of perfection. If this principle of music were followed there would be no need for an external religion, and someday music will be the means of expressing universal religion. Time is wanted for this, but there will come a day when music and its philosophy will become the religion of humanity.

This is no doubt one of the most surprising and far reaching statements ever made by Murshid, enough to warm the hearts of musicians, and to stir up the imagination of priests and prophets as to future developments of religion in the new age!

Inayat knew that among all sovereigns His Highness Mir Maheboob Ali Khan, the Nizam of Hyderabad, was the most highly qualified connoisseur of classical music and its mystical moment, but the jealousy of court musicians built an unassailable wall forbidding Inayat access to this great patron of arts and music for over six months. While patiently waiting, Inayat wrote his masterpiece on musical theory, *Minkar-i-Musiqar.*

He stayed with a Parsi family in Secunderabad; and to the joy of Dastur Hoschang, the priest, composed music to the Zoroastrian *Gathas*. His interest and enthusiasm for different religions was not always appreciated by the orthodox, yet he found in the midst of the highly cultured and noble Muslim society of the time a distinguished friend and teacher, an Arabic and Persian scholar who deepened him in his knowledge of Sufi poetry.

One day a friend took Inayat to see an old dervish woman who used to make unintelligible utterances, squatting by the roadside.

And then I happened to come in a place where a woman lived under the shade of a tree. They say she was in age more than a hundred years, but I do not know. And she never spoke to anyone; she just sat there. And a friend brought me to see this woman, and I at once felt that there was something wonderful about her. And at that time she had an earthen bowl in her hand, and she was eating from it, and as I went near her to greet her, in answer to my greeting she took a little food with the same hand as she was eating and gave it me. She had no fork. She held it before me. I first looked here and there, and my friend said "Take it," so I at once stretched out my hand and took what she gave me. And the same week I was called to the court, was presented at the court, and had what I desired at that time.

Who will tell us more of that mysterious dervish who silently blasted a surprising breakthrough in Inayat's early strivings in his musical career? How she reminds one of Hazrat Babajan, who had transfixed Meher Baba on his forehead; her face wizened by age, suffering and annihilation, held to be mad by her neighbors. One can imagine her speaking thus:

You come to see me! From me, you can never expect less than the truth. You want my food! You'll have to take it from my mouth. You'll have to accept that it is despicable but holy. Despicable from the point of view of the world, and holy because it is made holy by the consciousness of the divine presence. If you come to me and you are afraid, you will regret having got so near destruction. You say that you are shattered, but do you really long for it? I see you can stand the flashes in my eyes. Yours is a staunch heart, and that is why we believe in you. I was hoping for a long time that you would come, because I can't reach you unless you come to me. On the way to fulfilling your life's mission, you have to pass my way, if you wish for your desire to be fulfilled. I am the wishing well: yes, I wish you well. All is well that is wished by God. Do you wish God well? Then carry out his wish. Throw a penny in the well, and after a million years, it turns to gold. You make a wish, and someone else reaps the reward. If you wish for yourself, do not come to the well.

Truly enough, within a few days a friend, Deen Dayal, took Inayat for a drive to Mount Mowla, where the Nizam of Hyderabad and his chief of staff were due to celebrate a festival. They visited the court physician, Luoman Dowla, who was a Sufi engaged in writing a commentary on Rumi's *Masnavi*. Immediately he introduced Inayat to Prime Minister Maharajah Krishna Prasad. A Hindu, this unusually gifted and refined personality was at heart a Sufi adept and mystic, highly versed in Sufi literature and metaphysics, especially of the Chishtis, of which he had a unique library collection. At the time he happened to be most depressed, in fact, on the point of collapse; but the longer he spoke to Inayat, the better he seemed to become, until presently he was beaming again. Inayat deplored the onset of decadence of music once held so sacred, intimating how it acted upon the human soul, stirring to life aspects of one's being that feed on beauty; hence its use by the Chishtis to uplift the soul.

Presently messages were coming through at intervals, indicating the progress of the Nizam's procession, and the elaborate preparations were being speeded up. Expectations dragged on far into the night, until at long last, at two o'clock in the morning, the Nizam's own elephant, all richly caparisoned, stepped with dignity into the camp surrounded by the fanfare of bugles, the beating of drums, and a display of Arab sword dancers and torch bearers. Inayat was introduced to the Nizam, who was so overwhelmed by his singing that he stood out of respect while Inayat sang and explained the mystical significance of the songs, the modes, moods, rhythms, and emotions. Himself a poet, a musician, and an initiate, the Nizam knew how to appreciate every detail, and his casual simplicity impressed the young Inayat immensely.

Sound is the highest source of manifestation; whosoever therefore has knowledge thereof possesses the key to the universe.

The following morning, stirred by the exalted spirit coming to him through this unexpected message of music, the Nizam, who had slept little, wished to see again the one who had so uplifted his soul. Living the life of an ascetic behind the scenes of the royal splendor, he demonstrated his friendship by receiving Inayat in all simplicity, seated on a carpet on the floor and dressed in simple clothes. Inayat, at last able to express his music to one who could completely appreciate it, allowed his soul to be transported into the realms of the spirit peculiar to each raga, conveying its subtle nature through the magic of his art, finally reaching out to the only Being whose power enlivens all aspects of his Unity. The Nizam must have been intrigued by the destiny of this young yet magnetic being who, in the guise of a musician, had brought him ecstasy rarely experienced before. The Sufi sees in the friend who has been able to strike a light in his soul a message from above. The Nizam asked Inayat why he had come.

All motives and manifested things, and various people, have behind them the inner motive; should one meditate on causation one would see for oneself that there is one cause behind many causes.

At court the Nizam endowed Inayat with the title of Tansen of India, and took his own emerald ring from his finger to betoken him. History repeats itself; the emperor was granting recognition to the new Tansen, whose spiritual music teacher was once again a silent muni.

Having reached the summit any musician would dream of in his musical career, Inayat underwent a complete about-face. He inwardly renounced the performance of music in favor of the music of the soul. Years later, he taught his pupils to renounce an accomplishment, but only when one has achieved it. His last play, *The Living Dead*, ends with this teaching.

CHAPTER 4

"I Am Seeking
Another Kingdom"

INITIATION—THE GURU-CHELA RELATIONSHIP

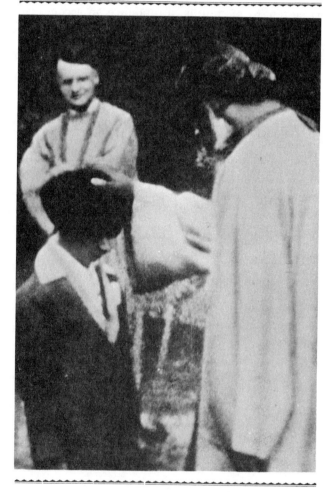

Initiation is taking a step forward in a direction which one does not know.—Gayan, 55

A change was now coming upon Inayat. He used to spend long night vigils meditating. Sleep would at times state its claim. But well he fought it, discounting its arguments; and morning found him singing so that he seemed illuminated by heavenly joy. While sleeping, often he heard a call; immediately he would rise and give himself to contemplation. Several times the beautiful face of a sage appeared as a vision, again and again. A friend versed in the art of interpreting dreams said this was God's summons to the chosen one and a sign that the time had come for him to look for a murshid (a spiritual guide). But each murshid he approached humbly declined the undertaking. This has often happened to masters in the past, to Krishna and Arjuna; St. John the Baptist felt unequal to baptize Jesus. But Jesus confirmed that such is the cosmic law.

Some people think that saints, masters, or sages have no need for initiation, but they forget that no soul can go further on the path without initiation.[1]

A friend took Inayat to see a dervish who was an uncompromising stickler for truth, known for his unpleasant forthrightness, telling people what he thought of them in no uncertain terms. This was his way of screening disciples rather than dallying with the sensationalism surrounding some gurus with thousands of followers. Contrary to his usual custom, he offered Inayat a welcome of distinction, and sat with him, meditating together in silence. His friend was able to ascertain that the dervish had not simply changed his mood, since he treated him as offhandedly as ever.

When a being becomes truth, he reads into the hearts of all beings like an open book.

One day Inayat visited the teacher Moulana Khair-ul-Mubin, famous for his brilliant speeches which drew thousands in Hyderabad; the Nizam himself would come and stand in reverence in a corner among the crowd. When he was prevailed upon to undertake Inayat's spiritual guidance, he said "I? I do not deserve that privilege; I am his servant." Hearing the arrival of a distinguished visitor, he said, "but wait to see who comes!"

Within a moment, there appeared, entering in at the door, a personality who seemed as if he had dropped from heaven, and was gently stepping on the earth that was not his place,

wrote Hazrat Inayat Khan recalling that moment.

"Who is this young man? He appears to my soul so intensely," exclaimed the Murshid Khwaja Abu Hashim Madani. In Oriental fashion, Inayat dropped to the teacher's feet. Lifting him, the Murshid said, "I have waited for you so long." This was the face Inayat had seen so repeatedly. The Murshid gave Inayat his initiation then and there. Those present were conscious of a happening of inconceivable moment: These two beings were so obviously made to meet. The destiny relating a Pir-o-Murshid to his successor had materialized, after having been revealed as a premonition.[2]

People often wonder what is the meaning of initiation. There are moments in the progress of a person, as he gains in realization or unfolds his personality, when there is a sudden change of state, a quantum leap, a milestone in his evolution. This is called esoterically a cosmic initiation.

The process of incubation can be initiated by a master through personal contact, called *darshan* by the Hindus and *tawwajeh* by the Sufis. This may occur in the course of a passing visit or constitute a deeper, and therefore stable, involvement. When initiation is so, it is formalized as a covenant, the oath of allegiance of the disciple having chosen his master, and the latter's acquiescence, which means that the initiator takes upon himself a serious involvement in the pupil's karma.

Initiation is a sacred trust, a trust given by the murshid to his mureed and a trust given by the mureed to the murshid. There should no longer be a wall from the moment of this initiation; for if there is a wall, then the initiation is not an initiation any more. And when the wall between the mureed and the murshid has been removed, then the next step will be for the wall to be removed that stands between God and the worshipper.[3]

Some people, although not all, will tell you of their experiences, and how at different times in their life a sudden change of outlook came to them. It is not usual experience to wake up suddenly one day from sleep and find that our point of view has changed; but it is no exaggeration to say that it takes but one moment to change one's outlook on life entirely. This is what an initiation is, an initiation which is above the initiations of the earth as we know them. One thing leads to another, and so we go on in life from one initiation to the next; and each step on the ladder that seems to be standing before us, for us to climb, becomes an initiation. And each step on that ladder changes our point of view if only we hold on to the ladder and do not drop down; for there is always the possibility of going either forward or backward.

One finds, too, that sometimes one goes through an illness or great suffering, and at the end of it one's whole outlook on life has changed. It also sometimes happens that someone who has traveled far returns apparently quite altered. Again, there often comes a sudden change of outlook after a person has formed a friendship, or has been somebody's pupil, or has married. There are even some cases where the change is so marked that one can say he has become an entirely new person.

They first take Bayat, initiation, from the hand of one whose presence gives them confidence that he will be a worthy counselor in life and a guide on the path as yet untrodden, and who at the same time shows them in life the image of the Rasul personality, the personality of the ideal man.

When this initiation takes place it then becomes the responsibility of the initiator to think of the welfare and well-being of his pupil; and it becomes the responsibility of the initiated to be faithful and true and steady and unshaken through all tests and trials. There are some who will go to one person and be initiated, and then afterwards they go to another to be initiated, and then to a third.[4]

The difference in outlook between the one who does not have a teacher and the initiated one is that the former simply follows his judgment or intuition, whereas the one who has handed his confidence over to his initiator expects to learn from him a point of view other than his own, and therefore hands himself into his hands.

When Hazrat Inayat Khan met Hazrat Abu Hashim Madani, he knew he could trust him with his life without knowing where he was going to lead him.

Khwaja Hashim Madani, an aristocratic Arab of the house of the ruling families of Medina, a great scholar of theology and erudite in Sufi lore and metaphysics, seemed to be continually rapt in the contemplation of God; his very being was the greatest lesson in the perfecting of the human nature and an example of nobility—of that aristocracy of the soul of which Inayat wrote later. Inayat used to visit him every evening at his bungalow in the rocky wilds in the neighborhood of a famous Sufi tomb, that of Khwaja Husain Wali Shah (a few miles from Hyderabad). With a selected few, he would then partake in the Sufi practices of meditations and repetitions which would last until the early hours of the morning. Some mureeds remember that as the hours of the night passed by, the tone was raised to a higher and yet higher pitch by the atmosphere of the Murshid's inspired countenance, drawing them ever further into ecstatic musings, which lifted them beyond their reach to disclose the mystery of a life such as can only be grasped through divine emotions; so that they returned home at sunrise sanctified.

The word initiation is interpreted by different people in different ways. By some it is considered to be a kind of attachment to a certain secret order, but what I mean by initiation is taking a step forward on a path unknown to oneself.[5]

Ghazali, a great Sufi writer of Persia, has said that entering the spiritual path is just like shooting an arrow at a point one cannot see, so that one does not know what the arrow is going to hit; one only knows one's own action, and one does not see the point aimed at. This is why the path of initiation is difficult for a wordly man.[6]

Khwaja Abu Hashim Madani had come to Hyderabad during his youth with his father as royal guests of the Nizam. Attending one day a recital of Sufi lore (*sama*), one by one the dervishes were moved to demonstrations of rapt appreciation for the hidden meaning of the words and the beauty of the relief in which they had been set by the musical rendering; Abu Hashim sat very dignified, as he disapproved of any emotional display. Suddenly he noticed that a masterly and magnetic personality, a great dervish, God-intoxicated while completely sovereign, seemed to be sounding into the depth of his heart; it was Khwaja Mohammed Hassan Kalimi Dehlevi, successor in the chain of the Chishti Sufis. After the ceremony was ended, he told Abu Hashim that he had orders to initiate him. "This cannot be," said Abu Hashim, "since it has already been arranged that I shall be initiated by my father's murshid upon my return to Medina, my hometown." "There can be no mistake in the orders received by me," replied the Murshid. The following night Abu Hashim dreamed that the murshid of his father instructed him to receive his initiation from Khwaja Mohammed Hassan. In the morning, the Murshid appeared, saying "I have come to initiate you." "But I said yesterday it could not be," replied Abu

Hashim. "Have you already forgotten your dream?" retorted the Murshid.

At first, training was very difficult for this personality used to measuring his wits with the most erudite commentators of the Qur'an or the subtle dialectics of Arab philosophers, but the Pir-o-Murshid had a learning to give that bypassed the meanderings of the mind for the sharper reality of being. When Abu Hashim submitted to his Murshid his most intricate queries regarding metaphysical problems, Khwaja Mohammed Hassan, who was the product of a knowledge unaccountable by words, could not answer. That night, as Abu Hashim was repeating his *dhikr* (invocation of God), in came Khwaja Mohammed Hassan, transfigured. "I am the answer to your problem," he said. Indeed, he was the answer in his being, which is more important than mental understanding. The distinguished and elegantly attired Abu Hashim surrendered the pride of his scholarly standing at the feet of the sovereign with the patched robe through whom God had suddenly become so vividly present. It is with human material so tried that the ranks of the Sufis are filled.

In his turn, Khwaja Abu Hashim taught metaphysics by developing the realization of the cosmic principles embodied in the being of his pupils. He did not try to fit into philosophical principles that which the human being senses when he stretches his faculties to their utmost reach. Rather, these murshids, who were artists in the psychology of human consciousness, knew how to sharpen all the faculties of their pupils in their soul-searching meditation to such a degree of sensitiveness as to permit them to perceive with their sense of feeling what the mind, in its inadequacy, can only render schematically. An academic approach to this learning would blunt this fine "sixth sense."

One day when the Murshid was perhaps more explicit when speaking about *wujud* (existence), *shuhud* (consciousness), *Tanzih* (transcendence), and *tashbih* (immanence), Inayat took a notebook; immediately the Murshid changed the subject, thus signifying to him that this was not the method of learning. Later when Inayat often returned home spellbound after his teacher had spoken so inspiringly, he realized that if he had tried to note the words down, he would not have sensed the mood or the sublime revelation of the ineffable reality which so moved him now; this spontaneous outpouring could never have been recorded by pen. The thoughts he noted in those days, later to be included in the book *Minkar-i-Musikar*, reflect the scruple he gained from his teacher about stereotyping a live realization in a philosophical concept.

O Inayat, you and this high talk. How dare you shout about the truth!

A fellow mureed criticized Inayat to the Murshid because he did not seem orthodox enough in his practice of Islam; his friends were mainly among Hindus, Parsis, Christians, and Jews. The Murshid admired Inayat for knowing the Hindu Shastras by heart, having rendered the Zoroastrian Gasthas to music, and keeping the Bible by the bedside, while being an authority on the Qur'an, and said, "He has a universal spirit; I cannot very well tell you what Inayat Sahib is, nor what he is to me."

It is difficult to describe the depth of the friendship of murshid and mureed in the East, especially the link of Inayat and his Murshid. Inayat always used to respond to the Murshid's inner call for him to visit him, precisely at the right moment. The Murshid would respond to his thoughts, talking about what had been on his mind for a long time. One day he noticed that the Murshid was wearing golden shoes, which contrasted with his usual sobriety. Immediately the Murshid said, impromptu: "The wealth of the world lies at my feet"; in other words, it does not govern me. And when he was seriously ill, Inayat thought, "Why are such high beings subject to illness?" Immediately the Murshid said, "Life on earth is subject to nature's laws."

"There are many ties that make people friends in the world," he used to say, "but there is one tie which is closest of all: the relationship between the murshid and the mureed."

What it meant for so self-willed and enterprising a personality as Inayat to subject his being entirely to the tuning of his Murshid's masterly hand, transpires in the verse of a poem that he addressed to him: "I have placed my pride in your hands."

One day, a servant of the Murshid came with a message; because of his humble attire, even the servants of the house took no notice of him. Inayat had at the time a reputation for elegance, moving in exclusive circles, so that the servant thought he would notice him still less. But such was the honor with which Inayat treated this servant that, much to the servant's dismay, he kissed his hands as a mark of respect for the one who had sent him. Such are feelings in the East!

Khwaja Abu Hashim had a most reverential regard for his wonderful pupil. Such was the delicacy in which their friendship grew that, though he loved Inayat's music, he did not like to prevail upon him to sing for him. Sometimes however, when his longing for music was very great, he would ask him to tell him something about such or such a raga. Then Inayat knew that he wished him to sing, and he did so. Many times Inayat's art, heightened under the spell of the Murshid's mystic mood, brought the latter a state of ecstasy. Inayat always knew when his Murshid wished for his presence, and never failed to respond. It was generally when the Murshid's spirit was soaring high and he wished to communicate to Inayat some particular aspect of the divine Nature discovered in his soul-searching contemplation while he was still immersed in it. The mureeds knew they need not bring their problems to their murshid, as he would invariably talk about them, giving a hint as to their solution without their having to broach the subject. Sometimes he would sit silently and everyone would remain silent, in reverence, rapt in an ineffable serenity.

Toward the end of his training, Inayat gives evidence of having undergone a deep experience of a mystical and initiatory nature, totally jolting him in his foundations:

I am losing all my consciousness and knowledge. . . . My name is the unknown.[7]

When the time of his passing was drawing nigh, Khwaja Abu Hashim Madani made Hazrat Pir-o-Murshid Inayat Khan his successor in the Chain of the Sufis, saying that he had received from Khwaja Muin-ud-din Chishti (the founder of the Order in India) instructions to tell him that he was missioned to carry the Sufi Message to the West. "Fare forth into the world my child and harmonize the East and the West with the harmony of thy music; spread the wisdom of Sufism abroad for to this end art thou gifted by God." "May God strengthen your faith," were the Murshid's words of blessing. When one knows how Hazrat Inayat Khan persevered on the strength of the conviction bestowed upon him at that moment, in the early years in the West at a time when odds seemed so hopeless and his music proved too unappreciated to become the medium of his Message, one can surmise what faith he had in the higher wisdom of his great predecessors—a faith which later proved so completely justified. It presently became evident that it was his knowledge of the moods of the soul stirred by music that gave him his mastery of tuning human souls to their highest pitch and blending them into the human brotherhood that was his message.

On the day he had foretold for his departure, intimating it to his wife six months before, the Khwaja Abu Hashim assembled his servants, asking them to forgive him if he ever had proffered a hard word or committed a deed that was hurtful. Then he asked to be alone and passed into the higher sphere repeating the *dhikr* (the testimony of the unity of God).

CHAPTER 5

Man, the Master
of His Destiny

TRAINING AND MASTERY

The purpose of life is to attain to mastery; this is the motive of the spirit, and it is through this motive at the back of it that the whole universe is created—IV, 119

By learning self-discipline one learns to suppress the outer inclinations in order to make way for the inner inclinations to rise and to flourish, which finally culminates in what we call mastery. In him is awakened that spirit by which the whole universe was created.—IV, 120

Murshid emerged from his training transformed beyond recognition. His being was magnetic, and diffused a holy atmosphere. His words came from the depth of his being. This is what he later taught his disciples, calling it the magnetism of the soul. And he spoke with the authority of one who had been promoted into the service of the spiritual government of the world. What was the secret in his training that had brought about these amazing results? He had undergone that very same discipline that he had witnessed throughout his childhood and youth among the ascetics and hermits. Now he had himself become a master in the art so that, having graduated, he was able to teach it.

In his later years he does give his disciples a clue to the art of mastery, making an adept a vehicle of that "very power that moves the universe." It is, of course, discipline from beginning to end.

Knowledge and wisdom are not enough; it takes power to make things happen, and one needs strength to withstand one's problems. Yet a wise and scrupulous person deprecates power because it can lead to dastardly abuse: in popular terms, an ego-trip. The great art consists in learning how to affirm the divine power instead of one's own, which those who have undergone that rare feat, a retreat in meditation, have experienced as they emerged from their seclusion. One feels so strong that one might transform the world, and on the other hand most precarious, volatile, and fragile, channeling a power that is almost too great for one to handle. One is never so strong as when one is broken, witnessing the divine power coming through. One discovers in oneself the same power that makes the planets revolve on their axes, and gravitate around the suns, the same power that moves the sap in the

71

trees, and the power of the storms, and of the sea and of the winds; the same power inhabits the human being. When one touches upon that power impersonally, when one experiences oneself as the impersonal wave of that ocean, as the instrument of that tremendous power, one is able to accomplish things that one could not do on one's own strength.

One night, as Murshid was sleeping in Rangoon, a strange character entered surreptitiously, literally summoning him under threat of arms to sing before the king of the Burmese underground gangsters, Masiti. Murshid's name had been in the papers; he had become a hero overnight, and Masiti wished to boost his own prestige by proving how he could commandeer the popular star to perform at his command. Murshid did not hesitate to take up the challenge; he had no qualms about appearing in person on the spot, and so impressed the robber king with his spiritual power that the latter could not bring himself to press him any further to sing.

It was this staggering combination of sovereign power with compassionate gentleness that gave Murshid his greatness and so deeply moved the souls of all those who came in contact with him. In fact, this was his very message: it is the tradition of the dervish kings, the magi or hierophants, to embody the divine power while being themselves selfless. This is the very application of the Sufi way of *fana*, annihilation, counterbalanced by *baqa*, a reinstatement by the divine operation in one's being without interference by the individual will. Here lies the secret of the power of the real spiritual master who can help people overcome their sense of limitation and helplessness. For Murshid:

Master is he who controls things and affairs, and he becomes a slave who is controlled by the things of the earth. . . . There is no worse enemy of many than helplessness. . . . Therefore the mystics have tried by exercises, by practices, and by studies to overcome limitation as much as possible.[1]

How did Murshid gain the mastery he displayed as a guest of the robber? Mastery is a power that one develops by practicing it on oneself. If the rishis and dervishes to whose company Murshid belonged free themselves from the conditioning of the limited concepts and automated behavior of the fellowmen, it does not mean that they become vagabonds at the mercy of the whim of their bodies or minds or emotions, but they control these by a determination that most people would shy away from exercising. Has one any idea of the willpower that it must have taken Buddha to sit under the tree at Bodh-Gaya for forty-nine days and nights of uninterrupted meditation amid the wild animals, the insects, the monsoon, enduring physical and mental exhaustion? The Sufi dervish Ibn Adham could hardly drag his body to the stream, and Khwaja Farid ud-Din Ganj-i Shaker hung upside down in a well for forty days repeating the dhikr. When a person has thus overcome himself while remaining selfless, people sense his determination and authenticity, and he is able to help them overcome themselves by the very power of his being.

By studying the lives of the ascetics who lived in the mountains and forests and in the wilderness, we learn that those who have really sought after truth have done their utmost to practice self-discipline; without it no soul in the world has ever arrived at a higher realization.[2]

It is therefore that the sages, in order to develop personal power, give one key, and that is the key to the whole mystery: the control of impulse, every impulse, whatever it may be.

Ascetics gain this extraordinary ascendency by sitting hours at a time without moving, however painful for the limbs, overcoming any desire to move; holding breath for periods unthinkable by the norm; looking into the sun for hours, when normally a retina exposed to the sun for more than a few seconds would be irremediably scorched. The secret of these initial practices consists in imposing upon the body, or the mind, or the personal will, a restraint, simply for the purpose of strengthening the will. It need not be practiced only in the wilderness. This is why Yoga has been adopted so extensively in the West; its advantage over gymnastics is that it fosters control of the will by sustaining an action and thereby enhances the higher being.

The next discipline is controlling one's breath, prolonging the inhaling, exhaling, retention, directing it in various azimuths in space, or to different parts of the body, synchronizing it with thoughts and harnessing it to tones and syllables. The next practice consists in controlling the glance. One learns this by fixing one's gaze on a nail in the wall, or a distant star, or the sun, without twitching one's eyelids; or an imaginary spotlight suspended in the void with closed eyes; or by casting one's eyes at infinity without allowing the physical scene to condition one's focus.

The first thing to do is to get control of the glance. The next is to get control of the feelings. And the third is to get control of the consciousness.[3]

Physical functions are brought under control, including slowing down the heartbeat.

Sometimes also there is a desire for food, a desire to drink, a desire to sleep, a desire to walk, or a desire to sit. Every one of these little desires can be checked;

and by checking them, by keeping them back, by controlling them, one can attain to this power of will.

Among the various kinds of physical culture known to modern world there is nothing that teaches the method or the secret of sustaining an action. For instance to be able to sit in the same posture without moving, to be able to look at the same spot without moving the eyes, to be able to listen to something without being disturbed by something else, to be able to experience hardness, softness, heat, or cold, while keeping one's vibrations even, or to be able to retain the taste of salt, sweet or sour.[4]

It takes a great deal of trouble to rule the body, for it is not willing to be ruled. Yogis, faqirs, Sufis may be seen sitting, standing in one posture for hours together. All the postures adopted are to control and govern every atom of the body, so that it may be under the control of the will. I do not mean that one should devote all one's time to these things, or even that one should have certain exercises for this. When one understands the matter, and carries it out in one's everyday life, then one's life becomes a continual progress.[5]

They have made a science out of this; there is a warrior's posture, a thinker's posture, an aristocratic posture, a lover's posture, a healer's posture; different postures for the attainment of different objects. These postures make it easier for man to learn the science of direction; posture does not denote anything but direction. It is an activity, an energy working in a certain direction which makes a certain form. That is why the way one sits makes a difference; it makes a difference whether one sleeps on the right side or on the left, whether one stands on one's feet or on one's head.[6]

It is a matter of being the boss of what one assumes is one's self, "seeing that neither our mind nor our body rules us, but that we rule our body and our mind."[7]

The next practice consists in controlling all compulsions, for example the impulse to speak without premeditating what one is going to say.

In human nature there is an inner urge to express oneself; and that urge pushes a word out of one, so to speak, before one has really thought of it; and all this shows lack of control over oneself. Very often a person tries to answer somebody who has not yet finished speaking; before a sentence is completed the answer is given.

Or the tendency to gossip about one another:

Expression or sentiment is an outlet given to the energy of the heart, which if it had been conserved would have been a power in itself. A person who expresses an opinion about another readily, a mist is produced by his word before his own eyes; he can see no further than what he sees. If he controlled that impulse of expressing his opinion, it would be an effort at that moment, but it would open before him the vision revealing all that he would wish to know.

Or the compulsion to answer back an insult:

One must check the wrong impulse, even as small as the thought of eating something that one likes, the wish to drink something that one wishes, an impulse to talk back to a person who insults, an impulse to pinch a person by saying a word, an impulse to hurt a person by cutting words, an impulse to get into the secret of others, to find out the secret of others, the impulse to criticize. All such undesirable impulses can be mastered. And it is not that one has mastered them, but one has gained a power over oneself.

A further discipline connected with the control of impulses is checking one's tendency to spill a secret; somebody in a relaxed moment may have confided to you his life's secret; or it may be one's own project that someone plagiarizes.

Especially when a person is not able to keep his secret he has much to suffer in life, because that power is most helpful, the power of keeping secret.

The next set of practices consists of checking emotion:

There are moments when laughter must be kept back, and there are times when tears must be withheld. And those who have arrived at the stage where they can act efficiently the part that they are meant to act in this life's drama, have even power over the expression of their face. . . . The child soul will give way to every feeling; the old soul will strike the higher note in spite of every difficulty.

In the orchestra there is a conductor and there are many who play the music; and every player of an instrument has to fulfill his part in the performance. If he does not do it rightly, it is his fault. The conductor will not listen if he says he did not do it properly because he was sad or because he was too glad.[8]

This will include giving expression to one's pain:

In Turkey a special education was given in the home in all good families. And that education was that how much pain, or trouble, or sorrow, or worry, or anxiety you have, as much as you can bear, you must bear, and not tell anybody. And the second stage of the control was not to show it on your face, you must bear it inwardly; no matter if you are going through the greatest torture, keep smiling to the world. And there are to be found wonderful examples of that practice. And there is a nobleness in it. A person whose heart is crying and laughs before the world is a brave man. And the person whose heart is laughing and whose tears are going out is a hyprocrite.

Self-control is best exercised when one can constrain one's anger.

This shows how a person can even fight and yet keep control over his anger and pain. As long as he is the master he can be blamed for nothing. But that is just the question: to be the master! Suppose a person is angry and you get cross with him too. It may bring a certain satisfaction to give an outlet to that anger at the moment, but if only you would discover the joy of being able to smile when the other person is cross, what a difference from the satisfaction one derives from the other act! The joy is so much greater because you keep control; it is just like not adding more fuel to a fire.[9]

Further, one must control fear: fear of danger, fear of defeat, fear of inadequacy, fear of death. "There is a Surah of the Koran which supports this, where it is said: 'There is no fear in the mastermind.' "

It takes nothing less than this kind of a will before one can undertake to control one's mind, which is what is meant by meditation.

A person who lacks control over his nervous and his muscular systems has no control over his mind; he eventually loses it. But by having control over one's muscular and nervous systems one gets control over the mind also. The means by which life draws in, one draws the life and power and intelligence from the unseen and unknown life. And when one knows the secret of posture, and draws from the unseen world the energy and power and inspiration, one gets the power of sustaining one's thought, one's word, one's experience, one's pleasure, one's joy.

One becomes master of one's thinking:

One should say to the mind, "Look here, you are my mind, you are my instrument, you are my slave and servant, you are here to help me, to work for me in this world. You have to listen to me. You will do whatever I wish, you will think whatever I wish, you will feel whatever I wish. You will not think or feel differently from my wishes, for you are my mind and you must prove in the end to be mine." By doing this we begin to analyze our mind. We begin to see where it is wrong and where it is right; what is wrong in it and what is right in it; whether it is clouded, whether it is rusted, whether it has become too cool or whether it has become over-heated. We can train it ourselves, in accordance with its condition, and it is we who are the best trainers of our mind, better than anybody else in the world. Mastery lies not merely in stilling the mind, but in directing it towards whatever point we desire, in allowing it to be active as far as we wish, in using it to fulfil our purpose, in causing it to be still when we want to still it. He who has come to this has created his heaven within himself.[10]

There is yet another aspect of self-discipline and that is . . . to practice the forgetting of things, so that certain thoughts may not get a hold over one's mind; and in the same way to check thoughts of agitation, anger, depression, prejudice, hatred. This gives moral discipline and by doing so one becomes the master of one's mind.[11]

Finally, the control applies to one's own will, checking unconscious actions.

The first exercise to help the will-power to develop would be to check every act, word, and thought which we do not wish to occur; to avoid unintentional actions, speech, and thoughts. The other exercise that is necessary for the development of will-power is that of seeing that neither our mind nor our body rules us, but that we rule our body and our mind.[12]

Sometimes it is absent-mindedness. The consciousness does not guard the action, and therefore one does an action which is not in the light of consciousness. Sometimes a person puts salt in the tea, or takes a knife of onions and uses it for the butter, or something like this. He knows that it is the onion knife, that he must not touch it. And yet he does not think until he eats it, and then he knows it. I have seen one person very capable of it. Always fish-tea or onion-toast. And then when he would eat he would know that it was wrong. When he would cook I always admired his skill.

If the hand is not trained enough, the mind is not satisfied.

The overall principle involved in mastery is to face and endure unpleasantness instead of running away from it; this is the way of strengthening one's being, whereas by protecting oneself against exposure, stress, and strain, one becomes weak.

Mastery comes from the evolution of the soul, and the sign of mastery is to conquer everything that revolts one.... The entire system of the Yogis, especially of the Hatha Yogis, is based upon making themselves acquainted with something their nature revolts against.[13]

This is why Shiva is always represented in Hindu mythology with a snake around his neck; he lets himself be bitten every day to immunize himself against the evil of creation.

The theory behind vaccination and inoculation is the same as the one taught as Hatha Yoga by Shiva, or Mahadeva as he is often called. It is said of Mahadeva that he used to drink poison, and by doing so he got over its effect. Mahadeva was the most venturesome among the ascetics. He is pictured carrying a serpent round his neck: If one can be such friends with a serpent as to keep it round one's neck, one can no doubt sit comfortably in the presence of someone one does not like. The hatred and prejudice and nervousness which are felt in the presence of someone one does not like would then not arise. The soul which has forgotten its battle with everything that made it fear and tremble and run away, has conquered life and has become the master of life; it attains the kingdom of heaven. No doubt the methods which Mahadeva adopted were extreme measures; no one could recommend them to his pupils and be thought sane in this modern world! The principle of Mahadeva, of the dervishes, of the great faqirs of all ages is this one principle: to drink all difficulties as a wine. Then there is no more difficulty.[14]

That aspect of destruction and knowing about destruction can be easier understood again by something which we see in the modern science, by the medium of what they call inoculation. By putting that destructive element in one's body one makes one's body disease-proof. That particular disease is no longer a disease, but the nature of that person. That is the method of the mystic from a spiritual point of view. That death is a death so long as man is unacquainted with it. When man eats it up, then he has eaten death; death cannot eat him. Then he knows the life eternal. That is the mystery of the Message of Jesus Christ. To seek eternal life from the beginning to the end. The mystery of eternal life is past once a person has tasted of death; then he is eternal.

The "immunity" against that which is irksome or corrosive or threatening to one's complacency and security is the very hallmark of the ascetic; it is indifference or detachment, called *vairagya.*

The real proof of one's progress in the spiritual path can be realized by testing in every situation of life how indifferent one is. There are calls from every side, from all that is good, from all that is beautiful, from all that is kind, from all that is comforting. And when one has shown indifference to all these calls, then one begins to hear calls from one's immediate surroundings, and those are a wish that one's goodness may be appreciated and that one's kindness may be gratefully received; that one's knowledge may be understood by others; one's rank must be recognized; one's piety must be observed by others; one's virtue must be valued; and one's good qualities must find response; one's good actions must bear fruit. The more one makes oneself free from all these calls the more one becomes raised above life. That is the true indifference, Vairagya, one must practice. And the strength that comes from this indifference is inexplicable and gives man mastery over life. Spiritual man is necessarily sensitive, and without this protection his life on earth would become miserable. To live among surroundings which are not conscious of the delicacy of his feelings may hurt him and cause him more harm than it would to a person like them. This is the only way to be among them and yet to be above them. The adept does not hear what he does not wish to hear, he does not see what he does not wish to see, and he does not feel what he does not wish to feel. This power is attained when one has learned how to ride on the Garuda [the winged steed], which in the terms of the Prophet is Burak.

The great objection that one hears rising in the mind of many is: Does this not kill the spontaneity of beings, make them inhibited and cagey and take away the sheer joy of living? Of course the Master was well aware of this argument. We know how perplexed a young girl was at a summer school to see how Murshid had indulged in cakes at a party, but surely the one who has undergone the most austere fasting and for years pulled himself out of bed after four hours of sleep can afford a banquet and knows how to relish it. Murshid tells the story of a murshid who, walking in the garden with his disciples, picked up a rose and kissed it. Whereupon, since it is a custom that disciples should follow the example of their master, they proceeded each in turn to kiss the rose. But shortly thereafter, the Murshid picked up the red-hot iron of an ironmonger. Now the disciples reluctantly demurred. Murshid's secretary remembered how when there was a chance to walk in a beautiful field of rare alpine lilies, the Master said, "Have we come here to work or to look at nature?" Knowing Murshid's need and longing for nature, we realize what a taskmaster he was to himself, because he knew the importance of mastery. His secretary tells how he used to work overtime, leaving no work undone for the morrow.

Murshid's answer to the question that grips us at present was to consider an impulse as a power placed at one's disposal: Either one can squander it by giving in to it, or harness it, thereby leading to a still greater power. In modern terms, an energy could be scattered in an explosion or channeled constructively in an implosion. The energy of the river or the wind can be transformed into an electric current. Do not inhibit, but transmute.

Every impulse is a power in itself, and every time when the will withdraws an impulse, the will is charged with a new strength and life; which makes the self-mastered man master of all. The process of alchemy is to control these expressions without killing them. There is a difference between controlling and killing. By controlling one possesses power without allowing it to express itself, but by killing it one loses that power which is life. Use everything where it will be most useful, where it will be of some advantage. All such things as passion and anger and irritation one looks upon as very bad, as evil; but if that evil were kept in hand it could be used for a good purpose, because it is a power, it is an energy. In other words, evil, properly used, becomes a virtue; and virtue wrongly used becomes an evil. For instance, when a person is in a rage, or when he really feels like being angry, if he controls that thought and does not express it in words, that gives him great power. . . . A person who has anger and control is to be preferred to the person who has got neither.

We are cutting into the heart of contemporary attitudes toward the outlet of emotions, for example, anger or sex, bearing and manners, outspokenness, or tidiness. The prevailing attitudes run counter to the austerity of the ascetics.

If we react automatically we are no better than a machine and no different from thousands and millions of people who do so. The only way to find in ourselves a trace of that divine heritage which is mastery, is by controlling our reactions against all influences.[15]

We know that self-consciousness in one's body movements makes one artificially stilted. There is a story of how Murshid, noticing how stiffly a soldier was walking in front of him, distended the soldier's muscles by thought transference, so that he began to walk more bouncingly.

No doubt there is also a meaning in controlling the movements. If a person is allowed to go on with his movements we do not know where it wlll end, but at the same time by repressing movements one can turn into a rock.[16]

But we also know how the immobility of the body poised in an *asana*, in contrast to the motion of the world outside, affects the mind, suspending it beyond the throes of agitation and restlessness. And that,

When the speech is controlled, the eyes speak; the glance says what words can never say,

and that the penetrating glance can sound the souls of people, and impose respect.

I have seen a father who could strike his children so that they could tremble, merely by his looks. Besides, a commander is not always so out of position, nor by his particular rank, nor by his loud voice, nor by his important appearance, but by his eyes; for through the eyes the will power of man goes out as a command, which is even stronger than words.

We know how we suffer from the faux pas we make by saying what later we regret. Murshid teaches that it can be cured by practicing periods of silence.

Q. Murshid, would you say, when one has a weakness and sometimes one says a thing which one very well knows one should not say, how can one cure or stop it?

A. By the habit of silence; every day make a habit of silence.

However, to fail to state one's ideas in no uncertain terms if a person whips a dog or does violence to an innocent human being is no self-constraint, it is simply weakness. Christ showed sublime detachment when insulted and tortured by the Romans, but expressed righteous indignation with whip in hand at the temple gates. Moreover, there is certainly danger in straining oneself overmuch in self-constraint. Remember, "Whom do you torture?" was Khwaja Abu Hashim's retort when Inayat asked his permission to increase his ascetic austerities; and Buddha, who had gone to the extremes of human endurance, called for the middle way. One may suffer from an inferiority complex from being thwarted by another person without being able to say anything about it.

But of course if it is not understood rightly one might endanger oneself.... If in order to avoid breaking another person's head he has broken his own head, he has done wrong too.... There is a danger in both cases; on the one side there is a pit, on the other side there is water. There may be a person who by being afraid of getting hurt or oppressed by someone, is always keeping his thoughts and feelings suppressed; if he had expressed them he would have become a very bad man, but by not having been able to express them he had been ruined. Therefore one should develop one's discrimination in order to analyse the reaction, to understand it before it is expressed.[17]

There are cases where one is fighting a losing battle by allowing oneself to be drawn onto the others' battlefield, using their weapons, so that they are at an advantage; in that case, one would best affirm an inner power that the opponent does not possess. One envisions Christ, his head held high, experiencing the way the divine perfection is being flouted, scorned, and violated on the earth plane; helpless on one level and all powerful on the other. We know how powerless we feel faced with tidal waves of thought, particularly if they become obsessive and imperious, and how we suffer from the restlessness of erratic thoughts if we are under stress. Giving in to them is no solution once we have lost the handle; therefore we value meditation.

A man who is helpless before his own mind is helpless before everything in the world; and therefore the great mastery is to stand before one's own mind and make it think what one wishes it to think, and make it feel what one wishes it to feel.[18]

We know how we get drawn by some people into their emotional netherworld by answering an insult with an insult. Our only saving is to lift ourselves above the pull of the emotions of antagonism or hatred by sublime detachment.

It means flying above things instead of standing against them as a material person does. How can one call oneself spiritual if one cannot fly? ... Only, in man there is the possibility of developing that spirit which is called the spirit of mastery, and that spirit is best developed by trying to gain control over one's reactions.[19]

We know how feelings can get the better of us; on the other hand, some of us may have enjoyed the wonderful feeling of having attained an inner sovereignty.

When every feeling is controlled from a free expression, in time it becomes a collected energy; the heart of the mystic becomes a reservoir of power, his every feeling begins to speak beyond words. The next sign of progress is that one begins to feel power. To some extent it may manifest physically and also mentally; and later the power may manifest in one's affairs in life. As spiritual pursuit is endless, so power has no end.[20]

For those who tread the path of mastery, a battery of power is necessary. This battery of power, no doubt, is created by three things: sympathy wakened, self discipline, and self-confidence.

In order to maintain this power, one thing must be observed in everyday life: to have control upon the desire of outgoing. Because for the time, for a moment one feels a satisfaction out of the passion of outgoing. But in the end one finds that one has lost more than gained. What use that generous one is who possesses no wealth?

What is magnetism? Magnetism is this reserved power. And the phenomenon that it shows and the wonders that are performed by this power are too great for words to express; nothing there is that this power cannot conquer, sooner or later. And it is of very great importance for those who walk in the path of meditation to preserve their magnetism.

No doubt all of the masteries examined are ultimately expressions of mastery over the self.

The weakness of the self betrays itself in our susceptibility to be influenced by people, our concern about what people think of us.

When a man is impressed by what others think, if that impression is of disappointment or distress or shame, his power is diminished; but when he is inspired by a thought, a feeling, an action he performs, then he is powerful.[21]

This is felt particularly by fine and sensitive people; the brasher type does not care if he shocks or disappoints other people. But when a sensitive person has himself in control by overcoming the self, then he has nothing to fear, and nothing to be ashamed of or to conceal.

No doubt, one of the greatest sources of power is the power of sincerity, the power of truth.

It is the power of truth that makes one stronger. Apart from those who know truth, even those who do not know truth, if they think rightly will have some power, the power of sincerity.[22]

Master is he who masters himself; teacher is he who teaches himself; governor is he who governs himself, and ruler is he who rules himself.[23] *The sage battles with his own ego, the ordinary man with other people's egos. And the difference in the result of these two battles is that the victory and failure of the ordinary man are momentary, but the victory of the sage is eternal. The former, when he has finished one battle, must begin another, but the latter, once he has succeeded, is victorious. All that the former gains, after all, is not his own; all he gains does not belong to him, but the sage is king in his own kingdom.*

True power is not in trying to gain power; true power is in becoming power. But how to become power? It requires an attempt to make a definite change in oneself, and that change is a kind of struggle with one's false self. When the false self is crucified, then the true self is resurrected. Before the world this crucifixion appears to be lack of power, but in truth all power is attained by this resurrection.[24]

It is an amazing discovery when one clearly sees the link between one's ascendency over oneself and one's control over circumstance; how, as soon as one has mastery over oneself, people treat one with respect, and circumstances begin to run favorably. It is a karmic law, although generally one cannot trace back the causal chain that makes it work. One cannot see how one's sitting for hours controlling one's glance, or one's breath, or one's thought flow, could influence circumstances that seem to be determined by fate, or by other people's wills.

This spirit of agitation shows itself as intolerance, as rivalry, as jealousy, as a dominating spirit, irritability, patronizing. When it is said in the life of Krishna that Krishna had a battle with Kansa, the monster, that monster was not outside of Krishna, that monster was inside of Krishna, that monster was that agitation spirit. Krishna had to fight it, and it is after conquering that spirit of agitation that Krishna became the Messenger of Love.

In fact, what is often ascribed to destiny is the working of a law incorporating the interaction and interplay of our will with that of all creatures in various degrees, and coordinated beyond our understanding.

Just imagine, man has been endowed with the power of determining his destiny.

Thought draws the line of fate. The one who goes the right way, he finds that key to that mastery, the mastery over his destiny. Well, now is the question how far is man granted that power of mastering his destiny and how far he stands in this life helpless? And the answer is, that it differs with every man. That a soul is born on earth helpless, and out of this helplessness it grows, and then learns to help itself.

Do we not see, even in our own limited experience, how things go wrong when we have become weak in will or mind in one affair or another? It is not possible to master the conditions of life until we have learned to control ourselves. Once we have mastery over our self everything will go right. It is just the same as when a rider has no strength in his fingers, so that he cannot hold the horse's reins. His fingers must obey his mind before the horse will obey. This is true of all circumstances in life, and of all the various conditions around us, our relations, our friends. We may complain that no one listens, that our servant does not do what we wish him to do, that our assistants do not carry out our orders. We may blame them when all the time it is ourselves who are to blame because we have not mastered ourselves first. After we have done this they will obey. The Vairagi learns his lesson mainly through abstinence. Why is this? Because things go wrong through our own weakness; we do not do what we wish to do; we consider ourselves so small that we cannot achieve our own wishes.[25]

All movements of the lights in the heavens influence the movements of the life on earth. Not only human beings, but even animals and birds live under the influence of the planets and stars above. But as man is the master of creation, he is in some ways above all influences, yet not every man. There is a stage of evolution in which man is the engineer who works with the machines. The man who has not realized the kingdom of heaven within him is as a machine, and the man who rises above that stage of evolution reigns not only on earth but in heaven.

From all this it is plain that man has two aspects of being: the servant aspect and the master aspect. When only the servant aspect is nourished and the master aspect is not, then the master aspect of his being longs to be master, and cannot be; and the whole conflict in life depends on that. When a person is interested in the master aspect and wishes it to be master, then he becomes master of himself; and he becomes not only master of his thoughts, feelings, and actions, but he becomes master of his affairs. Then the key to what we call fate is in his hands; he becomes the king of the kingdom that has been given to him from God.[26]

Here mastery applies to controlling conditions and circumstances. The master mind does not let himself be controlled by circumstances;

he therefore creates his own conditions and environment and does not allow himself to be coerced into fitting into the circumstances others would try to lay on him.

The balance of life lies in being as fine as a thread and as strong as a steel wire . . . . When a person progresses towards spirituality he must bear in mind that together with his spiritual progress he must strengthen himself against disturbing influences. If not he should know that however much he desires to make progress he will be pulled back against his will by conditions, by circumstances.[27]

It is the weakling who runs away from circumstances because he thinks he is too fine; the strong one intervenes in circumstances, shaping them to his ideal in terms of his divine briefing.

When he cannot put up with conditions around him he may think that he is a superior person, but in reality the conditions are stronger than he.[28]

When one has gained mastery over oneself, one's thoughts become so powerful that what one wishes comes true.

And people start carrying out one's wishes. This is, of course, the way creation is devised, so that a guidance, and therefore a government of the world, should at all be possible. Thus Murshid describes the power of the realized being:

If he were to admit before humanity the power that he has, thousands of people would go after him, and he would not have one moment to live his inner life. The enormous power that he possesses governs inwardly lands and countries, controlling them and keeping them safe from disasters such as floods and plagues, and also wars; keeping harmony in the country or in the place in which he lives; and all this is done by his silence, by his constant realization of the inner life. To a person who lacks deep insight he will seem a strange being. In the language of the East he is called *Madzub*. That same idea was known to the ancient Greeks and traces of it are still in existence in some places, but mostly in the East. There are souls to be found today in the East, living in this garb of a self-realized man who shows no trace outwardly of philosophy or mysticism or religion, or any particular morals; and yet his presence is a battery of power, his glance most inspiring, there is a commanding expression in his looks; and if he ever speaks, his word is the promise of God. What he says is truth; but he rarely speaks a word, it is difficult to get a word out of him; but once he has spoken, what he says is done.[29]

There is no doubt that the discovery of that power, unleashed in one as a result of gaining mastery over oneself, is staggering and awe-inspiring, and has gone to the head of many a well-meaning person because it was more than he could handle.

While using the inner power, beware, there are taps of water which, once opened, may flood the whole world, and there are volcanoes which, once made to burst, may set fire through the whole universe. Man must not play with the power latent in his soul; he must first know toward what end he uses the power, and to what extent he is able to control and use the power.

The secret of this discovery is a dawning realization:

In him is awakened that spirit by which the whole universe was created.[30]

It is all connected with one's realization of one's cosmic dimension, instead of identifying with one's personal sense of limitation. But this realization is distorted and betrayed if one continues to hang on to one's ego, equating the personal power with the divine power. This is what the Muslims blamed the Pharaoh for, contrasting his attitude to that of Moses.

The outer power. . . . eats up the inner power. So it is that the heroes, the kings, the emperors, the persons with great power of arms, wealth or outer influence, have become victims to the very power upon which they always depended.[31]

The great kings of the world very often have been pulled down from their thrones by those who for years bowed and bent and trembled at their command, but the Christlike souls who have washed the feet of the disciples are still held in esteem, and will be honored and loved by humanity forever.

Most people justify their weakness or limitation on the grounds of their humility, which is sometimes a false humility and a pretext for failing to make the effort needed to fulfill one's investiture on earth.

The spirit of limitation is always a hindrance to realizing the spirit of mastery and practising it. Man is powerless in spite of the power which is hidden in him. The powerlessness, the experience of being powerless, is his ignorance of the power within him.[32]

In reality his father had put a large sum in the bank, but he was not conscious of it. It is exactly the same with every soul.[33]

If you do not tell him he does not know. It seems as if the knowledge of his own being is buried within himself.

We should never allow that spirit of mastery which is in us to become blunted by a feeling of inability.[34]

It was the realization of the divine power within them that was the clue to the phenomenal power Murshid had witnessed in sadhus and fakirs and which he had now himself discovered.

It is like a king who does not know his kingship. The moment he is conscious of being a king, he is a king. Every soul is born a king; it is only afterward that he becomes a slave.

Murshid refers to this in the story of Rama from whom the beloved Sita was taken away. Every soul has to fight for this kingdom and to conquer it.[35]

When dervishes, who sometimes have patched sleeves or are scantily clad, who sometimes have food and sometimes not, address one another, they say, "O King of Kings, O Emperor of Emperors." It is the consciousness of what is king or emperor which is before them. The boundary of their kingdom is not limited. The whole universe is their kingdom. It is in this way that a soul proceeds towards perfection, by opening the consciousness and raising it higher. When the soul evolves spiritually, it rises to a height where it sees a wider horizon; therefore its possession becomes greater.[36]

The beauty of this realization is in being aware of one's personal precariousness and helplessness and, concurrently, of one's divine inheritance in incorporating the divine perfection.

The soul feels, "I am a king, but in this mortal casket I have become a pauper."[37]

Murshid often quotes a verse from his Murshid's lore:

I, the poor, have such a strength,
That if the eyes had eyes,
They could not see the rapidity of my steps,
This is the strength of the strong.

It is a matter of realization: If one realized that one's body is simply a product of the impersonal forces of the universe converging upon themselves and cannot be isolated from its ground, and is not, therefore, a divisible fraction of the planet; that one's mind is the thinking of the cosmos, so that one cannot think differently from the way all people think; and that one's soul dovetails inextricably with all souls; one could not think of oneself as a person anymore, and would therefore not experience limitation.

Once man has become conscious of his body, mind and soul, his power becomes greater than the power of the sun.[38]

Mastery is the nature of the Shuhud part of our being. Subjection to the laws, to conditions, and to one's own desires, which enslave man, is the nature of the Wujud part of our being. The consciousness of the Wujud part keeps one among the sheep, however good and pious that person may be; but the consciousness of the Shuhud part of our being makes the spirit lion, raising the spirit above all fears and doubts and above weaknesses.

How is this consciousness of Shuhud attained? By closing our eyes to our limited self and by opening our heart to God, not that God Who is called a king and pictured as being in Heaven, but the God Who is all perfection, Who is in Heaven and on earth and Who is within and without, the God who is all in all, Who is visible, tangible, audible, perceptible, intelligible, and yet beyond man's comprehension. It is the consciousness of the God Who is never absent which gives that illumination, those riches, that strength, that calm and peace to the soul, for which the soul has taken the journey through this world of limitations, and here on earth by experiencing life through the form of man it accomplishes its purpose and the wish with which it has started from Heaven is fulfilled on earth.

CHAPTER 6

Peering Beyond
the Veil

INTUITION—TELEPATHY—REVELATION

When the eyes open and begin to see with the divine sight, even the leaves of the trees become the pages of the sacred book—Sa'adi, Persian Sufi poet (in IV, 128)

To see without eyes, to hear without ears.—XII, 20

All faces are His Face.

The veil shall be lifted from thine eyes and thy sight shall become keen.—Qur'an

$\mathcal{M}$urshid Inayat was developing a startling intuition. Wherever he went the nature of people was revealed to him. It happened that just at this stage of his life he came across many seers who demonstrated this uncanny gift. Walking in the streets of Secunderabad, Murshid came across a fakir clad in rags, laughing madly, and uttering astonishing pronouncements, while throwing pennies to crowds of children who followed him. As he sat there, people soon gathered round, and the madhzub performed extraordinary feats of intuition by reading everyone's condition with alarming precision.

He told each one all about themselves, much to their embarrassment. To one he said: "Blackguard, you are complaining because you were given the sack from your job. Why did you embezzle the money entrusted to you?" And to a boy who was present, he said, "Do you know why you failed in your examination? At first you wrote the right answer on your slate, but then you doubted and copied from your neighbor's. That was your punishment."

There was a fakir who shielded himself from the kind of popular display that often surrounds gurus, by insulting those who came to him out of curiosity. Inayat's young friends kept this a secret, curious to see how the fakir would treat him. Upon seeing Inayat, he rose from his seat and sat with him in silent meditation, while he treated the man who accompanied him to his usual insults. There was the fakir who collected silver coins from those who came to have their fortunes told. He not only gave each one the answer to his question, but the question he intended to ask. To the Raja's brother, he said: "Now your intention is to test me, which I do not particularly appreciate, but here goes: You wish to know what the Raja is going to tell you when you see him next." Then he scribbled something on a piece of paper, placed it in an envelope, and bid him not to open it before he had actually had his conversation with the Raja. It was precisely right. There was the fakir who kept people away by sheer disagreeableness so that courage was needed to approach him. One desperate man overcame his fear and told him that he was facing a court case that very day and was so afraid lest he lose the trial and his family be financially ruined. The fakir wrote on a piece of paper: "I dismiss the case." And this was precisely what the judge decreed.

In India those who possess such powers (called *siddhis*) are held in awe. A man was afraid of facing the dervish who had once cursed him. Scared by the wrath of the dervish, he had inadvertently crossed the road and broken his leg; but he hastily added, "If I had not broken my leg, I would have taken that first flight of Pakistani Airlines that crashed." "If cursing you saved your life, why not let yourself be cursed again?" I asked. He replied, "Once was enough."

How can one doubt those powers? Once, during a war, there was a dervish who turned the cannons on the city wall in what seemed random directions, and one could see by the direction he gave them whether the state armies would be victorious or not.

Abu Sayed Mohammed Hashim Madani speaks of how he heard, in an assembly, a voice calling him by name, and the voice was heard by all present. He sprang up, saying that he was being called by his Murshid. He took the train and after some hours arrived at the house, where he found his Murshid about to pass from this earthly plane. The Murshid said to him, "My cup of life on this plane has already filled and the call has come since last night. I have been holding on that I might see you and bless you; and now I am passing on from this mortal plane to the life everlasting."

The biographical notes of disciples are replete with personal accounts of the way the Master picked up their thoughts or answered their unuttered questions at a lecture; or the answer came in silence. For example:

Once when I attended his lectures, there were many problems on my mind and I was looking for an answer. I did not have to wait till after the lecture to ask my questions, for during the lecture he answered all of them, looking at me all the while.

Another testimony says:

One day Murshid asked me if I should like to work for him. I said "I should

love it, but I am not free. I have a sister living with me." Murshid answered
"You will be free." After a few months, my sister married and I was free. Some
months passed. Then Murshid came to Holland and as soon as he saw me, he
said, "You are free." I had not let him know before. I asked (speaking about his
native country), "Do you think you will go back there?" "Yes, when my task is
fulfilled." This is exactly what happened. One night in Katwijk, in 1922, I
distinctly heard my name being called. I was immediately wide awake and got
up. There was nobody in the room and I lay down again. Then I heard the same
voice, asking "Will you work for the Message?" The next day, I was so full of
what I had heard that I asked Murshid: "Did you ask me that question this
night?"; Murshid looked at me long and seriously and said: "What is the
answer?" I knew that this was to be the most important moment in my life and
I said, "Yes, Murshid."

Once Murshid asked his disciples to let their thoughts express
themselves in symbols and then showed the meaning of what each one
had seen and explained these differences in terms of the differences of
their beings; he revealed their past and future and described how they
could be if they really wanted. Murshid gives us a peep into the
condition he was experiencing:

Then a person begins to communicate with all things and all beings. Wherever
his glance falls, on nature, on characters, he reads their history, he sees their
future. Every person he meets, before he has spoken one word with him, he
begins to communicate with his soul. Before he has asked any question, the
soul begins to tell its own history; every person and every object stands before
him as an open book.

How we would like to be able to have such insight into people! How
one would like to know for sure how one stands in relation to a friend
or acquaintance, since one's judgment of a person so often deceives
one. One would like to know if there is a karmic debt or bond or fate
involved.

Someone who is afraid of you, someone is against you, someone is in favor of
you, someone who is trying to help you, someone who is thinking of you,
someone who is going against your wishes, someone who is standing for you,
all this you can see from a distance if your mind is clear as a mirror.

How one would like to find a solution to people's problems when they
ask for advice.

The first impression tells a man whether he will be successful or not, whether a
person is right or not, whether there will be friendship between two people or
not.[1]

One receives warning of a coming danger, the promise of success, or the
premonition of failure; if any change is to take place in life one feels it.[2]

It is so interesting that in spite of all difficulties that the world presents one feels life worth living when one begins to notice how those who were going forward begin to go backward, and those who were going backward begin to go forward; when one observes how a person, without sinking into water, is drowned in life and how a person who was drowning begins to swim and is saved; when one sees how from the top a person comes down to the bottom in a moment and how a person who was creeping on the ground has at last arrived at the top; when one sees how friends turn into bitter enemies and how bitter enemies one day become friends. To one who observes human nature keenly it gives such interest in life that he becomes sufficiently strong to bear all, to endure all, to stand all things patiently. One may observe this moving picture all through life.

Most important of all, one would like to know more about oneself, about one's talents, idiosyncracies, the purpose of one's life. In fact, how one would like to know all things.

With the maturity of his soul, a man desires to probe the depths of life, he desires to discover the power latent within him, he longs to know the sources and goal of his life, he yearns to understand the aim and meaning of life, he wishes to understand the inner significance of things, and he wants to uncover all that is covered by name and form. He seeks for insight into cause and effect, he wants to touch the mystery of time and space and he wishes to find the missing link between God and man—where man ends, where God begins.[3]

In fact, many yearn for that ultimate knowledge called transcendental knowledge:

To understand cause and effect and to be able to find the cause of the cause and the effect of the effect; to be able to see the reason of the reason and the logic of the logic.[4]

How then were Murshid and the dervishes able to develop this faculty to the point of reading with such baffling precision? One paramount characteristic distinguishes these rare beings gifted with unimaginable power of insight and even intervention into other people's situations and sometimes cosmic events. As we have seen, they have lost themselves, and because they have lost the notion of who they are or what they are or say, are out of focus with the limited vantage point from which most people peer into the universe; they can see behind the veil that which is hidden from the sight of ordinary people.

The intuitive faculty develops most frequently among those who live a life of seclusion, or at least guard themselves from the kind of involvement at the personal level that most people are caught in.

How are the meditative souls awakened, how do they stay experienced to the inner life? In the first place, the adept values his object of attaining the inner life more than anything else, more than wealth, position, or rank. Seclusion, silence, thoughtfulness, meditation and gentleness, all these make the rhythm of one's life appropriate for receiving inspiration, revelation, communion. These ascetics who left everything in the world also attained a certain knowledge which they give us.[5]

Furthermore, one must be strong and pure enough to be entrusted with the secrets of one's fellow men.

When one rises morally above the tendency to devote one's time and thought to other people's affairs which do not concern one in any way, speaking about them, forming opinions about people, when all this is given up, then a person becomes entitled to spiritual attainment. Do you think the sages and saints try to see the thoughts of other people? Not at all; that does not concern them, but the thoughts of another person manifest themselves to the saint.

A person who is ready to give the secret of one to another, if he knew by this power the secrets of his fellowmen, what a terrible thing he would do. A person who is affectionate, afraid of any harm or hurt touching his dear ones, if he saw it coming, his nerves would be shattered to pieces.

The more trustworthy one is, the more another discloses his secret.

But if he were to indulge its secrets, his sight would become dimmer every day, because it is a trust given to him by God.

Nature obstructs intuition in a person until he has proven able to master it wisely. If one entrusted a loaded weapon into the hands of a child, imagine the harm he could do.

For everything there is an appointed time; and when that time comes, it is revealed. That is why, although on the one hand we may be eager to attain to a certain revelation, yet on the other hand, we must have patience to wait for the moment of its coming.

The knowledge of what is behind the scene is so overwhelming that it shatters the one who would venture over the drawbridge.

One should remember, however, that there are very few who enjoy reality compared with those who are afraid of it, and who, standing on top of a high mountain, are afraid of looking at the immensity of space. . . . What frightens them is the immensity of things; they seem lost and they hold on to their little selves.[6]

It is only for the strong, which explains why the dervishes and rishis gifted with insight distinguish themselves by the strength of their being.

As long as a person says, "When I look at the horizon from the top of the mountain I become dizzy; this immensity of space frightens me," he should not look at it. But if it does not make one dizzy, it is a great joy to look at life from above.[7]

The Sufi, therefore, is grateful for what he sees and hears and grateful for what he does not see and hear.

Why do so few people develop this faculty? In every person there exists to a greater or lesser degree a faculty of perceiving impressions, and that is the first step toward intuition. The finer the person, the greater his perception. But everyone feels, as an impression, the conditions of a place, the character of the people he meets, their tendencies, their motives, their desires, their grade of evolution. It is our doubt of the reliability of the warnings that are continually trying to break through the threshold of our awareness that causes us to discard them. We censure them before they have a chance of capturing our attention.

If there were a mirror sold for a million dollars which showed the condition of thought and feeling of every individual, there would be a great demand for it. . . . And as he does not believe in it, he would rather spend that much money and buy a mirror, than try and cultivate a thing in which he does not believe.[8]

Yet no sooner a hunch has been confirmed than we gain confidence in our ability. Therefore one should make a point of protecting one's hunch from one's doubts.

Besides, those who doubt intuition, their intuition doubts them. . . .

If one makes a habit of catching the first intuition and saving it from being destroyed by reason, then intuition is stronger.[9]

We ought to build a fence round intuitions as if they were delicate plants. . . . And when the intuitions become right then the dreams become right. We see what is really going to happen in every thought which comes to us; the truth of life. . . . To the illuminated one every night's dream becomes a book that tells the past, the present, and the future, both of himself and of all those whom he cares for or wishes to know about.[10]

We resolve to follow our intuition and then inadvertently again disregard it; the hunch was confirmed, so we decide next time to definitely take heed of it. So we train ourselves to be on the lookout for intuitions and check our inveterate habit of disregarding them. But then a case arises where what we had thought was a genuine intuition did not confirm itself, and we return to our tendency of doubting again.

How can one learn to distinguish between a genuine intuition and imagination at the moment of its onset? There are two methods. The first consists of suspending thought and action each time an intuition emerges. The second, if one misses the first chance, is to check and recollect precisely how one felt every time one had a hunch that was confirmed, as compared with how one felt the time when one took it to be real but it turned out to be amiss. One will be able to ascertain that every time that an intuition was genuine, one was passive with regard to the impression, albeit perhaps active in one's preoccupation, and where it failed one was actively projecting the hunch.

In our everyday life the moments when we catch without intention the thought of another, are such moments when our mind is open; that our mind is not occupied with any other thought, that our mind is in a passive, negative, respondent condition. As we catch thoughts of another in our daily life, in everyday life, so we catch the thoughts of others in our dreams. It is easier to catch the thought of another in the dream than in the wakeful state, because in the state of dream our mind is naturally focused.

We are generally geared to action, using our imagination creatively; therefore, to develop intuition, we have to reverse gears.

The mind can become a receptacle for the knowledge which comes from within. If we look at people we shall find that out of a hundred there are ninety-nine who are creative by nature, but only one who is receptive enough to receive it through his intuitive qualities.

Man is continually creating circumstances around himself by first representing them mentally and then pursuing actively what he desires. To intuit, the mind must be a blank, and then something is produced upon its surface.

One must bear in mind that, even if an intuition was genuine, it still has to be substantiated by imagination before it can stir the conscious mind. Imagination is the language through which our hunches are made intelligible. For example, a hunch about an accident may be manifested by the picture of the accident or a person who came to warn one. Therefore, the only difference between sheer fantasy and an intuition consolidated by creative imaginatinon is that, in the latter case, the imagination is monitored at a superpersonal level. However, should we attempt to reason out what is coming through to ensure that it fits into the categories of our understanding, we foil the transmutation of intuition into imagination and set off the creative process of imagination through our own volition.

The difference between imagination and intuition is sometimes puzzling to define. . . . Every imagination is intuition until it has been corrupted by reason and when the intuition is corrupted by reason it becomes fantasy.

For as soon as we begin to think it out, we at once descend from the higher, the spiritual source of information and use earthly means to establish what belongs to heaven.[11]

To develop intuition, one has to test oneself to reach inward and upward, as it were, to reach an impersonal level and abstain from any self-motivated imagination, while of course being able to continue one's activity in daily undertakings.

The first condition is to separate this outer knowledge from the inner knowing. . . . But intuition can be described as a glimpse of knowledge that one has stored within oneself, which comes at a time when it is needed, by chance. In a spiritual person it comes more, for the very reason that his mind is clear.

Indeed, the art of developing intuition, or telepathy, or revelation, is to feel inside our idiosyncracies as they react to the person we are reading. Do not let the thrust of your attention be captured by the person in front of you, but turn within to sense how you react.

The first step of the mystic is to see the side which is before him and his second step is to look at the side which is within him.[12]

Should the person before you be dishonest, if there is the slightest deviousness in your being, you will recognize that aspect of your being in his; if he is depressed, you will be more strongly conscious of a sadness that is in you in the depth and you might discover self-pity you had camouflaged from yourself; if he is agitated, you will feel uneasy and blocked, you will find difficulty in communicating; if he is a generous heart, you will open up to him; and if he is resentful, you will remember how it felt to be resentful. You discover his counterpart in you, and therefore discover him in yourself, even though he may be wearing a mask and dissimulate his being better than one could ever imagine. If you are reflecting him, he reflects you; therefore he manifests momentarily more strongly predominant idiosyncrasies in you that are present though recessive in him. One must capture those feelings in oneself which may be marginal, hardly noticeable, before they are averted by other thoughts.

Speaking about the science of telepathy, my Murshid once said, It is a disclosure of one's own spirit that unveils all things. It is by seeing the cause of every fault in oneself that one is able to have insight in human nature.

These premises may lead one degree further. For example, a man is having a court case; is he guilty or not? Or he intends to undertake an enterprise; is he going to be successful or not? Or he has difficulty deciding between two job offers; which is most in keeping with his idiosyncrasies? Or which would be the most propitious to his unfoldment as a person? Or what is standing in the way of his achieving success in his undertaking? Or what is obstructing his relationship with his wife, or friend, or acquaintance? A further step would be pointing out the people he may best get along with or cooperate with, or intuiting if a friend is deceiving or not, and in what way. The next step would be forecasting that a person is going to have an accident and thereby sparing him the misfortune, perceiving the things that a person is doing that he does not admit to you, forewarning a person against a move that would be damaging to him. Though insight into such situations is difficult to grasp, it can be clinched if, having experienced the other person's problem, one has oneself overcome it, or spotted its solution.

What makes one fail, what makes one succeed, what gives one happiness, what brings one sorrow. Then one should study the nature of pleasure and pain, whether it is a lasting pleasure, a momentary pleasure or a momentary pain; and then find out how under cover of pain there was pleasure, and how under cover of pleasure there was pain; how in the worst person there is some good to be found, and how in the best there is something bad to be traced.

And the next thing man has to do is control his activities, physical and mental.

Of course everyone has a hunch about others upon meeting for the first time. Here are the beginnings of intuition. How much may be ascribed to a common-sense induction based upon traits visible to a more-or-less experienced judgment and trained eye? It is because certain features in people seem to stand as the signs of an unmistakable characteristic that the pseudo-science of physiognomy became popular during the last century and the early part of this one.

The very walk, stance, and bearing of a person give a sure clue.

If one studies the walk of a person, the way he moves or looks, everything he does, one sees that whenever balance is lacking, something is lacking behind this which one may not have known but which one will find out in time. For instance, when a person is wobbling, do not believe that it is only an outside defect; it has something to do with that man's character. As he is wobbling in walking, so he will be wobbling in his determination, in his belief.[18]

One can show stubbornness, weakness, foolishness; all things can be traced when a person walks, or sits, or stands up. Stiffness in walking, also crookedness, is caused by self-consciousness, and sitting in a rigid position without any flexibility is caused by something. Self-consciousness gives hardness to the expression of the lips, and it stiffens the tongue, and makes the voice toneless, preventing a man from saying what he wishes to say. Self-consciousness is like a chain upon every feature and limb of the body and in the self-conscious person there is nothing of the smoothness that should flow like a fluid throughout every expression of life. Its only remedy is forgetting self and putting the whole mind into work on each occupation undertaken.

As a "musician of the soul," Murshid envisioned people as melodies, chords, and rhythms, and grasped how the features of the human being portray the dynamics of his soul.

Every person explains to us all that they contain in the form of music. A friendly person shows harmony in his voice, in his words, in his movement and manner. An unfriendly person in his very movements, in his glance and expression, in his walk, in everything, will show disharmony if one can but see it.

Even as all matter is a crystallized symphony of transcendental awareness and cosmic emotion, so the state of the soul is frozen into the flesh, physical tensions evidencing the stress of emotions become frozen in a prevailing facial expression, or recurrent stereotyped expressions, leaving permanent hallmarks engraved upon the flesh of the face.

The ends of the eyebrows turning upwards denotes egotism and shrewdness. The puckering of the lips suggests pleasure, as the twitching of the lips shows a tendency to humour or indicates confusion. The movement of the eyes toward the outer corners denotes a clever brain. The puffing of the cheeks denotes joy, the drawing in, sorrow.

Particularly the eyes, the windows of the soul:

Eyes, therefore, are the representatives of the soul at the surface, and they speak to a person more clearly than words can speak ... his eyes tell one whether he is favourably inclined or unfavourably inclined. Love or hate, pride or modesty, all can be seen in the eyes; even wisdom and ignorance.

The stability of the eyes expresses perplexity, confusion, fear, depression, distress and despair. When the eyes are downcast, then it is discouragement, disappointment with oneself and with another. And if the eyes are turned upward, then it is indifference. And when the eyes go right and left, then it is utter confusion. The contraction of the face shows the joy of the person. Eyebrows can smile without smiling, and eyebrows can shed tears without crying.

In graphology, too, the upward, descending, slanting, circular, fine, or dense features give a clue. However, there is a subjective element triggered by the objective feature. This is where intuition proper starts; but where is the dividing line? On the one hand, there are the tangible data: One may deduce some relevant information from the direction of a person's bodily movement.

No motion, to a seer, is without a direction; in other words, every movement is directed by a precedent cause.

On the other hand, the seer can sense an invisible but meaningful structure grafted, as it were, upon the actual physical expression of the face.

The form of thought also has its effect, upon the form and expression of someone. And there is a certain law which governs its work; and that law is the law of direction; if the forces are going to the right, or to the left, or upward, or downward. It is this direction of the vibrations of thought which produces a picture, so that a seer can see this picture as clearly as a letter.

Murshid assigns these almost imperceptible physiological changes in physiognomy, which we pick up and interpret subjectively, to the dilation or contraction of muscles owing to the variations in pressure of the blood in the arteries. He thus underlines the role of the cardiac plexus, which is what the Sufis mean when they refer to the heart as the governing brain of all emotions.

The veins, tubes and muscles, and the lines formed by their movements, are under the control of the heart, and every change that takes place in the heart shows on man's face so that one who knows the language can read it.

The changes in moisture demonstrated nowadays by the lie detector and other physiological signals are no doubt picked up by the sensitive.

No sooner you read this, no one can tell a lie before you. You at once know it, because words cannot hide then the thought. Mostly words are the cover over thought, but when one can read it in the face, then the words have no power to contradict. You can see it just like a mirror. Besides, there is a thought of humility, there is a thought of guilty conscience, there is a thought of shame, and however powerful a person may be he cannot hide it. It is so strong and you can see it in his face just like a moving picture.[14]

We realize that much of what we relegated to an unaccountable intuition could be accounted for by extrasensorial perception. Yet this threshold shifts when one feels the person's condition in his atmosphere rather than deducing one's assessment from any subliminal perception. If one's intuition is real, it is certainly more reliable than if based upon outer signs because of the failure of the human interpretation of sense data. It is a matter of displacing the center that observes from the personal level to the impersonal.

The eyes are given to see, the soul to see further. This no longer consists in reading the lines of the face, but sensing the atmosphere directly without any tutelage of the physical signals.

The thought reading of the atmosphere is as much easy as much difficult. It is easy because it at once strikes you. You do not have to examine the feature. You only have to be passive, and it strikes you at once, just like one shock.

The atmosphere is not audible to the ears, but it is audible to the ears of the heart.

We learn of the feats of telepathic connection attained behind the Iron Curtain—a technique used by the rishis in the caves and dervishes since time immemorial to communicate with each other or the outer world in the absence of telegraphy—and much cheaper! In the new age, if we go back to the windmill and the dung heap in order to move forward into new dimensions of living, will it not be a feature of human progress in the twenty-first century to cultivate this latent faculty not prevalent in earlier civilizations? Murshid tells how, in the presence of his Murshid, he thought of an engagement he had elsewhere; immediately Abu Hashim Madani said, "Yes, it is all right, you may take a leave." Even as there are soundwaves, there are thought waves in the mental sphere, in which our minds live, move, and have their being. Not unlike radio sets, we pick up those sound waves, but they are only meaningful if we exercise our will to tune in to the desired frequency.

The thought waves are just like voice waves. It is quite possible for the thought of another person to float into that field of which one is conscious, and one may hear it and think it is one's intuition. . . . It happens frequently to everyone during the day that there come thoughts and feelings and imaginings which he has never had himself or which he had no reason to have. It would not be right to call these intuition. . . . The thoughts which come and go, floating on the surface, are not to be depended upon; real intuition is to be found in the depth of one's being.[15]

Telepathy may be considered as a special case of intuition or insight, picking up a specific thought rather than reading character or past events or forecasting. The clue lies deeper than the place where thoughts burst forth, actually in feeling, since the moving power behind every thought is feeling.

You become a highly evolved personality when the feelings of another can tell you much more than his words and actions can.[16]

In fact, telepathy may be extended to picking up the inception of a thought in the unconscious, even if it never skips across the threshold from the unconscious to the conscious.

A mystic can know the thought of another person even before the person who is thinking, and he can feel the feeling of another even more deeply than he can.

Having started by reconnoitering the state of mind of a person, one reaches more deeply into the concerns and aspirations of the person and then yet clearer information hits the unconscious of the reader. Two people may wish to communicate at a distance.

Those whose sympathy is awakened, those who have feelings, those whose thoughts are deep, those whose imagination rises high, will never deny the fact that thought reaches beyond the boundaries of land and water, that feelings are reflected from thousands of miles away. Two souls can communicate, wherever they may be, in one instant. If this is true then the next world is not very far away; the unseen world has not been drowned, it is there, it is before us, and we live and move and make our being in it. There were many instances of this during the war when mothers and wives of soldiers, in the times of pain, illness, or death, were conscious of their distress without any source of communication. How often when people are in close touch do they perceive each other's condition, not only by thought waves, but in the realm of feeling also; this shows that there is one body, and that in that body there is one life which continually circulates as the blood does in our veins.[17]

How does one develop telepathy? No doubt it happens to people connected by deep bonds of love or sympathy; these need not train themselves to do it, but there are methods that are helpful in ordinary cases. It is best to practice it with two people:

1. Ensure that you sit absolutely facing one another.
2. Decide who is the transmitter and who is the receiver.

There are two actions of sense, which are in fact two actions of the whole being: expressiveness and responsiveness. . . . As soon as the expressing spirit expresses itself, the responsive spirit receives its impressions, just as a person whose picture is taken by a camera yields his impression.[18]

3. Synchronize your breaths, so that as the transmitter exhales, the receiver inhales, and vice versa. This can be done by prearranging a system of signals; i.e., the transmitter taps the receiver on the knee when he exhales, and in turn the receiver taps the transmitter on the knee when he wishes to exhale.
4. The transmitter must concentrate with all his mental energy, reinforced by his will, upon a point in the uppermost part of the receiver's brain.

We must learn the process of "throwing the ball" to hit a certain goal. We must direct our aim right, and we must put enough force in it to enable it to reach the goal. It is the force of the will that sends the thought to reach another person, and the aiming, whereby one focuses one's mental eye upon the other is telepathy, is concentration. In brief, two things are necessary for telepathy: strength of will and power of concentration.[19]

5. The receiver must switch off all outgoing activity and gear himself to being absolutely receptive. Do not strive to receive, just become blank and sensitive.

The mind is likened to a photographic plate, and it must be kept open, that the impression of another person's thought may fall upon it. That makes the impression. The thought of another comes as a reflection falling upon a mirror.

Looking into the past is just like looking deep down from great heights. It means probing the depth of life. Looking into the present is just like observing a wide horizon, as wide as we can see. Looking into the future is like looking upward to the zenith. And the feeling we experience is different with each of the ways of looking. One gives knowledge; the other gives power; and the third gives peace.[20]

There are moments when the records of the past of a person or an object suddenly emerge in one's consciousness; or again, in a flash the entire future is thrown into perspective. Then one's sense of time begins to totter and falter; for how can the past still live and the future be already present, without our exploring our confinement in the present?

Man is floating on the ocean of wordly activity, not knowing what he is doing, not knowing where he is going. What seems to him of importance is only the moment which he calls the present. The past is a dream, the future is in a mist, and the only clear thing to him is the present.[21]

If time is subjective, it is because it is the measure of our inability to grasp reality in one take, like the cine-cameraman who has a pan to cover a landscape, rotating to take sections of the scenery in sequence, unless his camera is fitted with a panoramic lens. The advantage of the panning arises from the fact that consciousness is able to absorb more detail if impressions are meted out gradually than if it were exposed to the whole panorama at once. The advantage of the panoramic span is that one can spot the interrelationship between the parts. In any case, when faced with a large screen, the viewer makes up for the camera-man's failure to pan by panning himself, or oscillating between fixing one particular spot or scanning the total view.

The conductor of an orchestra may hear the whole orchestra at the same time, and yet he may want to hear one instrument alone to know in how far it is correct.

The same would apply to seeing the events of one's life in sequence, as we do when we reminisce, as opposed to trying to envision the entire sweep at once. In the latter case, the causal sequences stand out with more clarity. For a given capacity of absorption of consciousness, one can either see more and more of less and less, or less and less of more and more. The lens of our camera can be focused to flash upon the figure in the foreground at the expense of the background horizon, or it may sharpen the background and leave hazy the branches of nearby trees in the foreground.

Exposed to a giant screen of high-quality photography, showing infinite detail, consciousness staggers, overwhelmed because over-loaded. A strange euphoria is experienced due to a sharp sense of one's smallness in relationship to the cosmic dimension of reality. It is this bewilderment and perplexity in the soul of the Sufi dervish enhanced by adoration of the divine presence which he espies everywhere that endows him with a prophetic perspective; he has overtaxed his con-sciousness through looking at reality face to face, while allowing the vision of divine glory to annihilate his sense of himself.

This, then, is the secret of developing intuition or insight. We observed that if the Hyderabad dervish knew everything about everybody else, it was because he had lost the notion of himself. He had exploded the mental framework which normally shields consciousness by confining it within the ordinary notion of the present.

Just as there are some who have short sight, and others who have long sight, so there are some who see things at a far distance with the eye of their mind, but who cannot see what is near them. They have long sight. Then there are others, who have short sight; they see all that is near them but they cannot see further.[22]

There are some who can see far beyond, or long before events, and there is the person who only sees what is immediately before him and what is next to him; he sees nothing of what is behind him. His influence reaches only as far as the thing that is just beside him, and it is that which influences him. But there is another person who reasons about what he sees; his can be called medium sight. He reasons about it as far as his reason allows. He cannot see beyond his reasoning; he goes so far and no further. Naturally if these three persons meet and speak together, each has his own language. It is not surprising if one does not understand the point of view of the other, because each one has his own vision according to which he looks at things. No one can give his own sight to another person in order to make him see differently.[23]

What happens then to consciousness? Its entire perspective becomes completely transformed by dint of some mystic spell, and therefore it sees behind the curtain, the effect of the past still operating in the present, and the future on its way.

It is very difficult for man to realize his true self because the self to which he is awakened from the time of birth, the self which has made within him a conception of himself, is most limited. However proud and conceited he may be, however good his idea of himself, yet in his innermost being he knows his limitation, the smallness of his being. If there is anything that can make him great, it is only the effacing of himself and the establishing of God instead. The one who wants to begin with self-realization may have many intellectual and philosophical principles, but he will get into a muddle and arrive nowhere. These are wrong methods.[24]

It is not by self-realization that man realizes God; it is by God-realization that man realizes self.

In the self-knowledge of past and present and future one has to learn what was the origin of the soul, how the soul has formed itself, how it has come to manifest, the knowledge of the process of manifestation, and the different stages through which it has passed towards manifestation. Regarding the present one should learn one's own condition, the condition of one's spirit, of relationship to others; one should also realize how far the soul reaches in the spiritual spheres. And regarding the future one should find the answers to the questions, "Am I preparing for something that is to come, and what is there to come? If life is a journey, what is the object of this journey? What is the destination and how shall I reach it? What preparations must I make for this journey and what must I carry to make the journey easy? What are the difficulties that I may meet on my way?"[25]

Imagine the difference between the worm's-eye view and the eagle's! For the worm the little clod of earth he climbed over a few moments ago is no more; it belongs to the past. And the next one belongs to the future unknown. But for the eagle that hill he flew over a few minutes ago is still there, although he may be vertically over a spot miles away. The sense of the present for some beings is narrower than for others. Indeed, as one grows in awareness, one perceives the way the past is still working in the present. And this widens one's grasp of the potentialities inherent in the present. Not only are the footprints of the past indelibly engraved in the records, but the effects of the actions have set the wheels of that enormous machine that is the universe into operation; therefore, they can be checked on at any time in the course of the operation, just as a criminal action may be reconstructed even though the circumstances have since changed. Or to take another example, the past action of sowing seeds is to be traced in them at every stage of their unfoldment. Or again, one can tell how old a tree is by the rings in its trunk, or a relic by its effect on the carbon spectrum. Further, if we experience today the twinkle in a distant star which occurred two billion years ago, our time, it is because that action is still flashing in the universe and has reached the range in which we are located.

Every word once it is spoken, every deed that is done, every sentiment felt is recorded somewhere; it has not gone, it is not lost. We do not see it because it is not always recorded on the surface.[26]

The hill left behind by the eagle is not in the past for him, because he can see it now inside the wide framework of his present. We demonstrate our limitation by storing into our concept of the irrevocable past all those beings and events we experience in the cross-section of that reference framework which we call the present, rather than looking upon all things and beings dynamically as currents (*santana*, in

Buddhism) or processions. If we widen our sense of the present to include the posthumous condition of beings thought of as having died, or the situations that have evolved out of actions we ascribe to the past, we shall live in an extended eternal present and know things in this extended present that other people still refer to as past.

Furthermore, one might ask, something which is past, where is it? And if it is, it must be standing still. But in reality there is nothing that is past, all that is past is working on. Therefore every word we speak is going on repeating itself, every action, every imagination, every thought, that we let out, is working on towards its desired goal.

How does the psychic read the past of an object, maybe a ring or a piece of furniture, a house or a castle? He abandons his personal consciousness, and experiences himself as the totality of which the object is a part.

By self-realization a man becomes larger than the universe. The world in which he lives becomes as a drop in the ocean of his heart.[27]

Indeed, behind the superficial strata of individual, or rather individualized, consciousness and memory, lies the whole consciousness of humanity, which includes the consciousness and memory of the minerals, plants, and animals and the whole human race; planetary consciousness and behind that cosmic consciousness; and beyond, transcendental consciousness.

Every child born on earth possesses, besides what he has inherited from his parents and and ancestors, a power and knowledge quite peculiar to himself and different from that which his parents and ancestors possessed; . . . he shows from the beginning of his life on earth signs of having known things which he has never been taught.[28]

C. G. Jung stumbled upon this discovery in the course of his research on memory in pathological patients, and he called it the collective unconscious. When these subliminal forces in the unconscious strata burst over the threshold between unconscious and conscious, they form a pattern, which deserves the label of collective conscious. Not only does our unconscious memory store impressions transmitted by the whole planet, but also we carry the memory of our heavenly inheritance, and beyond that, our divine inheritance.

Murshid often refers to the storehouse of cosmic memory and universal knowledge that lies at our disposal if we are armed with Aladdin's lamp, which represents awakened consciousness.

Whatever we know today is the result of thousands of years of experience. No country or nation can say, "We were the only discoverer of this or that." No, the discovery of the very least thing is the discovery of the whole of humanity. . . . All have helped so much that no one can say that something is only due to a particular person or nation. The whole of humanity has shared in everything that we think new today.[29]

There is a still deeper sphere to which our memory is linked, and that sphere is the universal memory, in other words the divine Mind. . . . where we can even touch something we have never learnt or heard or known or seen. Only for this the doors of memory should be laid open.[30]

Divine Mind is the stream of the fountain, and each individual mind is just like a drop. But each stream of the fountain is connected with the stem of the fountain, is it not?

The storehouse I spoke of . . . is the subconscious mind. In that storehouse, there are things and they live; all thoughts and impressions are living things. There is nothing in the mind that dies. It lives and it lives long; but when we are not conscious of it, it is in our subconscious mind.[31]

There is another form of this which is attained by a greater enlightenment, by a greater awakening of the soul; and this form can be pictured as a person going through a large room where there are all kinds of things exhibited, and yet there is no light, except a searchlight in his own hand. If he throws his light on colour, all colours become distinct; if he throws his light on line, all lines in the most harmonious and beautiful form become clearly visible to him. This searchlight may become greater still, and may reach still further. It may be thrown on the past, and the past may become as clear as it was to the prophets of ancient times. It may be thrown on the future; and it is not only a sense of precaution that a person may gain by it, but also a glimpse into the future. This light may be thrown upon living beings, and the living beings may become like open books to him. It may be thrown on objects and the objects may reveal to him their nature and secrets. If this light were thrown within oneself, then the self would be revealed to him and would become enlightened as to his own nature and his own character.[32]

We should distinguish the level at which memory is transmitted. Memory may be carried by the body, for example, the muscular movements required to play a piece of piano music, or type, or drive a car. Memory may be carried by the mind, as in a recurring thought. A memory may be carried by the soul, and this is what Murshid is referring to.

There is a knowledge which one can perceive with the senses, and there is a knowledge which one can perceive with the mind alone. And a knowledge which can be realized by the soul.

To earmark the memory of an event witnessed bodily by an ancestor, one has to envisage oneself as a continuation of that ancestor and abstain from thinking of the ancestor as a different person from oneself and relegating him to the past. One should experience him as living further in one. We know how difficult it may be to recollect an event from our childhood. In order to be able to remember oneself as a child, one has to think of oneself as a continuity in change. One may proceed in a similar way by identifying oneself with the entire continuity of one's inheritance from all ancestors, including the whole planet.

Your mother may be amazed to find that you are tying your shoes precisely the odd way your grandfather did, although you never saw him doing it. And now, for having been made conscious of this transmission through bodily inheritance, you may discover him continuing to live in a certain manner in your being. You may realize that you are a stage in a continuity of being that transcends your individuality. It may prove easier to capture the memory through the network registered at the mental level than at the physical. Do you feel in your blood how your father would have reacted to a given situation? And even remember his feelings regarding such a situation although you were not present? Memory transmitted at the soul level sometimes comes readily. For example, one can find the being of Christ on the cross or Buddha under the tree somewhere within the collective unconscious. This is why psychometrists, when holding an object they are asked to read, feel from the condition of their own soul.

When the intelligence experiences life through the medium or vehicle of the body and mind then, no doubt, it remains limited. If we want to go to a particular street or place with our body it will take a certain time, but if we go there in our mind we can get there in a moment's time. It may take much time and effort to accomplish something in the physical world, but it takes less time and effort to accomplish the same when we work mentally.

Doubtless one can only use the circuit of soul memory if one identifies with one's soul; here lies the secret.

Man experiences heaven, when conscious of his soul: he experiences the earth when conscious of his body. Man experiences that plane which is between heaven and earth when he is conscious of his mind.[33]

The psychiatrists probe into the unconscious memory, consisting of the representation of events or emotions as experienced at the mind level they call the psyche. The gurus probe into the memory of what one might call a superconsciousness as experienced at soul level. Therefore they are not always speaking the same language.

When the three who have travelled the same way, on foot, in the car, and by aeroplane meet together and speak of their experiences, we shall find a great difference in what they tell: and this explains why people who have gone through the same life, who have lived under the same sun, who have been born on the same earth are yet so different in their mentality.

Memory is transmitted from body to mind and then from mind to soul, and conversely from soul to mind and mind to body by virtue of the same principle whereby the spirit experiences bodiliness in the flesh and matter experiences consciousness through the soul, or that the condition of the soul may manifest bodily in a lovely smile and earthly features are transmitted in a transfigured form in resurrection. The psychometrist has to know how to consciously expose himself to the impressions stored in his soul memory, triggered by the presence of the object.

Thought is activity of the consciousness impressed by the external world. When the light within is thrown upon this [worldly] knowledge then the knowledge from outer life and the life coming from within make a perfect wisdom.[34]

All life is convergence, so the inextricably intertwined lines of communication and awareness in memory build a mighty network in the universe. Within this network one may discover certain tracks followed by microwave communication at high speed, which might well be compared with communication at soul level. Here information is screened and broken down to its quintessence. The soul only admits highly digested and transfigured values after they have been distilled from their contingent dross.

Concerning the future, we know that some have the gift of prophesying a coming event with surprising infallibility. So had some of the dervishes described by Murshid from his early experiences, the ones who read precise forecasts in teacups or smoke rings. This art, called divination or the hieratic art, used to be very much practised by the ancients, particularly the Greeks at Delphi and other temples of the oracle. It was based on the postulate that every atom in the universe is linked with every other, and therefore in each the conditions of every other can be discerned. Thus the fate of a being on earth is written in the stars, and the astrologer is supposed to be able to read the language of the stars.

The seer's discerning of the condition of those before him and away from him is likened to the process of eating and digesting. The food, of whatever sort it may be, cereals or vegetable, sweet or sour, it is felt in the mouth. Once it is swallowed then what is felt about it is the feeling, not out of distinctions but the inner essence. This is the assimilation of its subtle properties. What happens is that man's mind is fully occupied in distinguishing by the experience of the mouth. And therefore he remains unaware of those subtle distinctions which also he makes after he has swallowed the food.

Therefore the seer reanalyzes something which the person whom he sees has analyzed with his mind. In the case of a seer it is becoming one with another person, experiencing what his mind has experienced, the same thing with one's soul. It does not mean that the seer cannot perceive mind, but by perceiving mind he limits his powers, because he descends.

A man sees his future in the teacup, with limited light; similarly he sees it in the cards, in the crystal, in the coals of the fire, in smoke. All these things have the future written in them; it is the same light that shines upon them and begins to reveal itself in them. It is not only books, but all things in nature which begin to reveal the secrets of nature to him.[35]

We know that animals have uncanny premonitions; for example, all the dogs of Agadir left the area before the earthquake, and dogs howl when there is going to be a death in the family. Rats leave a ship long before the accident that causes it to sink.

Small insects know about human happenings and give a warning to those who can understand it; and it is true. Besides, birds always give a warning of storm and wind, and of rain and the absence of rain. Mankind naturally is more capable of intuition.[36]

We humans sometimes make use of ths instincts of animals, although our capacity for intuition is far superior.

The ancient physicians used to follow wild animals, such as the bear and others, who sought for different herbs when they were in need of a cure for some illness, because their intuition was clear.

We often have hunches, later to be confirmed; for instance, an inner voice warns us not to take the car; later on, we discover the car has had a crash. Or one may feel fate on meeting a person, or finding oneself in a new place or involved in a new situation. Our theories tend to attribute these chance meetings to karma, since we do not understand the mechanisms of the future.

Intuitively one feels: this person will one day deceive me; or he will prove faithful to me, sincere, to be relied upon. Or in this particular business I will have success or not.[37]

Without enquiry a thought comes to you which tells you of a coming event. People sometimes take this to be "spirit-communication"; sometimes they take it to be a thought transference from someone else. But intuition is a greater and higher thing than a spirit-communication or thought-reading, because it is pure; it is your own property; it belongs to you. In this you do not depend on a spirit or upon another person sending a thought to you. In this you are perfectly independent. You receive the knowledge from within, which is far superior, and greater and higher.[38]

Sometimes we have a sure hunch about our friends' lives. If we once gained the reputation of being a good soothsayer, people would soon crowd for advice.

Then about affairs, one's own affairs and the affairs of others, the appearance or even the thought of the affair has in it a hidden voice, telling: "yes" or "no," "right" or "wrong," "success" or "failure," "do it" or "do not do it."

The master guards against fortune telling.

To say, "I know the future" is the work of a fortune teller. It is not the work of a mystic. At one time you may know the future, and may tell another person. Another time that person may be depending upon your word and you do not know the future. To know and to say nothing is the work of the mystic. To know and to help. To say to another, "Take care. There is a pit."

The reason is that events cannot always be forecast because of the interplay of the planning and freewill. Murshid explains that the very reason why premonitions do not always materialize is that, while the forces set into action in the complex machinery of the universe have inevitable results (called karma by Hindu philosophy), the eversprouting fresh forces on their way down to manifestation from the unmanifest have to pass through the volition of untold numbers of beings, archangels, angels, djinns, each delegating his hierarchic superior yet each endowed with a measure of free will or initiative within a given framework. In addition, one has to take into account the wills of those humans involved in the situation. The forces representing human free will interplay with the karmic forces, interfering with the strict karmic causality, thus introducing grace beyond law. This unpredictable element evidences a free will that may well be infinitesimal in comparison with the irrevocable momentum of the mechanism of the universe, yet nevertheless plays some role.

Imagine a machine, piloted by a computer, which offers several alternatives in its programing. Now plug in a human brain between the computer and the machine, which freely selects the program from several possible ones.

The machine part of his being is dependent upon climatic changes, upon what is given to it, what is put into it, upon what it depends upon in order to keep in working condition. And there is another machine, a fine mechanism which works as the inner part of this machine, that is finer than its outer part. And that fine part feels atmosphere, feels vibrations, feels pleasures and displeasures, enjoys comforts and rejects discomforts; every kind of feeling exists there. Then the mystic looks on life in this manner: that this machine is made for the use of the other part of one's being, which is the engineer. But as long as that engineer is asleep, and that engineer in unaware of this machine, he does not run it, it is just left to conditions and environment; they run it.

Compare the program fed into the computer, which may include several alternatives, to the planning generally ascribed to destiny, which is working its way down into manifestation; and compare destiny to a machine. The potentialities built into the computer are not noticeable to most people until they affect the actual functioning of the machine. But a sensitive observer is able to espy the programing on its way down. However, most observers, owing to their limitations, could possibly notice only one among the different alternatives. If they happen upon the very course chosen by the person among all the possible alternatives, they will be proven right, otherwise not; for example, if it is predestined that a car or plane will crash, you still have your freewill expressed in your choice to take it or not. That is why some wise astrologers, seeing the alternatives, say, "If you do this, such and such will ensue, but if you decide to do that, the following will ensue." The forecaster also has to take into account the time that it takes the planning to materialize and the stages of growth through which it passes in the machine. Sometimes time works for us and we lose our chance by hurrying our plan through.

The length of time that the thought is held has also much to do with its accomplishment, for the thought-vibrations have to be active for a certain time to bring about a certain result. A certain length of time is required for the baking of a cake; if it is hurried the cake will be uncooked; with too great a heat it will burn. If the operator of the mental vibrations lacks patience then the power of thought will be wasted, even if it were half-way to its destiny, or still nearer to a successful issue. If too great a power of thought is given to the accomplishment of a certain thing, it destroys it while preparing it.[39]

Also, our intuition can pilot our free will by determining what stage in a cycle is propitious to our undertaking; for example, start an enterprise on the approach of the ebb of an energy wave, instead of upon the flow.

So there is a cycle of the life of the world, and the cycle of the creation of man and his destruction, the cycles of the reign of races and nations, and cycles of time, such as a year, a month, a week, a day and hour. The nature of each of these cycles has three aspects: the beginning, the culmination, and the end, which are named Uruj, Kemal, and Zeval; like for example, new moon, full moon, and waning moon; sunrise, zenith, and sunset. These cycles, sub-cycles and under-cycles, and the three aspects of their nature, are divided and distinguished by the nature and course of light. As the light of the sun and moon and of the planets plays the most important part in the life of the world, individually and collectively, so the light of the Spirit of Guidance also divides time into cycles.

The seer watches continually the potentialities of attributes vying to manifest in a person or in a problematic situation: These attributes are trying to embody themselves in actual happenings. Thus the seer acts as a midwife, contriving to make these virtualities materialize. One could extend one's sense of the present to include all that is eternally present, and look upon the present in the manifested world as a framework within which all reality may or may not appear to view.

Most people's ignorance of the answer to their soul-searching questions arises out of their inability to see the future as already virtually present in the form of potentialities; however, a seer may be able to grasp these potentialities as chess players may foresee two or three moves, possibly more, ahead. Most people judge a person by his visible personality, while the seer sees his real being, including all his potentialities. The secret of expanding the span of the present consists in lifting one's consciousness. Murshid evidences the point of view of the man who is attuned to the eternal present. The future, he said, does not seem to lie ahead, but above; you do not move into it, it descends upon you because it is on its way, in the process of formation. Reality always supersedes anything that one can encompass, but when one's vantage point has been raised, the present includes not only the past that lives on, but the future which one can already anticipate. The sense of the eternity of the present is certainly vaster to some than others, but may still be infinitesimal in comparison with the real dimensions of eternity.

Intuition reaches its apogee in revelation. It is grasping meaningfulness beyond circumstances and events, beyond psychometry or telepathy or forecasting. In its first stage, it consists in earmarking the cause of a situation instead of just picking up on a situation.

There is a difference between eternal and everlasting. The word eternal *can never be attached to the soul, for that which has birth and a death, a beginning and an end, cannot be eternal, though it can be everlasting. It is everlasting according to our conception; it lasts beyond all that we can conceive and comprehend, but when we come to the eternal, that is God alone.*

The next step toward the understanding of human psychology is to find out the cause behind the faults people have. While an ordinary person can see the action of another, the seer can see the reason of the action also, and if his sight is keener still he can see the reason of the person. A person who sees cause and effect of every word, of every thought, of every movement, of every change of expression, that is the person who reads between the lines, that is the person whose glance is like an X ray; it sees through a person. No doubt it is this person who will find more faults, lacks, wants in human nature naturally, and it is this person who will be less affected by it or at least react less upon it, overlook it and rise above it; the person who sees the most complains the least, the person who sees the least complains the most. The reason is that he does not see the lack, but he sees the cause; and when he sees the cause he sees the effect.

At the next stage, the seer reaches even beyond insight into the cause of the situation, for it flashes into the cause beyond the cause.

Besides this, in all affairs of this world, of individuals and multitudes, which confuse people, which bring them despair, and cause them depression, which give joy and pleasure, which amuse them, he sees through all. He knows why it comes, whence it comes, what is behind it, what is the cause of it, and behind the seeming cause what is the hidden cause; and if he wished to trace the cause behind the cause he could trace back to the primal cause, for the inner life is lived by living with the primal cause, by being in unity with the primal cause.

In the third stage, instead of just understanding the functioning of the machine by seeing the causal links between people's action and what happens to them as a consequence, the seer sees into the planning itself, grasping the divine intention, not just the way the machine is made, for he now discerns what that person was intended to become if he so wills. It is this "intention" that is "the purpose, even beyond the cause behind the cause."

To gain insight into things the mystic enters into the depths of the whole mechanism of the universe by educating his senses to be keen enough to see and hear the working through it all, through the whole cosmic system. Taking these two senses as his means of investigation he dives deep into the universal life. He, so to speak, touches the soul of the thought. It is just as by seeing the plant one may get an idea of the root. And in this way things unknown are known and things unseen are perceived by the mystic, and he calls it revelation. When one is able to see the works of God in life, another world is opened before one; then a man does not look at the world as everybody else does, for he begins to see not only the machine going on but the engineer standing by its side, making the machine work.

The answer wells up from the depth of all existence, like the sound of a bell being struck, or the splash of water, or the crackle of the firecracker; each reveals its condition when struck, like the knock on the door.

There is a stage in the evolution of a man's life when every question is answered by the life around him. He may have a living being before him, or be surrounded by nature; he may be awake or asleep, but the answer to his question comes as an echo of the question itself. Just as certain things become an accomodation for the air, turning it into a sound, so everything becomes an accomodation for each thought of the sage, helping it to resound; and in this resonance there is an answer. In point of fact, the answer is contained in the question itself. A question has no existence without an answer. It is man's limited vision that makes him see only the question without the answer. While all things have their opposites, it is also true that in each the spirit of the opposite exists. The closer one approaches reality, the nearer one comes to unity. The evidence of this realization is that no sooner has a question arisen in the heart, than the answer comes as its echo either within or without. If we look in front of ourselves, the answer is before us; if we look behind, the answer is behind; if we look up, the answer awaits us in the sky; if we look down, the answer is engraved for us on the earth; if we close our eyes we will find the answer within us.

Murshid gives two diametrically opposite clues. The answer comes within and without.

The whole of life, everything he looks at, is the answer to his question. And if he does not wish to look at the objective world, he has only to close his eyes and find the answer within himself. The objective answer is waiting for him in the outer world and the answer from the inner is waiting within.[40]

The answer dawns upon one as soon as one sees the flaw in the question. This is the "answer that uproots the question."

And as he progresses, the moment the mystic has reached the state where he has no questions, he himself becomes the answer to every question.

There comes a time when we begin to see every action, everything that is going on is an answer to that which is going on within ourselves. For example, a man is walking in the street, thinking about his business, or his domestic affairs, and then suddenly a horse becomes restive and breaks a carriage it was drawing, upsetting the coachman. Now there are two different things. The man is thinking about something, and the horse with which he has nothing to do upsets the carriage. It is another thing altogether, but at the same time, for the mystic everything is connected; there is no condition which is detached from another condition. Every condition has a correspondence, a relation with another condition, because for a mystic, there is no divided life; there is only one life, one being and one mechanism which is running. And therefore a mechanism is always running in relation to another mechanism; however different and disconnected they may seem, they are not disconnected.[41]

CHAPTER 7

The Inner Odyssey

STAGES ON THE PATH

Blessed is he who sees the star of his soul as the light that is seen in the port from the sea.—Gayan, 89

The purpose of life is like the horizon; the further one advances, the further it recedes.

The court life of Hyderabad had become stifling to Murshid since he had known a real sovereign. But he could not leave India yet on his mission because this would have dealt a fatal blow to his ailing father.

Now Murshid had a struggle with himself. Shall I adopt the life of a dervish? Then I shall be burdensome upon my fellow men. Shall I enjoy my livelihood by selling my musical talent? This proves degrading to the sacred value of music. The only solution was actually to live the life of an adept under the guise of a musician, communicating his own spiritual realization in the form of lectures on the sacred role of music, and illustrating these by singing. Thus he traveled throughout India on a last pilgrimage of homage to its holy men before setting out on his great mission.

During my pilgrimage to the holy men of India, I saw some whose presence was more illuminating than reading books. They do not need to speak, they become living lights, fountains of love. One feels uplifted and full of joy, ecstasy, happiness and enlightenment.

It took three days and nights driving in a rough bullock cart on out-of-the-way country roads to reach the temple of Manek Prabhu, the seat of a great guru among the Brahmins. Not being a Hindu, Murshid was placed in the worst room near the stable. Nearby, a tinny, scratchy band shrieked out its tune regularly every three hours, which Murshid much appreciated, as it helped him awaken for his night vigils. The following morning the guru's son caught a glimpse of Murshid and obviously was intrigued, he called for him. "I cannot understand why you should choose this out-of-the-way temple instead of visiting a

119

Muslim saint!" was his first query. "Muslim or Hindu are only outer distinctions," was the reply. Asked to what creed he belonged, Murshid answered that he saw the divine everywhere. Suddenly the young man recognized Hazrat Inayat Khan from articles in the papers as the person who had received outstanding distinctions from the hand of the Nizam. He was at a complete loss to understand why he should abandon the palace to come here: "I must speak with my father." "No," said Murshid, "you are removing my shield: I was contented staying in a corner." But it was inevitable.

"What is the purpose of your visit?" asked the Swami. "I am seeking the image of my Murshid in various forms, and especially to recognize his countenance in the faces of the holy ones," was the reply. The guru then evidenced his interest in Sufism by showing Murshid the flagstaff of Khwaja Abdel Qader Jilani, a great Sufi saint, in his collection. Countering Pir-o-Murshid Inayat Khan's assertion of the identity between Vedanta and Sufism, he pointed out the difference on the issue of reincarnation. Pir-o-Murshid responded that the concern about one's personal genesis and survival strengthened ego consciousness and deterred one from divine consciousness, pointing out that the very Hindu teaching of *mukti* (or *moksha*) posits emancipation from the individual self, and Advaita Vedanta considers the self as illusory. The guru found no quarrel with Murshid's deep realization on the subject and donned him with the shawl of the sanyasin (the Hindu recluse), a recognition of spiritual kinship.

It is ironic that the theory of reincarnation which had been devised to prompt people in the East into liberating themselves in order to avoid having to come back to earth again, suffer once more, and repeat the same mistakes all over again, should have been exploited in the West to give people hope in coming back!

The thought of reincarnation is helpful to those who do not believe in God or know His being, also to those who neither believe in an everlasting life nor can understand it. For some people it is very consoling to think that they will come to this earthly plane again and again, brought there by their Karma, rather than to think, as many materialists do, that when we are dead we are done with for ever.

It always appeals to the hearts whose treasure is on the earth to think that even if we passed from this earth we shall not be taken away forever, we shall come back again.

The law of karma is a logical concomitant of the theory of reincarnation.

The law of Karma or action is the philosophy which a reasoning brain holds in support of reincarnation, saying, there is no such being as God as an intervener in our life's affairs, but it is we who by our actions produce results similar to them. There is the ever-ruling law of cause and effect, therefore every occurence in life must be in accordance with it. If we do not get the results of our good or wicked deeds immediately that is because they need time to mature so as to produce similar results; if they do not do so in this life, then the law forces us to be born again.[1]

The law of Karma is very gratifying for several reasons. First, because it answers immediately the question of why one is well off in life and why another suffers. Second, because:

Those who have not experienced the life of the earth sufficiently and who have not achieved their desire in this life, they are only content to think that next time they will come and accomplish it. Then there are some who find that there is little time left in life and they have not yet improved themselves. They can hope that perhaps at their next visit to the earth they will finish the task.

The consolation that it gives to the ego is paid for by waylaying one from seeking resurrection. One fallacy in attributing causation exclusively to karmic law is that it does not account for the one gratifying factor in life: grace, compassion, mercy. The theory of reincarnation accounts for those factors in our lives that are determined by causal vectors: law. But much of what happens evidences an ever renewed test with a view to encouraging people into the next step toward greater progress. This evidences freedom rather than law, an underlying future-oriented purpose rather than just the cause begun in the past, an ever recurring divine intention instead of its fossilization in the form of habit.

Some believers in God say in support of reincarnation, "God is just. There are many who are lame or blind or unhappy in life, and this is the punishment for the faults they have committed before, in a former incarnation. If it were not so, that would be injustice on the part of God." That makes God only a reckoner and not a lover, and it restricts Him to His justice like a judge bound by the law. The judge is the slave of law, the forgiver its matter.[2]

This is also the answer of Christianity:

Jesus answered: "Neither hath this man sinned, nor his parents, but that the works of God should be made manifest in him."[3]

A rishi in a cave in the Himalayas once answered to my question on reincarnation: That is what they teach in the Temple. In other words, for the masses.

Reincarnation is an integral part of the caste system.

Owing to the inclination of the higher caste to keep itself pure from further admixture of the lower classes, a religious rule was made enforcing the belief that the Sundra, the lowest, could not become a Vaisha, the Vaisha could not become a Kshattria, nor a Kshattria be admitted among Brahmins ... unless by his good actions he had made it possible that he should be born in the next incarnation, in a family of the higher caste.[4]

However, the idea of Reincarnation and Karma, which came from the race of Hindus, never has given the full satisfaction to that race itself. The influence of Islam, the ideas of the Sufis, made a great change in the Hindu outlook for many centuries, and great Hindu poets like Nanak and Kabir, Sundar and Dadu, Ram Das and Tukaram, and religious performers of India like Swami Narayan and Babu Keshewe Chandra Sen, Dayananda Saraswathi, Devendranath Tagore, all these, although they could not entirely erase this idea from the surface of the Indian mentality, upon which it had been engraved for ages, yet modified it to such an extent that hardly anyone speaks about these things.

The West received the theory through the Theosophical Society.

If it were not for the theory of Karma and Reincarnation which the Theosophical Society has brought forward as its special doctrine, on which the whole theosophical theory is based, it would have had great difficulty in touching the Western mind, which wants food for reason first before accepting any faith.

The second fallacy is that reincarnation focuses on the individual, whereas, if we knew how the strands of life converging from and dispersing into all the bountiful components of the universe, physical and beyond, intertwine momentarily, cross-pollinate, then proliferate the qualities thus acquired, while their essence is extracted and transmuted, we would question our naive notion of individuality.

The only thing which contradicts this theory is the failure to prove an exclusive individuality when the idea of individuality is x-rayed.

According to Buddhism, there is no such thing as a person, since we are not even the same person as when we were a baby, but there is continuity in change. This crucial view of Buddhism is equally to be found in Sufi metaphysics and indeed in *Advaita Vedanta*.

Whatever we call *I* is an evershifting conglomeration of various so-called bodies or sheaths, which are themselves continually being coalesced then disintegrated. The interrelation of the bodies is ensured by the fact that the characteristics of the subtler sheaths may be communicated to the grosser ones, which may be called embodiment— the Christian Fathers call it incarnation—and the qualities of the grosser ones or those acquired by the grosser ones are a consequence of osmosis from their environment, and may be communicated to the subtler sheaths, providing they undergo a process of sublimation. To simplify, at the cost of accounting for the extreme complexity of the mystery of life: The seed, having unfolded into a plant by drawing its environment into itself, reappears at the end of the growth process, generating further plants that inherit its idiosyncrasies. Are they different plants? One may well say that the plant continues to exist in its progeny. On the other hand, the plant continues to live, but in a subtler way, in the form of the perfume of its flowers, while also continuing to live in its progeny.

The personality, being a picture, is reflected in the mind-world. Therefore, as a reflection of a person on a photographic plate does not rob the person of his existence, so the reflection fallen upon a soul from a soul does not rob the soul of its personality. It is this reflection which builds another personality on the same design, which is known as reincarnation.

The continuity between the links in the reincarnation chain is, according to Murshid, the creative perpetuation of impressions marking a being sometimes more deeply than his congenital heritage.

In the plane of the jinn a sympathetic link is established between two souls. In this way it is natural for the spirit of Shakespeare to continue to inspire the Shakespeare personality on earth. The question if there can be more than one incarnation of the same person at the same time, may be answered: yes, a person can have many pictures, so there can be many reflections of one personality manifested on the earth.

More generally, one might say that reincarnation designates the continuity of personality in its progress on the plane of the mind, which may well be quickened by a different soul from its previous patron; in fact, this is the meaning of quickening. It is not the alliance of two bodies or two personalities, but the infusion of an entity by one of a subtler nature—a different kind of parenthood. In fact, a rare exemplification of this principle on the physical plane is the swapping of souls, of which the finest example is in the transmissions of Lama souls. At the death of a Tibetan Lama, a child receives something of his being and proves it by being tested and giving identical instructions to his predecessor's.

In conclusion, there is a horizontal and a vertical continuity, both going on simultaneously:

There are two deaths, the inner and the external. The first is going into the centre, the second going into the vastness. It is like a pebble thrown in the water: what one sees are the horizontal circles which become wider and wider;

there are other lines which go deeper and deeper. These two sorts form the cross.

The first one ensures, at the physical level, the continuity of the body, albeit in cooperation with another body; at the personality level, reincarnation (which is the meaning of *samsara*); at the soul level, its continuity in the spheres yonder. The second Ariadnean thread ensures the transference of the qualities of the soul to the personality, then to the body; and conversely, the qualities acquired by the body are transmitted to the personality and the qualities thus acquired to the soul, and further upward.

On his pilgrimage, Murshid ran across danger. On arriving at the tomb of a great Sufi Bandanawaz at Gulburga, he had fever. It so happened that the plague had declared itself, and the authorities were out of preventive measures, putting an end to the lives of anybody showing the slightest sign of the plague. A miracle happened: When Murshid was due for medical inspection, his fever had disappeared. An hour before he had asked help from the entombed pir.

A reverent and soulful reception welcomed him, the pride of the family, as he briefly called back at Baroda house. The high attunement of his soul had left a mark on his face and in his eyes.

Once a person has absorbed the thought of reality, it is not only that this ennobles his soul, but it gives him a kingly spirit. It is like being crowned.

His father found him very changed. His atmosphere had become more calm, his thoughts collected, and his voice, too, had changed; his father, who had never been able to reach him completely, now treated him with high regard. "How I wish I were young so that I might sit at your feet," said father to son. But life at Baroda had lost its purpose for Murshid.

Curiously enough, now that in his heart Murshid had given up music as his motivation, people were clamoring for it. Consequently, wherever he went he brought through his music a spiritual message, sharing with his audience the uplift he enjoyed. In Madras there was an ovation. Presently Mysore, the city of his illustrious great-great-grandfather, Tippu Sultan, the city where his grandfather Moula Bakhsh had gained recognition, now fifty years later was acclaiming him. But the gold medal he received did not mean anything to him anymore. He was practicing what a few years later he was to preach in the West:

What is made for man, man may hold; he must not be held by it.

Renounce the world before the world renounces you.

He knew how vain is worldly fame. Music was his language, not his objective anymore. His way of life lay with the holy men and sages. He was on a holy pilgrimage to meet the sages of India before he set off on his great task ahead. He discovered a great Sufi sage, Pir Jemat Ali Shah, who had a following of thousands of people but was drawn to Murshid alone.

In Bangalore, as Murshid sat every night after sunset singing, surrounded by friends who used to drop in, a madhzub used to stand at a distance listening. As the hours passed, his soul seemed to soar ever higher in divine rhapsody. When Murshid urged him in, he said, "I know you and know what you shall have to go through and my heart will follow you everywhere." Again chance had it that Murshid met a great Sufi sage who drew crowds of Hindus and Muslims, "his eyes inspiring, his atmosphere uplifting," so that "in this the purpose of my coming to Bangalore is fulfilled."

A sparkling soul flashes out through the eyes.

Now Murshid submitted his musical talent to the greatest challenge ever, the very place where his grandfather, Moula Bakhsh, had gained recognition. Kumba Koman was the most orthodox Brahmin center of the South, a real test place for Southern (Karnatic) music and where connoisseurs were most critical. Murshid's rendering of the Tyagaraja's style won in the hearts of these Brahmins the place of his grandfather, but such were the local customs that no non-Brahmin could be accommodated in the houses. A dilapidated shed was pointed out to him in the open countryside. As the ground was uneven, Murshid found it difficult to sleep and thought it a good opportunity spend the night in contemplation. As light dawned, he noticed that a dervish was sitting outside. Greeting Murshid, he told him how he had enjoyed his long night's vigil and said that he had come there every night for twenty years to sleep. Murshid regretted having found this accommodation uncomfortable for one night, when the fakir had put up with it for twenty years!

As a guest of the Raja of Tanjore, home of the most celebrated musicians of the Karnatic style, Murshid could witness the grandeur of the India of the princes, already crumbling in his time.

An aristocratic family with their traditions and culture, albeit worn out, that fineness, that gentleness and modesty they showed, which proved their aristocracy much more than did their palaces and stately environments.

They were deeply moved by the kingly spirit of their musician guest.

Now the scene changes, and the pilgrim finds himself at Tricknapoli in the midst of the orphans to whom the great social worker Saiyed Mustapha Khan Bahadur dedicated his life's work. The classical Hindu temples of Madurai struck Murshid as "an education in human life for the unlettered men of the past," and he welcomed "the new consciousness" that was emerging among the Muslims at Coimbatore, where he was received by the Anjuman Islam. The natural simplicity of life of the Malabar coast and the watery land of Cochin were now a peaceful interlude.

Visiting the Maharaja of Travancore brought home once more to Murshid how:

the princes and potentates of India, upon whom depends the welfare of the country, are unaware of the progress of the world in general, absorbed only in their little narrow groove, and conscious of their little kingship.

Someone remarked that the power of sincerity emanating from Murshid overwhelmed the Maharaja. In Ceylon he found Markas Muslims "most restricted in their faith and afraid to go where there was a danger of hearing music," but also,

younger musicians who were trying to come out of their old restrictions, and who, besides their appreciation of Inayat as a musician, found in him a young reformer.

One day in Rangoon Murshid found that all his funds had been stolen from his trunk. He went several days without eating, refusing however all invitations by Burmese merchants to be a guest at their homes. His servant offered to lend him some money, but he refused. Finally, in awe before Murshid's asceticism and faith in God, the servant returned all the money he had stolen. Murshid found in Burma an ideal of brotherhood that inspired him in much that he said later of the brotherhood of man in the fatherhood of God.

At Calcutta, a great center of Indian culture where Murshid projected founding a music school, he encountered someone who bore a grudge against his family, put obstructions in his way, and later admitted it. It was that great sage, Babu Lahiri, who insisted on opening the door for him to the students at the university, on a memorable evening under the patronage of Rabindranath Tagore.

At this point Murshid received the news of the passing of his father, which brought him great sadness. Rahmat Khan had been so genuine and endearing a personality, so true, kindhearted, and endowed with a sense of responsibility and righteousness; he had shown increasing understanding of Murshid's indomitable genius.

Murshid seemed to undergo an intensive process of inner preparation, spending most of the nights in meditation and sleeping for the remaining two or three hours on a tiger skin. A great Sufi, Moulana Ektedarul Huq, who addressed masses of people, foresaw Murshid's future: "Here is a hidden soul in which the expression of the divine is now budding," he said.

Refusing an invitation of the Ruler of Silhet, Murshid founded a school of music in Calcutta. Among the students, an odd personality—a madhzub—used to attend, and when he could not find Murshid would inquire: "Where is my Lord and Master?" Murshid said: "All great souls call even undeserving souls great because of their own greatness." Another sage who became Murshid's greatest friend was Babu Hiran Maya.

Murshid's life so far had been a long pilgrimage. Yet well he knew that the greatest trek of his life now lay ahead, heading West, although he was aware that the real odyssey takes place inside.

There is a place which one cannot reach by going anywhere.[5]

Later, he drew a sketch of the milestones marking the stages (called *maqamat* by the Sufis) through which the adept passes in his spiritual progress. We are all pilgrims through life, and our progress is in our realization, which manifests in our change of outlook on things, assessment of situations, insight into being.

We are all on the journey; life itself is a journey. No one is settled here; we are all passing onward, and therefore it is not true to say, that if we are taking a spiritual journey we have to break our settled life; there is no one living a settled life here; all are unsettled, all are on their way.[6]

He often used to ponder upon the meaningfulness of his trek in the Himalayas. Was it not the metaphor of life?

The joy of life is the joy of the journey. If one could close one's eyes and be put immediately on top of the Himalayas, one would not enjoy it as much as the one who climbs and goes from one peak to another, and sees the different scenery and meets the different people on the way. The whole joy is in the journey.[7]

We are heading for goals which we cannot know before we reach them, and any ideas that we might form as to our objective have to be superceded ever and anon, for as we approach what we had envisioned, a further objective looms ahead, which a short time earlier we would not have been able to discern at all. One's objective is the ideal that one forms in one's mind. But as one draws nearer to it, if one were to cleave to it, one would become insensitive to the next milestone that beckons out of the haze, which can only stand out more clearly as one approaches it.

The ideal is the means, but its breaking is the goal. The reason for this is that mostly what we think is our ideal is only the picture of our ideal, which becomes clearer as we advance.

However beautiful a picture of our ideal we make, the ideal itself is still more beautiful.

Furthermore, we must understand that what we depict here as advancing on the path is really growing in realization and stature. Hence that toward which we thought we were moving is nothing other than what we already are but have only to realize.

As great as is a person's ideal, so great is that person. It is the ideal that makes a person great, but at the same time if he is not great his ideal cannot be great.[8]

Progress means a traveling on the path of motive to the destination which may be called its fulfillment. There is not a single thought or imagination—speech or action apart—which does not in time reach its destination, which may be called fulfillment.

Sometimes we regress instead of progressing, or remain stationary mid-stream, or stall, stalemated. Sometimes we zigzag, dilly-dallying, loosing our bearings, or waylaid by our lack of resolve or inconsistency and negligence. Sometimes, we proceed two steps forward and one backward, and sometimes, one forward and two sideways.

From the hosts of ideas that come to him, man must select; he can only follow one path at a time. As man advances along his chosen path, he finds that it branches right and left.[9]

Not knowing the way and the lay of the land, and since the signposts of our next objective most often lie in the haze, we seek an experienced guide. But our personal appraisal of him may be as fallible as our evaluation of our ideal. Consequently, some disenchanted wayfarers abandon the quest; others, doubting their guide's ability, struggle alone; and others swap guides and so change itinerary midway. Others follow a guide who guides them toward a different milestone from the one originally planned, and then find it difficult to retrace their tracks when left to their own devices.

As the pilgrimage is internal, it does not so much consist in changing the outer conditions of one's life, like a sanyasin who leaves his job and family to live as an ascetic, but rather in doing something internally, like ceasing to be insincere or jealous, irate or bumptious. However, when one's outlook has changed through reaching a higher realization, and one's sensitivity is consequently refined, one cannot always continue doing what one was doing before.

We make a great mistake today when we consider every man's evolution as the same. There are great differences between people. One is creeping, one is walking, one is running, and another is flying. And yet they all live under the same sun. Very often people ask, "How long has one to go on the spiritual path?" There is no limit to the length of this path and yet if one is ready, it does not need a long time. It is a moment and one is there.[10]

Nevertheless, what is most necessary is to connect the outward action with the inward journey. . . . And once this harmony is established one begins to see the cause of all things much more clearly. Everyone knows what he is doing, but not everyone necessarily knows where he is going.[11]

Everyone goes through changes of heart; one passes through phases where one is filled with a certain emotion, or enthused by a certain way of looking at things; then, entering into the next phase, one is in a completely different mood and one's outlook may be utterly shifted.

What is it? What is it like? Spiritual progress is the changing of the point of view.[12]

There is no spiritual progress in knowing more things than one has known. On the contrary, the spiritual progress is to be seen in the attitude one takes toward things, in one's outlook on life.

For example, one might be in a state of remorse, or in a state of achievement, or in a state of contentment, or in a state of irony, or in a state of delight, or of detachment, or of love, or of bewilderment, or of glorification. The Sufis have made a point of revealing the importance of the experience of those states, called *hal*, for the unfoldment of one's being and then outlining the sequence of stages, called *maqamat*, through which one passes on one's itinerary (or even sketching out different itineraries), composing a real topography of the soul.

This latter gives the map of the journey to the soul travelling towards manifestation. It is from this map that the travelling soul strikes his path rightly or wrongly. One soul may have one kind of instruction, another soul may have another kind; one soul may be clear, another may be confused. Yet they all go forward as the travellers of a caravan, taking with them all the precious information, all the things which they have learned from the others on the journey.[13]

The journey requires careful planning:

The inner life is a journey, and before starting to take it there is a certain preparation necessary. If one is not prepared, there is always the risk of having to return before one has arrived at one's destination. When a person goes on a journey, and when he has to accomplish something, he must know what is necessary on the path and what he must take with him, in order that his journey may become easy and that he may accomplish what he has started to accomplish.[14]

Progressing means jettisoning a lot of ballast that one does not need and which has become a burden one could well spare oneself. One learns to leave behind irrelevant fantasies in one's life.

In order to be aware of the temptation one has to meet with, it is well to keep before one the goal one wishes to attain and always to reason out before taking a step toward anything whether it will help or hinder the attainment of one's desired end. For the boat to be able to sail, various conditions must be fulfilled: for instance, that it is not more heavily laden than its capacity. Thus our heart should not be heavily laden with the things that we attach ourselves to, because then the boat will not float.

Any resentment or grudge that one holds against anyone would constitute a burden bogging one down and slowing down one's progress, even sometimes to a halt. The same applies to despondency about life, even without placing the blame on a person but upon "blind fate."

There must be no grudge against anybody and no complaining of anyone having done him harm, for all these things which belong to this world, if man took them along, would become a burden on the spiritual path. The journey is difficult enough, and it becomes more difficult if there is a burden to be carried.... It is a path to freedom, and to start on this path to freedom man must free himself; no attachment should pull him back, no pleasure should lure him back.[15]

Before setting sail, one must first be sure that one has not left anything unfulfilled, an opportunity one might have availed oneself of, anything one would still like to experience for one's personal satisfaction; otherwise that very thought will be pulling one back in the opposite direction to the line of advance.

Also the boat should not be tied to this one port, for then it is held back and will not go to the port for which it is bound. Every desire, every ambition, every aspiration that he has in life must be gratified. Not only this, man must have no remorse of any kind when starting on his journey, and no repentance afterwards.

Man must also consider, before starting on his journey, whether he has learned all he desired to learn from this world. If there is anything he has not learned, he must finish it before starting the journey.[16]

This is why Murshid was not in favor of our overstressing ourselves, like accelerating the ripening of an apple or cooking food too fast: It gives mediocre results.

Particularly important is to ascertain that one has not left behind a debt to anyone.

Every soul has a certain debt to pay in life; it may be to his mother or father, his brother or sister, to husband or wife or friend, or to his children, his race, or to humanity; and if he has not paid what is due, then there are cords with which he is inwardly tied, and they pull him back. Life in the world is fair trade, if one could only understand it, if one knew how many souls there are in this world with whom one is connected or related in some way, or whom we meet freshly every day. To everyone there is something due; and if one has not paid one's obligations, the result is that afterwards one has to pay with interest.[17]

When there is money to be paid to a money-lender it must be paid whether he deserves it or not. And so it is on the spiritual path. Those we have to pay we must pay, in the way of attention, services, respect. All that is due to anyone, we have to pay. In the first place, apart from spiritual realization, we feel such a release at having paid our debt to everyone to whom it is due.[18]

My mother has brought me up from infancy, she has sacrificed her sleep, rest, and comfort for me and loved me with a love which is beyond any other love in this world, and she has shown in life that mercy to me which is the compassion of God.[19]

The consequence may well be that one might have to carry the weight of one or more people for whom one has assumed responsibility, making one's advance much more laborious, for the sake of being true to one's sense of honor, even if it would seem obvious that it would be easier to undertake the journey alone. Since the standards of behavior become more exacting as one advances, the damaging effect ensuing from the protraction of the debt becomes more noticeable. If the debt is not met, its effect will soon be felt in one's restlessness and irritability, which transpire just as one wishes to meditate. This is the way in which one's conscience urges redress, preventing one from putting off one's coming to terms with reality.

A person may give his valuable time to contemplation, to a spiritual life, yet at the same time his mind is disturbed, his heart is not at rest, for he feels he has not done his duty, he has a debt to pay to someone.

To negotiate heavy seas, one needs a strong disposition, manly courage, a sense of responsibility, great reliability; one must overcome any whimsical moodiness, and scatter-brained lightheartedness.

Life is a sea, and the futher one travels on the sea the heavier the ship one needs. So for a wise man, a certain amount of weight is requiped in order to live, which gives balance to his personality.[20] One no longer sways with every wind that blows but stays on the water like a heavy ship, not like a small boat that moves with every wave that passes.[21]

One also must be sensitive to any favorable forces that may be harnessed to propel one toward one's objective.

Furthermore, the boat must have the responsiveness to the wind which will take it to that port; and this is the feeling a soul gets from the spiritual side of life. That feeling, that wind, helps one to go forward to the port for which we are all bound. Once it is fully concentrated, the mind should become like a compass in a boat, always pointing in the same direction.

The Murshid gives a final briefing to the wanderer on life's paradoxical journey:

On this journey certain coins are necessary also, to spend on the way. And what are these coins? They are thoughtful expressions in word and in action. On this journey man must take provision to eat and drink, and that provision is life and light. And on this journey man has to take something in which to clothe himself against wind, and storm, and heat, and cold; and that garment is the vow of secrecy, the tendency to silence. On this journey man has to bid farewell to others when starting, and that farewell is loving detachment; before starting on this journey he has to leave something behind with his friends, and that is happy memories of the past.[22]

What are the *maqamat*, the stages, the psychological hurdles, or horizons of understanding that one reaches one life's journey? Some Sufi teachers have gone into great detail in distinguishing innumerable stages, resulting in numerous systems; and one may well wonder how useful it is to know the stages ahead before one has reached their threshold. Yet it does give one motivation and incentive to have a general preview of where one is going.

Murshid refers to the seven valleys outlined by the Persian Sufi poet Farid-ud-Din Attar in the *Mantiq at-Tair*, translated as the *Conference of the Birds*. A bright one among the birds, the hoopoe, erstwhile guide to King Solomon and crowned by him, convoked an assembly of all the birds the world over, known or unknown. The whole range of human characters and feelings is here so realistically typified in each bird, and men's arguments to justify systematic postponement of the great issue of their lives is most convincingly brought home in ornithological language! It begins with the most far-reaching decision in the life of a human being: whether one is prepared to seek the supreme fulfillment. "I have traveled by sea and over land, over mountain and valley, and have measured the bounds of the world," says the hoopoe. And he describes the seven valleys, which are not places but conditions of the soul.

However, each Sufi teacher outlines the stages according to his own vision. According to Murshid, the wayfarers are at first simply enthused by all that captures their attention, or strikes their imagination, or touches their emotions. Life opens itself up, to their great astonishment, in all its bounty, exciting, apparently inexhaustible and mysteriously unfathomed. This is the *maqam* of the quest.

It is the soul's infancy when life to the soul is attractive, everything, right or wrong, good or bad, has an attraction for that soul. It is ready to jump in a pit, to fall in a ditch, to run into thorns, to fall in the mud. Everything is attractive, good or bad, which comes along. That is the soul's infancy. The soul at that time is new and vigorous, appreciative and observing, just like an infant. For an infant even fire is most beautiful. It would like to put some fire in its pocket. And that is the condition of the generality.

In the second stage, the enchantment of life involves the wayfarer more deeply in a relationship of concupiscence. One forms an attachment to all that means so much to one.

All that the soul has taken to heart, it is that which attracts. Their heart is where their treasure is. That is the time when there comes the time of temptation. Everything that one desires, one wishes to have, one values, one gives importance to; it is that after which one goes. That is where his temptation is. What very often happens is a disappointment. But still if one thing disappoints there is another thing ready again to make him forget it. And so he goes on, one thing after another, always building hopes, always fixing his mind upon things, always finding it comes to nothing, and again always ready to be given into temptation. And so he goes on through life. There is never an end to his temptations. If not one thing, there is another thing. And there is never satisfaction gained in the things that he is tempted with. For they are only the shadows covering reality.

At the third stage, one experiences a need to understand what makes things work, how they are related, how one situation ensues from another, why things happen the way they do. It is the stage of knowledge.

It offers him an interest to look through it, to study, to understand it. And this very world in which he has lived several years, then begins to change at every moment. His field of study becomes vast. Every experience, every condition, every action, every person, teaches him. What he has learned today he unlearns tomorrow, because there is a raw experience, perhaps contradicting what he has known yesterday. And so he goes along the way of unfoldment, and life offers greater and greater wonders in all things one sees. He observes and he sees and he wonders and at times he is completely bewildered at it. Nature apart, its mystery, its secret, its character aside, human nature that one sees from morning till evening, the ways of the wise and the ways of the foolish, and the ways of the rightdoer and the ways of the wrongdoer, and how things change and turn, and hide and manifest, it gives one so much to think about and to study and to observe that not one moment in his life seems to have been wasted; it is filled with a wonderful vision.

At the fourth stage, the wayfarer is disenchanted with the very things that used to attract him, and he sees through much of the sham which builds up our common but elusive illusions. He unmasks the hoax. This is the valley of detachment and renunciation.

And then there is a stage further, when the soul begins to lift the curtain which hides hopes. He begins to lift, so to speak, the curtain which hides human nature. It seems as if a veil is lifted from all things and from all conditions, and that the colours which once seemed bright become faded, the light of gems and jewels becomes pale. He sees behind attachments and detachments, and love and hate, thin threads sustaining them. He sees, as Omar Khayyam says "a hair's difference" between right and wrong. Heaven and earth seem to him touching one another. Gulfs between things which are opposed seem removed from his sight. Then he begins to feel indifferent, he begins to feel independent. He is not hurt at the pinpricks of everyday life nor does he feel exalted by red roses. He builds hopes, but not as every person. He has only one hope, and that hope is in reality. All other hopes for him mean nothing. His indifference is not unfriendly, his independence is not conceited. By indifference he does not neglect others; only his indifference is his independence. He does not mind if he is neglected. By his indifference he does not avoid doing all he must do for others, only he is independent of the doing of others for himself. It is to that right kind of independence and indifference, which is called in the language of the Hindus Vairagya, that that spirit becomes developed.

Completing the cycle, curiously enough, at the fifth stage he returns to life, playing with the children of the world, while enjoying what used to make his sensitivity cringe, without getting in any way disturbed by the selfishness, dishonesty, and cruelty of his fellow creatures.

The great Indian poet Tulsides has said, "Everyone does and says as much as he has understood." Why should a man blame another for what he cannot understand?[23]

Therefore the person living the inner life never condemns and does not criticize the objects of another, however small or ridiculous they may appear, for he knows that every object in the life of a person is but a stepping-stone, which leads him forward if he only wishes to go forward.[24]

In all forms of life he sees God, and thereby he has toward everybody that attitude which a lover of God, a worshipper of God has toward God. Therefore the Sufi complains no more, has no grudge against anyone, has nothing to grumble about: "That person insulted me," or "treated me badly," or "behaved unjustly," or "acted unkindly"—no complaint whatever, for complaint comes to a person who thinks of himself most of the time. And then follows that ideal stage of the soul's unfoldment; when the world with all its limitations and people with all their faults, they are all tolerated, they are all forgiven, there is a continual expansion of sympathy and love, which continues to expand, just like a little pool of water expanding and turning into an ocean. And in this expansion the Divine Spirit expresses, and man with all his limitations stands only as a cover hiding that Divine Perfection which is expressing behind it. To that soul then the world is not attractive nor tempting nor is it wonderful nor futile, it is most beautiful. God is beautiful and He loves beauty. Also he makes no pretence of knowing something, or of being something. Outwardly to be like everyone, inwardly to be what one is.

This is the way of the sages. Their first moral principle is constantly to avoid hurting the feeling of another. The second principle is to avoid allowing themselves to be affected by the constantly jarring influences which every soul has to meet in life. The third principle is to keep their balance under all different situations and conditions which upset this tranquil state of mind. The fourth principle is to love unceasingly all those who deserve love, and to give to the undeserving their forgiveness; and this is continually practiced by them. The fifth principle is detachment amidst the crowd; but by detachment I do not mean separation. By detachment is only meant rising above those bondages which bind man and keep him back from his journey towards the goal.[25]

It is like living in the world and not being of the world, touching the world and not being touched by it. It needs a clear perception of life, keen intelligence and thorough understanding, together with great courage, strength, and bravery.

There is yet a further stage, the sixth, called the valley of bewilderment, when one sees that everything is different from what one thought; one is shattered by the sheer meaningfulness of life and singed by one's confrontation with the power of truth flaring forcefully through the camouflage of maya.

This bewilderment is such that it becomes wonderfully amusing to look at life.[26]

For in the first place the mystical life is a puzzle, in the second place a bewilderment, and in the third place a miracle.[27]

Imagine an evolved person being more bewildered than an unevolved one! And yet it is so, for at this stage a man begins to see that things are not as they seem to be but as they are. This causes a kind of conflict; he does not know whether to call a thing good or bad, love or hate. There comes a time when all that he had accepted in his mind, all that he believed in, now appears to be quite the contrary to what it seemed before: his friends, his relations, those whom he loved, everything; wealth, position, all the things he has pursued, all change their appearance and sometimes seem to become quite the opposite of what they seemed.

The one reaching the seventh stage displays the temperament of the mystic. People say the mystic is unpredictable, paradoxical, and unaccountable.

Therefore the one who has realized the inner life is a mystery to everyone; no one can fathom the depth of that person, except that he promises sincerity, he emits love, he commands trust, he spreads goodness, and gives an impression of God and the truth.[28]

A mystic may take one step outwardly, inwardly he has taken a thousand; he may be in one city, and may be working in another place at the same time. A mystic is a phenomenon in himself and a confusion to those around him. He himself cannot tell them what he is doing, nor will they understand the real secret of the mystic. For it is someone who is living the inner life, and at the same time covering that inner life by outer action; his word or movement is nothing but the cover of some inner action. Therefore those who understand the mystic never dispute with him. Very often people find that a mystic has a paradoxical temperament. He may suddenly think during the night, "I must go to the North," and in the morning he sets out on his journey; he does not know why, he does not know what he is to accomplish there, he only knows that he must go. By going there he finds something he has to do and sees that it was the hand of destiny pushing him towards the accomplishment of that purpose, which inspired him to go to the North. Or a mystic will tell a person to do or not to do a thing. If that person asks the reason he cannot tell him. His feeling comes by intuition, a knowledge which comes from the world unseen, and according to the knowledge he acts.[29]

The reason for his mystery is that the mystic does not see things from the limited vantage point of any particular person. For example, a person forms an opinion about another person, about a situation, judging a certain action to be good or bad, assessing a situation as a failure or a success, or attributing a certain happening to a cause as he sees it. On the other hand, the mystic sees another cause that escaped the person's perspicacity, or the cause behind the cause that the person was not able to detect, or the right where the other only saw the wrong, or the wrong of what the other only saw as the right, or the ultimate gain ensuing from what the other estimates as a loss, or the disadvantage of what the other assumes to be an advantage. He may unmask the unimportance of what some people attach so much importance to and may take a most serious view of what another considers unimportant. This is because he looks upon things in a more far-reaching perspective and peers behind the curtain, because he has given up his personal view.

The first sign one notices after the awakening of the soul is that one begins to see from two points of view. One begins to see the right of the wrong and the wrong of the right. One begins to see the good of the bad and the bad of the good. One begins to see that everything is reflected in its opposite. In this way one rises above intellectuality, which then begins to appear as a primitive or elementary knowledge. One sees the dark in the bright and the light in the dark, death in birth and birth in death. It is a kind of double view of things. And when one has reached this, then reason has made way for higher reasoning. No doubt one's language will become gibberish to others; people will not understand it. They will be confused by what one says. To some it will be too simple, to others too subtle; too simple for those who only hear words without meaning, and too subtle for those who strive to understand the meaning and do not reach it. The third aspect is that in failure one will not feel such disappointment, and in success not such a great joy. In adverse conditions one will not be so dejected, in favourable conditions not so conceited. And these continual changes we experience in this world, such as friends turning into enemies, love sometimes turning to hate, sense to senselessness; these little surprises we experience every day in this world.

Things which seem real to an average person are unreal in the eyes of the mystic; and the things that seem unreal in the eyes of the average person are real in the eyes of the mystic.[30]

Little things that people take to heart will seem to him of little importance; things that people become confused with will become clear to him; things that matter so much to everyone will not matter to him; many things that frighten and horrify people will not have the same effect upon him; disappointments and failures will not take away his hope and courage. His thought, speech and action, as his outlook becomes wide, so everything he says or does will be different. Every good and bad experience he accepts as a lesson, and he thinks that all of them lead him onward. If it is a bad experience it is also a lesson; if it is a good experience, so much the better; but they are all leading him towards the purpose of his life.[31]

It is a matter of encompassing the overall dimensions, and therefore the implications, of every problem, whereas most people tend to treat problems ad hoc, isolating each from its ramifications.

Yet one often sees that the mystic lives above the world, and many think that he is not conscious of the world. But they do not know that for the very reason that he lives above it, he is more conscious of it.

CHAPTER 8

I Am the Wine
of the Holy Sacrament

ECSTASY

I am the Wine of the Holy Sacrament; my very being is intoxication; those who drink of my cup and yet keep sober will certainly be illuminated; but those who do not assimilate it will be beside themselves and exposed to the ridicule of the world.—Gayan, 246

If he tries to obtain ecstasy through drugs or intoxicants, he only becomes a slave to them. If, failing these, he seeks to gain his desire through other vices, he will never find the contentment he seeks.

Come to the mystic, then, and sit with him when you are tired of all these other remedies that you have employed in vain; come and take a glass of wine with him. The mystic wine is the inner absorption, which removes all the worries and anxieties and troubles and cares of the physical and mental plane.

Thy music causeth my soul to dance; in the murmur of the wind I hear Thy flute; the waves of the sea keep the rhythm of my dancing steps. Through the whole of nature I hear Thy music played, my Beloved; my soul while dancing speaketh of its joy in song.—Gayan, 87–88

The time came when Murshid was able to pay his respects to the earthly shroud of his great predecessor, Khwaja Muin-ud-Din Chishti, who had founded the Sufi Order in India in the twelfth century. So great was his influence and ascendency over all the ancient Sufis that he was given the surname of the Sultan-i-Hind, the real emperor of India. "These parched frocks conceal the valiant arms of the emperors of emperors," says the Persian Sufi poet. At Khwaja Muin-ud-Din's tomb in Ajmer, Sufis from all parts of India, Pakistan, and even from Iran, Afghanistan, Turkestan, the Arab countries, and as far as China assemble annually to celebrate the anniversary of the passing of the saint. Apart from Muslims, one may find among the throngs of pilgrims, amounting sometimes to millions, Hindus, Buddhists, Jains, Sikhs, Zoroastrians, Jews, and Christians, and even free thinkers. This popular display, although chiefly Muslim, proceeds under the flag of tolerance, or better still, brotherhood. Surely this bears witness to the impulse communicated to the masses by the influence of Khwaja Muin-ud-Din Chishti. At night the Mausoleum, or *dargah* (which literally means the court of a spiritual king), is wrapt in a mysterious garb of silence and awe at the majesty of the presence of the Khwaja that has drawn emperors and beggars for unbroken centures; whereas on the hillside outside the town, near the lake, the dome-shaped cave of the Khwaja is a haven of peace where recitation of *suras* of *wazifa* (the names of God) creates harmonics that link up with the higher spheres.

As Murshid watched the pilgrims flock through the superb "gate of paradise," open only for annual celebrations, he was struck by the whole gamut of expressions, of atmospheres, of attitudes, of rhythms, of radiance, of these beings, all so different yet all moved by the same purpose of offering their reverence to one whom they hold as their ideal and whose good graces they beseech. He noticed how each reflected in his atmosphere the "presence" felt, according to his capacity of sensing it. Each seemed to see in the saint that which was predominantly beautiful in himself, thus enhancing the cherished feature of the saint which may have been dormant in himself. Some seemed to be completely oblivious of what was going on around them. Some ceased to emit any thought of their own, thus channeling the saint's thoughts, offering whatever material was in them as a means of substantiating these.

To appreciate the power that draws people from all walks of life to this sacred spot, one would have to live with the pilgrim this intense spiritual life (which our concern with material well-being has relegated to odd outposts like this one); one would have to grasp all that is being enacted behind the coarseness of the human throng whose sentiments appear sometimes to be so inconsistent with the outer demonstrations of devotion to the saint, whose sentimentality rebuffs those who love little or do not tolerate its exhibition in others; one would have to assess all that happens at soul level in the encounters of dervishes or initiates unknown to each other yet saluting one another with noble reverence, while no outward sign would seem to the layman to brand them with the trappings of spiritual dignity.

Here Murshid Inayat, designated by the founder of the Order to bring it to the West, knelt in sacred communion at the feet of his great predecessor before setting on his mission throughout the world. Could we ever fathom what took place at that moment? The thoughts and prayers of pilgrims draw the presence of the saint nigh; therefore, the mausoleum is called the dargah, the court of the king. There is a treasured tradition that any bona fide wish formulated here is granted, and there are many examples to this effect. If this can be the case for those who ask for themselves, imagine how bountiful could be the spiritual heritage conferred upon Murshid who asked nothing for himself but offered service in whichever way was asked of him.

Once more the call of solitude made itself felt in Hazrat Inayat's soul, and he made his way into the jungle, not knowing his destination. Presently he reached a cemetery, where dervishes wearing patched robes were sitting on green expanses of grass. Now came the Pir-O-Murshid, surrounded by mureeds who were chanting: "Be conscious of your every breath, and watch every step you take and thus experience solitude in the crowd." [1] The form of mutual greeting adopted in this circle was "Ishq Allah Ma'Abud L'illah" (God is love, God is the beloved), and this reminded Hazrat Inayat of the words of the Persian poet Hafiz: "Do not befool thyself by sleeves full of patches, for most powerful arms are hidden under them."[2] Hazrat Inayat was most intrigued to hear each dervish address the other "Oh king of kings," and mused over the dependence of worldly sovereigns upon their environment, while these enjoyed an invulnerable kingship—that of the soul. They sang Sufi songs on the words of Rumi, Jami, Hafiz, and Shems-i Trabriz.

Each one revealed a peculiar mood of ecstasy; some expressed it in a sigh, some in tears, some in dance, and some in the calm of meditation.[3]

Murshid was enthralled by the majestic demeanor of these dervishes met among the dusty tombs of their great predecessors, who treated each other with the respect due to a king, even with reverence, and spoke eloquently about just that insight and realization of the way things look behind the scene of the world, which he was now developing increasingly and was later to teach his pupils. As he was musing upon the extraordinary blissfulness of these dervishes, they began to sing and play their musical instruments. Murshid was spellbound by the feeling of ecstasy that emanated from them to the extent that he felt that even the trees and the whole environment were caught up in their rapture.

The heart is made alive by the Sufi who gives an outlet to his intense feelings in tears and sighs. By so doing the clouds of Jelal, the power which gathers with his psychic development, fall in tears as drops of rain; and the sky of his heart is clear, allowing the soul to shine. This condition is regarded by Sufis as the sacred ecstasy.[4]

After sundown, the massed pilgrims would gather to participate in *nafil*, a musical ceremony where qawwals, singers and musicians, would extemporize on the verses of cherished Sufi poets like Rumi, Hafiz, Attar of Ghalib, and sometimes even converse by quoting these, under the aegis of the spiritual deacons or pirs, ceremonially seated according to protocol under a dais. (The secular Maharajas were accorded pride of place on either side.) The psychological temperature would rise, particularly under the impact of the dervishes spread among the crowds, who would express their ecstasy in sighs and gesticulations of delight and reverence.

Ecstasy manifests in various aspects. Sometimes a Sufi may be in tears, sometimes he will sigh, sometimes it expresses itself in *rakhs*, motion. All this is regarded with respect and reverence by those present at the Suma assembly, as ecstasy is considered to be divine bliss. The sighing of the devotee clears a path for him into the world unseen, and his tears wash away the sins of ages. All revelation follows the ecstasy; all knowledge that a book can never contain, that a language can never express, nor a teacher teach, comes to him of itself.

Finally one, carried beyond himself, would start whirling. All present would then stand in a sign of respect for the miracle that swept this piece of flesh into what seemed like an accretion of dust caught in a cyclone by sheer wonderment. Presently he would regain personal consciousness and fall upon the carpet, an inert mass, until the pirs and murshids would restore him.

The Sufis in the East work for years together to tune themselves to the spheres where they wish to be, as the Yogis do. Therefore the beginning of music in India was at the time of Shiva, Lord of the Yogis. Since the time of Rumi, music has become a part of the devotions in the Mevlevi Order of the Sufis. The masses in general, owing to their narrow orthodox views, have cast out the Sufis, and opposed them for their freedom of thought; thus misinterpreting the Prophet's teaching, which prohibited the abuse of music, not music in the real sense of the word. For this reason a language of music was made by the Sufis, so that only the initiated could understand the meaning of the songs. Many in the East hear and enjoy these songs not understanding what they really mean.[5]

There is an inherent need in the human being for exaltation. Man cannot live by bread alone; he also needs wine.

As much as we need sensation in life to make our experience of life concrete, so much or even more do we need exaltation in order to live life fully.[6]

Every soul is born with the capacity by which it can draw all the spiritual bliss and ecstasy which is needed for its evolution.[7]

Ecstasy is the intoxicant that relieves humdrum existence of its tedium, transfigures the ego into its quintessence, pure spirit, and makes people stir and throb and dance into life, like Shiva dancing the cosmic dance of whirling planets after sitting immobile for aeons on the summit of Mount Kailas. It is pure nostalgia—man's aspiration to reach beyond himself, not only faced with the immensity of space, or the endlessness of time, or the infinity of numbers, or the limitlessness of possibilities, but the vastness of widening and unending dimensions of understanding and all-encompassing love. It is enhanced by surpassing oneself, continually beating one's own record, overstepping one's reach, being lacerated by life's tests, then reinstated, passing the portals of death, then being resurrected, touching upon the secret spring of existence, and merging the self in the Self.

There is a time in life when a passion is awakened in the soul which gives the soul a longing for the unattainable, and if the soul does not take that direction, then it certainly misses something in life for which it has an innate longing and in which lies its ultimate satisfaction.

Ecstasy is a communion with all beings made possible through the loss of the notion of the self, and is the most contagious addiction there is. Even the rocks and trees and birds join in the rapture of ecstasy at dusk and sunset, and when nature's heart is stirred by gigantic emotional storms and the ensuing peace.

Even birds have their moments of exaltation. At the setting or the rising of the sun, the breaking of dawn, in moonlight, come times when birds and animals feel exalted. There are moments when even rocks become exalted and trees fall into ecstasy. There are times when even the trees are in a complete state of ecstasy. Those who live naturally, who open the doors of their heart, whose soul is in contact with nature, find nature singing, dancing, communicating. It is not only a legend, a story of the past, that saints used to speak with the trees. It is an actual fact and is the same today as in the past.[8]

There are traumatic events or sudden flashes of realization which, by their violence or the extent of their reach, overwhelm a being into an emotion too intense to be considered as joy or suffering; in fact it lies beyond the limits of both, and may well cumulate extremes of jubilation and despair in one undefinable emotion. Suddenly everything seems ignited, whereas previously it seemed bleak; the scene assumes a new brightness, the events a new vivacity, the people a new intelligence, like live effigies lit up by the wand of an uncanny fairy Godmother. Everything makes supreme sense, whereas before one was in a continual quandary, and one merges into the overall Self in a world of wonder and delight and meaningfulness. What does it take to initiate this magic spell? The more fortuitous, the greater the psychological impact it will have as it hits one unaware and off-guard, although admittedly one may seek to surround oneself with favorable circumstances conducive to making one high.

For an incurable romantic, a flaming sunrise where the sky is dappled with the most glorious array of resplendent hues, varying in exquisite patterns from bright red to dark blue, passing through mauve and orange and green into an ever changing kaleidoscopic latticework, will lead to ecstasy. The pure magnificence of it! When one suddenly discovers one's soul's identity with this incandescent effulgence, something of moment happens.

For a more serene experience, contrasting with the rush and tear of daily life, a crystalline spring of bubbling water, trickling among rocks, preferably studded with icicles on a moonlit night, is likely to induce a feeling of déjà vu (something that one seems to have seen before, that one recognizes), switching one's entire outlook into another dimension. For the valiant, the reckless, facing fear in a close encounter with death, as in rock climbing, deep-sea diving, hang-gliding, being caught in the high mountains in the middle of a furious lightning, or of course on the battlefield, may trigger the heart leap that makes for ecstasy. Another experience is scanning the sky and imagining oneself flying in outer space in the hope of landing on some distant star, extracting oneself from one's roots on planet Earth, and enjoying the vastness of sidereal space beyond the stratosphere.

There is a physical aspect of exaltation which comes as a reaction or result of having seen the immensity of space, having looked at the wide horizon, or having seen the clear sky, the moonlit night and nature at dawn. Looking at the rising sun, watching the setting sun, looking at the world from the top of a mountain, all these experiences, even such an experience as watching the little smiles of an innocent infant, these experiences lift one up and give one a feeling which one cannot call sensation. It is exaltation.[9]

For the one whose heart leaps at the enchantment of music, and who is possessed of the fine sense to appreciate its subtle cosmic language, a strain of sublime rhythmic notes will transport him into a state that defies words, speaking of horizons after horizons of pure emotion, whether through the sacred worshipfulness of plainsong, or the more lavish flourish of glorification of Monteverdi, or the sublime immaculacy of Allegri, or the angelic landscapes of Victoria, or the effervescent pure mastery of J.S. Bach, or Beethoven's heroism, or Mozart's elegance, or Brahms's glowing soulfulness, or Debussy's dream world; and the intangible horizons reached in Indian, Chinese, or Japanese music; or Persian or Arabic or Aztec music, and so on.

Penetrating in deep communion, with a feeling of solidarity, into the souls of those suffering, thereupon reflecting upon the significance of life and death, and strife and despair, then giving counsel, will give one a yet more soulful euphoria. But rescuing a victim of a fire, or drowning, or accident; or wresting the hands of two men fighting; or preventing a murder or suicide; all act upon the soul of the rescuer with still more force.

The beautiful gesture of forgiving a person who has done one a serious wrong, or being the recipient of such a gesture, or welcoming a rival, or overcoming jealousy, will make one feel like walking on air.

When we have asked forgiveness, and humbled ourselves before someone towards whom we were inconsiderate, we have humbled our pride then. Or when we felt a deep gratitude to someone who had done something for us; when we have felt love, sympathy, devotion which seems endless and which seems so great that our heart cannot accommodate it; when we have felt so much pity for someone that we have forgotten ourselves; when we have found a profound happiness in rendering a humble service to someone in need; when we have said a prayer which has come from the bottom of our heart; when we have realized our own limitation and smallness in comparison with the greatness of God; all these experiences lift man up.[10]

Of course, being deeply, madly in love is an enchantment that will leave an indelible impression; all life smiles around one, while one incurs an agony of fear of losing this treasure by inadequacy or clumsiness. The loss of the self in the merging in the loved one precipitates ecstasy.

The power of love accomplishes all things in life as does the power of dynamite that conquers the world. But when dynamite explodes it sets everything on fire, and so it is with love: everything goes amiss in the life of the lover. That is the mystery that accounts for all the pain and misery in the life of the lover. Still, the lover is the gainer in both cases. If he has mastered the situation he is a master; if he has lost everything he is a saint.[11]

Of course ecstasy flourishes in the love for all beings.

Ecstasy is a feeling that only comes when the heart is tuned to that pitch of love, which makes it melted, which makes it tender, which gives one gentleness, which makes one humble.

The trauma of losing all one's possessions, or incurring a fateful defeat when all breaks down around one, unleashes the discharge of a devastating energy that can be exploited positively by switching its momentum in the opposite direction: experiencing freedom from all that was weighing one down.

Suddenly grasping something pertinent that one had just not perceived before, as in children's puzzles where one exclaims "Eureka!" like Archimedes, particularly if it affects one personally and intensely, releases pent-up forces of joy. These reach a still higher degree of intensity when one finds oneself zeroing in on the reason behind the reason, and the reason behind that. There is high ecstasy in the consternation of the mind (the mind is blown, they say); it is something like breaking the sound barrier, the frontiers of the mind are burst at the seams.

Murshid points to yet a further dimension of ecstasy.

The third aspect of exaltation comes by touching the reason of reasons and by realizing the essence of wisdom; by feeling the depth, the profound depth of one's heart, by widening one's outlook on life; by broadening one's conception, by deepening one's sympathies and by soaring upward to those spheres where spiritual exaltation manifests.[12]

This dimension of understanding sets the soul rocketing into far reaches of meaningfulness. One has the impression of peering behind the curtain of the scene of life where most everybody is befooled and befuddled. Freedom from precarious mental constructions of banal understanding is such ecstasy!

The poet when he is developed reads the mind of the universe, although it very often happens that the poet himself does not know the real meaning of what he has said. Very often one finds that a poet has said something, and after many years there comes a moment when he realizes the true meaning of what he said. And this shows that behind all these different activities the divine Spirit is hidden, and the divine Spirit often manifests through an individual without his realizing that it is divine.[13]

Murshid guides one into a still subtler source of ecstasy; it consists in touching upon the force that sets the universe into motion. When one realizes that one partakes of this force, incorporates this force, delegates this force, that one is the very expression of this force, one comes upon the very foundation of one's being: the will behind one's will. This is the ecstasy of the dervish: to feel the power of God operating in one's very flesh!

Sticking to truthfulness, or adhering to one's principle, against withering odds stirs the soul into a paroxysm of ecstasy, as has been experienced by the really great.

By following a certain principle in life one gains a power which comes as an intoxication, but when one breaks that principle one feels the want of that intoxication, which is power.

Maybe the most stirring encounter with ecstasy is the feeling of the limitation in which one functions on the earth plane—no doubt carried to its most exasperating incongruity in the case of a person held prisoner as a martyr for having fought for justice, righteousness, and human freedom. Of course, the forces of cosmic karma released on the planet could not have failed to mark Christ as the scapegoat or sacrificial lamb for this experience: being delivered bodily in the hands of the Roman soldiers, yet sovereign; hands and feet nailed, the body lacerated, but the soul is jubilant. The Master often refers to his experience of the divine perfection operating in him, while being battered and constrained and foiled by having to function within the straight-jacket of limitation.

The supreme exaltation is hinted at in the Bible: "Be ye perfect, even as your Father in heaven is perfect." [14]

Numberless are the martyrs who have been thwarted and buffeted by human bigotry. To some degree all human beings experience this incompatibility between what could be and can be, or how things could be if circumstances would be what they should be! The reason for this is that, owing to the obstruction on the earth plane frustrating fulfillment of the ideal, one is obliged to seek its attainment at the soul level.

It is as though it is not intended that things should happen ideally on the earth plane; what is programed is that beings should attain higher realization themselves, because this attainment can never be taken away. In so doing, one touches upon the reality that really counts, beyond the peripheral projection of that reality on the earth plane, which we generally take to be reality.

There is a stage at which, by touching a particular phase of existence, one feels raised above the limitations of life, and given that power and peace and freedom, that light and life, which belong to the source of all beings. In other words, in that moment of supreme exaltation one is not only united with the source of all beings, but dissolved in it; for the source is one's self.

Not only souls resurrect, but even happenings, abortive on earth, triumph in heaven. For example, the crucifixion of Christ on earth, which seemed like a disaster when everyone abandoned him, was cosmically a coronation in heaven, and later turned out to be a victory on earth.

Of course, the ultimate ecstasy which is the magic behind all forms of ecstasy is the transformation—one should say the transfiguration—of the sense of reality. It is our banal sense of reality that is our prison, a mind-bind to which we have become so accustomed that we can't believe things could look different viewed from a different vantage point. Do we realize how we restrict ourselves by assuming that we are what we think we are, or that things are the way they look?

If we now review the few cases conducive to ecstasy that we have scanned, it is clear that the trauma of the experience, hitting one unwittingly, throws the sense of the ego off balance to the point that it is eclipsed, or at least partly eclipsed. Yes, ecstasy arises out of the annihilation of the sense of "me," and gaining a more universal identity; ecstasy is being shattered and overwhelmed by something so much greater than oneself that one cannot cling to one's identity any longer.

In selflessness lies a deep ecstasy.

There is a curious relish in being annihilated; it is being really emancipated from the tyranny of the ego that weighs upon one very heavily.

There are many ideas which intoxicate man; many feelings act upon the soul as wine, but there is no stronger wine than selflessness.[15]

In the encounter with splendor, or vastness, or death, or the void, or suffering, the ego is shattered.

One can provoke the spell of ecstasy by switching on a certain built-in mechanism; yes, one can be high without drugs. It is a matter of shifting the focus of one's vantage point by a certain increment, and letting go of oneself and of one's relationship with the environment. A sudden "swish" is sensed by the body, which feels as though the whole network of cells were being pulverized and scattered by a sharp electric shock. Of a sudden, the whole physical scenery is thrown off focus, appearing as a dream world from which one has emerged into a strange wakefulness; and time seems to linger, the past seems to be living on, even way back into childhood, and one is not confined by the environmental space.

How does this compare with the use of a drug? The foreign agent forcibly releases a perspective upon reality that is ordinarily eclipsed by the physical vantage point, and lies latent in the unconscious, but which is so much out of step with the usual appearance of things that the experimenter is rarely able to relate it to physical reality and runs the risk of being maladjusted, for having seen what nature spared him from seeing until he became strong enough to integrate it into a multidimensional picture. Should a person be able to do this, as through meditation, the experience comes of itself. This is awakening, and ecstasy is the emotion thereby experienced. If one knew how much damage is done to the brain by a single hallucinogenic trip, let alone the hard drugs, one would think better about jeopardizing that most wonderful organ with which one is graced at birth, together with its astral and other counterparts. One would hesitate to overload one's consciousness while being deprived of the ability to protect it.

Everything intoxicating deadens the nerves, more or less, and the centers which are the factors for spiritual realization become dead. The centers which show sensitiveness during the time of intoxication, after its influence become weary and lifeless. Fakirs and dervishes who take intoxicants in order to excite the centers become dependent for their spiritual progress on a material substance; in the end they find their seeming advancement a set-back.

The word *maya*, coined by the Hindus, refers to this feeling of unreality in respect to the physical fabric of the world experienced when one is awakened. Philosophical speculations about the nature of physical reality are as illusory as our notion of reality, and will deter from the experience of ecstasy. No sooner does one contrive, when in meditation, to stare physical reality in the face than one's focus shifts right back to the usual and one loses one's perspective; this is why Lot's wife was told not to look back.

Murshid used to provoke ecstasy just by his presence. One was exalted under the impact of a consciousness seeping deep down into one's being from lofty spheres—a consciousness old as the universe that knew all things from inside and made us see all things from the pitch of the soul.

Murshid often recounts the story of the Hyderabad dervish who kept laughing his head off at all he saw as he walked down the streets in a state of mystical inebriation. When one is sensitive to the suffering that people undergo, this would seem unkind, unless indeed he were concealing his tears and only showing his mirth. "Laugh, and the world laughs with you; cry and you cry alone," is a Chinese proverb.

Once I saw a Madhzub, a man who pretends to be insane, who though living in the world does not wish to be of the world, standing in the street of a large city, laughing. I stood there, feeling curious to know what made him laugh at that moment. And I understood that it was the sight of so many drunken men, each one having had his particular wine.

It is most amusing when we look at it in this way. There is no one single being on earth who does not drink wine; only, the wine of one is different from the wine of the other. A man does not only drink during the day but the whole night long, and he awakens in the morning intoxicated by whatever wine he has been drinking.[16]

What was it that amused the dervish so? Imagine that you awake, and you are surrounded by people dream-walking, and taking the effigies of their dreams for real; for example, fighting against the dragon that isn't there, or taking a rogue as their savior, or scrambling for sham values. The king thinks he is a king because he sits upon a throne; that young man thinks he is poor, ignorant of the fact that his father has put a fortune in his bank; this man thinks he loves an ideal woman, only to find that it was a hoax; that little girl is distraught because her dolls were broken, or that woman, because her jewels were stolen.

A man's environment and condition in life create for him an illusion and an intoxication, so that he no longer sees the condition of the people around him, the people of the city or country in which he lives.[17]

If a man can observe his actions in everyday life, and if he has an awakened sense of justice and understanding, he will often find himself doing something which he had not intended to do, or saying something that he did not wish to say, or behaving in such a way that he asks himself "Why was I such a fool!" Sometimes he allows himself to love someone, to admire someone; it may go on for days, for weeks, for months, even years, although years may be very long; and then perhaps he feels that he was wrong, or something more attractive comes along.[18]

One goes from one intoxication to another, as one progresses. What are these?

There is the intoxication of childhood. Imagine what attention, what service, what care the child demands at that time when it still does not know who takes the trouble or who takes care of it! It plays with its toys, it plays with its playmates, it knows not what is awaiting it in the future. What it wants, what it plays with, is what is immediately around it; it does not see further. Nobody in his childhood has ever known the value of his mother or his father or of those who care for him, until he reaches that stage when he begins to see for himself. And when we observe the condition of youth, that again is another intoxication, it is the time of blossoming, of the fullness of energy. The soul in that springtime never thinks that it can be anything else; the soul never thinks that this is a passing stage. The soul at that time is full of intoxication; it knows nothing apart from itself. How many errors a youth commits, how many faults he has, how many thoughtless, inconsiderate things he does of which he afterwards repents but about which he never thinks at the time! It is not the fault of the soul, it is the intoxication of that time of life. The person who is intoxicated is not responsible for what he does; neither is the child to be blamed for not being responsible or appreciative enough, nor the youth for being blind in his energy; it is natural.

The intoxication remains as a person goes on in life; there is only a change of wine. The wine of childhood is different from the wine of youth, and when the wine of youth is finished some other wine is taken. Then, according to what walk of life a man follows, he drinks that wine which absorbs his life, either collecting wealth or acquiring power or seeking a position; all these are wines which intoxicate man. And if one goes even further in life, intoxication still pursues one. It may be one is interested in music or fond of poetry, or one may love art or delight in learning: it is all intoxication. If all these different occupations and interests are like different wines, what is there then in the world that can be called a state of soberness? It is wine indeed from beginning to end. Even those who are good and advanced, spiritual and moral, they also have a certain wine. One has to take wine all the way; but there are different wines. A highly advanced artist, a great poet, an inspired musician will admit that there are moments of intoxication which come to him through his art as a joy, as an upliftment, and it makes him exalted; it is as if he were not living in this world.[19]

This is, however, not the only intoxication. A man's absorption in the affairs of his life also keeps him intoxicated; and besides the intoxication of his work and affairs in which his mind is absorbed, there is a third intoxication, and that is the attachment that a man has to himself, the sympathy he has with himself. It is this intoxication which makes him selfish, greedy, and very often unjust towards his fellow-men. The effect of this intoxication is that a man is continually feeling, thinking, and acting with the idea in mind of what would be to his interest, what could bring him an advantage; and in this idea his whole life and all his time become fully involved. It is this intoxication that makes him say, "This one is my friend and that one is my enemy, this one is my well-wisher, but that one is against me"; and it is this intoxication that builds the ego, the false ego of man.[20]

In fact, if one could see keenly, one would realize that everyone is infatuated by a certain whim. There is the football fan, the bridge fan, the stamp collector, the butterfly collector, the collector of antiques and even museum pieces, the man who is sold on hunting, or the family man or the music fan, the meditation fan, the sanctimonious and pious, or the man thirsting for wealth or success, or prestige or adulation. We develop attachments to certain addictive emotions: There is the angry type, or the demure type, or the affectionate type, or the dashing type.

Perusing Persian poetry, one often comes across references to intoxication, wine, or being drunk. This is the Sufis' way of expressing their divine ecstasy in love with the Divine Beloved.

This concept of drinking is used in various connections and conveys many different meanings. In the first place, imagine that there is a magic tavern where there are many different kinds of wine. Each wine has a different effect upon the person who drinks it. One drinks a wine which makes him light-hearted, frivolous, humorous; another drinks a wine which makes him sympathetic, kind, tender, gentle. Someone else drinks and finds his way into the ditch. One becomes angry after drinking while another becomes passionate. One drinks and is drowned into despair. Another drinks and begins to feel loving and affectionate; yet another drinks a wine that makes him discouraged with everything. In point of fact we live in that very tavern and we see it every day; only, we do not take proper notice of it.[21]

The higher intoxication cannot be compared with the lower intoxication of this world, but it is still intoxication. What is joy? What is fear? What is anger? What is passion? What is the feeling of attachment, and what is the feeling of detachment? All these have the effect of wine, all produce intoxication.

Understanding this mystery, the Sufis have founded their culture upon the principle of intoxication. They call this intoxication Hál, and Hál means literally condition or state. There is a saying of the Sufis, "Man speaks and acts according to his condition." One cannot speak or act differently from the wine one has drunk. With the one who has drunk the wine of anger, whatever he says or does is irritating; with the one who has drunk the wine of detachment, in his thought, speech and action you will find nothing but detachment; with the one who drinks the wine of attachment, you will find in his presence that all are drawn to him and that he is drawn to all. Everything a person does and says is according to the wine that he has taken. That is why the Sufi says, "Heaven and hell are in the hand of man, if only he knew their mystery." To a Sufi the world is like a wine-cellar, a store in which all kinds of wine are collected. He has only to choose what wine he will have and what wine will bring him the delight which is the longing of his soul.[22]

The Sufis recognize grades of wine; there is all the difference between the *vin ordinaire* and the Chateauneuf du Pape or Champagne. Each person will choose the wine corresponding to his degree of evolution. That is "where he is at," as the saying goes.

Hafiz pictures the whole world as a wine-press, and every person takes that wine which is in accord with his own evolution. The wine of one is not the wine of another. He wishes to express the idea that every person, whether evolved or ignorant, whether honest or dishonest, whether he realizes it or not, whether he has a great belief or no belief at all, is in every case taking a certain wine. It is the type of intoxication produced by that particular wine which is his individuality, and when a person changes, he does so by drinking another wine. Every different kind of wine changes the outlook on life, and every change in life is like taking a different wine.[23]

The Sufi teaches the divine art of alchemy. The secret of this teaching is to wean the pupil from the more vulgar kind of ecstasy into the more sublime.

They discovered the alchemy, the chemical process, by which to change the wine that a person drinks, and give another wine to see how this works. The work of the Sufi teacher with his pupil is of that kind. He first finds out which blend of wine his mureed drinks, and then he finds out which blend he must have.[24]

Undoubtedly, the experience that presses ecstasy to its supreme apotheosis is the discovery of the presence of God as the one whom one has always loved, inside, outside, everywhere, no particular where, just ever present. Flouting the constraints of people wallowing in their sense of self-importance or priding themselves on conforming to the consensus of propriety, the dervish invites one to join him in his special kind of libation, and does not have any qualms about giving vent to cosmic ecstasy, leading one into the whirling dance.

There is a verse of Abdul Qadir Jilani of Baghdad, "I am the bird of the spiritual spheres dwelling at present in earthly spheres, but my food is the knowledge of God and my drink is His beauty in manifestation."

Having joy in your nature and disposition, you bring it to everybody you meet. Well, that is the state of the dervish. He says to himself, "If I may not dance, what shall I do?" Possessing the joy of the presence of his Beloved, he feels the sublimity of nature; he is conscious of all the motion going on throughout nature. It intoxicates him like wine.[25]

There is a wine which the mystic drinks, and that wine is ecstasy. A wine so powerful that the presence of the mystic becomes as wine for everyone who comes in to his presence. This wine is the wine of the real sacrament, whose symbol is found in the church. What is it, where does it come from, what is it made of? It may be called a power, life, a strength which comes through the mysic, through the spheres which every man is attached to. By his attachment to these spheres the mystic drinks the wine which is the sustenance of the human soul, and that wine is ecstacy, the mystic's intoxication.[26]

Wine is anathema among Muslims, and of course it is the divine intoxication that is meant by the Sufi metaphor; but its very use is a way of scorning the veneer of righteousness of the sanctimonious because ecstasy is always a shock to the complacency of the ego. The dance which offends those who are "uptight" evidences a freedom from the fossilization that sets in when people have become entrenched in their ways and beliefs.

As Hafiz says, "If those pious ones of long robes listen to my verse, my songs, they will immediately begin to get up and dance." And then he says at the end of the poem, "Forgive me, O pious ones, for I am drunk just now."[27]

The spontaneous expression of emotion in motion gives vent to the nostalgia of reaching toward one's spiritual calling. It is always leaving the place where you are to go to the place you want to be, as on a pilgrimage. But as the gravity pull of one's ego counterweighs one's nostalgia, a point of balance between the centripetal and centrifugal forces is reached, but the energy offsetting that inertia propels it into a whirl.

We see in the life of an infant that there comes a moment when it smiles to itself and moves its little feet and legs as if dancing, bringing delight to the one who looks on and creating life in the atmosphere. What is it that suddenly springs into being in the heart of the infant, ignorant of the pains and pleasures of life, that gives expression to its eyes, that inspires its movements and voice? In ancient times people said, "This is the spirit coming"; they thought it was an angel or fairy speaking to the child. But in reality it is the soul which at that moment rises in ecstasy, making all things dance. There are many delightful experiences in life, but joy is something greater and deeper than delight; it springs from the innermost being, and there can be no better description of the spring of joy than the dance of the soul.

To nearly all animals there come moments when the blessing of heaven descends upon them, and they respond by dancing.[28]

In all other living beings, the soul is lying asleep, but when once the soul has awakened, called by beauty, it leaps up dancing, and its every movement makes a picture whether in writing, poetry, music or whatever it may be. A dancing soul will always express the most subtle and intricate harmonies in the realm of music or poetry.[29]

Your mind, body, and whole being go through a certain rhythm, called *Sabtal* in Sufi terms. This is a rhythm whereby your mind, body and soul come to feel an exaltation, an inclination towards higher things. It is just like the rising of a wave. A heart frozen through cold, through selfishness, has become liquid through some emotion, affection, love, or distress, sorrow, or despair. It becomes like an ocean when the waves form. The waves make a rhythm, a rhythm which soothes the mind, and which gives you joy and peace and a feeling of being inclined towards a higher truth.

Obviously, this is exactly what happens to the planets. When man gives expression to the cosmic harmony felt in his being, he integrates himself into cosmic gravitation. The physical movement implements the dance of the soul when stirred by the intoxication of ecstasy.

If Shiva sits immobile on Mount Kailas, his *chakras* (spiritual centers) rotate; if he projects the dance of the soul into space, the body whirls. As Buddha says, "There is a place you cannot reach by going anywhere." Truly enough, the dance of the dervish can be extended to the dimensions of understanding instead of space. It means abandoning the point of view in which one has settled, to reach into further horizons of understanding. Once more, one is impeded by gravity, caused by the limitation of one's mind; consequently, one strikes a point of continual circumvolution. The mind spins between its own bigotry and its intuition of the immensity of transcendental knowledge; one is impelled ever further by one's nostalgia for understanding. Indeed, one sinks in a kind of death every time that one tries to interpret the vastness of realization within the framework of one's limitation, and one rises in a kind of survival by unlearning all one took for real, following conventional opinion.

The dervish dance may equally be experienced in the choreography of love; it means leaving oneself behind in one's nostalgia for the divine Beloved. One is suspended between one's desire to merge into the One, and one's desperate clinging to one's personal identity. By some transcendental planning, even those who really wish to fuse in the totality of Being must maintain the vortex of their egos, albeit transfigured, as instruments in which the totality might be exemplified. However, as the pendulum oscillates between divine consciousness and personal consciousness, there may be a supreme moment of absorption in God consciousness.

If anyone has claimed divinity, it is only after having drunk that wine of divine life which intoxicated him, and in his ecstasy the secret came out as it comes out of a drunken man, who if he had been sober would never have let it escape.

Facing such exaltation one may seek sobriety. What is sobriety?

There are moments when there are no feelings, and these moments are the most exalting.

The whole of life is interesting because it is all intoxicating; but what is really desired by the soul is one thing only, and that is a glimpse of soberness. What is this glimpse of soberness and how does one experience this glimpse of soberness which is the continual longing of the soul? One experiences it by means of meditation, by means of concentration.[30]

The awakened person seems to be asleep to the sleeping one, and so the one who has become sober also appears to be drunk; for the condition of life is such that no one appears to be sober. It is this soberness which is called Nirvana *by* Buddhists *and* Mukti *by* Hindus. *But if I were asked if it is then desirable for us to be sober, my reply would be, no. What is desirable for us is to know what soberness is, and after knowing what soberness is, then to take any wine we may choose.*

When euphoric ecstasy is overcome, one experiences beatitude, and even beyond: serenity. This is often found among those who have fulfilled all they had to accomplish but are alienated from life. One can be sober in relation to the intoxication of the generality, and thereby be uplifted into a peaceful aloneness. Yet the temptation of complacency can make the peaceful one very smug, unless he can enjoy everybody's drunkenness while taking in the quintessence in a sublimated state.

What were the mysterious utterances that Murshid overheard the dervishes exchange that day during their mystic encounter? Most such locutions are kept confidential because average people would not understand them. But they make a higher sense to those who are capable of grasping a further dimension of thinking.

When the spirit rises above flesh like the sun above the horizon, and the soul is moved to ecstasy, that ecstasy becomes the very substance of life. It becomes the yeast in the bread, it's wine, the wine of the holy sacrament. It's the poison of Shiva, it's the divine ambrosia, and all are carried by divine emotion into the vision of God. When a glimpse of that emotion is experienced on earth, it is like a drop of the nectar of the Kumba that falls in the Ganges, and people scramble to have an infinitely small drop of that essence of life. The dance of the soul expresses freedom, freedom from all the stale fossilized forms which are the tombs of God in the ego of men. It's the freedom to move out in space, out of matter, into infinite dimensions, vastness of the spirit. The most wonderful dance is the dance of the one who is apparently still and around whom the whole world dances. Because the dance is the sparkling of his spirit and he dances in every being, yet he seems to remain motionless, unmoved by his emotions. The dance of the soul streams out of the silent life, and becomes heavier as one goes down the planes, and there are planes where it is simply the flicker of enlightenment of the soul in the fireworks of joy. Dance your sorrows away, dance yourself away. Dance your body to the floor, dance your soul to the sky, dance your thoughts into a whirlwind, dance your emotions into a spiral, dance your soul into the spirit. And then realize the scintillating footsteps are lost in the vastness of space and whisper drops to the depths of the ocean to form pearls. And the sun of the planetary system is paled by the light of the crown of God. Yes, the dance of the soul is the scintillation. Oh ye of little faith, how I wish you could see. Each one is separated from the Beloved by the strength of his ego, and each is united to the Beloved by the strength of his love. Am I here? Am I there? Why do you think I am anywhere? The dance takes you from where you were to nowhere, and from that you were into nobody. And if you think you know me, you may have a surprise: I may appear to you as yourself until you are so confused that you do not know anymore who yourself is. God is all in one and One in all. And One in each, and each in each other; unity in multiplicity and multiplicity in unity; and all may be found in each, and each in all; and the One may become that all and the all return to the One. There is no understanding without faith, and there is no faith without understanding. I rejoice in your joy when it leads to a great ovation in the cosmos, and I suffer in your suffering, when it alienates you from contact with God.

The secret of the dance is that one never remains where one is, although one remains equally distant from the goal and the abyss outside. The centrifugal power holds one back from union, because the centripetal power, the longing, spells annihilation by merging in the Loved One.

If you have overcome the self, each soul you will greet will recognize in you the divine Beloved, and if for one moment you presume that they love you for yourself, you will be plunged into a death of oblivion in the ocean of the self. This is death, where the divine impulse becomes stale in the isolation of the ego. Where there is life, there is movement, away from where you are into something beyond. Come let me lead you into the cosmic dance and leave your phantom behind. You can only survive by joining in the cosmic dance. Let my heart illuminate your heart. If you remember yourself, I shall scatter your body; if you indulge in self-satisfaction in your understanding, I shall wound your heart; and if you try to grasp reality with your mind, I shall make your mind run amok; if you are disloyal to your calling, I shall torment your soul. Beware to those who approach me, I give ecstasy, but I am terrifying to the faint-hearted. I can smite people in the face out of love, and beckon upon them to awaken. Shake yourselves. Look at them scratching each others' eyes out! Killing one another violently or in slow stages! O the tyranny of humans! If only they knew how they make us suffer. We laugh and we cry, and God is still dancing, His feet bleeding from the thorns, and his entrails scorched by the fire of hell.[31]

CHAPTER 9

The Call of the Dervish

AWAKENING

Befool not, O night, the morn will break; beware, O darkness, the sun will shine; be not vain, O mist, it will once more be clear; my sorrow, forget not, once more joy will arise.—Gayan, 257

Awake for the morning, in the bowl of night has flung the stone that sets the stars to flight. And lo, the hunter of the East has caught the sultan's turret in a noose of light.—Omar Kayyam, Rubaiyat

Every atom, every object, every condition and every living being has a time of awakening.—VIII, 318

The Message is the awakening of humanity to the divinity in man.

Among the dervishes, Murshid was himself becoming more and more of a dervish, and undergoing an even greater awakening than ever before, for the effect of contact with a dervish is traumatic awakening. This is precisely what, later, he did to his disciples, and his objective reached its culmination on a prophetic scale in the awakening of humanity to the divinity in man.

You have heard of the dervish. But have you heard his steps as he chases away the night of ignorance? A day or two ago he was unknown to you, except through cryptic references in books or travelers' tales of the haunts of this mysterious being. But somehow you have picked up his call from the ether. The very prospect of meeting one has led you to read about the Sufis, enquire about their whereabouts, and finally lured you on this wild goose chase when you might have spent a comfortable holiday on the Riviera. So here you go along the pilgrim trail that leads yearly thousands to that shrine, the dargah, of the great twelfth century saint, Khwaja Muin-ud-Din Chishti, at Ajmer in India. Yesterday the name was one among many on the map; today it has gained a sharp meaningfulness.

You brave the conditions, shocking, squalid, and miserable, calling upon whatever strength you can muster for the sake of experiencing things genuinely in their context, and you meekly let yourself be escorted by one of the *khadim* (guardians of the tomb) into some run-down lodgings, which would qualify as a slum in the West. Perhaps it helped to imagine it as the forsaken guest room of some ex–movie star's counterfeit castle. You remember having scrambled into your brand-new sleeping bag on the concrete floor, after having borrowed a rustic broom, hoping to escape the fleas and other crawling creatures of

God. You are dozing on one ear, knowing the value of vigilance in these outposts, when . . . there is a tap on the door, now it's a bang, in fact, a roar. Your startled shudder is no less dramatic than the threatening of the door on its hinges, but it is the desperate insistence in the call of the man at the door that sets your soul aquiver, the very urgency of his appeal. What amazes you most is the velvety quality of the voice that wells up from the depth of a sensitive soul, intonation on another plane. There seems to be refinement in his strength and mercy in his heroic willfulness. He had been singing the verses of Rumi, or Ghalib, or Amir Khusrau, or a verse from the Qur'an, "We shall lift the veil from thine eye and thy sight shall be clear." What you heard in the street was the serenade of the man of God to your balcony, and you had not taken heed! Your vigilance had been set for the thief in the night, not for the hunter of the East who beckons you to awaken you. You wonder, why should he bother to awaken me? I do not know him. In fact, I am afraid to open the door; his imperative presence strikes me with terror. How can he possibly know me? Why did he pick on this door rather than another? Or does he knock on every door?

Later, as the other members of the household wash the haze of slumber from their eyes and rise, you will ask that question over a cup of tea. Yes, is the answer, there is nothing that the dervish does not know. He knows how nostalgia lured you all this way, and he knows your complacency in burying your head under the covers instead of facing reality. He knows that if God knocked at the door you would be afraid of answering. He knows that you were turning round in your sleep, and it is his task to awaken you. The awakened one is entrusted with the task of awakening only those who are seeking after awakening.

In the East it is regarded as a sin to wake a sleeping person. Let him rest. He is comfortable. It is not time yet for him to wake up. So, if you went and woke him up you would make him unhappy and even resentful. Let him go on sleeping till the time comes when he will wake up naturally. A person is asleep when he says there is no such thing as telepathy, no such thing as heaven, no such thing as God, and so on. Let such a one be. He is not ready.

This is why Murshid, later in his life, reserved the higher teaching for more advanced initiates, lest others awaken too soon.

So mystics do not openly talk about mysticism, but keep their knowledge for the few that have woken up. And when a person wakes up, he will see for himself! (The sage or mystic only fulfills the purpose of taking his hand when this happens.) "It is now his time to wake—I must give him help." This is called "initiation" and from that time a person is ready to go into the mysteries of life.

The Message is a call to those whose hour has come to awake, and it is a lullaby to those who are still meant to sleep.[1]

If one sleeps, one is not aware of those awakening; but the one who is awake notices everywhere around him those who are awakening. This accounts for Murshid's vision, which he communicates to us:

Every atom, every object, every condition, and every living being has a time of awakening. Sometimes this is a gradual awakening and sometimes it is sudden. To some people it comes in a moment's time by some blow or disappointment, or because their heart has broken through something that happened suddenly. It may have appeared cruel, but at the same time the result was a sudden awakening, and this awakening brought a blessing beyond words. The outlook changed, the insight deepened; joy, quiet, indifference, and freedom were felt and compassion was showed in the attitude.[2]

Then there is a further awakening, a continuation of what I have called the awakening of the soul. And the sign of this awakening is that the awakened person throws light, the light of his soul, upon every creature and every object, and sees that object, person, or condition in this light. It is his own soul which becomes a torch in his hand; it is his own light that illuminates his path. It is just like directing a searchlight into dark corners which one could not see before, and the corners become clear and illuminated; it is like throwing light upon problems that one did not understand before, like seeing through people with x-rays when they were a riddle before.[3]

In fact, most sensitive people seek for that crystal-clear awareness and overall understanding of all things that the spiritual tradition calls awakening.

After the soul has been caught by the physical body there comes a time when the soul awakens. As long as it is asleep it is in a kind of dream in the physical body. That is the condition of the average man; a kind of dream. The mystic is the one who is awakened. The amusing thing is that the average man will call the mystic a dreamer, whereas in reality it is he himself who is dreaming!

If we could see things from a pinnacle beyond our human standpoint, we would realize that what we assume to be our understanding is the overall intelligence which, although ordinarily functioning within the limitations of those wonderful psycho-physiological instruments that are our mind-brain complexes, tends increasingly in the course of evolution to bypass this limitation and excels increasingly in the higher operations of understanding, intuition, and a sense of meaningfulness.

One may ask how one awakens to this inner life, what makes one awaken, and whether it is necessary for one to be awakened. The answer is that the whole of creation was made in order to awaken. But this awakening is chiefly of two kinds; one kind is called birth, the birth of the body when the soul awakens in a condition where it is limited, in the physical sphere, in the physical body, and so this man becomes captive; and there is another awakening, which is to awaken to reality, and that is called the birth of the soul. The one awakening is to the world of illusion. The other to the world of reality.[4]

When this happens, a person feels as though he is awakening beyond the scope of his usual understanding. The ordinary activities of people in everyday life circumscribe within the immediate environment (Murshid says the surface of life) any intelligence that may filter through the framework of the mind, for whatever is perceived is doctored by our human reason before it reaches our consciousness. As intelligence progresses, however, in the course of the evolution of the human species, it extends its scope beyond the limits of man-made logic, manifesting as intuition rather than reason. Therefore the master encourages one to grasp a cause behind the apparent cause.

If we can close ourselves to the outer world, we shall see the inner world. If we can close our outward senses, our mind will turn inward.

When the venture of our intuition has been confirmed, there can be no further doubt that it is a knowledge that was not based upon anything perceived by the senses or which one might have deduced from any sequence of rational inferences. It breaks through the mind even in defiance of the evidence of the senses or of reason; in fact, it is a sign of consciousness that has freed itself from the conditioning of the physical world and touched upon the deeper reality.

Why does the awakened one venture to awaken the one turning in his sleep? Because he remembers having taken things to be as they appeared and now he realizes that they are the crystallization of a reality which is not structured in three-dimensional forms. Similarly, a vibration projected on an oscillograph will appear as a visible form, or a chromosome will manifest as a form in the embryo. The physical scene exercises a gravity pull upon intelligence, coercing it into functioning through the instrumentality of the mind and brain circuits. Once one has seen through this, one begins to assess physical reality in its true perspective as the projection into form of something that is formless; one no longer assumes that it is reality. Once one sees one's own personality as a germ of one's real being, one cannot be deceived by appearance; one awakens as from a dream, and thus one is prone to help those who are beginning to realize that which one realizes oneself. Such is the state of that dervish who was trying to awaken you.

When the soul is awakened, it is as if that person were to wake up in the middle of the night among hundreds and thousands of people who were fast asleep. He is sitting or standing among them, he is looking at them, hearing about their sorrows and miseries and their conditions, hundreds of them moving about in their sleep, in their own dream, not awakened to his condition although he is near them. They may be friends or relations, acquaintances or enemies; whatever be their relationship, they know little about him as each one is absorbed in his own trouble. This awakened soul, standing among them all, will listen to everyone, will see everyone, will recognize all that they think and feel; but his language no one understands; his thoughts he cannot explain to anyone, his feelings he cannot expect anyone to feel. He feels lonely; but no doubt in this loneliness there is also the sense of perfection, for perfection is always lonely. Imagine living in a world where nobody speaks our language! Yet he can live in the world, for he knows its language.

What is the sign that one is ready to awaken from sleep? It is when a person begins to think:

All that I have learned and understood seems so unreal; there are some realities of which I am vaguely aware, and yet compared with them all I have studied and done seems to be of no account. As the dawn comes after the night of darkness, so he sees the light appearing; but he has not yet seen the sun; he is only beginning to awaken. And yet, for us limited beings to say that this world has no reality seems a blasphemy. It is all right for us to feel this, but it is not right to say it because, if you are to say it, you must prove it by your independence of this illusion. A claim that has not been yet put into practice is not a good claim. That is why a mystic will always refrain from saying such a thing as that all this is an illusion; but he tries to feel it more and more every day.[5]

No sooner has one ceased to think of oneself as one's personality than the consciousness of one's eternal being, of a greater scope and range, emerges beyond the limits of the personality consciousness. One feels as though one has awakened from the hoax not only of the physical scene but also of one's personal self. Of course, at some stage the consciousness of one's cosmic reality refuses to let itself be hampered by the consciousness of its instrument, the personality, and breaks through.

How can the Unlimited Being be limited, since all that seems limited is in its depth beyond all limitations?

Therefore, Buddhism defines awakening as the liberation from the self. One discovers oneself as the self of all beings and things. The dervish sees yourself as the self of that which he also is.

When someone has attained to God-consciousness, he experiences everything as the self of each being. If an elephant comes before him, he is the elephant. Whatever comes before him, he is. When the consciousness of the external self is gone, then whatever appears before him is his self.

Maybe that dervish knocking at your door took you to be himself and you did not recognize yourself in him because you have not yet awakened to the Self of selves.

All faces are His faces, and from all lips it is His word that comes.[6]

In your sleep you were guarding the door to your higher self, to which he was awakened. The best way of seeing an awakened soul is to wake up oneself. You were asleep, while he was wandering in the night awake. He was seeking to awaken you to his realization—the realization of the awakened one—that he is your real self, because he is awakened.

I know of a God-conscious soul who was once walking in the city of Baroda where the rule was that no one should go about after ten o'clock at night. And this sage was wandering about unconscious of time. A policeman asked, "Where are you going?" But he did not hear. Perhaps he was far away from the place where he was wandering. But when he heard the policeman say, "Are you a thief?" he smiled and said, "Yes." The policeman took him to the police station and made him sit there all night long. In the morning the officer came and asked "What is the report?" This policeman said, "I have caught one thief. I found him in the street." When the officer went and saw this man, he knew that he was a great soul and that people respected him very much. He asked his pardon. "But," he said, "when the policeman asked you that question, why did you say that you were a thief?" The answer was, "What am I not? I am everything."[7]

If you came all that way to see the dervish it was because, at least unconsciously, you were fascinated by the prospect of a traumatic encounter that could possibly precipitate awakening. Yet when the time came, you were afraid to open the door. Why? Because one feels safer, more secure, experiencing and enjoying the immediate environment on the miniaturized human scale and through the embrasure of the senses and the mind, than facing the breathtaking realness behind the surface that squelches one's sense of oneself. The experience of the average person is like projecting a three-dimensional reality on a two-dimensional screen, like reducing a live scene to a play of shadows, or freezing a symphony into stone.

The principle of the one who experiences the inner life, is to become all things to all men throughout his life.[8]

And if you go still further, then you can only realize that you are connected with all beings. That there is nothing and no one who is divided or separate from you, and that you are not only connected by chains with those you love, but with all those you have known and do not know—connected by a consciousness which binds you faster than any chains.[9]

When a person awakens to the spirit of unity and sees the oneness behind all things, his point of view becomes different, and his attitude changes thereby. He no longer says to his friend, "I love you because you are my friend." He says, "I love you because you are myself." He says, as a mystic would say, "Whether you have done wrong or whether I have done wrong does not matter. What matters is to right the wrong."

It is "just now" which gives us the feeling of reality, and it is that which we are experiencing which becomes real to us, whereas that which we are not experiencing, of which we are not conscious, does not exist for us at this moment. Thus everyone has his own life and his own world. His world is that of which he is conscious; and in this way everyone has his heaven and his hell made by himself. We live in the world to which we are awakened, and to the world to which we are not awakened we are asleep. We are asleep to that part of life which we do not know.[10]

One feels more secure in the confined space of the personal self. But there is an inveterate idealism struggling through the personality of many that cannot be satisfied by being fed on watered-down effigies of reality. They hasten to stand up and face the entire length and breadth of meaningfulness whatever the blow to their sense of security. This is where we enjoy discovering our familiarity with the stalwart dervish soul whom we met yet failed to invite in. It requires courage to venture beyond the trodden path into the unknown vastness of understanding, threatened by the awe of the dissolution of consciousness.

Thus among the seekers after truth, we find only one who is courageous enough to look at the immensity of truth. But there are many who take an interest in illusion, and they are inclined, out of curiosity, to look at mental illusions because they are different from the illusion of the physical life.

The mind is staggered by the discovery of the programing that controls the functioning of this enormous machine that is the universe, of which we can have only experienced a fraction. As soon as one ceases to take the end-product to be the ultimate reality, one awakens to the archetypes behind all creatures and the intention of the engineer behind all events. Rather, a deeper and wider consciousness that has been operating behind one's personal awareness emerges, affirming its wider and truer vision of the potentialities in creatures and the meaningfulness of events. The very magnitude of this vision works upon the personality right away. Therefore, as the adept advances, his being exercises a fascinating influence upon all beings. As he identifies with the Divine Being, upon whose presence he muses continually, he manifests the many-splendored attributes thus revealed to him in his personality, which becomes a source of exaltation for those who approach it.

Since the way of the Sufis tends toward awakening to the consciousness that God has of the universe rather than awakening from existence, as in the *Arupa Jnanas* of Buddhism, Sufis attach much importance to the personality of the accomplished being (that fruit of the tree of life, as Murshid calls the personality of man) as the manifestation of the divine perfection.

All were moved to become my friend, but none knew why.[11]

Such is the net or the feminine aspect of God, the magic charm of the God-conscious. It takes nothing less than this to harness people's energy in the service of a cause greater than their own vision allows them to grasp. It may be that it is nature's purpose in furnishing it. This is the charm that conjures so much delight, that Sufis and Kabalists refer to as "the curl of the Beloved." It is portrayed by murshids and khasidim, and it lured the gopis to rally around Krishna. One who exercises this divine charm exhibits the manner of God, called *Akhlak Allah* by the Sufis.

In Sufi terms the divine manner is called Akhlak-e Allah. Man thinks, speaks and acts according to the pitch to which his soul is tuned. The highest note he can be tuned to is the divine note, and once man has arrived at that pitch, he begins to express the manner of God in everything he does. And what is the manner of God? It is the kingly manner which is not known even to the kings, for only the King of heaven and of the earth knows it.[12]

It is the kingship of God which manifests in the blossoming of every soul. When a soul arrives at its full bloom, it begins to show the colour and spread the fragrance of the divine spirit of God.[13]

The person conscious of the divine perfection displays a greatness, a majesty, a sovereignty epitomized in the idyllic and utopian image of a king; that is to say, a king in the real sense of the word, as one appears sometimes in legend and children's fairy books. In fact, it dwells in the collective unconscious of humanity. And indeed, if you had opened the door to that dervish, whose voice sent a thrill through your soul, you would have confronted a being magnanimous and of human splendor such as one would hope to see among temporal rulers.

He is king just the same wherever he is. Neither money, a coat, nor life in the world can take away his kingship from him. If he chooses to live in solitude, it is his own affair. If he wishes to be in the crowd, he may just as well be there. Whether a person sits in a remote place in the forest or in a baker's shop, if he is thinking of a high ideal his surroundings cannot touch him; he does not see them. There is no aspect of life that can deprive a mystic of his mystical spirit.

If one identifies with one's individuality, one is confining one's personality and thereby hampering it from manifesting the latent richness within. Confidence in this innate bounty will open the possibility for these exquisite buds to bloom. This confidence is gained as soon as one realizes that one inherits not only from one's parents but from the whole universe. It is possible to identify the traces of a mighty inheritance beyond anything transmitted by the body.

That goal was the discovery of the traces of the King of kings within himself, a spark of that divine light which is the illumination of his own heart, a ray of that Sun which is the light of the whole universe.[14]

Mevlana Jelal-ud-Din Rumi, the great Persian Sufi poet, witnessed this phenomenon in the dervish Shems-i Tabriz as he approached him for the first time in Konia, transfigured by the awareness of the divine presence.

The God whom I have worshipped all this time appeared to me today in the form of man.

Awakening consists in grasping, not just with the mind but with the entire consciousness, a realization that had not dawned upon one before. Imagine the consciousness that a cell of your body may enjoy, being a fraction of your total body consciousness. Inasmuch as the cell is aware of itself as an entity, one may assume that it is conscious of the pressure and interference of the adjacent cells, but one may also assume that it has a vague awareness of the general condition of the body: tired, healthy, etc., and maybe the overall consciousness of the body seeps through to it. The global consciousness of the body includes an awareness of the cells neighboring the specific cell we have chosen, which this cell itself could not possibly possess. For example, the overall body consciousness could be aware of a growing inflammation before it has reached the precincts of the given cell, or the mind may know of a psychological condition long before it has affected the body. Thus the overall awareness of the total being underlying the fractional or focalized center knows the condition of the entire being because it *is* the consciousness of the total being. The same applies on a larger scale to the consciousness of the planet underlying individual creatures, and further, to universal consciousness. As the fractional center allows the knowledge of the larger center to seep through, so the individual awakens to the wider or more universal consciousness. Yet, conversely, by giving vent to the scope and action of universal consciousness, individual consciousness awakens universal consciousness. The master awakens the individual; the prophet awakens the soul of humanity.

One may ask how one awakens to this inner life, what makes one awaken, and whether it is necessary for one to be awakened. The answer is that the whole of creation was made in order to awaken.

Behind the awakenings of people who hoist themselves above their human condition, which we can witness, looms the very awakening that God experiences through the awakening of the individual cells, as it were, of his being. For surely that is what is happening behind what we think is happening to us in our limited thinking. Our awakening must affect his awakening, as the transformation of the cells of a body must affect the body; or rather, it is the other way round: The transformation of the cells in parts of the body are the symptoms of what is happening to the body as a whole. Murshid compares it with an intelligent being who is sleeping and awakens to discover the scope of his understanding, which extends to becoming aware of his own cells. Imagine that, having been absorbed in contemplating at an abstract level the principles governing your life, envisioned overall, your consciousness started to pay attention to the motions, the functions, the strivings, even the thinking of your cells. Reality is always more far-reaching and amazing than we could ever possibly fathom. Imagine (what is hardly possible to imagine) that, by paying attention to his cells, the Overall Being were to make them existent, passing them from latency to actuality, so that they gain a concreteness on the physical plane that they did not enjoy before. Now, as they awaken to his consciousness, his consciousness descends more deeply into their consciousness.

It would follow that the awakened person awakens to this infusion of the Divine Consciousness into the more primal forms of evolution, thus awakening them. Thus the awakened person is able to enter into the thinking and feeling of people and feel at one with them. Playing with the children of the world means thinking as that little child does and enjoying it. Then one becomes so much more conscious of the condition of God's lovely creatures, the animals, and the secret life of the plants, and the mysterious effervescence in the rocks, especially the crystals, to right down into the microscopic life of the atoms; and thence right back into the early descent of life, backward through the jinn and angelic planes, and even further back.

The journey towards the goal is passed by a mureed through the same planes and phases which he has crossed once before and which he has had hidden in his nature all the time. The process of evolution is not a straight way, it is more like a wheel which is ever turning. So the experience of the person who treads the spiritual path begins to show a downward tendency, and from that again upwards. For instance, in the spiritual path a person goes backwards, he experiences youth again, for spirituality gives health to the mind and to the body, it being the real life. He experiences vigor, strength, aspiration, enthusiasm, energy, and a living spirit that makes him feel youthful, whatever be his age. Then he becomes as a little child, eager to play, ready to laugh, happy among children; he shows in his personality childlike traits, especially that look one sees in children, where there is no worry, anxiety, or bitter feeling against anyone, where there is a desire to be friendly with all, where there is no pride or conceit, but readiness to associate with anybody, whatever be his class or caste, nation or race. So the spiritual person becomes like a child. The tendency to tears, the readiness for laughter, all these are found in the spiritual person. As the spiritual person goes further he shows in his nature infancy. This can be perceived in his innocence. His heart may be lighted with wisdom, yet he is innocent; he is easily deceived, even knowingly, besides being happy under all conditions, like an infant. As the infant has no regard for honour or for insult, neither has the spiritual person. When he arrives at this stage, he answers insult with a smile. Honours given to him are like honours given to a little baby, who does not know to whom they are offered. Only the person who has given the honours knows that they have been given to somebody. The spiritual one is not conscious of it, nor happy in it, nor proud of it. It is nothing to him. The one who has honoured him has honoured himself, since to the baby it is nothing if somebody should speak in favour of him or against him; the baby does not mind, he is ready to smile at both; so is the spiritual soul.

But as he grows he continues also to grow backwards. He now shows the signs of the animal kingdom: for instance, such a quality as that of the elephant, which, with all its strength and power of giant bulk, is ready to take the load put upon; the horse, which is ready to serve the rider; and the cow, which lives in the world harmoniously, comes home without being driven, gives milk which is the right of her calf.[15]

The characteristic of the deer, as described by the poets of India, is that when it is thirsty it runs about in the forests looking for water, and it is greatly delighted on hearing the sound of thunder and runs about with a desire to drink; but sometimes there is only thunder and no rain afterwards, or if it rains it is perhaps only a shower and not enough to drink, and the deer still remains thirsty. And so is the thirst of a fine soul in this world. The soul of the spiritually inclined man is constantly thirsty, looking for something, seeking for something; and when it thinks it has found it, the thing turns out to be different; and so life becomes a continual struggle and disappointment. And the result is that instead of taking interest in all things, a kind of indifference is produced; and yet in the real character of this soul there is no indifference, there is only love.[16]

When the Vairagi is still more developed in this feeling of Vairagya, then he becomes a lion. He is no more the serpent seeking solitude, although he loves it still; he is no more the deer running away from the crowd. He is the lion, who stands and faces all difficulties. No longer sensitive, but with all strength and power, with all balance, with patience, he endures, and with a brave spirit he stands in the crowd in the world. For what? To bear all things that come to him; to endure all the jarring influences that the world offers to a sensitive person; to look into the eyes of all, being brave in spirit and strengthened in truth and clear of conscience.

He then develops a bird-like nature and floats in the spheres of imagination, quite unconscious of the earth and its surroundings. He seeks the society of those of a like interest just as a bird would be with a bird, and makes his home on high, in the world of thought, just like the nest of a bird in the top of a tree. He advances still further and becomes as an insect, admiring the Immanence of God in nature and absorbing rapture from divine wisdom, just like a bee gathering honey from the flowers. And he like a moth concentrates on and hovers round the light until his self is sacrificed in the vision of his ideal. He in the end becomes like a germ, an object to be lying at the feet of the walker; anybody may walk upon him who may so choose. He cares for neither light nor knowledge for he has passed far beyond all that.

When he goes on further still there develops in him the quality of the vegetable kingdom, of the plants which bring forth fruit and flowers; patiently waiting for the rain from above; never asking any return from those who come to gather flowers and fruit, giving and never expecting a return, desiring only to bring forth beauty according to the capability which is hidden in them, and letting it be taken by the worthy or unworthy, whoever it be, without any expectation of appreciation or thanks.[17]

The one who can reach the branch of the tree can take the fruit. People throw stones at trees and cut them, but although no doubt this hurts the tree, the tree does not blame them. It has borne fruit and it is willing to give it to them; and this becomes the condition of the spiritual person: willing to serve all who need his service, bearing fruits and flowers which may nourish and release others.[18]

He adopts harmlessness, usefulness, and medicinal and healing properties, and self-sacrifice for the purpose of another, all such qualities of the vegetable. He shows in his personality the sweetness of the fruit, the perfume, the colour, and delicacy of a flower. And when the spiritual person advances still further he arrives at the stage of the mineral kingdom. He becomes as a rock; a rock for others to lean on, to depend upon; a rock that stands unmoved amidst the constantly moving waves of the sea of life; a rock to endure all things of this world whose influence has a jarring effect upon sensitive human beings; a rock of constancy in friendship, of steadfastness in love, of loyalty to every ideal for which he has taken his stand. One can depend upon him through life and death, here and hereafter. In this world where nothing is dependable, which is full of changes every moment, such a soul has arrived at the stage where he shows through all these changes that rock-like quality, proving thereby his advancement to the mineral kingdom.[19]

Then he acquires the quality of the rock when it has no effect upon him for what purpose he may be used, whether to crown a dome, or for the base of a building. Neither climate, nor day nor night can make any difference to him, neither sorrow nor joy can touch him, he becomes free from all affects.

There have been many kings and rich people in the history of the world, but they have never been so loved and honoured and held in so much esteem by human beings as the spiritual souls. Why is this? Because it is out of the rock that the idol of God is made; and when man has become a rock, then he is worshipped, then he becomes a living idol. And if one asks why man has to become a rock in order to be worshipped, the answer is because the rock is not conscious of itself; that is why. People prefer to worship a rock rather than a man, so when the spiritual soul has reached the stage of becoming a rock, no more conscious of his little self, unaware of his limitation, not concerned with anything, detached from all things and beings, then that soul is to be worshipped.[20]

As the spiritual soul proceeds further he begins to show the real traits of humanity, for here humanity really begins. One can see in such a soul the signs which are the pure characteristics of the human being, devoid of the animal traits. For instance, there is a tendency in him to appreciate every little good deed done by anyone, to admire good wherever he sees it in any person; a tendency to sympathize, whatever be the condition of the person, saint or sinner; a tendency to take interest in the affairs of his friends when called upon to do so; a tendency to sacrifice.[21]

When man advances in age he shows a return of the same qualities. First the jinn quality; when he has had all the experience of the world and has reached a certain age he becomes most keen to express all that is beautiful. At this age human beings become intelligent, they speak, they teach, they understand things which young people cannot understand; the jinn quality develops. And when he advances further in age, then the angelic quality develops, then innocence comes with its engaging smiles, then all malice and prejudice are gone and a quality of continually giving out begins to manifest.[22]

Then a mureed arrives to a condition where he sojourns in a star, planet, moon or sun, in other words he himself becomes a soul. His star-quality brightens him, his planet-quality produces within him a world of his own, his moon-quality becomes the receiver of all Divine Light and his sun-quality produces in his voice, word and glance the power of illumination.

Afterwards he acquires the all-pervading quality of sound, communication with all hearts and souls in the universe, with whom he would wish. He also becomes a spirit in all its aspects. Then a Sufi acquires the quality of consciousness, conscious and awakened in every phase of life until he acquires the quality of unconsciousness when he can become unaware of all signs of life.

Yes, one may distinguish several awakenings. First, awakening to the way things look behind the curtain, like looking into an artist's dressing room backstage. This is what is meant by *samadhi*, which might include the *Sabija* samadhis, which means viewing the divine perfection at the causal or archetypal level. Second, one might wake up to the consciousness of the totality of being in existence, which includes the awareness that the total being acquires through the eyes of all beings. Third, consciousness of the divine perfection working its way down into one's being and manifesting everywhere: consciousness awakened at its cosmic setting sees divine perfection where individuated consciousness fails to see it. Fourth, an awakening that can only take place gradually and could only be possibly perfected at the end of time, or at least of the present cycle of evolution: awaking to the consciousness that the total being acquires through the consciousness of awakened beings. Doubtless, these listings do not exhaust in any manner the dimensions of awakening (*bhojanga*, in Pali) which Buddha steers into states of further and further abstraction, and

Murshid weaves into states incorporating more and more concreteness.

This is what is happening in our time, at the advent of the new age, and this is new age consciousness: The convergence of the thinking and awareness of individuals, by calling upon the deeper strata of thinking and awareness, awakens humanity as a whole to its consciousness as a being. This is what Hazrat Pir-o-Murshid Inayat Khan calls "the awakening of the soul of humanity to the divinity of man."

Part II

THE CONGRUENCE
OF THE STRANDS
OF THE UNIVERSE

CHAPTER 10

Sleep in the Night of Time

DREAMS OR METAPHYSICS?

La Vida es sueno. *(Life is a dream.)—Calderon de la Barca*

God lost in manifestation is the state which we call awakening. Manifestation lost in God is realization. In my language I would call the former dream and the latter awakening.

O sleep, it is thou who makes the king unaware of his kingdom, and the suffering patient forget his illness, and prisoners are free when they are asleep.

Something occurred to Murshid that no doubt marks the apex of his mission in India, before setting off on his task; he experienced the state of samadhi, the far reach in meditation.

He used to rise to that state in an instant. No sooner did he begin his music, than he would rise above the spheres of the earth. It developed to such an extent, that not only he himself, but those sitting around him, would become spell-bound, and feel exalted, in which Inayat found the fulfillment of his having the talent of music. They did not know where they were, or what they were hearing, and could not realize to what sphere they were lifted from the earth. After finishing his music, Inayat was drowned in ecstasy and they all seemed as lost in a mist. As they opened their eyes, their attitude towards him changed, and he whom they had at first taken for a singer, then became a mystery.

He used to sit for hours at night meditating; and dawn saw him up again, musing in the higher sphere of consciousness. The physical world would fall out of focus like a dream of the past as he abandoned his body to the physical substance of which it was part, to the extent that he knew not where he could reach it, since he was voided of physical consciousness. At first, he seemed to be pure energy, a high-powered magnetic field, filling the room; then he realized he was a being of light, a flamboyant aura, burning by a bright flame and radiating thunderbolts. All thoughts connected with the personal self had disappeared so that he became aware that the nature of all being is cosmic, impersonal. It was like peering behind the veil of existence, and experiencing the reality behind the appearance of things in the sphere of causes, suspended motionless beyond the procession of becoming, so that existence in time and space seemed to have faded away as in a dream in the night of time. His consciousness seemed to be like a wave in the ocean of consciouness and there was no object of which consciousness could be aware since all was potentially present in this crystal-clear intelligence. Now he lost all sense of being an individual consciousness. Yes, this is God-realization. Having peered beyond the veil, one can never be the same again!

When we sit still, musing on our lives, cogitating upon the miracle of life on the planet, on the very fact of existence; when we look upon our consciousness as a mere flash in the thinking of mankind, indeed of the planet; if then in our meditation we grasp the continuity in change beyond our existence, or even beyond the history of the planet, or the solar system, or the galaxy, consciousness flowing through us into the unknown beyond the beyond and before the beginning, we may sense a stillness, a darkness, and touch upon the eve of existence, the potency of all forms, all activity, all thought, the latency of consciousness before its awakening.

Contemplatives testify to this state as in the *Asamprajnata samadhi* of Yoga; or the *Vimokka* of the Buddhists; or the state corresponding to the *En Sof* of Kabala; or Tawhid at the level of *'al 'ama*, the dark mist of unknowing, according to the Sufis; or the "Dark Cloud of Unknowing," as in the title of a beautiful medieval anonymous text.

Sleep, the unconscious condition, is the original state of life from which all has come. As the body sleeps and the mind sleeps, so the soul sleeps. This sleep of the soul is experienced only by mystics.

The ordinary person knows that after deep sleep he is calm, reposed, his feeling is better, his thoughts clearer. The condition of Hal, or Samadhi, the highest condition, is the same as that of deep sleep, the difference being only that it is experienced at will. The difference between the perfect person and the ordinary person is only this, that the perfect person experiences consciously what the imperfect person experiences unconsciously.

When the mind is dispersed, no impression will remain on the soul, nothing will retain it from merging into the whole consciousness.

This is the condition of nonexistence or beyond existence or, as Buddha called it, cessation of causality or determination.

What was Murshid experiencing as he sat for hours lost in samadhi?

When I open my eyes to the outer world I feel myself as a drop in the sea; but when I close my eyes and look within, I see the whole universe as a bubble raised in the ocean of my heart.[1]

Was he dwelling on the planes we have touched upon all the while? He never spoke about anything that he had not actually experienced or realized himself.

I do not give you my ideas; what I give you is my personal knowledge.[2]

We would have to peek into the states he describes by tuning in to our unconscious memories of our descent through the spheres.

The Sufis refer to seven steps in the descent (*tanazulat*, in Sufic terms), seven stages, or seven planes, or seven levels of consciousness, as in the Kabala. In our dreams we focus sometimes on one level, sometimes on another, while sometimes straddling several planes; this is also true of meditation, except that in meditation, one can steer oneself a little more deliberately or consciously; or, at least, one does not lose the Ariadnean thread of memory of the higher planes, as one does more readily in sleep.

Murshid had a vision of the progressive materialization of reality, one might say of the Only Being, out of the night of time, beyond existence, beyond the beyond, becoming gradually more concrete and tangible. Samadhi in its highest form (Asamprajnata, or Tawhid) reaches into strata beyond multiplicity, or beings, or attributes; in fact, beyond consciousness. Murshid describes it as the sleeping condition of the Only Being, whose body is the universe prior to the proliferation of existence, a condition which is still going on in the depth, while part of the Total Being is involved in activity—not really a part, but an aspect. Indeed, while the active part (aspect) experiences consciousness, the somnolent aspect basks in a blissfulness more primal than experience, thought, and emotion. In fact, inasmuch as all beings are part of the One Being—at the physical level as the fraction of a totality, at the personality level as the exemplars of a model, and at the level of consciousness—yet at the supreme level all beings are coexistential to the One. Since in samadhi the sense of individuality has been lost, one basks in the primeval blissfulness and transconscious awareness of the One, aware of the way reality looks beyond form, time, space, qualities, individuation, even consciousness in his (our) deep sleep in the night of time. This state is called by the Sufis *Ahadiat*, and the corresponding plane, *Hahut*.

The first step of the descent denotes a convergence, a focalization, a quantum leap from latency into being.

In the first plane there is no other but the only existing One, free of form and matter. This Heaven the Sufis name Ahadiat. "The world was created out of darkness," says the Koran; this darkness may be explained as the Unknown, the Unseen, as that which is beyond human perception and imagination and explanation; as that state of existence which language fails to describe. The knowers have spoken of One Only Being; the absolute; omnipotent and omnipresent; nameless; formless; birthless and deathless; while the mystics speak of a perfect restful and peaceful state. It is this background of the universe that is meant by the word darkness, the beginning and end of all.

In this the consciousness touches the innermost depth of its own being.

In this first plane it is no other but the only existing One free of form and matter. Before manifestation, what existed? "Dhat," the truly Existing, the Only Being. In what form? In no form. As what? As nothing. The only definition that words can give is the Absolute.

Bringing back the memory of that state, Murshid, confirming the impressions gathered by those who ever reached that state, described it as the way things look when existence has fallen out of focus: only unity prevails. This is why the Sufis call it Tawhid, which means unity, often translated as *unio mystica*. Murshid compares it to the deepest strata of sleep, where the primal Intelligence is not aware of any activity. Therefore samadhi or Tawhid requires an extreme peacefulness, beyond joy. One adduces similes like darkness or the state of unknowing.

Since Murshid, in consonance with all Sufis, attached the importance that he did to life in the world, he tended to stress the states experienced during the descent from samadhi or Tawhid, rather than describe the method of ascent, as do the Yogis. Thus he describes the first step downwards from Ahad, as one would the condition of a great Being who was awakening out of the sleep in which he was solely aware of the principle behind existence, to the awareness of his existence in the second Heaven, called *Wahdat*.

In the beginning when there was no earth, no heaven, there was no other plane of existence than eternal awareness, which may be called a silent, inactive state of life, or unawakened intelligence that men have idealized as God, the Only Being. Within it, there awakened of its own nature, the awareness of Its own existence, unlimited by knowledge of form and space—as a mirror in which, as yet, nothing is reflected.

This is sometimes called *Lahut*. Murshid said we all experience it, albeit elusively.

In the life of every man there is a moment during the wakeful state, a moment when he rises above all limitations of life, but so swiftly does it come and go, in the twinkling of an eye, that he cannot catch it, that he does not realize it. This is called Lahut. It is just like a bird which came and flew away, and you only heard the flutter of its wings. But those who wish to catch this bird, who wish to see where this bird goes, and when it comes and when it goes, look out for it and sit waiting and watching for the moment when it comes; and that watching is called meditation.[3]

Here is the birth of primal Intelligence, already latent within the One, before the advent of existence. It is the consciousness of being, not the consciousness of existence, for there is no consciousness of phenomena; in fact, at this stage, there are no phenomena yet.

We recognize intelligence in its manifestation, but we do not know it in its essence. In its essence it is all-pervading, and that is why philosophically minded people have called God omniscient.

Then, the innate quality of consciousness shines forth, conscious of its own existence, and conscious of being. It is just like a man who is intelligent, but when he is asleep, his intelligence is not actively intelligent; it is only when he is awake that he knows of his existence.[4]

One may notice that Murshid speaks here of the innate nature of consciousness, rather than consciousness which has not yet emerged.

It is intelligence when there is nothing to be conscious of; when there is something intelligible before it, the same intelligence becomes consciousness.

Consciousness must always be conscious of something. When consciousness is not conscious of anything it is pure intelligence. It is in this realization that the greatest secret of life can be revealed.

Consciousness means the loaded intelligence, intelligence charged with knowledge, with impressions carrying ideas.[5]

Imagine envisioning yourself as pure intelligence, completely impersonal. And then, opening your eyes, observe how the gravity pull of the physical world draws intelligence into a focal center that assumes it is a personal conscious subject.

Here Murshid gives us an invaluable clue to understand samadhi, or most particularly the *Turya* state of Vedanta: If intelligence becomes consciousness when faced with an object—that is, when involved in existence—then conversely where existence falls out of the focus of consciousness, consciousness dissolves into its ground: intelligence. It is the sense of existence that brings the contemplative back into conscious life, the first step being an overall consciousness of existence (Wahdat) or Lahut and the next of one's existence as a person (Wahdaniat) or *Jabrut*.

Out of this consciousness of existence, a sense developed, a sense that "I exist"—a development of the consciousness of existence. It was this development which formed the first "ego," the Logos.

To grasp the plethora of manifested idiosyncrasies, consciousness initially had to split itself into galaxies of individual focus, each of which could grasp only a fragment of the totality, with the resultant limitation and illusory impressions of the parts.

To put it plainly, the first aspect may be called unawakened intelligence (at the level of Ahadiat), the next awakened intelligence (at the level of Wahdat), and the third divided and limited intelligence (at the level of Wahdaniat).

The Intelligence confined to knowledge of phenomena becomes limited, but when it is free from all knowledge then it experiences its own essence, its own being.

Paradoxically one may represent the One and only Being as awakening into existence, or, alternately, as awakening from existence into his (our) sleep in the night of time, according to whether one considers reality to be the transcendent Absolute or existence. One experiences all the above states both in sleep and in meditation.

One does frequently reach a yet higher level in sleep when all images subside and vanish, and all that remains is pure consciousness without object. This is called deep sleep (stage four according to current sleep research). One cannot remember this state when back into the diurnal state, as there are no images to hang onto, so one can only connect up this experience in one's memory by maintaining the continuity of consciousness and even intensifying awareness while sinking physical, mental, and even archetypal levels of consciousness into oblivion.

Both Sufi and Hindu adepts practice the feat of staying awake during sleep. What then is considered sleep from the everyday vantage point is actually waking up into higher spheres—an adventure into higher dimensions of the cosmos—in fact, precisely what one seeks to experience in meditation. Let it be pointed out that meditation in its highest forms consists essentially in doing this while maintaining the thread of memory without breaking it when passing the threshold from diurnal to sleep consciousness and vice versa.

Indeed, though most people lose the continuity of memory when returning from sleep and therefore recall very little of the experience, one learns in meditation to maintain the continuity of consciousness throughout sleep: It is a great art called *Nidra Yoga*. The *Mandukya Upanishad* draws the parallel between the states of diurnal consciousness, sleep with dreams, deep sleep, and awakening beyond existence on one hand; and the stage of meditation on the other. And Guadapada and Shankaracharya researched it further in what is called *Advaita Vedanta*. To achieve this, one should try to remember the diurnal scene and events while being awake to the dream of one's creative mind. If one manages this, one will maintain the continuity of consciousness. Needless to say, this is a tremendous feat of will power. Such is meditation—it requires a strong resolve. The key to doing this consists in being able to accept that one is the same person though so different, and hence to envision the continuity to one's being in its different dimensions.

The all-encompassing grasp is at such a monumental scale that the contemplative is shaken out of his sense of himself. Here the "I" does not make sense any longer. Evidencing this state, the Master says:

It is just like touching the Presence of God, when one's consciousness has become so light and so liberated and free that it can raise itself and dive and touch the depths of one's being.

This explains why, when mystics have reached a certain level, they lose their sense of identity and testify to the unity of being; consequently the word I refers to God or the Self as the One and only Being. This obviously is the level reached by the Sufi al-Hallaj. "The transcendent I circulates among the multiplicity of individual I's," he says.

The mystery of sleep presents perhaps the greatest challenge to man's thinking, especially since there is such a profusion of evidence of premonitions in dreams, later confirmed, and since research in psycho-physiology reveals the therapeutic value of sleep. No doubt, one of the great advantages of the phenomenon of sleep for psychotherapists is that it removes the censorship, both logical and moral, of the personality.

The mind has its full play when a person is asleep. In the waking state, man has a rein over the mind, but in sleep mostly that rein is lost and the mind is free to produce pictures, natural or unnatural, broken or unbroken, as it happens to produce.

Therefore dreams reveal rarely trodden no-man's lands of the psyche, if not remote planes of existence endowed with a reality of so different a nature from the physical that psychiatrists tend to write it off as subjective, and therefore unreal.

It is so obvious that if one makes the physical world the measuring rod of reality, anything belonging to other dimensions will not fit into one's prefigured hypothesis. If the scientific mind is an open mind, then at least it should accept that "physical reality is a condition of reality"—a Hindu maxim—rather than take for granted that it is the only reality.

Yes, we fool ourselves that we sleep ourselves into oblivion, out of the here and now, as lethargy estranges us from our physical environment, and we let ourselves be transported beyond our will and knowing into the uncharted reaches of mind and soul. Many a glass of wine, a soporific, or a water-pipe has surreptitiously relieved a weary being from his agony of mind or body or of his desperate soul searchings by catapulting him to a pinnacle from which earthly problems have lost their meaning.

The mystic, who realizes the Creator within himself, thinks that his dream is the Creator's dream: if the Creator's dream is all this which we call reality, then the dream of the mystic is the same.

If one could remember while dreaming what life was like on the physical plane, what indeed would it seem like? Of course, like a dream. How real is reality?

To a mystic the reality of the external world is not more real than the reality of the mental plane.

Physical reality is just a condition of reality, as ice is a condition of H_2O.

Why do we assume that the way things look is the way things are? From the worm's-eye view, the grass is more real than a star; from the eagle's, the blades of grass fall out of perspective as he soars higher and higher. For some the experience of the heavens testified by a few are sheer wishful hallucinations; for the contemplative, the image of earthly things has fallen out of perspective and appears as the product of maya.

The more closely a person is drawn to heaven, the more the things of the earth lose their colour and taste. To him who has experienced only materially by his five senses, without even a glimpse of an idea of something else, this seems real, and we cannot blame him for thinking it real. It is only when he awakens from his life that he sees that it is unreal. While you are dreaming, if someone would come and tell you, "Do not believe it, it is a dream," you would never believe that; you would think, "it is real." The dream is recognized as a dream, because of the contrast of the physical life, as everything is recognized by its contrast.

An ironic feature of our unconsidered slant about the nature of reality is our assumption, unquestioned by most people, that we "wake up" from a dream. Has it ever occurred to you that it could well be the other way around? Does anybody remember what everyday life seemed like when one was dreaming? If one remembers a dream when back into the diurnal state, can one not remember the diurnal state when dreaming?

If a person were asked when he is dreaming, "What about the experience of yesterday?" he would say, "It was a dream." "And what about everyday life?" "It was all a dream."

Chung Fu woke up one day and said, "Last night I dreamt that I was a butterfly; and this morning, I do not know whether I am a man who had dreamt that he was a butterfly, or whether I am a butterfly who is dreaming that he is a man."

In fact, when in the dream state one does remember the diurnal state and has the impression of having awakened from the diurnal state; but when back in the diurnal state, most people only remember a few impressions or images of the dream and fail to remember the psychological condition they were experiencing, because one seems to have been so completely a different person. One's relationship with whatever is experienced was so completely out of step with the diurnal state that one cannot fit it into one's diurnal *imago mundi*; and consequently it escapes one's grasp when back into the physical perspective of things. Yet the impression lingers, although somehow one cannot lay a hand on it. By contrast, the impressions of the diurnal state when dreaming do not bear any likeness to one's dream personality and therefore seem as unreal as the dream when one is in the diurnal state.

It seems as though one has an aspect of one's being on every plane, yet one's being in the heavens has so much greater a dimension than one's being on earth that it is difficult for memory to refer events to the same being. When one is dreaming or in a higher state of meditation, one finds it so hard to accept that the things that one vaguely remembers really happened. One feels oneself to be another person, yet the continuation of the same person.

The soul in its manifestation on earth is not at all disconnected with the higher spheres. It lives in all spheres, though it is generally conscious on only one plane. Thus it becomes deprived of the heavenly bliss, and conscious of the troubles and limitations of life on the earth.

Maybe we are ordinarily trapped on the physical or mental planes in a mind-bind, not realizing that we are free, like the fly in the bottle or the man hanging on a branch the whole night, oblivious of the fact that he was few inches above the ground. Maybe it is the other way round: In sleep we awaken from earth consciousness. Then it is clear that it is the personal focus of consciousness that hampers one's reach. We do not always know how to modulate it by our free will. Sometimes the impact of a gripping situation launches consciousness aloft like a kite borne by a gust of wind. To control it consciously and intentional-ly is what is called meditation. Yet one may sometimes wonder whether part of one is conscious of the heavens while part is tuned to the earth frequency.

Man can only be really happy when he connects his soul with the spheres of heaven.

As I assume the reader is in the diurnal state perusing this book, we will have to use that state as a point of reference. How then do our dreams appear to the diurnal mind? Like a confused mass of impres-sions that one feels unable to coordinate, and therefore one possesses an a priori judgment as to the state of dreaming, calling it disorderly, even chaotic. However, in this chaotic amalgamate, some impresssions may stand out with astonishing precision; we normally remember only a fraction of the experience, generally the more pictorial aspect; the psychological conditions vanish as we try to grasp them with our conscious will, yet keep recurring when we are less centered in our diurnal personality. In fact, it is the influence of our personal will upon the focus of our consciousness that offsets the focus needed to recollect a dream. This explains why we remember dreams better when we are suspended on the threshold between sleep and day conscious-ness; our notion of ourselves is less definite and therefore involves other dimensions of our being than those experienced and identified within our everyday thinking. In everyday consciousness, we seem to be in the world; in a dream consciousness, the world is inside us.

Here in the physcial plane, though we appear to be one separate from the other, in the plane of the dream upon the surface of the individual's mind the whole world exists. He who is one single being in the physical plane inverts the whole world in the plane of the dream, although he holds still fast his individuality even there where he is alone.

A further reason the dream appears so confused is that because in the dream impressions from numerous sources are intertwined and woven into a multidimensional pattern, making sense according to the level at which it is experienced. Let us unravel these components. Murshid distinguishes four types of dreams:

First of all the reflex, almost photographic reproduction of scenes of everyday life projected pictorially as a mirage on a nonexisting screen in front of consciousness.

There is Khwabi Khayli, when a person sees in the night what he has been doing during the day. When your mind is so much engaged in all the thoughts, the occupations, the cares of the day, that these appear before you in the dream. This dream has not much effect upon the mind because it is not very deep.

Second, a regurgitation of psychological impressions of fear, pleasure, desire, anger, or inadequacy, sometimes reexperienced as pure emotion, but hardly communicated to the diurnal memory except when it bursts forth as a symbol portraying the emotion. Some of these impressions may well up from unconscious reactions, normally inhibited in everyday life, triggered by encounters with the outside world.

During this dream the soul knows nothing except what appears before it, for instance desires, habits, wishes, experiences, environment, actions, throughts, and impressions.

Third, the repressed forces of the unconscious, uncalled for as far as we know from outside, may project in morbid or even diabolical symbols.

Dreams produced before the view of man either caused by the unbalanced activity of mind or by the disorder of the health.

Fourth, impressions originating inside at various levels, which cannot possibly be explained away as personal inhibitions of the unconscious psyche, but definitely depicting other spheres of being, including other beings than oneself, which may well convey a message or a warning. Here we can sometimes capture future events in our dreams as they are on their way to materializing in manifestations.

Every accident, pleasant or unpleasant, has a long preparation before it; first it exists in the mind, then on the physical plane. A dream shows the depth of life.[6]

The next plane encountered, after the regurgitation of mental impressions has dwindled into a peaceful interlude, betrays astral activity. Most people linger here in sleep, while a few reach higher. It is because of the incompatability of this state with the physical one that most people cannot make the transition into it while maintaining the continuity of consciousness, and so one remembers this state as a hazy one.

Laboratory research conducted during the last few years by Loomis, Kleitman, Dement, and Aserinsky confirms the existence of a sleep pattern alternating between an increasingly deepening sleep progressing from stage one to stage four and lasting at first approximately one and a half hours; and a "paradoxal" type of sleep, accompanied by rapid-eye movement, denoting mental and imaginative activity, while the body becomes cataleptic. This condition may well point to astral projection, given an acclerated EEG frequency wave, and reduced heart rate, blood pressure, and breathing. Perhaps one of the features that identify the astral state is that the phenomena experienced appear as being undoubtedly outside oneself, and one experiences oneself as buoyant or made of a fine fabric.

When in a dream man is able to see himself, what does that show? That after what is called death, man is still not formless.[7]

One is conscious of pulsing with a strange quiver; furthermore, one's sense of space and distance is completely altered. One realizes that one is living without a body.

There is a difference of time, for in dreams a man may pass from one land to another in a flash instead of taking a month.

The astral dream contrasts with the more ponderous recurrence of diurnal impressions, conjuring symbols and archetypes from the unconscious. One can distinguish the astral dream by the fact that one remembers having moved during sleep into different surroundings and being visited by people, or all kinds of beings, known or unknown, still incarnated or having died. If, as in some exceptional cases, one is able to maintain the continuity of consciousness and remember having left one's body behind, one will discover that one can change environment at will by the sheer thought of a place which one wishes to visit.

The astral dream is the real experience of the soul dwelling in the higher spheres with the vehicle of the mind. There are three aspects of the astral dream. One aspect is that a person knows the real happening, not contrary or symbolical; the real happening manifests on the surface. The next aspect is that a person meets the living or dead friend and sees his actual condition. The third kind is that the astral part of the living or dead comes and visits a person. By means of the astral dream a great many things are accomplished. Those who become masters of life control the astral plane and bring about these abovesaid three experiences at will.

At a higher level of our being, we reach a totally different type of dream world, called *Khwabi Khayal* by the Sufis, populated with beings we think of as thoughts when in diurnal consciousness, to which we have imparted life. Having once been conceived, they are endowed with a certain autonomy, of which normally we may be oblivious. If we have any reminiscence of that level during sleep, we will recall that we not only projected thoughts but we moved in a world of thoughts that assumed a reality they certainly fail to assume in the diurnal state; in fact, they seemed like phantoms, live effigies, called elementals, some of which we ourselves projected into the fabric of this palace of mirrors, as the Sufis call it. Furthermore, other beings are created by the mind beings we have created.

A keen observer will certainly distinguish within this world several strata, of which one could distinguish at least between the mental plane and the plane of jinns.

And in the mind our every thought and feeling is as alive as we, even such beings as the elementals, demons, and angels, which are created within us, from us, and of us, and yet may as fitly be called individuals as we. So in the end of the examination, it is hard for a man to find out whether he exists as one or many. In our dreams all the inhabitants of our mind resurrect, forming a world within ourselves. We see in the dream things and beings, a friend, a foe, and an animal, a bird, and they come from nowhere but are created out of our own selves. The mind of an individual constitutes a world in itself, which is created and destroyed by the conscious or unconscious action of the will, which has two aspects: intention and accident. We have experience of this world of mind even while awake, but the contrast between the world within and without makes the world without concrete and the world within abstract.

It is at this mind level that telepathy operates during sleep. Such impressions are immediately translated into symbols. One of the essential functions of the mind consists of digesting experiences, "eternalizing" them as symbols after having divested them of their contingent temporal dimensions. Dreams convey their meaningfulness in the form of symbols, so that a psychologist positing, like any scientist, that there is reason and meaning in everything, avails himself of the material of dreams to decipher the condition of the psyche in its depths. Murshids or rishis read a message in the symbols otherwise considered as fortuitous, intended to warn the dreamer or make him aware of something affecting his life or unfoldment, or promoting his understanding.

The distinctive feature of a symbol is that it stands for a whole category or range of being instead of being confined to its outer form. For example, the eye in Egyptian hieroglyphs represents consciousness, not just the human eye but the human "I"; the cross in Christianity represents disintegration and resurrection, not just the wooden cross on which the body of Christ was suspended.

To a person who sees only the surface of things in life, symbols mean nothing; the secret of symbols is revealed to souls whose glance penetrates through objects. Verily, before the seer the things of the world open themselves. First the intuitive faculty must be opened and then the whole meaning of the symbols will be understood; and often it will be quite a different meaning from what the object seems to represent.

Dreams, of course, affect one's day thinking and their memory remains ever present in the unconscious. Murshid showed how we are continually working out creatively, in the world, the dreams of our soul.

The reason why mental dreams should have an effect upon the life of a person is that the line of our fate is made on the lines of the impressions that our mind creates before our soul.

A problem arises in our understanding because in our diurnal consciousness we are used to assuming that objects are other than ourselves, but, in fact, they are only a fragment of an ever created reality that has become fossilized, not the whole of reality or the only reality. In the dream our identity does not distinguish itself from the environment in the same way as it does in the physical plane; it merges with the landscape of the soul, and this is why it is so difficult to translate the experience in terms of the dual subjective–objective perspective of everyday consciousness. In fact, even as we project, in the dream, the formless meaningfulness of transcendental spheres into imaginary scenery, so do we also project the effigy of ourselves as the subject contemplating the scene.

Someone may ask: "If all that we see in the dreams are we ourselves, then why do we see, even in the dreams, ourselves as an identity separate from all other things before us in the dream?" The answer is: "Because the soul is deluded by our external form, and this picture it recognizes as I and all other images and forms manifesting before it in the dreams stand in contrast to this I."

It is because one has difficulty in identifying oneself as the same person as in the dream that the impressions are distorted when recollected, and sometimes even reversed, so that one misinterprets the happenings or misappropriates the qualities appearing in the dream.

This is *Khwabi Ghalti*. In this case you see the opposite of the real happening. Your friend may be ill and you see him as being well. When the mirror of the mind is distorted, then the image falling upon it is distorted also, just as there are some mirrors in which a thin person appears very fat, a tall person appears short, everything appears reversed. He may see the death of the father when it is the death of the mother, or the illness of the daughter when it is the illness of the son. But if he is absolutely pious he sees the exact event. Everything, either the printer's block, the photographic plate, the humorous mirror, and all things of a negative character will show opposite before they manifest aright.

Another type of dream shows things the way they are.

The third sort is *Khwabi Ruhi,* vision. In this the happening is shown exactly as it is. This dream is seen by the pious persons, by the pure minds. It comes only to the few, to the chosen ones. One can see what a person is. Then the dream does not seem a dream; it is real as life on the physical plane.

The reasons one questions the reality of a subjective impression are that one is not only a spectator but also its creator; and that it dissolves as soon as one's creative act ceases, whereas the objective world remains and can be experienced by others at the same time as one is experiencing it oneself.

But we say: "Yes, but when we awake we find a house."[8] Actually, we are only the instruments through which creative yet unformed reality is projected into mental pictures. These are not pure fantasy, but correspond to a cosmic order or reality that is continually being projected into forms.

The palaces which are built in that world are as much our own, are much more our own. . . . We create a world for us to live in. This is the secret of the whole life.[9]

Have you ever returned over and over again to the same place or scene in a dream? Can one, while dreaming, remember a previous dream, just as memory of earthly events may be interrupted by sleep but return after the recovery of diurnal consciousness? Yes, the house is still there, the only difference is that it is not palpable with the body; so has a symphony of Beethoven an indestructible reality, once composed, even if it is never played and even if every script or score has been physically destroyed. In fact, the whole physical world, says the Veda, is the dream of Brahma petrified into matter.

Vedanta it is called, "the dream of Brahma," that is "the dream of God." Each of us experiences a part of the dream, and only God, the Whole Being, experiences, all the time, the whole of the dream. People say it is only imagination, a working of the mind. But what is mind? Mind is that in which the world is reflected. . . . In comparison the physical body is like a drop in the ocean.[10]

At the next level, the sleeper reaches a sphere described by the Sufis as the plane of *Arwah* (or *Malakut),* where creative and inspirational thoughts originate, the plane of souls, angels.

A person who can experience joy and sorrow by raising his consciousness to that plane can make heaven in himself.[11]

That state of Malakut is reached while in the waking state by the great thinkers, the great inventive minds and the gifted artists; and it is experienced by the seers and sages. It is to experience this that all the concentrations are given by spiritual teachers to their disciples.[12]

It is a luminous plane of pure splendor, horizons of light, zones of vibrations inhabited by beings whose bodies are constituted of light and sound. All events on the physical plane have their counterpart at this level, which divides into the akashic and the auric plane prior to manifestation.

The spiritual dream is that during which the light of the soul has fully illuminated the mind, and the mind is able to create and perceive the clear picture of past, present, and future. In the spiritual dream one sees actually what is happening at a distance or what has happened or what is going to take place.

Since at this level the dichotomy of object-subject is overcome, the landscapes of beings are neither within nor without. It is undoubtedly the notion of the self that tends to restrain one from reaching this high. Consequently, this plane is more often reached in dream, and can only be encompassed in full consciousness by more advanced meditators who are capable of surrendering their self-consciousness without any hope of ever recovering it. Of course, most people have glimpses of this plane under the cover of sleep, but the impressions collected here are so inextricably enmeshed into the fabric of one's dream that it is difficult to spot them.

If his soul can rise at will from the lower planes of existence, he can dwell in the spiritual sphere with mastery. The greatest hindrance that veils man's eyes from the spiritual dream is the thought of self.

CHAPTER 11

Raindrops in a Pool

VIBRATIONS—THE SYMPHONY OF THE SPHERES

The all-pervading life is silent in its original nature and inactive. It is this condition of inertia which is called by Vedantists, Sattva; and the beginning of its activity is the formation of capacity, and it is this capacity which allows the activity of the all pervading life to become audible. And therefore the first manifestation of the all pervading life is called in the Bible "word," and in Vedanta Nada Brahma, meaning "creator-word," or "the word of the Creator." And this is the explanation of what is said in the Bible, "First was the word, and the word was God."

Now a world of pure vibration opened to Murshid, the musician of the soul. It was remotely familiar, judging from his experience of ecstasy while singing or playing the vina, yet now more vivid than ever.

As man is the miniature universe himself, in him also the word is born. When the capacity allows the word which is breath to reecho itself, it manifests in an audible sound. It is this sound that the adept hears. It is breath, life itself. When it raises itself into motion, and when the capacity allows it to echo, then the sound becomes audible—which means, the all pervading life which was silent, has been allowed to manifest itself, first in the realm of sound, this being the original state of the whole creation which naturally reminds the soul of its origin; therefore it puts the soul into ecstasy.

Raindrops upon a pool, fireworks in the clear atmosphere, thunder on the high peaks!

Have you ever watched the concentric fanning out of widening circles of ripples somersaulting, frolicking, and scintillating in the moonlight, as each fresh splashing crystalline drop sets a stir in the heart of molecules, thrust into a magic design, displaying some abstract pattern of cosmic rhythm? Have you ever witnessed the sparkling ballet of fireworks sprinkling radially, criss-crossing flurries of blinding flashes that spurt harmonically, flaring into a multicolored pulverised rainbow spectrum, and then dispersing beyond your sight into the dark vastness beyond? Have you ever heard the ominous tremor of angry thunder boomeranging back and forth from near and distant peaks as it wraps you with recurrent waves of sound, blurring out into a fringe of plaints, still woven into an undecipherable symmetry, way

195

into distant shores of space? Have you ever harkened to the symphony of the spheres, crowned by the choirs beyond, from plane to plane into transcendental dimensions of astral space, and then echoing yet remoter overtones, luring you even further like the Valkyries?

If a pebble thrown into the sea puts the water in action, one hardly stops to think to what extent this vibration acts upon the sea. It takes in everything, and it brings it up; it rears it and it allows it to grow.[1]

Our preconditioned ideas assume that we are the subject, and the universe is the object. However, Murshid has shown us that in the experience of samadhi, at the highest level, there is only awareness of being without any form or qualities, which he calls intelligence. Now he shows that at a certain stage, as consciousness descends from that pinnacle, it observes a polarization of the one reality into consciousness on the one hand and the manifested on the other—we say subject and object—by projecting what will become the objective world out of the original state where there was only Divine Intelligence, thus manifesting himself to his own view.

It is the consciousness itself which has involved a part of itself in its creation, while a part remains as Creator, as water frozen turns into ice and yet water abides within.[2]

Intelligence is not only a knowing faculty, but is creative at the same time. The whole of manifestation is the creation of the intelligence.[3]

In the third Heaven Consciousness manifests to its own view. This is the plane of the Abstract, in which consciousness evolves into waves of activity, into vibrations that are first audible and then become visible. The first activity of consciousness produces Sound, and the clashings and groupings of vibrations produce Light. The third Heaven is called Wahdaniat.

This may be called the causal plane, where the secret causes or archetypes of all created things are found in the form of pure vibrations. We will recall that, at the previous stage, the first notion of the Self (*Zat*) emerged. At the present stage, what is known is the attributes (*Sifat*) of the Self.

Intelligence becomes intelligible by turning into denseness, that denseness being manifest to its own view.[4]

It is the tendency of the intelligence to seek an object; even as the eyes seek something to look at, and the ears desire to hear. This first activity of the intelligence may be called love, or will, or desire—the Sufis name it Ishk.

This projection of the makings of creation in the form of vibrations, the signature tune of the archetypes of all things to come, is attributed by the Sufis to an innate nostalgia heaving within the depth of the Divine Intelligence, which is the primal energy out of which love evolved, called *Ishk*. And there is an inner necessity in love to polarize into the duality of lover and beloved, in order to become a concrete reality. This indeed is the original duality. Consequently, that primeval energy burst forth projecting the virtualities of a Beloved: The arch-image of God came into view in the form of the "names behind all forms," those unheard vibrations that express the spectrum of the many-splendored attributes behind all creation, while simultaneously incubating the consciousness of the Divine Lover: the Self.

When Ahad, the only Being, became conscious of his Wahdat, only existence, through His own consciousness, then His predisposition toward love made Him project Himself to establish His dual aspect, that He might be able to love someone. This made God the lover and manifestation the beloved; the next inversion makes manifestation the lover, and God the beloved. This force of love has been working through several evolutions and involutions which end in man, who is the ultimate aim of God.[5]

The primeval image of the Beloved is an expression of pure splendor in the form of vibrations. Yes, the reality we witness in our body, in the subtler counterparts of our being, and in the universe around us is the growth of the early stirrings of vibration in the night of time.

The life Absolute from which has sprung all that is felt, seen, and perceived, and into which all again merges in time, is a silent, motionless and eternal life which among the Sufis is called Zàt. Every motion that springs forth from this silent life is a vibration and a creator of vibrations. Within one vibration are created many vibrations; as motion causes motion so the silent life becomes active in a certain part, and creates every moment more and more activity, losing thereby the peace of the original silent life. It is the grade of activity of these vibrations that accounts for the various planes of existence.[6]

Behind the whole metaphysics of sound of the Sufis lurks a lovely Qur'anic allegory: The souls of men could not be persuaded to enter into bodies of clay, whereupon God commanded the angels to play music; immediately the souls condescended to accept that limitation for the advantage of hearing music more concretely through the senses. Those who strive back to the source will turn into the abstract music, because by it we are attuned to the silent life.

It was the Saut-e Sarmad, the sound of the abstract plane, which Mohammad heard in the cave of Ghar-e Hirá when he became lost in his divine ideal. The Qur'an refers to this sound in the words: "Be! and all became." Moses heard this very sound on Mount Sinai, when in communion with God; and the same word was audible to Christ when absorbed in his Heavenly Father in the wilderness. Shiva heard the name Anahad Nada during his Samadhi in the cave of the Himalayas.

The sound of the abstract is always going on within, around and about man. Man does not hear it as a rule, because his consciousness is entirely centred in his material existence.[7]

It is through vibration, through motion, that spirit turns into matter. Hindus call it Nada, and they always combine this word with Brahma.[8]

If we have a counterpart of our being on every plane, then a part— the quintessence of our being—is pure vibration.

Creation begins with the activity of consciousness, which may be called vibration, and every vibration starting from its original source is the same, differing only in its tone and rhythm caused by a greater or lesser degree of force behind it. On the plane of sound, vibration causes diversity of tone, and in the world of atoms, diversity of color. It is by massing together that the vibrations become audible, but at each step towards the surface they multiply, and as they advance they materialize. Sound gives to the consciousness an evidence of its existence, although it is in fact the active part of consciousness itself which turns into sound. The knower so to speak becomes known to himself, in other words the consciousness bears witness to its own voice.[9]

This then is the constituent beyond the soul, which forms later out of the fabric of light, since metaphysically sound is prior to light.

The Sound, or Divine Music of the Abstract, projected from itself Light; and this Light, responsive and yet expressive, broke again into the rays that form Arwah, the spiritual heaven of souls. And the souls, each responsive and yet in itself expressive, bringing forth and partaking of the various attributes of the Abstract, grouping them together in manifold forms and variations, created this world, Sifat, the expression of the Absolute.

Thus the primal sound of the Absolute breaks up into multitudes of notes or chords before manifesting as light and so fanning out into a multitude of rays that constitute the souls. The signature tune that constitutes beings continually emerges out of that bass-continuum, the undertone that is the sound of the Absolute.

With the music of the Absolute the bass, the undertone, is going on continuously; but on the surface beneath the various keys of all the instruments of nature's music, the undertone is hidden and subdued. Every being with life comes to the surface and again returns whence it came, as each note has its return to the ocean of sound.[10]

However, before reaching the highly specific individuation of the personal signature tune of each being, the Absolute Sound broke up into galactic and planetary chords, and it is these that Pythagoras referred to as the music of the spheres.

When one looks at the cosmos, the movements of the stars and planets, the law of vibration and rhythm, all perfect and unchanging, it shows that the cosmic system is working by the law of music, the law of harmony.[11]

Some may interpret this Sound as the sound produced by planets in their circumvolutions, and even include the sound on the surface and inside the planets, like the sound of the sunflower revolving upon its axis in its nostalgia to face the sun, as described by Proclus, or the sound of the windharp, or the crackling of thawing ice, or incandescent molten matter splintering—such natural sounds as are now the fabric of electronic music.

There is nothing in this world which does not speak and every being is continually calling out its nature.... I have found in every word a certain musical value, a melody in every thought, harmony in every feeling.[12]

Everything and every being Murshid envisioned as a crystallized vibration, pulsing, throbbing, and resounding. This knowledge was based upon a way of looking upon sounds as endowed with an entity of their own, as pure vibration, like radio waves of varying frequency, or sound current, having a life span, a consciousness, and the faculty of perpetuating and reproducing themselves.

Sound has its birth, death, sex, form, planet, colour, childhood, youth and age.[13]

Vibrations as a rule have length as well as breadth; and they may last the least fraction of a moment or the greater part of the age of the universe. They make different forms, figures and colours as they shoot forth, one vibration creating another; and thus myriads arise out of one. In this way there are circles beneath circles and circles above circles, all of which form the universe. Every vibration after its manifestation becomes merged again in its original source. The reach of vibrations is according to the fineness of the plane of their starting-point.[14]

In fact, Murshid sketched a monumental representation of vibrations as life forces and live beings that are opening up new vistas in contemporary music; vibrations may be considered as latent behind all structure and thus as a creative force in the hands of man.

Vibrations broadcast radially from outer space into sidereal space assume a direction:

It is the direction of the activity of vibrations that accounts for the variety of things and beings.[15]

Differences of frequency determine the degree of subtlety or grossness of the heavenly planes.

It is a certain degree of vibration which brings to the earth the things of the inner world . . . and a change of vibrations takes away the things that are seen into the unseen world.

It is the gradually increasing activity which causes vibrations to materialize, and it is the gradual decrease of the same which transmutes them again into spirit.[16]

One may divide the spectrum of vibrations into three stages: slow, moderate, and quick, or as they are called in Sanskrit: Satva, Rajas, and Tamas. The first stage is creative in its effect, the second stage is progressive, and the third stage is destructive.[17]

For it is the nature of activity to become more active every moment . . . by so producing energy, its own strength throws it out of its normal rhythm.

When the frequencies of vibration increase beyond a threshold, they manifest as light, conforming to a scientific theory according to which light waves figure in a higher frequency range, and are both vibration and particle; the particles arose out of the collision of vibrations.

It depends upon the speed of the vibrations as to whether a thing is visible or audible, perceptible or imperceptible.[18]

The interference or collision of vibrations may reach a still further stage and freeze the resultant vibration into molecules or atoms, displaying the splendid musings in the imagination of the Divine Planner into a kaleidoscope of shimmering tangible patterns, gifted with the miracle of the breath of life.

Vibrations turn to atoms and atoms generate what we call life . . . and as the breath manifests through the form so the body becomes conscious.[19]

And in turn, these atoms vibrate and spin, and throb; in fact all bodies have their pulsings; in the human body, one may recognize the rhythm of the breath, of the heart beat, and a mysterious pulsing vector of the order of seven to eight beats per second, and beyond, unteemed pulsings whose frequency rockets up beyond recognition. These rhythms can be altered by the control of the will.

All existing things which we see or hear, which we perceive, vibrate. If it were not for vibration, the precious stones would not show their colour and their brilliance; it is vibration which makes the trees grow, the fruit ripen, and the flowers bloom.[20]

All man's inner bodies are vibrating, and they are related to each other by the speed of their vibrations. The etheric and astral bodies vibrate at the same or proportional rates to the human body.

What the soul perceives are the vibrations of the feelings; what the mind conceives are the vibrations of the thoughts; what the eyes see are the vibrations solidified from their ethereal state and turned into atoms which appear in the physical world, constituting the elements ether, air, fire, water, and earth. The finest vibrations are imperceptible even to the soul. The soul itself is formed of these vibrations; it is their activity which makes it conscious. Perhaps the day might come when scientists will be able to check thought waves in the atmosphere with sensitive instruments.

The phenomenon of sound is, then, a privileged form assumed by the cosmic harmony in that it communicates the harmony in a more direct understanding of meaningfulness. Since it is an index of one's degree of realization, music can be used as a means of helping people evolve. For a like reason, the language and technique of music can and will be applied in the future to psychological, and perhaps even physical, therapy; for example, to attune people to their real being or compensate undesired idiosyncrasies by those programed by the musician–psychologist.

If one knew what rhythm was needed for a particular individual in his trouble and despair, what tone was needed, and to what pitch that person's soul should be raised, one would then be able to heal him with music.

In his pulsation, in the beat of his heart, in his vibration, rhythm and tone, his health or illness, his joy or discomfort, all show the music or lack of music in his life.

And what does music teach us? Music helps us to train ourselves in harmony, and it is this which is the magic or the secret behind music.

Vibrations can be changed by understanding the vibrations of one's own life, which means one's own self. In the first place one can study the vibrations of the physical body.

The pulsation of the heart, head, and body, upon which circulation depends, is based upon the rhythm of breath. The next step is to understand the rhythm of the mind. People who think, "I will do this," and then at once decide to do something else, or who begin one thing and then go on to another, show that their mind is not in its proper rhythm.[21]

This would require a whole study in the psychology of music therapy, pioneered by Murshid, the musician of the soul.

The whole universe is one symphony; in this every individual is one note and his happiness lies in becoming perfectly attuned to the harmony of the universe.

Man, being a miniature of the universe, shows harmonious and inharmonious chords. The gradual progress of all creation from a lower to a higher evolution, its change from one aspect to another, is shown as in music where a melody is transposed from one key into another. The friendship and enmity among men, and their likes and dislikes, are as chords and discords. The harmony of human nature, and the human tendency to attraction and repulsion, are like the effect of the consonant and dissonant intervals in music.

The tone of one personality is hard like a horn; while the tone of another is soft like the high notes of a flute.

In tenderness of heart the tone turns into a half-tone; and with the breaking of the heart the tone breaks into microtones. The more tender the heart becomes, the fuller the tone becomes; the harder the heart grows, the more dead it sounds.

CHAPTER 12

Rainbows Fanning
Out into Rays

THE GENESIS OF THE SOUL

When the soul is clear from all earthly shadows then heavenly pictures appear upon the curtain of man's heart.

Murshid described the breathtaking spectacle in the cosmos experienced during his samadhi as the symphony of cosmic vibrations crystallizing into matter. Just as a crystal displays a structure of vibrations expressing divine ecstasy frozen into symmetrically ordered molecules, so abstract light, having structured itself in the auras of the archangels and angels, acts on the earth plane as a catalyst and sets off the breakdown of matter into light rays. In this way vibrations, which manifest life, are the functional molds of atomic matter and effect incarnation, while light, which manifests intelligence, effects the transmutation of matter.

Should one suspend one's consciousness between sleep and everyday consciousness, visual and auditory impressions may be jumbled; but if the mind is particularly serene, as happens to people who master meditation, one may be graced by a vision looming crystal-clear against the meanderings of the mind, or an audition as sharp as a bell. Like dreams, these states have their relevance if judiciously interpreted. If a vision can prove to be relevant when confirmed as a premonition of something which actually happens, can it not also be a communication with a higher being, which cannot be confirmed so readily?

Although it bears some resemblance to a voice, an audition differs greatly from ordinary sense perception. The ears are not trained and focused upon some source of the sound located in space (presumed to be outside), but the sound seems to emerge out of an inner space, where the dichotomy of the subject and the object governing perception in outer space no longer applies. Therefore, people call it an inner voice.

This is why psychologists often dismiss these auditions as subjective, which may be interpreted as hallucinatory in nature, hence completely fanciful. Disagreeing, esotericists attach importance and validity to "subjective" impressions, since they actualize a reality that is endeavoring to break through a mind otherwise too prepossessed and maybe prejudiced.

In the physical world, you are here, and everything else is without you. You are contained in the space. In the dream, all that you see is contained within you.

Why a person does not observe the unseen world is that he is accustomed to observe only what is before him.[1]

In other words, the obstacle to vision or audition of higher planes is our habit of thinking of the objective world as other than ourselves and outside ourselves, instead of merging with the object in what Patanjali calls *dhyana*.

Vision may be experienced in sleep, in the awakened state, and in the twilight state, suspended between sleep and wakefulness.

Murshid points out the difference between a vision during sleep and an ordinary dream: Vision is like an unusually clear sleep projection, standing in contrast to ever moving and evanescent kaleidoscopic flashes of a dream, and it generally is pregnant with a purpose, like a warning or a revelation important to one at that particular moment.

It is not like a dream, which goes on like an act on the stage, but it is a picture. To those who are developed spiritually this vision often comes, sometimes as an answer to their question, sometimes to warn them of an unforeseen danger, and sometimes to guide them toward some accomplishment in life.

In the ordinary vision a person sees past, present, and future exactly as it is. For instance, if some friend or relation is about to come unexpectedly the vision first shows his arrival.

The message the vision is trying to convey is often obstructed on its way to reaching one's awareness by preconceived ideas that assume the form of logical thinking, and consequently it attempts to capture one's attention when the censorship of the conscious mind is off-guard in sleep; but if a person is able to keep his rational mind in its right place, and restrain it wherever necessary, he may be graced with a vision in the diurnal state.

Vision can be said to be a dream which one experiences in the wakeful state.

A clear case of a vision occurred when Murshid, in danger, saw the face of his Murshid, and the threat was averted.

I have had many experiences of the vision of my murshid, one of which is the following. Once we were making a three days' journey through the jungle, in a place where there was great danger from robbers, and every night two or three travellers were killed. Ours was the smallest caravan. Generally the caravans were of twenty wagons, but it happened that ours was of three wagons only. I had with me very precious gems given to me by the Nizam of Hyderabad, and instead of arms I had musical instruments with me. All the night I saw the form of my murshid, at first faintly, afterwards distinctly, walking with the wagon. The two other wagons were attacked and robbed, and a few worthless bundles were taken, but my wagon was safe. This is not the only instance I have had in my life; I have had a thousand experiences of the sort.

A vision may catch a person unawares, as it did the young girl waiting in a bus queue in London who saw her long-dead grandmother warning her not to take the bus. Her fright delayed her getting on the bus, so she missed it. Later she heard that the bus that she was about to take had had an accident.

One need not see a vision only in a dream, one can also have a vision when awake. There is nothing to be frightened of in this. It is only clearness of the inner sight. Knowledge comes in a flash and a problem is solved; a philosophical problem or a certain hidden law of life or nature has become manifest in a very clear form. Or one has got in touch with something or with someone at an unimaginable distance.[2]

It seems as though information from the higher strata of our being strives to pierce through the layers of fossilized assumptions and opinions and representations of the universe as seen from the perspective of the individual. Even if it finds an outlet in dreams, when we return to the diurnal state we preclude even the chance of remembering the dream by our prejudgment that it is fanciful and unlikely. The secret of receiving this information is to believe in these marginal impressions, even if they do not fit into our *imago mundi*. Once one has allowed them to flow over the threshold from sleep to the diurnal state when recollecting dreams, they will begin to emerge in day consciousness in the middle of our occupations and preoccupations. Here lies the clue to developing that very precise form of intuition that manifests as vision.

The effect of this vision is certainly greater than the effect of a dream; the reason is that the imagination which can stand before one's mind in one's wakeful state is naturally stronger than the imagination which was active in one's state of sleep.[3]

This is the reason why visions are vouchsafed to the spiritually attuned or increase when a person meditates a lot. Rishis and dervishes are continually contacting wonderful beings.

Every soul has visions at very important times in his life, but there comes a time
of the clearness of the soul when every dream becomes a vision; and it can
increase to such an extent that a person may have twenty visions in the day.

As man evolves he naturally ceases to look down on earth, but looks up to
the cosmos, the heavens. And so if one wants to seek heaven one must change
the direction of looking.[4]

Vision is generally vouchsafed to those who are pious, righteous in their
action, and of tranquil mind; for an untranquil mind is just like moving water,
which does not take a clear reflection. The view is often coloured by the
personality of the one who sees. His favour or disfavour, his liking or
disliking, stands between the eyes of the one who sees and the one who is
seen. Therefore sometimes innocent people have a better understanding of a
person than clever people with deceitful minds.

However, one should not assess the spiritual rank of a person on the
strength of his gift of vision; and those claiming such rank are in for
some serious deflation.

A person may have gone far on the spiritual path, and he may not have visions.
Visions are a temperament. There is a type of person, a visionary type,
imaginative, dreamy, interested in dreams and whims, and if he is spiritual, the
same type produces real visions. It also comes to those who have gone through
a long illness, who are perhaps abnormal in mind or weak in body.

When visions reveal conditions in the heavenly spheres, they qualify
for the term *revelation*.

It is the opening of the sight to a higher plane of one's being.

When the soul is clear from all earthly shadows then heavenly pictures appear
upon the curtain of man's heart more clearly than one's eyes can see.

What did Murshid experience during those early hours of samadhi as
his consciousness gradually recovered from the sleep in the night of
time, the sense of a more and more individualized "I exist" while it
descended through the spheres of vibration and light? Impressions can
be culled from scattered references, since his metaphysics is always
reflections and experience defying description.

The unseen, incomprehensible and imperceptible life becomes gradually
known, by first becoming audible and then visible. It is the outcome of
vibrations which manifested in radiant atoms. As the fine waves of vibrations
produce sound, so the gross waves produce light. Activities in the light of
intelligence cause the light of the abstract at the time when the abstract sound
turns into light.

What Murshid calls abstract light is no doubt what Gregory of Nyssa,

Simeon the Theologian, Jakob Boehme, and St. John of the Cross called "uncreated light," which is no doubt the *Chaitanya* of the Vedas and the *Nur al Anwar* of al Ghazali, the light upon a light of the Qur'an. One may indeed experience in meditation a fragmentation taking place within the ocean of light in the formation of eddies, whirlpools of light, like the *galganim* seen by Ezekiel, envisioned as the wheels of the divine chariot, the *Merkaba*.

Meditating on different spheres, Murshid experienced a fanning out of rays at the Arwah level from the unbroken collective light beyond. Above the plane of Arwah, light is just pure effulgence; there are no structures, rays, or colors; and beyond, just the light of pure intelligence that becomes luminous consciousness.

At the source from which the rays of light start they do not start singly, separate from each other; but it is a collective light; at every step forward it separates more, until at its end it takes the form of a separate ray.

The vortices of light represent focalizations of the original undifferentiated effulgence breaking up at the first stage into planetary beings of light. The Sufis call the archangel of the sun Prince Huraksh.

The real sun is light itself. But as there is a point which is the central vortex of light, we call that point the sun.

Murshid looks upon the physical sun as the crystallization of abstract light. On a larger scale he envisions the unbroken fabric of abstract light, of which the firmament is a star-studded network, broken up by wider spaces. Murshid is speaking about:

atoms which existed before the sun. It is the centralizing of the all-pervading radiance that made the sun, and the atoms afterwards became different from the atoms which existed before.

With the feeling of I-ness the innate power of the Absolute, so to speak, pulled itself together; . . . thus the all-pervading radiance formed its center, the Center which is the divine spirit or the Nur, in Sufi terms called Arwah.[5]

There are moments in our meditation when we remember our solar origin. It is a memory concealed in the unconscious, more especially in the collective unconsicious, which is communicated even at the cellular level. It is an inherited memory, since the planet, of which the body is made, is itself an agglomeration of cooled gases from the sun. At the soul level there is a memory of the soul, which is part of the soul of the sun. Having interpenetrated the flaming fabric of the sun, this now gravitates at some distance from its original home, while still being connected with its origin. Moreover, the soul of the sun, called Prince

Huraksh, is a fraction of the soul of the galaxy Milky Way. Further, it is a network of hierarchically related luminous consciousnesses, each deriving its light from the one hierarchically above it and radiating it to those hierarchically subordinated.

The fire that comes from coal or wood is in reality the part of the sun that is in them; and when the soul qualities arise in the heart of a man and show themselves, this proves that it is the divine part in him that rises, like the flame in the fire.

Remember the intense concentration of light in the center of the heavens; the nostalgia of souls for the light, from which they originated and of which they are a part, draws them inevitably into an aura or halo surrounding what is known as the Throne of the King of Kings, so great that all beings are part of his being.

The angelic souls, who are in direct touch with the spirit of God . . . whose food is divine light, make around the divine Spirit an aura which is called the Highest Heaven.[6]

They fly around this light like the moth around the lantern. . . . They live and move and have their being in the divine light.[7] Therefore in the angelic heavens which is the sphere of radiance, the soul collects the atoms of radiance.[8]

On the other hand, this nostalgia is outweighed by the desire for autonomy, and also by the desire to experience reality more concretely instead of only in principle: to contemplate the image that one embodies in some other oneself, cast into form and set among the fantastic prodigality of multiplicity. Thus there is a concentration and a scattering of souls.

The light which is the eternal spirit spreads forth its rays, each ray containing attributes differing in quality and quantity under the influence of time and space. Each ray is equally the potential soul of a thing or living being. Each ray is detached, and each distinguishes itself as an individual soul, separate from the Universal Spirit, upon which, nevertheless their existence as an individual depends. This world of rays has been called the world of Fereshtaha, or angels. In this Heaven are souls that will proceed further, and also souls who have not sufficient desire to manifest further. In ancient tradition the beings of this Heaven are described as spending their lives in listening to the Sound of the Abstract, which is divine music; and in rejoicing in the Divine Light, the Nur; and therefore these are depicted as holding harps and trumpets, or flaming torches: the symbols of sound and light.

From out of this conglomeration of sparks that forms a central sun, the

Nur al Anwar, the Light of Lights of the Sufis, or Xvarnah of the Zoroastrians, some sparks shoot out centrifugally, as rays gaining further individuality as they move further and further from their origin.

Riding upon the tidal waves of vibrations and the tranfusing matter, abstract light undergoes a conversion. This is why the Sufi Najm-ud-Din Kubra speaks of the light that descends and the light that ascends. In its descent uncreated light, just like the soul of the planet, breaks up into rays; in its ascent the astral, auric, and further highest bodies are tranfigured so that the souls of men are resurrected, merging finally into the unity of pure undifferentiated effulgence.

Every Atom of the universe, having come from the divine sun, makes every effort to return to it.

But passing through the human condition, something of moment is achieved. Mechanically generated music, however beautiful—in the case of the windharp, for example—can never convey the emotional uplift of composed music because it is at the human stage of evolution that compassion arises. This is what Teilhard de Chardin meant by the word *hominization*. Divine understanding, passing through the human instrument, the confrontation of luminous consciousness with factual reality, becomes wisdom, the end achievement of incarnation.

If the planet is an ocean, then the individual is a drop. But inwardly the planet is a drop in the ocean of man.

Something in us warns of the illusion and self-deception we are laying ourselves open to by disclosing our visions or representations of the glories of the heavens. They may seem to be the best recollection we can summon from the memory of the ages transmitted to us and through us. But how different these things looked before we tried to pigeonhole them in our minds' space-time reference system! To make them comparable with the human experience we had to distort our vision by refracting reality into space and time and into our concept of solid matter and form; whereas in reality every spark of light or vibration is part of every other spark or wave. Now when we wish to remember them they seem barely recognizable as we try to recall how they appeared in the cosmic perspective. Everyone is everywhere, at the same time and in the same space, every being in each being. Every being is the totality and at the same time a part of the totality. The knowledge of God is mirrored in a million mirrors which simply evidence the amplification of a knowledge which is complete, beyond any mirroring or amplification. For example, radio waves are everywhere in the ether, yet you have to use a receiver to hear them because of the limitated range of the human ear. But where there is no limitation there is no need of lens or mirror or receiver. Thus the entire universe appears to be like a palace of mirrors, a hall of echoes studded with vortices of cosmic consciousness which, having segregated themselves partially from the overall perspective, are caught up in the mirroring or echoing and therefore distort and misconstrue the vibrations that are being resonated or the light that is being refracted or the archetype that is being exemplified. It is also a mirage appearing to confused minds stubbornly arguing illusive opinions.

And yet, and yet . . . could it be that the distorted impoverished recollection might lever our ponderous thoughts back into their original perspective? Are we going through an experience now? Together? Do we not go through an experience when we try to remember a dream? And who knows what is remembered by other parts of us while that part of ourselves which we think we know thinks it remembers the things it thinks it remembers? So let us once more wake from the oblivion which shrouds our memory with the immediate environment and with the ephemeral moment into awareness of the miracle of the genesis of our existence.

In our descent we have traversed the sphere of roving uncreated light beams, pulverizing into pyrotechnics of sparks whence our souls emerged into consciousness. Remember! It seemed at first like a plethora of unending dove-tailed rainbows fanning out into rays, crisscrossing in kaleidoscopic flickering figures: pure splendor. Then, suddenly, as you shifted your focus, tidal waves intertwining with tidal waves crashed into overwhelming breakers at the surface of the cosmic ocean. Rainbows float shimmering through the sprayed galaxies of effervescent ephemeral atoms below, churned up by the heaving cosmic spasms, a diaphanous glow in the dark abyss of nothingness.

At the level of light the same scene is transposed in terms of souls. Souls may be conceived as luminous focal centers of consciousness, but they appear as light. Now the luminous consciousness of all creatures reproduces invisibly the same magic pattern: Each spark becomes a focal center around which others gravitate and each gravitates around a yet higher vortex of consciousness into a gigantic interplay of consciousness functioning at the level called Arwah, where we are aware of the ebb and flow of creation. At what appears like the inhaling of the divine breath there is a convergence or centering of the light activity, as in the formation of the sun. At what appears like the exhaling of the divine breath, the light mass of the sun is broken up in fragments.

Are souls made of light? Or are souls vibrations? This question betrays the limitation of our human understanding, as we try to represent things in terms of what we know physically, even if called uncreated light or akashic vibrations. The soul is a new condition of reality emerging as we descend to the plane of Arwah, varying in its manifestation according to the vantage point with which one approaches it. In fact, it may be seen as pure energy loaded with consciousness, representing a further step in the vector of evolution which marks a descent from higher spheres, rather than the vector generally considered, which is the evolutionary procession from the geosphere to the noosphere. The word *involution* would be appropriate. Musically minded people will note the difference between electronic music and Brahms, in that a factor is missing in the former—compassion, which marks a further step in the forward march of life. Similarly, the abstract reality of the spheres of Wahdat and Wahdaniat becomes hominized, to borrow Teilhard's term, at the Arwah level, through the advent of the soul.

Souls appear, souls after souls, generated and incubated from each other, legions of souls interacting with each other, billions interfusing and compounding with one another like proliferating cells run amuk with sinister alacrity. Contemplate the spectrum of consciousness converging like beams, scattering like sparks, filtering out the vibrations of the symphony of the spheres, like a ray of light riding a tidal wave: consciousness rising high at the dawning of individual awareness, as the soul of souls comminutes itself into infintesimal focal centers—consciousnesses counterchanging, sparking one another off into a phantasmagoria of optical phenomena in the cosmic harmony of the heaven, sometimes even challenging, refuting, rejecting one another, confronting and vying, in the dimension of understanding.

Thus out of the plane of Wahdaniat, where there are only cosmic vibrations and rays, emerges the plane where individuality has reached a further stage: the sphere of Arwah, the birth place of individual souls.

Indeed, a change has been brought about in the cosmos: Each note of the symphony has become a being as it grows in awareness and ventures into greater autonomy. Each note with its train of overtones conjugates, more and more intentionally and of its own free will, with other notes, forming chords, which themselves merge and coalesce. Chords harmonize in consonance and resonance with kindred chords, attuning with one another as they take over individually the onus of ensuring the overall harmony of the entire symphony, resounding with one another in a wealth of inexhaustible variations.

There is not one inch of space where no beings exist. . . . The light with which an object . . . shows itself is . . . more clear to our inner perception and it is more dim to our outer sight.[9]

Our ability to peer into the heavens is comparable to our ability to espy the stars while the sun is above the horizon. Imagine: It is our own light that conceals the light of heavenly beings from our sight!

It is the glow and radiance of the human body which is so great that it hides the beings in space. In reality they are all visible; but the radiance of man's form stands out and hides all that is less visible compared with it.[10]

There were moments when the Master, surrounded by trusted pupils, revealed some of the more hidden experiences vouchsafed to an adept. The vision of being on higher planes may take place on the astral or angelic planes, depending upon the level of the residence of the being thus appearing to our sight and the level that we are able to reach. It is rare, but possible, that very high beings should materialize on the astral plane, but it must be as unpleasant for them as deep-sea diving for humans, because of the pressure of the astral matter.

Astral vision is the seeing of the unseen beings, such as spirits, jinns, fairies, or angels. In an astral vision a relation or a friend may appear to a person and tell him something about the other side of life, before another saint or sage may appear, who may guide him still further; to another an angel may appear, as Gabriel to Moses, and may give him the message of God. One may see the vision of one's friends, relations, past and present. One may see faces never seen before and yet faces that have once existed in the world. One may see the vision of his Rasul, his Saviour, his Lord, Master, or Prophet, or Teacher.

Murshid's dreams became more and more vivid, and included not only premonitions of his mission but encounters with higher beings in the different spheres, and masters.

As a person advances spiritually, his dreams become more beautiful and prophetic.

In order to be attuned to the vision, the seer has to focus himself on the relevant level; for example, for astral vision he has to experience

himself as being ethereal, floating in an unreal world in wide spaces
having a dimension different from the physical. This is done by
turning away from the outer world and discovering a space within.

What is it that . . . debars man from the vision of objects and beings in the
unseen world? . . . The next world is the same world as this, and this world is
the same as the next; only, what is veiled from our eyes . . . we call it the
unseen world. But in so far as man is capable of seeing the seen world, to that
extent he is also capable of observing the unseen world, on condition that he
first sees and observes his own unseen world. And why a person does not
observe the unseen world is that he is accustomed to observe only what is
before him; he never turns within to see what is within him.[11]

To communicate on levels above the astral, one has to remove not only
the consciousness of the physical environment but any vestige of
thought connected with it, and recollect one's angelic origin.

When one ponders upon heavenly conditions, angelic beings are
drawn to manifest because one is vibrating at their wavelength. But, as
Swedenborg says, the angel must use the substance of our creative
imagination to reveal itself.

When the visions are clear it is the moment when the soul is clear from all
earthly shadows and therefore heavenly pictures, so to speak, appear upon the
curtain of man's heart. Every unseen form that we see in a vision, be it of a
spirit, fairy or angel, or of a teacher, sage, or saint, is according to man's
evolution. As highly evolved a person is, so high is his vision. Sometimes he
attracts the object of his vision, sometimes the object of his vision wishes to
manifest to him, and sometimes he creates the object of his vision before him.

This would answer the question why the Chinese seers picture Buddha
with Chinese features, and the Indians with Indian features, and
medieval European seers picture Christ with European traits, even
Anglo-Saxon.

*There is a language of forms and symbols. When one does not know this the
visions to him make no meaning, and there cannot be made a standard of this
language. Yet spiritual vision is not necessarily symbolical, sometimes it is as
clear as it manifests on the surface.*

The visions of a master can only be captured from a very high
sphere. Those of prophets are understandably extremely rare, normally
only vouchsafed to hermits living under austere conditions, or very
evolved beings, living a very pure life.

The traditions of the world are mostly based upon visions. The vision of
Valmiki brought Rama, the great king and prophet of Hindus; Solomon,

Jamshyd, Joseph, even Abraham, the Father of religions, were known and accepted as prophets by reason of their visions; the foundation of the life of Jesus Christ was the vision of the Virgin Mary; the beginning of the prophethood of Mohammed was the vision of Amina, his mother.

Murshid gives the clue: one has to create the accommodation within oneself. This accommodation for the savior manifested itself physically as stigmata in Saint Francis of Assisi. We have to distinguish between that which is:

self-created, and that which comes by response. For instance, a devotee by the fullness of his devotion may create the picture of the Savior in his heart or one who is responsive, in his full response, and waiting, may attract the spirit of the Savior. Every vision springs forth from the heart of man with as fine and delicate a form as his own personality, and in as picturesque a form as his artistic capabilities, and in such metaphor, or so symbolical as his poetic gift. Those who have seen or otherwise perceived such things and beings have described them to us in the form of legends. They have called them fairies and spirits and jinns and by many other names, and artists have also helped people to form a certain idea of such beings. But this does not mean that it is all imagination and that nothing exists save that which we can perceive through our organs of sense. Everything shows itself by its own light. Our eyes are capable of seeing certain forms, and there are other forms which our eyes cannot see.

The muridan (disciples) of Sufi pirs (elders) and murshids (spiritual preceptors) are taught to keep the picture of their teacher continually before their minds, so that the teacher's being avers itself to be the tangible answer to their questions. This enables the teacher to communicate the answer at a distance by changing his countenance, which the pupil then perceives as giving a clue to his problem.

To them, at times when it is necessary, a warning or a guidance appears in the form of that ideal as a vision. Those who master Tassawur, meaning the concrete production of the ideal in thought, their first experience is that every form they see seems covered with the form of their ideal. This is the first step toward progress, which in the Sufi term is named Fana-fi-Sheikh.

This vision appears just like the audition referred to earlier, "inside," as one places (as Buddha says) "a sentinel at the doors of perception."

The purer the soul is, the clearer the vision becomes. It is the bowl of Jamshyd, the seven-ringed cup, which is the head with seven openings. And in this head the vision rises, and shows him all whose sight is keen.

When one becomes sensitive, one becomes aware, for example, of the shadow of the earth ingrained in the expression of many passers-by in the street. Imagine, the very same and sole divine reality may be reflected by an earth-bound being in the form of a dark shadow upon his brow, and assumes in a being who has become immaculate in his thoughts and feelings a crystal-clear luminosity.

Murshid outlines two methods of developing the art of seership: One is turning the eyes within so that the light of the soul will be filtered into a lattice work encompassing the impressions projected upon earth from the heavenly spheres.

The reflection in the looking glass, the shadow upon the earth, the reflection in the water, are different from one another. The shadow upon the earth is dark, because the earth has no light, is dark. These are the external shadows. There are also the shadows and reflections within: What is called clairvoyance is to allow the light within to pass through one so that these reflections are seen within.

Then there are the internal shadows, the shadows that fall upon the mind, all the shadows of the earth.

The other methods consist in gazing into space, setting the focus of one's eyes at infinity, but using the eyes as lamps rather than organs of perception, as the Tibetan monks do. It means resisting any temptation to view the physical scene, which would, of course, immediately focus the eyes to the range of the object, thus conditioning one's sight.

The shadow falls upon the earth, it falls also upon the space. And there it is much clearer. In the space the colours of the elements are reflected. It is very difficult to see this reflection in the space, because our eyes are so much accustomed to look at the things of the earth that they have become material, and they do not see that which is finer. The mystics, the Sufis, have ways of developing the eyes. They show you ways of looking into the space, that make the eyes capable of seeing what is reflected there. From these reflections the past, present, and future can be told, and all that surrounds a person.

Following are practices observed by anchorites which develop vision:

All that one sees during the day and night is not what one intended to see, but what one is compelled by the life around us to see. That is why the thinkers and sages of the East in ancient times used to have mantles put over their heads, so that they did not see anything or anybody and could control their sight. The Sufis of ancient times used to keep their heads covered like this for many years, and in doing so they developed such powers that their one glance would penetrate rocks and mountains. It is only control of the sight. Yogis in all ages have worked not only with their minds but even with their eyes, attaining such a stability of glance that they could direct their sight to anything they wished to examine or penetrate.

To develop this "second sight," one has to practice assiduously, following the different stages of the method in their sequence: First of all, turn within, as previously described, which not only means turning one's attention away from the senses, but also pivoting and converging the physical eyeball upwards, which exercises an action upon the third eye.

In order to get an insight into the unseen world the first thing is to open our own sight to the unseen being that is within us. It only means opening the third eye, as it is called in occult terms.[12]

In order to see into the intuitive centres one has to turn the eyes back, turn the eyes within; then the same eyes which are able to see without are able to see within. But that is only one phase of seeing.[13]

The next phase consists in centering oneself in the third eye, using the physical eyes somewhat as an engine uses the railway tracks, without allowing the activity of the physical eyes to draw away one's attention in the slightest from the impressions drawn up into the beam of the third eye. Then the physical scene of nature seems to be adumbrated with a silver lining, or even a golden one, like a strange kind of phosphorescence or magical glow.

Sometimes that third eye sees through these two eyes and then the same eyes see things more clearly than they would otherwise. By the help of the third eye one's eyes can penetrate through the wall of physical existence and see into the minds of people, into the words of people, and even further. When one begins to see, what happens first is that everything one's eyes see has a deeper meaning, a greater significance than one knew before. Every movement, every gesture, the form, features, voice, words, expression, atmosphere, all become expressive of the person's nature and character.[14]

And every little detail is clear, whereas what we see with our eyes is mostly only the outline.[15]

Through any study we take up, no matter what it be, we shall be able to find out that when we look at things they first appear in a certain form, but as we go on looking at them they appear differently.[16]

According to some holistic thinkers a part of the energy of the electrostatic field of the body is continual by being transmuted into a phosphorescent shroud. However, for esotericists, it is the fragmentation of the cherubic light before it sets off the disintegration of the physical atom into rays. Maybe the day will come when one will be able to confirm that the aura is the interference pattern (compare

Newton's rings) of the ascending and descending light. This idea is corroborated by the fact that a person who gives the impression of being radiant—a purely subjective impression—invariably radiates a brighter aura, which signifies that where there is such a transformation of atmosphere, the physical factor is influenced by a psychological factor. Furthermore, it has been ascertained that adepts practicing with light radiate most intensely during meditation. This is ostensibly an application of the cosmic law that any function operated consciously is intensified.

This is the method advocated to develop the ability to see auras. One has to learn to overcome the localizing action of the physical scene into the retina. Then they appear as colors.

The visible atmosphere is called the aura. Those who do not feel its vibrations sometimes see it in the form of colours or light.[17]

There is no doubt that, as the sight becomes keen, first the colours of different elements working in nature manifest to the view; secondly, the atmosphere that is created around man, which is composed of semi-material atoms also becomes manifest.[18]

Nevertheless, Murshid warns against the temptation of occult phenomena, and that seeing auras is no indication of spiritual evolution. And it must be reiterated:

There are some quite unevolved people who see auras for the same reasons that some very unevolved people also communicate with spirits, which is really something that only an evolved person should venture upon. But they are made like that by nature, and it is the same as someone who has never been trained in the technique of art yet he draws a beautiful picture. It is in him, it is a gift, it is his finer soul and his nervous temperament that are susceptible to finer vibrations.[19]

Just as different degrees of the vibrations of the atmosphere have a distinct influence upon the person who perceives them, so the different colours of the aura have their particular effect upon those who see this aura.[20]

A selfless person tends to scatter the atoms of the astral and auric substance of his being, causing it to radiate, while the more selfish person condenses the atoms within the confines of his body. Consequently, the auras of the more selfless people assume a kind of crystal-clear transparency and therefore become more visible than those of the denser beings.

The next stage consists in displacing the "observation post" backward, as it were, to look as if one were peering from the deeper or loftier recesses of one's being into a space that transpires through physical reality.

The other phase of seeing within cannot be seen by the eyes; it is the heart that sees. And when one is able to see that way, the pain and pleasure and joy and sorrow of every person that comes before one manifest in one's own heart; one actually sees it.[21]

And the fourth stage consists in displacing the "observation post" still further back into the soul. This happens when one is able to identify oneself with one's soul.

Even the heart is a telescope which helps one to perceive and to conceive all that one seeks. Yet . . . it is the soul that sees.[22]

The great moment comes when one is able to forgo any instrument, whether physical eyes or ears or third eye, and rely directly upon the vision of the soul.

Although these instruments give the soul knowledge of things clearly, these instruments at the same time limit the power of the soul.

When this happens, the glance acquires an uncanny power, which can be observed by watching the eyes of the seers.

The eyes of the seer become a sword which cuts open, so to speak, all things, including the hearts of men, and see clearly through all they contain.

Murshid gave his disciples numerous practices with light, including visualizations of the sun, crescent moon, stars, rainbow and crystals refracting light. Pupils diligently practicing these concentrations taken to the point of contemplation were sometimes transfigured beyond recognition; no doubt it was the underlying dwelling upon the sparkling luminosity of Murshid that triggered the phenomenon, unfolding vision.

CHAPTER 13

Whence and Whither

THE CELESTIAL SPHERES

I first believed without any hesitation in the existence of the soul and then I wondered about the secret of its nature. I persevered and strove in search of the soul, and found at last that I myself was the cover over my own soul. I realized that that in me which believed and that in me which wondered, that which persevered in me, and that which was found at last, was no other than my soul. I thanked the darkness that brought me to the light, and I valued the veil which prepared for me the vision in which I saw myself reflected, the vision produced in the mirror of my soul. Since then I have seen all souls as my soul, and realized my soul as the soul of all; and what bewilderment it was when I realized that I alone was, if there were anyone; that I am whatever and whoever exists; and that I shall be whoever there will be in the future. And there was no end to my happiness and joy. Verily, I am the seed and I am the root, and I am the fruit of this tree of life.—V, 137

Murshid was discovering the sphere where cosmic light becomes personalized as souls. Later on, many of the pupils of the Master remember him sitting under a tree in the garden of Fazal Manzil, our home near Paris, lost in eternal consciousness, surrounded by a group of a few mureeds rapt by his words as he told about the experience of a soul in the different spheres, describing these planes with an authenticity that spelled a genuine memory. Here was no book learning. The recounting of these reminiscences no doubt catalyzed the memory of many of those present. In fact, it all seemed so very familiar. Indeed, is not the art of meditation that of the recovery of the Ariadnean thread of memory of the reality one had forgotten by confining oneself to the immediate environment?

The Master was describing his reminiscences of the descent of the soul through the angelic and jinn spheres to the earth plane, and then its return.

Do you remember the birth of your soul at the beginning of time, like a light ignited by another light? Each soul switches other souls into existence as a candle may kindle innumerable candles. Even so does life call life into life that it may sprout and thrive, fulfilling itself in its inexorable advance, breaking through ever more concrete horizons of reality, requiring ever more ingenuity from the new-born soul.

A problem in our minds is exactly what we mean by individuality.

All that exists on the earth plane has its existence on the higher planes too; but what is individual? What one calls an individual is a conception of our imagination; and the true meaning of that conception will be realized on the day when the ultimate truth throws its light upon life.

So when that ray we think of as man's indiviual consciousness merges into its origin, the divine consciousness working through him, he is carried beyond himself, he is able to see what God sees; but as soon as he circumscribes himself again within his notion of himself, then that which he saw no longer makes sense because he has cut himself away from the divine consciousness. Seen from the vantage point of the sun, the rays are extensions of itself; but if one isolates oneself into the consciousness of a particular ray, it appears as a cylindrical volume in which the sun is threaded. This accounts for the fact that the mystic, at a certain stage of realization, may think he is the eyes through which God sees, and at a more advanced stage realizes that he is the divine glance.

The connection between the consciousness and the soul is in the connection between the sun and the ray. The ray is formed by the activity of the sun shooting forth its light. The activity of the consciousness shoots forth its ray, which is called the soul. Activity in a certain part of the consciousness makes the part project itself towards manifestation. The ray is the sun; but to distinguish the ray as a part, distinct in itself, longer or shorter, stronger or fading away, according to the state of activity is the basic illusion.

It is capacity which makes the soul a soul; otherwise it would be spirit.

The sun may be likened to the spirit, and its entry through the window, which is a capacity and which gives it a form—triangular, square, or whatever it may be—may be called the soul. The soul becomes identified with qualities and merits because of the capacity through which it expresses itself; if not it would be spirit.

In fact, it is only the identification with its limitations that causes the soul to visualize itself as an individual entity, for no sooner does it free itself from its self-reflection than it realizes itself as the totality.

The soul is an individual portion of the all-pervading consciousness. It is undivided because it is the absolute Being; it is completely filled with the whole Existence. The portion of it that is reflected by a certain name or form becomes comparatively more conscious of the object reflected in it than of all other objects. Our minds and body, being reflected upon a portion of the all-pervading consciousness, make that part of consciousness an all-pervading soul which in reality is a Universal spirit. This individual soul experiences the external world through the medium of the bodies reflected in it, namely our mind and body. The soul in itself alone is no other than consciousness, which is all-pervading. But when the same consciousness is caught in a limitation through being surrounded by elements, in that state of captivity it is called soul.

The intelligence of its original aspect is the essence of life, the spirit, or God.

But when this intelligence is caught in an accommodation such as body and mind, its original nature of knowing then knows, and the knowing intelligence becomes consciousness. The difference between consciousness and the soul is that the soul is like a mirror, and the consciousness is a mirror which shows a reflection in it.

Out of Himself, God produced His manifestation, His means of becoming conscious, and now each manifestation of Himself calls out "I," not knowing its true Self.

What dies is the view that a soul has of itself as an individual.

The soul may be considered to be a condition of God, a condition which makes the Only Being limited for a time. A soul only exists as an individual soul from the time that it shoots out as a current through the different spheres until the time when it goes back and meets its original being. A new ray vivifies each incarnation; for the action of the soul is not to go out and to come half-way back and to go out and again from there. The action of the soul is the same as the action of the breath. It goes out fully and it is drawn in fully. As the air, by being caught in water, becomes a bubble for the moment, and as the waves of the air, being caught in a hollow vessel, become a sound, so Intelligence, being caught by the mind and body, becomes the soul. It is only a condition of the intelligence which is the soul. In reality before this journey the soul is not a soul, nor does the soul remain as a soul after this journey.

If one could see oneself as a continuity in change one would be aware of one's immortality. Imagine the consciousness of a drop in the fountain that got more distinctly separated, thus envisioning itself as a reality per se, only to lose this point suddenly when it merged in the pool; compare this with the consciousness of the drops that, remaining closer to the center, were more aware of the continuity of their being throughout the flow. The same could apply to the waves of the sea, the sparks of fireworks, or the vibration of the symphony of the spheres.

In the fountain there are two kinds of drops: the one constantly touching the source as goal; the other rises, breaks on the way, and so drops in the source disconnected on the way. The latter is the life of the people who simply live and die. There is no gap in reality; it is only a temporary condition of the rising of the water that makes a space between two waves; these two waves are a temporary condition of the water of the sea. The water of the sea remains, but these waves formed for a moment rise and fall again.

As people are so used to the understanding peculiar to the mind, they have no clue as to what is the understanding of the soul. The soul thinks that it is a person, and its awakening comes when it realizes it is God. The soul longs to be free, but, in seeking freedom, it binds itself in the ego and only in the divine consciousness is it free. The communion of the souls is the realization of identity. The presumption of difference is the crucifixion of the soul. "I distinguish myself from you," is the hell of the ego. The punishment of the soul is to be set in a corner in deep isolation.

Therefore the soul is really immortal; it is the consciousness of the individuality which is transient.

No soul perishes; the soul was not born to perish. If the spirit is eternal, then the souls are eternal. If the sun is eternal, the rays are eternal because the sun and the rays are not two things; rays are the unfoldment of the sun and souls are the unfolding of the spirit. The soul has no birth, no death, no beginning, no end. Sin cannot touch it, nor can virtue exalt it. Wisdom cannot open it up, nor can ignorance darken it. It has been always and always it will be. This is the very being of man, and all else is its cover, like a globe on the light. The soul's unfoldment comes from its own power, which ends in its breaking through the ties of the lower planes. It is free by nature, and looks for freedom during its captivity. All the Holy Beings of the world have become so by freeing the soul, its freedom being the only object there is in life. Our very souls are angels. Every soul passes through the angelic heavens; in other words, every soul is an angel before it touches the earthly plane. Those who do not become human beings remain angels.

They are in the highest glory.

Those who are satisfied in the angelic sphere remain there. There are others who feel uncomfortable until they have penetrated into another sphere. Some are not content in that sphere either and look for another. Those who settle in the angelic sphere have exhausted their creative powers in manifesting as angels. If they had greater power they would certainly have gone further, even to the physical plane, and preferably would have manifested as human beings; for the desire of every soul is to reach the culmination in manifestation and that culmination is the stage of the human plane.

Thus one may distinguish between two sorts of angels: the *Fereshta*, who are absorbed in the nostalgia for beauty, and the *Hur* or *Malik*, which is the state the human being undergoes on his return journey at the moment when he reenters the angelic plane. Each soul ventures to project itself as far as it can.

To reach the human condition souls have to pass through the angelic and jinn spheres. The latter is the realm of ideas, of creative imagination, of genius. Whether souls become jinns or humans depends upon the strength of their nostalgia for tangible reality, or a purpose they have to fulfill.

It is as if a thousand birds had started from Paris for England, and some went as far as Rouen, where they remained, as they liked the place; and enjoying themselves, they forgot about England. Some went to Le Havre and stopped there; some crossed the Channel and arrived in England. The ones who stayed in Rouen did not have far to go when they returned to Paris, but the ones who reached England had farther to go on the return journey.[1]

When the desire for more experience urges the soul on further than the angelic plane, it reaches the plane of the jinns (called *peri* or *gulman* by the Persians). It is this further descent of the soul that is epitomized in the legend of Adam's banishment from paradise. The wish for more experience causes the soul to leave the world of the angels and go to the astral or physical plane.

In the further step—incarnation on the physical plane in the form of man—the purpose of creation is fulfilled.

Man is Ashraf al Mukhlaqat, the Khalif of Creation. All angels were command-ed to bow before him, but while all the other angels prostrated themselves, Azazil (Lucifer) alone rebelled, saying: I have been the chief of the angels. I will never bow before this thing made of earth.[2]

Therefore, a Fereshta has not reached the adulthood of man; but the Hur or Malik has, since he passed through the state of man. Yet children and infants who die also come to spiritual maturity, often on the jinn plane and sometimes on the plane of the angels.

The little that we are able to glean of the angels trickles over the threshold of our memory. A few beings entertain a more vivid memory of preincarnate states than others.

One soul is perhaps more impressed by the angelic heavens, and that impres-sion has remained more deeply with it throughout the whole journey; another is more impressed by the sphere of the jinns, and that impression lasts through the whole journey. Then there is another soul who is not deeply impressed with the angelic heavens or the world of the jinn, and that soul does not know of these worlds; he comes through blindly, and is only interested in things of the earth when he reaches it.[3]

Reminiscence of the angelic plane is not comparable with recollection of a past event experienced in terms of substance, form, time, space, sensory impressions, mental associations, emotions of covetousness; rather, it filters into our awareness as a revelation. We may know something perfectly well that we are nevertheless unable to describe. Reminiscence comes unexpectedly from "hearing the call of higher spheres," no doubt an answer to our homesickness.

A black-out marked our crossing the threshold of creation in order to save us from the shock of a sudden switch of focus, but the conse-quence has been a gap in our memory.

Sometimes impressions are communicated within our momentary

consciousness by the direct initiative of angels who, having themselves gone through the human condition and risen to their present vision, wish to be helpful to the denizens of the planet. These are the Hur and Malik.

The Soul comes with closed eyes.

It is the work of the souls who return from the earth to communicate with the earth very often, and it is such angels who are generally known to men.[4]

Such visitations occur particularly frequently when one is about to die; just at the moment when one is poised on the threshold, one may communicate with both worlds, albeit in a somewhat nebulous way.

There is another aspect of the contact with the angels, and that is at the time of death. Many have seen in their lives the angels of death, yet when death's call comes some have seen them in human form. Others have not seen them, but have heard them speak.[5]

The ancient belief was that after a dead person is put into his grave and buried, two angels come to ask him questions, and by this cross-examination to prove their arguments for and against. Their names are Munkir and Nakir.

Often a discussion takes place between those who keep the record of the good deeds and those who record the evil deeds. The former do not believe in the evil deeds because they are only conscious of man's goodness; they cannot believe that one who is good can be bad also. In Sufi terms these two are called the angels of Khair and Khar.[6]

We often wonder whether beings in the higher spheres know what is going on upon the earth.

Do they know of the conditions of the earth? If they care to.

To understand our understanding, they have to borrow our minds, work through our consciousness. This is precisely what is done by the Fereshta, those who never incarnated. But they do not reveal themselves to us or communicate their views since they do not wish to involve themselves with earthly conditions.

Angels who have never manifested as men on earth, only experience life on earth by the medium of other minds and bodies, which by their evolution come closer to the angelic heavens. They take these as their instruments, and at times reflect themselves in them, and at times have them reflected in themselves. This is not obsession, but inspiration.[7]

But to experience the Hur and Malik, one has to let oneself be hoisted from one's understanding to their understanding, one has to wend one's way into their souls, into a different time–space reference. For example, what seemed to be the immensity of space appears at this level to be immensity of consciousness. In the human condition one thinks that one is experiencing something, but in the angelic plane the universe does the experiencing; in the human condition one thinks one understands, but here it is the divine mind that does the understanding. As the angels have no guile, they can see things with the clarity of the disarming truthfulness of the innocent.

The relation of angels to human beings is that of a little child to a grown-up person; they can help human beings as an infant can help its elders.[8]

People wished to know from Hazrat Inayat Khan, "What do angels look like?" Those who have, at exceptional moments, had visions of angels clothed them in a form of their own imagination and heard the voice of the angels in their own language.

We are accustomed to consider every form like our own; therefore, when we picture angels, fairies, or ghosts, we picture them like ourselves. The fairies of the Chinese have Chinese features, the fairies of the Russians wear Russian hats. The form we imagine covers the angelic form.[9]

For instance, the angel Gabriel spoke to Moses in the Hebrew language, and to Mohammad in Arabic. One would ask, which was the language of the angel Gabriel, Arabic or Hebrew? Neither Arabic nor Hebrew was the language of Gabriel; his language was the language of the soul and the soul knows the language of the soul; it is when a person interprets what he hears, even to himself, that he clothes the words he hears in his own language. When the Spirit descended upon the twelve apostles they began to speak all languages, and the meaning of this is, that when they were inspired by the angelic world, by the . . . Holy Ghost . . . they heard before the men spoke to them.[10]

Untold numbers of personal witnesses, the scriptures, folklore, abound with testimonies to encounters with visions and auditions of angels. If only we would tune in to the sensitivity of our inner eye and ear, we would discover worlds of beings so numerous that we would be staggered. They are flying, floating, roaming, leaping all around us in the entire scene of the universe near and far. Like Alice's Wonderland, an enchanted world of fascinating, inspiring beings would emerge; brownies popping their heads out of crevices in the earth, pixies dancing in the grass, gnomes peering out of trees, undines surfacing in the brook, or nymphs out of the sea; salamanders wrestling with the flames and sylphs skimming the whistling wind, hovering over the clouds; thunder devas of the elements in a storm or the elves that hover above a whole landscape and the mountain gods haloed over the peaks; the archangels of the planets and galaxies, and also simply those angels that are the souls of men.

Angels visit in a dream or a vision; angels are attracted by celebrations, lovemaking, catastrophes, meditation, the moment of death, or whenever there is a call for help. Archangels appeared to the Virgin Mary, Abraham, Zachariah, Mohammed; Seraphim, to Isaiah; Ezekiel saw the denizens of all seven planes and Elijah was advised by the angel of the Lord. Krishna and Vishnu were visited by Narada; the suras and devas greeted Buddha; Christ declared: "Thinkest thou that I cannot now pray to my Father and He shall presently give me more than twelve legions of angels?"[11]

The reason any description of an angel is inadequate is that physical reality is projected onto what we believe is an object, whereas reality at the angelic level is subjective. Swedenborg said: "It is the angel who sees himself through you." Therefore, if you see yourself through him, you will somehow partake of his vision of himself. Ibn Arabi, the great Sufi metaphysician, says, "I see him through his eyes and he sees me through my eyes." Reality in its continually or recurrently recreated genesis, as opposed to its relatively petrified condition in physical matter, naturally becomes less distinctive: The edges fall away like a glow, as compared with an incandescent coal: there is no outline.

One cannot give a definite picture of the likeness between those bodies, but they all develop towards the image of man. The physical body is the most distinct and clear; the jinn body is less clear, more phantom-like; and the body of the angel is still less distinct, that is to say less distinct to human eyes.[12]

In order to conceive, to picture, the form or the face of an angel, one needs to become an angel oneself.

The ever changing expressions on a face burst through the limits of the profile. In a face there may be many faces, one cannot pin it down to an outline; even more so with angels.

Our imaginations have the faces we give them . . . our feelings too.[13]

The glow extends beyond the coal, and therefore it appears larger.

The size of the body that the soul brings from the sphere of the jinn is much larger than the size of the physical body, and the size of the . . . body brought by the soul from the angelic heavens is larger still.[14]

The best way to describe the fabric of the angelic bodies is to say they seem like ethereal interwoven meshes of light and, simultaneously, high-frequency waves of pure vibration.

Theirs is a life of illumination and of praise; they are much nearer to the universal, everlasting sound, the universal, eternal light, much nearer to God, than we are. They have luminous bodies, as solid, as concrete, as the light one sees.[15]

Emotionally, they differ from most human beings in their absolute lack of earthly ego. One may discern something of the condition of the angel in infants who come to earth with their angelic qualities, and pass away without having experienced the life of a grown-up man or woman.

The impressions the Master communicated of the heavenly and jinn spheres could be borne out by those human beings who feature these qualities.

Souls on earth retain something of the angelic quality; therefore they readily respond and are attracted without resistance to the innocence, happiness, and goodness of another person. If they knew that it is because this is the original quality of the soul they would develop the same [qualities] in their own being.[16]

In beings who have been able to retain their angelic qualities, yet have been "concretized," "hominized" through incarnation at the human stage, we find our models of spiritual perfection, for they epitomize the next step after death, the condition of the Malik and Hur.

Spirituality, therefore, is the development of the angelic quality; and love of spirituality is the longing for the angelic heavens; it is homesickness.[17]
The soul of a saint and murshid has remained long in the world of the angels, and being more impressed by it . . . it brings with it angelic qualities.[18]

The moments when we experience the emotional condition of the angels stand out indelibly in our lives and certainly represent our partaking in the heavenly glory on a cosmic scale. Our hearts leap at the slightest echo of the ovations in the celestial spheres reaching into our exile, as if our emotions are being churned within by some inexplicable feeling of ecstasy.

The person whose heart is tuned to the pitch of the angelic heavens will show on earth heavenly bliss; therefore the wise seek the association of spiritual beings.[19]

At such moments one is functioning precisely as the angels do; since they are not limited by our mode of perception, based on the polarization of subject and object, they do not perceive as we do in terms of form, but attune themselves to the vibrations of all creatures and all existence. How does one steer oneself in those planes? Simply by tuning to the relevant frequency.

In the angelic heavens there are no distinct impressions; but there is a tuning. The soul is tuned to a certain pitch by the law of vibration, high or low according to the impression it receives from the souls coming back home. In this tuning, it gets, so to speak, a tone and rhythm which directs its path to the world of the jinn.[20]

This we experience when we do not distinguish our egos from all beings and things, but merge with the rhythm of a greater unity, adjusting our pulse to their pulse.

If [the soul] is in tune it takes its place in the music of the heavens as a note in the tune; if it is not in tune it falls short of this, producing discordant effects for itself and for others.[21]

One soul is more harmonious than another, but in the music of the heavens they all fit in, just as in our music we would not want everything to be alike. And the souls who are still out of rhythm will continue to have the choice of becoming harmonious; for there is a choice at every step in the heavens too.[22]

Sensitive humans like to hear music or play music, because we are bound in the dichotomy of the perceiver and the perceived; but do we know what it is like to be music? This is the condition of the angel. This is why Murshid describes them as being vibrations in addition to being light beings.

Souls when they start from the angelic heavens are vibrations.
The picture of the angels that we read of in the scriptures as sitting upon clouds and playing harps is but an expression of a mystical secret. Playing the harp is vibrating harmoniously; the angels have no actual harps, they themselves are the harps; they are living vibrations; they are life itself.[23]

Something of this nature happens to us when we engage in a very high meditation; we are able to hear the music of the spheres only if we cease trying to pick it up through the ears, thinking of ourselves as a center perceiving sound at a distance, but take the plunge and scatter ourselves in the ocean of vibrations, dissolving into and identifying with them. The laws of physical perception do not apply at the angelic level.

Life in the heaven of the angels is one continual music.

Therefore it is that the wise of all ages have called music celestial, a divine art; the reason is that the heaven of the angels is all music; the activity, the repose, and the atmosphere there is all one symphony continually working towards greater and greater harmony. The intoxication that music gives excels all other forms of intoxication. Then imagine the music of the heavens where harmony is in its fulness; man here on earth cannot imagine the joy which that can give. If the experience of that music is known to anyone, it is to the awakened souls whose bodies are here, whose hearts are in the spheres of the jinn and whose souls are in the heaven of the angels; who, while on earth, can experience all the planes of existence. They call the music of the angelic spheres Saut-e Sarmad *and find in it a happiness which carries them to the highest heavens, lifting them from worries and anxieties and from all the limitations of the plane of this earth.*[24]

CHAPTER 14

Where the Blueprints of Minds Are Made

THE JINN PLANE

What the soul is impressed with, that it becomes.

As the soul descends, or rather focuses itself further downward, it assumes more specific characteristics or idiosyncrasies. From the human viewpoint it seems as though, from being a center of light and vibrational energy animated by consciousness, the soul at this stage is stamped with the imprint of those qualities or attributes which distinguish each being from each other. Seen from the transcendental viewpoint, may it not be that souls are the custodians of the attributes of the causal world, or plane of archetypes, which they embody? Or are beings at this level not simply divine attributes that have become hominized? For example, power or intelligence or joy might have become this person or that person as these qualities particularize in their descent. It could be seen in yet another light. The jinns, the beings we are about to consider, are the product of the interfusion of the stuff of which souls are formed on the one hand, and on the other hand the fabric of the causal world, a hybrid consciousness developed through the descent of the attributes. Spirit does not interfuse with matter any more than light does with a crystal; but since matter is viewed as crystallized spirit, one could use the simile of water flowing upon the ice.

In the next grade of manifestation the soul, with its collected attributes, waits to turn into matter. Into this heaven, each ray has projected itself from the spiritual plane in diverse forms, under the influence of the five elements already produced by activity; Ishk. . . . This plane corresponds to the realm of the soul of each being on earth; it is the realm of ideas. In it resides the experience of earth. It has been called Ajsam; and those beings who inhabit it have been called Djinn or Peri, in the tradition.

Every step manifestation has taken has resulted in a variety of forms made by the different substances which are produced during the process of spirit turning into matter.[1]

It is in the nature of the soul, this vortex of light–sound energy, this current running through all planes of life, to act like a magnet. As it individuates itself from its undifferentiated ground, it becomes increasingly self-centered, acting as a focal center, drawing toward itself more and more of the environment through which it passes, like an advancing whirlwind or whirlpool, and organizing the fabric of the planes through which it passes according to its own desiderata.

The nature of the soul is to gather on its way all that it can gather and to make a mould out of it. The soul coming through different planes and spheres of existence partakes of different attributes; and the attributes of the lower world become so collected and gathered around the soul, that it almost forgets its very first experience of itself, its purest being.[2]

In the angelic sphere the soul attracts angelic atoms, in the jinn sphere it attracts jinn atoms, and on the earth, physical atoms. Thus mankind is clothed in the garb of an angel, of a jinn, and of a human being; but when he sees himself in the garb of a human being without seeing the other garbs, he believes he is nothing but a human being.[3]

Besides, from infancy and childhood man begins to show the qualities which he has gathered from the different spheres. For instance, infancy shows the sign of the angelic world; in the form and face of the infant, in its expression, in its smiles, we can see the angelic world . . . [furthermore,] the love for all that is good and beautiful, all that attracts the senses, these qualities of the jinn world manifest in a child.[4]

Murshid sees the soul as a capacity that draws to itself on each plane those qualities adequate to its own inner predispositions; one picks up those impressions of which one has the counterpart in oneself.

On its way it gathers around it properties produced from itself and borrowed continually from the elements which compose the universe, and as our possessions are not necessarily ourselves, so the properties are not the soul.[5]

From Ajsam, the realm of ideas, the ray focuses itself upon an earthly object akin to itself, and it penetrates direct to that plane of the physical existence where it finds its own attributes. Thus the soul with the attributes of a tiger will seek its means among tigers.

The soul proves its divine origin on all planes of existence, in creating for itself all that it desires, in producing for itself the wish of its heart, in attracting and drawing to itself all that it wants. The source of the soul is perfect, and so is its goal; therefore even in its limitation the soul has the spark of perfection.[6]

To understand the functioning of the soul, one must once more divest oneself of one's habit of thinking; on the earth plane, earth is fertilized by water, a stone may be dented by the impact of a stone, but the soul is not subject to transformation, albeit it shows forth its own qualities by identifying with those it is exposed to, as a chameleon shows the colors of the environment.

Souls in the angelic heavens live as a breath. The soul in its nature is a current ... the nature of which is to envelop itself with all that may come along and meet it on its way ... therefore, it becomes different from its original condition.[7]

But this is only a temporary condition. The soul does not interfuse with the substance of the planes.

The soul, during its life on earth and after, does not change its plane of existence. It simply quickens it and transfuses it with consciousness, and identifies itself with all things that it sees, and changes its own identity with the change of its constantly changing vision.[8]

The soul, coming from the highest source but having identified itself with a smaller domain, the domain of the body and the mind, has conceived in itself a false idea of itself; and it is this false idea which is called Nafs. Yet in its real being the soul is a vibration, the soul is a breath, and the soul is intelligence, and the soul is the essence of the personality.

This is the real meaning of maya:

What the soul thinks, it becomes. What the soul is impressed with, that it becomes. The soul is likened to the caterpillar. As a caterpillar reflects all the beauty of colours that it sees, and out of it turns itself into a butterfly, so does the soul. When in the angelic world, it reflects the angelic beauty, manifesting itself in the form of an angel; when in the world of genius, it reflects the jinn qualities, covering itself thereby with the form of a jinn; when in the world of men, it reflects human qualities, manifesting itself therefore in the form of man.

It may identify so completely with an impression that it shows it forth.

The soul manifesting as a body has diminished its power considerably, even to the extent that it is not capable of imagining for one moment the great power, life, and light it has in itself. Once the soul realizes itself by becoming independent of the body that surrounds it, the soul naturally begins to see in itself the being of the spirit.

Yet such is the freedom of the soul that by one switch over, it can shake off the impression in an instant.

The soul acquires only those qualities in which it is interested. If the soul is not interested in the qualities, it will never take them. And the soul keeps only those attributes in which it is interested. If it is not interested in them, it loses them. However wicked a person may be, however many undesirable attributes he may have, he can lose them all if he does not approve of them.[9]

You will say: "But can we change our physical body? Can we change our face?" We can. People become like those of whom they think strongly, or with whom they associate. All things exposed to the eye are reflected in it for the moment, and when the eye is turned away the reflection is in it no more. It had received it for the moment only.

Amir Minai, the Hindustani poet says, "However fast I am bound by earthly ties, it will not take a moment to break them. I shall break them by changing sides." Every experience on the physical or astral plane is just a dream before the soul. It is ignorance when it takes this experience to be real. It does so because it cannot see itself; as the eye sees all things but not itself.[10]

In reality, no sin, no virtue can be engraved upon the soul; it can only cover the soul.

One may distinguish between those qualities that the soul has inherited from its Divine Origin, those it has collected on its focus downward and whose counterparts were already latent within it and those qualities the soul has gleaned without being able to assimilate them, because they are foreign to it.

Every infant brings with it to the earth soul qualities, but as it goes it forgets them and learns the qualities of the earth.[11]

However wicked a person may be, be assured that his soul has the best qualities, as a spiritual inheritance, but they are covered up by all that has been gathered afterwards. And so, there is always possibility of spiritual progress for every soul, even the most wicked.[12]

How can one distinguish soul qualities from earth ones? The answer is probably that the qualities originally brought down by the soul from the angelic planes bear the mark of those planes; we may reminisce.

There are, however, soul qualities, distinct and different from the qualities of mind and body ... The principal soul quality is innocence. There is a great difference between innocence and ignorance. The ignorant one does not know; the innocent one both knows and does not know.[13]

Another soul quality is harmony. It is a natural inclination of an illuminated soul to create harmony, for it is in harmony that an illuminated soul finds peace; the one who is without illumination finds his satisfaction in struggle.

When one sees generosity in someone who is poor and humility in someone who is honored, when one notices simplicity in a great soul and fineness in a strong personality, when one discerns an unassuming quality in a brave man and a desire to learn in a man who knows and understands, then one may realize that all these are qualities which belong to the soul, and they win the heart of man more than anything in the world. Fearlessness is also a soul quality.[14]

It is the soul carrying an impression of the mind that Murshid calls a jinn.

The sphere of the jinn is the universe of minds. The words genius and jinn come from a Sanscrit word Jnana, which means knowledge.[15]

Yet the minds of the jinns are not so developed as the minds of men. The reason for this is that the experience of life on the earth completes the making of mind. In the world of the jinns the mind is only a design, an outline; a design which is not yet embroidered.[16]

If it is true that wisdom is born of the contact of consciousness with matter, one might well say that before descending, or rather focusing upon the physical plane, the soul lives and moves and has its being in a world of archetypes. The eternal models of all things and beings proliferate and individuate in nature: for example, the species instead of the individual, roseness instead of roses, lion-ness instead of lions, and beauty instead of beautiful things or beings. As consciousness passes through the funnel of individuality on earth, it focuses on objects rather than archetypes. But as it refocuses into the jinn plane, it broadens its outlook.

The mind is not the same there, with all the thoughts and imaginations which it carries from the earth to this plane. Mind which is a mind here on earth is the whole being there.

Therefore a jinn's thinking is more abstract, while that of the mind of a human is more concrete.

While the soul of every person is looking for the beauty which is outward, the attention of the jinn soul is directed not so much to the beauty which is reflected outwardly as it is to the source of the beauty which is within.[17]

The jinns are the architects working actively prior to manifestation, on the features and shapes of things to be projected into the physical world.

We all have passed through the jinn plane, and therefore have been jinns or enjoyed the jinn consciousness. Better still, we are jinns who have incarnated, in the sense that we have become caught up in identification with bodiness. Many remember that state, particularly those who feel the vocation of a genius; we seek to connect up with our source of inspiration in the blueprints of all created things. When we realize with what infinite ingenuity, skill, and craftsmanship every little detail of things and beings has been devised, it is clear how much planning must be taking place behind the scene.

In the jinn there is something like the mind which is completed in man. All the intuitive and inspirational properties are possessed by the jinn, because that is the only source that the jinn has of receiving its knowledge. Subjects such as poetry, music, art, inventive science, philosophy and morals are akin to the nature of the jinn.[18]

It is a world of music, art, poetry; a world of intelligence, cheerfulness and joy; a world of thought, imagination, and sentiment; a world that a poet would long for and a musician would crave to dwell in. The life of the jinn is an ideal life for a thinker.[19]

We would naturally like to know how that world looks, what jinns look like. The same law applies as in the case of the angels.

One generally finds among artists, poets, musicians, thinkers, as well as among philosophers, great politicians and inventors, souls of the world of the jinns, who have brought with them to the earth some deep impression which causes them in their lives to be what men term great geniuses. Impression is a great phenomenon in itself; as a man thinketh so is he.[20]

There is much that can be said in support of man's imagination, which pictures the angel or jinn more or less in the form of man. For everything in the world proves on examination that it is striving to culminate in the form of man.[21]

It is this idea which is expressed in the words of the scriptures, "We have made man in our own image." If I were to add a word of explanation I would say, "We have made all forms in order to complete the image of man."

As everything on the jinn plane is internalized, what we do remember does not tally with our present *Weltanschauung* (picture of the world), therefore we unconsciously dismiss it; but if we try to remember our dream personality, it gingerly flashes back so long as one dismisses the usual image of oneself.

The sphere of the jinn has as many worlds as there are planets in the universe . . . yet not so much out of communication with each other.

Are there suns, are there moons, in their worlds as in ours? Yes, this outer solar system is the reflection of the inner solar system. What difference is there between time, our conception of time, and the idea of time they have there? . . . For the sake of convenience let us say that our year is the hour of the jinns and the moment of the angels.[22]

Of course, creativity is an act of imagination, which is something that happens internally. On the jinn plane, in the act of imagining, the jinn participates actively and consciously in carrying his own creation one step further, and helps in that of other beings.

If the soul wishes, it can be changed according to its own ideal.[23]

Are there differences among the jinns and the angels as among men of different kinds? Indeed there are; but among the jinns not so many as among men; still less among the angels.

However exhilarating the inexhaustible inventiveness of the mind, there certainly is at this level a departure from the joyous state of the angelic spheres, since the jinns have to take the limitations of earthly conditions into consideration in their designs as they receive feedback from the earth through beings returning on the upward journey. This is why the Master says, "In Ajsam, the realm of ideas, the ray focused itself."

In its pure condition the soul is joy, and when it is without joy its natural condition is changed; then it depends upon the names and forms of the earth and is deprived of the dance of the soul, and therein lies the whole tragedy of life. The wrath of Indra symbolizes the breach of the law that the highest love must be for God alone.[24]

CHAPTER 15

Spirit Communication

GHOSTS, MEDIUMS, OBSESSION

The soul that has passed from the earth can see all that is going on in this world almost as clearly as one sees life during one's lifetime. It can experience life on the earth through the organs of those living in the world.

As the soul proceeds further down through the planes, it passes through the astral plane, sometimes called the plane of spirits (not to be confused with the plane of pure spirit). As in every preceding sphere, the soul collects the substance of this particular sphere, fashioning for itself astral and etheric bodies before it finally links up with the substance of the earth in the womb of an earthly mother. As it voyages back, after having cast off the human body, the soul hovers for a while in the astral and etheric shroud. Some tarry for some time in this limbo state before facing the death of the astral and release into the jinn and then angelic planes on the way aloft.

Some people can experience communication with beings on the spirit plane, either in astral projection or in a state of clairvoyance or clairaudience. There are ample testimonies of spirits and out-of-body projectors having seen or conversed with them. According to these reports, many are encapsulated within their own thoughts and emotions, regurgitating impressions of the earth plane, often involving fear and pain. A few dedicated beings have offered their services to release them. Murshid left a detailed account of some of his experiences early in life with ghosts and spirits:

I had my first experience of the spirits when a boy. One night I awoke in the middle of the night feeling a wish to look out of the window into our courtyard at the beautiful moonlight shining there. I went to the window, and looking out I saw some way off a man of saintly appearance, clothed in a long white robe, with long snow-white hair and beard. I saw him as plainly as in full daylight. I was amazed at the sight of him, wondering how it had been possible for him to enter our courtyard, all the doors being locked. But for his

241

saintly appearance I might have supposed him to be a thief, but the nearer he came the taller he grew. At each step his height increased, until I could no longer see his head, and as he came forward his figure became a mist, until at last he was like a shadow, and in a moment he vanished from my sight. My hair stood on end and I was completely overcome by bewilderment.

The next morning when I told my family what I had seen, they tried to make nothing of it in order to keep me from superstitious beliefs; but others told me that they too had often seen this phantom appearing in this quarter. This taught me that spirits are attached to those places in which they are interested, just as we are, and they are constantly drawn to the places of their interest. Their form is not solid but ethereal, and can expand. This phantom which I saw was that of a Pir who lived in the well in our courtyard.

After a few years of these first experiences I was trying to forget and disbelieve this impression, fearing that it might lead me towards superstitions. But one day, happening to arrive at our country cottage in the middle of the night, I found on our land a huge person at a distance of three yards from me, making a sign that he wished to wrestle with me in the way Indians do, who give a challenge by slapping their thighs and crossing and slapping their arms. I did not for one moment take him to be a man; I at once thought that he was a spirit. At first I was terrified, comparing my size and strength with this gigantic spirit. But I had heard that the spirits swallow the fearful, so although I did not know the art of wrestling, I determined to fight with him, and I advanced, quite prepared to give him a blow. At each step that I took forward he drew back, which naturally gave me courage to close in upon him. He retreated until he was against the wall. I was glad that now I had got him, and approaching I struck him a strong blow, which, instead of hurting the spirit, knocked my hand against the wall, and the spirit disappeared.

The reason why the spirit appears and yet has no solid form is that it exists in a vaporous state, and the image seen in this vaporous form is nothing but the impressions of his former body when on earth.

Among very many different experiences I cannot forget one which made a great impression upon my mind. I had purposely rented a haunted house in James' Street, Sekunderabad, although my friends advised me not to, and in order to experience any manifestations there I slept there alone without even a servant. After a few days I began to find that whenever I played upon the vina at night, sitting on my bed, the bed would gradually begin to move as if levitating, and to rock to and fro. It would seem to rise for an instant some way into the air, but the movement was so smooth that there was no shock. I was playing with my eyes closed, and I thought that perhaps this was the effect of imagination under the spell of music. This went on for some time. Then I happened to send my vina to be repaired, and one night to my great horror I heard a noise as if all the windows of my house were being smashed. I got up and looked everywhere. The window-panes were unbroken, and there was no reason to suppose that there might be anyone in the house who had caused the noise. For three days this went on and I could not sleep. I had no peace at night until my vina came back. The spirits seemed to be so much interested in my music that they rejoiced in it and showed their appreciation by lifting me up; when the food of their soul was not given they rebelled.

You might ask by what power the bed was lifted. The answer is that the finer forces are much more powerful than the external forces. There is nothing that they cannot lift up or carry.

There are some who master the spirits so that the spirits bring them whatever they desire from anywhere, jewels, money, fruits, food. The spirits can even carry a person from one place to another. But those who work evil by the help of a spirit, train that spirit in evil and one day that spirit throws the bomb of evil back at them.

Sometimes spirits bring news for him who has mastered them. From whatever distance it may be they can bring the news in a moment of time. Sometimes the spirits go and cause trouble to someone if they are so directed by a spiritualist master. I have myself seen a case where the spirits would set fire to a man's house. Sometimes his clothes would catch fire, sometimes his papers burned, sometimes the food disappeared from the dish in which it had been put and dirt was found in the dish instead.[1]

Murshid had visited the tomb of Miran Datar, a Sufi reputed to have cured obsessions in his lifetime. Still today the obsessed hope for a miraculous cure at his shrine.

On the steps of the tomb a man was sitting who seemed a quiet and thoughtful person. I asked him, "Why are you here?" He said, "Do not ask me such a question." I said "Why not?" He said, "Because I am afraid. Now that I am near this holy tomb I have a little strength to answer you; if I were not here I could not even do that."[2]

Exorcism is a rare art, used occasionally by a few dedicated priests, including Catholics. Exorcists have to exercise great will power. Sometimes the situation is dramatic, when the obsessing spirit, living like a parasite on the energy of the obsessed, is deprived of his sustenance and wiles, after struggling like a grim death to hold his life-grip upon his victim.

As soon as the patient's secret is known to the healer, he has really made a successful operation in the invisible heart and taken out all the poisonous substance which was causing the sickness and leading the patient to his death. He then releases him from this by words of consolation, by fragrance, by music, by the recitation of the names of God, and by reflecting upon the heart of the obsessed his own wisdom and piety. No doubt there are very few, even in the East, who could give the right treatment; and mostly there are real devils amongst those who profess to cast our devils.[3]

The spirits of the departed may choose to use the mind and even the body of a being incarnated on the earth plane as an instrument to function on the earth.

They see, if they care to see, conditions of the world as clearly as we do, and even more so. They must have a medium on the earth as their instrument; for they need the physical eyes to see, the physical ears to hear, and the physical senses to experience life in the physical world. They seek for an accommodation in the heart of a being on the earth, and they focus themselves on the mind of that person, and receive through this medium all the knowledge and experience of this earth that they desire as clearly as the person himself. Thus they can still live on the earth in one way, by obsessing another soul.

The phenomenon of obsession is probably more frequent than most people realize, particularly among people debilitated through illness or overstrain.

But there are many living dead in the good or bad sense of the words. It is in these cases that a single-pointed spirit takes hold of their minds and bodies as its own instrument, using them to the best advantage. In point of fact there is no soul which has not experienced obsession in the true sense of the word; for there are moments in everyday life when those on the other side take the souls on the earth as their medium through which to experience life on the physical plane.[4]

There are, however, cases where a spirit is trying to help a person and his influence is beneficent.

The souls who are attached to the earth are either earthbound, or the inspirers or the protectors of the earth. The love of those inspirers and protectors of the earth comes like a stream.

Most of the great souls, poets, musicians, writers, composers, inventors have had a reflection of some personality upon them. Those who are devoted to the pursuit of beauty in knowledge and art, are liable to become obsessed, and many times by spirits who were themselves devoted to the same pursuit, but who were separated from their bodies before their interest and hope in this life was sated. By focusing their minds on the work of a great personality, they come in contact with that personality and derive benefit from it, very often without knowing the secret.

Murshid advises anyone, when dealing with spirit communication through a medium, to discriminate between obsession and telepathy.

The soul that has passed from the earth can see all that is going on in this world almost as clearly as one sees life during one's lifetime. It can experience life on the earth through the organs of those living in this world. Therefore those who wish to offer food, clothes, flowers, prayers to the dead, they themselves become mediums.

The difference is that a professional medium knows he is one; the medium only focuses his heart to the heart of the person who asks for a message. Therefore, when the medium says what he reads already from the heart of the one who asks the question, the questioner cannot but say "Yes, yes." Mediumistic knowledge comes either by a continual obsession or by a momentary obsession, by a voluntary obsession or by an involuntary obsession.

Much as Murshid deprecates using a medium to satisfy curiosity, he still feels that the development of intuitive faculties is part of spiritual progress. It could be said to be the next step in evolution.

But I should consider clairvoyance as a natural effect of spiritual progress, and mediumism is a kind of temperament, which can be a kind of unbalanced condition. A person in an abnormally negative state also gets reflection from the inner world; for you will find in the insane asylum many cases of mediums.

What Murshid objected to very strongly was the use experimenters made of mediumistically inclined people. They became the easy victims of people's curiosity about the other side, and at the cost of their balance, sometimes their sanity, for they can lose all sense of reality. Murshid discouraged spirit communication in no uncertain terms.

The soul is hindered in its progress by being called back to the earth.... Suppose a person is going somewhere, and all the time people call out, "Please stop, we want you"; he will never be able to get to his destination.... It is better to help the soul to go forward, and that one does by sending one's loving thought.[5]

He also deprecates it for the effect that it has upon us:

In regard to spirit communion, which is a subtle subject, I will say that it is better to have more connection with the beings living upon earth than to be obsessed with the desire to meet with the people on the other side of life. It is here that we are meant to evolve, and by being absorbed in those who have passed on we are taken away from the life we are meant to have and we live on earth as if we were dead. People in pursuit of the spirits have a dead expression on their faces.[6]

There are some who, if once they have become interested in a soul on the other side, focus their attention on this particular soul. Then a connection is formed, and it is natural that day and night, or on many occasions, communication is established. But there is danger in this play. It is interesting to begin with, but later it can be most difficult to get rid of. The story is known of a person who had put himself in spirit communication so profoundly that the spirits would not leave him alone for one moment. It was just like a ringing at any time of the day. When once these fine nerves have become sensitive, then the communication is open with the other side. But then the difficulty is that the gross vibrations of the earth are too hard on the nerves; and the nerves cannot answer the demands of this gross world, this material world; they become too fine. The result is nervous illness.

Murshid had witnessed so many cases of this abuse that he felt it a duty to warn people against it.

If they want to experience, they must experience themselves and take the consequences. But this way of taking an innocent young person, a weak person, a mediumistic person, putting him into a trance, and profiting out of his ruination, neither brings a blessing nor brings that knowledge which illuminates the soul.

Of course, when one becomes sensitive, one begins to be aware of beings on the other side without the intercession of a medium. Murshid even tells us something of how it is done.

The intuitive centres in the body are made of fine nerves, finer than one can imagine. When once these fine nerves have become sensitive then the communication is open with the other side. In order to know of the existence of the spirit we must ourselves live in the spirit, and above matter. If a person loses someone in whom he was quite absorbed, and he goes about lost in the thought of that person, whenever he goes in the crowds, in the jungle, he feels the presence of that person, because his self is no more before his view.

Murshid distinguished between obsession and impression (which is, of course, telepathy).

Obsession can be caused not only by the dead but also by a living person; in the case of the former it is called obsession, in the case of the latter it is called impression.

Imagine Murshid's surprise to find that in the West scarcely any distinction is made by a psychiatrist between an insane and an obsessed person; consequently, hospitals incarcerate numberless people whose therapy should be dealt with quite differently from clear cases of psychosis—paranoia, schizophrenia, and such.

When I came to the Western world I was curious to know whether it is only we in the East who have so many obsessed people, or whether there are obsessed people in the West also. They said to me, "Here if someone were to show such a condition, we should put him in a lunatic asylum. If you wish to see cases such as you mention, you must go there." I went, and there found that there were many who were mad and also many who were obsessed. I wanted to try some experiments in casting out the influence, but the doctors would not let me, because they wanted a medical diploma, which unfortunately I lacked.[7]

Murshid gives us a few typical cases of obsession from his experience in the East.

I have seen some very curious and remarkable cases of obsession. One was in a Parsi family. There was a young lady who sometimes once a day and sometimes two or three times, would change her mood and would speak in Arabic and

Persian; and she spoke about philosophy and metaphysics which she had never been taught. She was so strongly obsessed that she did not care to speak to her father and mother or her brothers and sisters or anyone else; nor would she ever go out. She always had incense burning in her room and led a very retired life. They brought learned people to speak with her, and she discussed with them like a great philosopher and got the better of the argument. Then she would forget it all again. At Sekunderabad there was a boy who sang Telagu songs. He had never learnt them, because Telagu is not spoken there among Muslims. Sometimes he would sing many songs, and then later on he could not sing one.[8]

The disciples of Khwaja Nizam-ud-Din Wali, a great saint of Delhi, were once sitting waiting for him to come and speak upon a very abstruse and difficult matter, when to their astonishment they saw his servant come into the room and sit down on the murshid's seat; Nizam-ud-Din then came in, made a very deep bow to the servant and took his seat before him. The servant began to speak and spoke for some time, explaining some very subtle and deep questions. Then a change came over his face, he looked around, and ran from the room in great confusion. Afterwards Nizam-ud-Din told his disciples that he had asked his murshid for the answer to some very difficult question, and that the subject was so complex that the murshid needed a human form in order to explain it exactly, and that was why he had spoken through the servant.[9]

A pupil reported:

I have met lately a woman who had never learned English, who was very much interested in you, and I gave her your photograph. She got in a trance by helping someone else who was ill. And when she had done that, she turned to the chimney piece where your photograph was standing, and took it in her hands, and addressed in English beautiful things.

Murshid healed a number of cases personally by exorcism.

For Murshid, the whole universe is a phenomenon of reflection. It is the palace of mirrors: Every atom, every being, every planet, every plane is in continual sensitive and intelligent contact with every other through an invisible network, which is the overall consciousness of the universe, eternally fragmented and reinstated.

The more intelligent person, the person who is more living, is more susceptible to reflections; and if that person happens to be more spiritual, then he has reflections from both sides, from the earth and from the other side.[10]

CHAPTER 16

Why Do Things Happen
the Way They Do?

PREDESTINATION AND FREE WILL

The purpose seems to be in the cause,
but it is finished in the effect.

Indifference and independence are the two wings
which enable the soul to fly.—Gayan, 23

I caught this morning, morning's minion kingdom
*   of daylight's dauphin*
dapple-dawn-drawn falcon in his riding of the
*   rolling level underneath him steady air, and striding*
High there, how he rung upon the rein of a wimpling
*   wing in his ecstasy!—Gerard Manley Hopkins, Windhover*

Oh, I have slipped the surly bonds of earth
*   And danced the skies on laughter-silvered wings*
Sun-ward I've climbed and joined the tumbling mirth
*   of Sunsplit clouds*
And done a hundred things you have not dreamt of.
—John Gillipsie Magee

From the pinnacle of his samadhi, Murshid was watching the course of things, of happenings on the planet: men and women rushing about, having forgotten their origin because adorned with the fabric of the planet, and unaware of all the conditioning monitoring their actions, and aspirations, and judgments. And behind all this striving, and surging, and worrying, and enjoying, and soul-searching, the overall laws governing the causal procession of circumstances—the forces set into motion in the great machine; and further behind this, the ever spontaneous free will and inexhaustible inventiveness of the One who pulls the strings of his own being with what sometimes appears a foolhardy verve, perplexing wit, and compassion in the gift of himself.

Pursuing further his sounding of the nature of happenings around him, while preserving the wakefulness of one who has maintained the continuity of his memory of the way things looked in the night of time all the way into manifestation, Murshid was remarking in all events human and divine crowding in around him the free divine act, ordinarily camouflaged by what seems like the mechanistic effect of the laws governing the forces set off by actions. Everywhere he saw the divine free will intervening, altering what many think is predestination, and which is nothing less than the fossilization of the earlier free act of the One, now become a custom in the universe.

Emerging out of his odyssey in the night of time, and contemplating the phenomenon of manifestation in an overall survey, Murshid saw clearly that the ulterior objective behind all existence is achievement, and behind achievement, realization; that is, understanding why things happen the way they do, and the ultimate realization: discovering that one is free!

Many a thoughtful person has been staggered by the thought of an accident that killed a wonderful person in the prime of life; or some preposterous crime, so shocking to the most elementary sense of decency; or the illness that struck a friend while he was accomplishing something great; or the collapse of that plan that was so admirable, and the success of a crook—why such injustice to the innocent?

Why did Mozart die at thirty-five, and Bach go blind, and Beethoven deaf? Why did Gandhi have to be assassinated? And Ramana Maharishi die of cancer? Why did Akhenaton's religion fail? And Dara Shiku lose his throne and life to Aurangzeb? Why was Christ crucified? And Al Hallaj? Why did those miners die asphyxiated in their tunnel, and those sailors drown? Why was that child born retarded, or blind? Why did those Jews die in the gas chambers? And Noor, my sister—why was she beaten to death by a Nazi? Why does that false guru have thousands of followers? Why, why, oh why? *Why* is the greatest mountain there is.

How can we believe in God, or even in a basic law of justice in the universe when we witness things happening that way? Look at the faces of people in the streets: There is so much despondency written in the expressions of those who hoped and now feel that they have been dealt with unfairly by certain people, or sometimes just by destiny, fate. How we would like to know why such things happen the way they do!

It is like climbing a mountain, a mountain whose name is *Why*.[1]

Of course, we all look for meaning. And the first thing we discover is a consistency in the sequence of phenomena, which is what we mean by law or causality.

There comes a stage in the evolution of an illuminated soul, when it begins to see the law hidden behind nature.[2]

Sometimes, all of a sudden, the mind boggles at the thought of our interdependence with the most distant star, our interrelation with every atom and being, the force that we set in motion by our thought, word or deed.

Verily, every atom sets in motion each atom of the universe.[3]

Every activity that is once set to run on its wheels goes on running. And we call it lost when it disappears from our sight. But sooner or later, in some form or other, it arrives at its destination. Man forms his future by his actions; his

every good or bad action spreads out its vibrations and becomes know
throughout the universe.

The next step is applying this knowledge to everyday life, which we
call wisdom.

All things in life are materials for wisdom to work with.[4]

Few indeed know what effect every action has upon one's life, what power a
right action can give, and what effect a wrong action can have. Man is only on
the look-out for what others think of his actions, instead of being concerned
with their effect.[5]

Several factors enter into the account of any single event. Let us
unravel these. There is the simple law of reckoning:

Life is a fair trade wherein all adjusts itself in time. For all you take from it, you
must pay the price sooner or later. For some things you may pay in advance; for
some you should pay on delivery; and for some later on, when the bill is
presented.

Then there is the law: "As you sow, so shall you reap"; that which is
put into the machine returns:

When a child who has been disrespectul to its parents itself becomes a parent,
it will find the same attitude in its own children. A soldier who does not
observe discipline under his captain or colonel will experience the same from
his subordinates when later he holds that position.[6]

A person however rich, powerful, highly placed, capable, efficient, supported
by many in life, by armies, can be thrown down to the depths of the earth by
the smallest hurt he may have caused, which then rebounds. No protection, no
support can ward off the blow of the reaction of any hurt a person causes to
anybody.

There is a further law that seems paradoxical:

He who has spent has used; he who has collected has lost; but he who has
given has saved his treasure forever.[7]

And yet still another law that seems to contradict this:

All that one holds is conserved; all that one lets go is dispersed.

The reason for this contradiction is a difference between giving and
letting go by neglect. There are things that are not ours to give—a
charge, a responsibility; and things we may dispose of—the fruit of
action. One can more readily give away that which one has earned
than things that have been passed on to one, for example, presents,
because they often have the character of a charge.

Things that pass from one hand to the other are but changing things, and be sure that when you gain a thing from another you may have to pass it on to another also when the time comes, willingly or unwillingly. Therefore be always in search of things that will endure, that will last long, and adopt ways of attaining them by right and just means.

The next law we should account for is the influence of personality on events and events on personality. Perhaps we failed to see why a certain situation occurred ten years ago. Perhaps I realize now that if I had been then as I am now, it would not have happened. But if I am what I am now, it is because of what happened many years ago:

Since the nature of life is action and reaction, every outer experience has a reaction within, and every inner experience has its reaction in the outer life.

Everything which is once felt, thought, or spoken is born as a living being with a destiny, with a purpose to fulfill; and as it has birth it necessarily has death. Therefore, besides living beings, feelings, words, thoughts and the effects of one's actions float in the air, rise up and come down, and swing hither and thither, and seek their locations in objects and in living beings.

Beyond the cause of a known effect, one must also take into account the cause behind the cause, just as a good doctor does not just prescribe a medication for a symptom but tries to diagnose a prior cause: For example, a heart condition could be due to infected tonsils, the reason your erstwhile friend harms you now is because you let him down (maybe inadvertently). This is the cause of the effect. But the reason you let him down was because you were disappointed in him (maybe unconsciously). This is the cause of the cause of the effect. And there might be a yet prior cause: he scoffed at your ideal. And a still further cause: he was brought up in a different environment, where values other than your own were treasured. And so, we could climb the ladder of causes ad infinitum. But the reason it all happened was because the Planner is trying to make you learn to forgive or to tolerate, and is using your relationship as a test case. This is the purpose, rather than the cause. So if you go on blaming your friend, you have failed to see what it is all about.

The unconscious specter of karma has stifled many into self-pity or despondency. What is meant by fate? A whimsical situation where there is no consistent or intelligent planning? In the absence of being able to grasp an intention, some believe there is none; whereas some of us may even be so bold as to think that in our particular case, there is an adverse planning. We say: Fate is against me!

We cannot be very objective. The conservative religious attitude is that everything is planned, but most people are unaware of the causal relationships involved. As far as the popular Hindu dogma is concerned, the solution is simple: The causes lie beyond our memory's reach in past incarnations. Nobody can verify this, so the doctrine is safe. The mind's limitation stands in the way of most people's insight, says Murshid, revealing the point of view of the rishis and murshids who see the cause behind the cause, the loss that avers itself to be a gain and the gain that proves to be a loss, the good in the bad and the bad in the good. The reason is that the plan is devised to coax us into ever greater evolution rather than to fit our own plans or our sense of justice. We are trying to apply our measuring rod to issues that reach far beyond our scope. It is the mark of a great being to overcome the appearance of situations by dismissing personal judgment. Then he may discover that the answer is more often the testing exercised by the divine planning rather than the expiation of karmic debts. On the cross Al Hallaj says:

Thy abandonment of me is a proof of Thy love, for Thou testest most those Thou lovest most.

These are among the most revealing words ever proffered in the history of human thinking.

Do we know how beautiful the girl who was mutilated by a car accident has become? Do we know what functions are being fulfilled by those who were suddenly recalled to the higher spheres? That man was a good man, but do we know that he became a saint when he was killed? Do we know with what symphonies and choirs Mozart fills the heavens? And the vision that awaited Bach? Murshid quotes the Muslim legends of Moses, who was told by his guide Khidr the reason things happened which at first seemed to him so perplexing.

The Sufis call the purpose the divine intention, which is rooted in love. This is the spontaneous flow behind the law of harmony of the universe; the divine intention becomes fossilized as the causal chain, but the fresh outpouring breaks the routine.

We understand now why it is so difficult for our finite minds to understand why things happen the way they do. "All situations in life work towards some definite end." This is the tacit hypothesis behind all scientific thinking: The programing of phenomena makes sense to human understanding, although this understanding is forever being strained to its extreme limits and assumes that if there is anything that is still perplexing, it is simply because our intelligence has not yet been able to clinch it. We can safely affirm that scientists entertain, maybe unconsciously, a tacit belief in the wisdom of the planning. It is obvious in the foregoing examples that free will played a part in setting off causal chain reactions, and came in at each step. So we have to account for this interplay of free will and law. In the domain of science this bears out Heisenberg's principle of indetermination: There is an area that escapes reckoning, and scientific laws apply only to averages in a range of large number, allowing scope and play within those limits to individual freedom.

What, then, can the astrologer foresee reading the language of the stars, or the phrenologist presage from the shape of the infant's head or ears, or the palmist from the lines of the palm? They can testify to

what you could be if you would be what you should be.

Whether this ever materializes depends upon your free choice. But how free are we?

Children running naked on the beach, building on earth the sand castles of their minds; the skylark wheeling in the breeze. With what purpose? The butterfly fluttering by, apparently aimlessly; the deer loitering among the fallen leaves; the young man dangling under a hang-glider; the young woman daydreaming, or the invalid seeking freedom in astral flight: How free are they? Is it fantasy that directs their courses or some law more elusive than those that have so far succumbed to the scrutiny of human intelligence? All we sense is that if, indeed, they are moved by invisible strings, they are enjoying a freedom of which a lion or eagle is deprived in a cage. If only man knew what is behind his free will he would never call it so. What certainly is true is that there is a desperate need in man for freedom.

There is a longing hidden beneath all the other longings which man has, and that longing is for freedom. This longing is sometimes satisfied by walking in the solitude, in the woods, when one is left alone for a time, when one is fast asleep, when even dreams do not trouble one; and when one is in meditation, in which for a moment the activities of body and mind are both suspended. Therefore the sages have preferred solitude, and have always shown love for nature; and they have adopted meditation as the method of attaining that goal which is the freedom of the soul.[8]

As freedom is the nature of every soul, so the child, even from infancy, seeks freedom. We want the child to sit in our arms, but it prefers to go and play. An animal, a dog, or a cat, which depends so much on the sympathy of mankind, still does not wish to be deprived of freedom.[9]

Man's affirmation of his free will seems to be challenging the divine order.

Man, a legion squirming like ants in the capitals of that tiny speck of dust in the starry universe called planet Earth, has transformed the face of that planet, changed deserts and stretches of sea into arable land, flattened hills, excavated mines, diverted the course of rivers, created rain artificially, deforested vast areas, replanted new regions, eliminated whole species from the animal kingdom and propagated man-bred ones. Scientists have wrested the secret that could flood the earth with monsters; atomic power or the use of gases could eliminate whole populations, even lay the planet waste, while inoculations and hygiene and "the pill" change the balance of population. The undaunted spirit of man does not falter at scaling the most forbidding mountains, penetrating the unexplored depths of the sea inhabited by giant octopi, threading his intelligence through telescopes and satellites into outer space and through microscopes into the atoms. The ingenuity of human incentive is boundless. Is this the divine will working through the fragments of himself? Where does the individual initiative end and the Divine consciousness begin? Obviously, an overall intelligence is continually gaining new ground in the evolutionary process, although at the human scale it looks as though individual people had thought things out themselves. But when the human mind intervenes, it certainly spoils the original harmony, called the order of the universe. Man pollutes the earth, the water, and the air; spoliates the planet with non-biodegradable waste, including the dangerous by-products of fission; and brandishes a landscape of questionable taste, like the gardens of Versailles or the Tivoli, or the outlines of modern cities, the artificial harbors, the artificial lakes of hydroelectric stations, and the cable-cars in the mountains. Maybe he is instrumental in replacing an old order with a new order and a new sensitivity that values the aesthetic line of a Guarini or a modern villa above the silent beauty of the fjords and an oasis in the desert or the Weisshorn at dawn. But at times one feels that he is sticking his neck out too far and pitting his wits *against* the divine order. So we do come up against a dichotomy between individuated will and an overall will ascribed to God.

Thy will be done on earth as it is in heaven.

Who has not deliberated silently in himself, or debated with others upon the meaning of this line, unrelentingly quoted by Murshid when witnessing how modern civilization is flouting the natural order. Can the will of the part go counter to the Will of the Whole?

But if our individual will is a branch of the divine will, if its source is the same, how can it ever be out of harmony? Sometimes the hand sympathizes with the foot, at other times it does not. We hurt ourselves many times just because of disharmony; we may cut ourselves, our fingers for instance. If then, I, who am one person, can cause harm to myself, and suffer thereby, why should it not be possible that the human will should be out of harmony with the divine, so that the divine suffers thereby? It is possible to act in a way contrary to the divine will, even though one is only a branch of it.[10]

There are two forces, Kaza and Kadr. Kaza is the force which is all powerful, and Kadr is the force of an individual will-power. An individual goes on running his hoop as far as his power allows him to, but there comes a wagon which blocks the road, and the hoop cannot go further. It is that wagon which is Kaza, the all powerful, which comes into conflict with the individual power. This idea is so well expressed in the saying, "Man proposes but God disposes."

One may distinguish between forces set into motion and the forces of the prevailing circumstances in mechanics—momentum and inertia. The billiard ball may hit several billiard balls, or the atom several atoms, before its energy is absorbed by these, which energy will be resorbed by others until it is exhausted. Inertia should not be envisaged as a negative, opposing force, but as a real, active force that one will have to contend with. However great one's initial drive, at some stage it will be offset and brought to a halt by this paramount power called *Kaza* by the Sufis. In other words, however great a scope of freedom has been delegated to the individual, God has the final word. We find this very strongly outlined in Zoroastrianism in the contention between Spenta Mainu, the Holy Spirit, and Angra Mainu, the challenging force of personal egotism. If this were not so, the universe would be in a state of chaos. Such is the principle of all government. Curiously enough, the very will that you are delegating can override you if you overstep the bounds.

Sometimes it looks like a mother giving her child some leeway, yet catching up with it should it stray into danger; or a boxing match between a professional boxer and a teenaged pupil—the former may sometimes step back to give the youth a chance of affirming himself, but he knows that he can always win in the end.

One may not have an inkling of the force, or even the reality of this power until one has come right up against it. Certainly one of the most traumatic encounters with this power is in an accident in which a dearly loved one dies; or fighting the death of a loved one, doing everything in one's power to avoid it; or finding that everything one has built up for years suddenly collapses for reasons outside one's control.

It is only by getting in touch with the Almighty Power that he will begin to realize the All-powerful and the phenomenon of the Almighty.[11]

Yes, we think that we are hampered in our freedom by circumstances which we attribute to fate, or our duty to which we feel committed. Yet limitation, built into man's scope with its many frustrations, fulfills a purpose.

If we watch carefully, we are likely to discover a scope of freedom within our field of action that we had failed to discern, having been so obsessed by the apparent limitation in our possibilities of action. Murshid tells the story of a young man of an aristocratic family in India who fell upon difficult financial circumstances and so worked as a groom. A wise man who had known him before said, "It makes me sad to think that you at whose house there were so many horses should work as a groom," and advised him to become a horse trainer, at which he was most successful. His karma lay with horses, but within this field he had the choice between being a groom or being a trainer. His brother became a bird catcher; the wise man advised him to catch the king's falcon, which changed his luck. His karma lay with birds.[12] He did not have to change the direction of his activity, only find further scope.

As evolution advances, there is a fragmentation in the original undivided will, giving a measure of autonomy to the part which may override the original order, as this order was prior to the fragmentation. It looks as though by granting free will to the fragments of himself, God took the consequence that his overall Will would not always be carried out—except his Will that we should benefit by some measure of freedom is fulfilled.

Yet the scope of this individuated will is limited. For example, a personal will challenging the original harmony of nature may create a tadpole with two heads, but only if protected exceptionally and artificially could it ever develop into a two-headed frog; delivered into the forces of nature, it would never survive. Mankind has so artificially altered that protection that we are exposed to greater hazards than before. Truly enough, many minds today are reacting against pollution, artificial fertilizers, the violation of ecology, etc. In so doing, they are incorporating the divine counteraction to the reckless challenge of the individual.

How can we tell the difference, whether we are exercising our own will or the divine will?

The difference between the divine and the human will is like the difference between the trunk of a tree and its branches; and as from the boughs other twigs and branches spring, so the will of one powerful individual has branches going through the will of other individuals. In a tree there is a trunk, and there are some prominent or large branches; from these there spring many smaller branches. So there are the powerful beings, the masters of humanity. Their will is God's, their word is God's word, and yet they are branches, because the trunk is the will of the Almighty. As the branches grow, so we too grow; as the branches develop, so we develop; as the branches flourish, we flourish; as the branches bear fruit, we bear fruit; as the branches are capable of rising, we too rise. Whether the branch be large or small, every branch has the same origin and the same root as the stem. Therefore, whether a person be holy or wicked, wise or foolish, he has in his innermost spirit the same essence and the same power that the wise have.[13]

The essential problem is man's ability to decide whether to submit to the overall divine will or to assert his individual will by submitting to the wish of his body, or mind, or emotion! The whole problem of freedom is involved here.

When man takes his own responsibility into his hands, calling it free will, he loses, so to speak, that dependence on God which holds him and which makes God responsible. Therefore, it is the saintly person who arrives at resigning himself to the will of God; and afterwards this may develop into his free will, which will then be the will of God. This is what marks the difference between the saintly character and the character of the master: the character of the saint is to be resigned fully to the will of God, and the character of the master is to find the will of God in his own free will.[14]

But how can one tell which of these two alternatives one is applying? Murshid points out a clue:

How can we distinguish between these two aspects of will: the will of God and the obstacle which is the will of man? It is easy for a person with a clear mind and open heart to distinguish between them, if he only knows the secret of it. For to that which is the will of God his whole being responds, and in doing His will his whole being becomes satisfied. When it is his own will, only one side of his being is perhaps satisfied for a certain time, and a conflict arises in him.

This is assuming of course that one is fully using one's intuition, and requires a fine awareness. If you allow the sore in your foot to prevent you from walking, the body has given into the wish of the part; if you force your foot to walk, the body has overridden the wish of the part. If you give in to your stomach's wish to pick an apple in your neighbor's garden, the body has been dragged to the tree by the wish of the part— the stomach—and if you override your stomach's will it is obliged to conform to your overall decision.

There seems to be a whole range of wills in each person strung hierarchically; at one end whim, or fantasy, at the other end, the Divine Will. Free will is ultimately an affirmation of one's real freedom over one's whims, selfishness, and slothfulness, and is strengthened by overcoming these.

The will is a slave to the experience of the joy and pleasure that we obtain out of all manner of kinds of comfort. The joy and sense of pleasure make the will into a slave. For instance, there is no greater comfort than sleep. So when you have to get up before dawn, you do not wish to get up to repeat the name of the Lord: you fight the greatest comfort you can experience each day. Once you begin to fight you begin to crush the power (that is, pleasure, comfort) on the surface. It is this ego, fed on pleasures and comforts of all kinds, which is your enemy. Therefore, once you crush this ego, your will is master, and becomes the ruler over your pleasures, and when the will is master, you are master. The variety of your past life is now submitted to the unity of your being. There is one part of your being which you can call "myself," and that one part must control the many beings—the nose, eyes, ears, etc.—which belong to you.

Desire is all that produces longing in one. To desire is to be bound; the heart deprives it of its freedom.[15]

However, Murshid does not treat desire contemptuously; he considers it as an energy that was originally a divine impulse, which has become diverted by passing through the human ego. Murshid distinguishes between fancy, desire, wish, and will:

When an idea or a thought that one would like a certain thing is not yet made clear in one's mind, when one's own mind has not taken a decision, then it is a desire, a fancy. When it is a little more developed then it is a wish; then it stays there and is not dispersed like the clouds. It is tangible, it is there. When the wish develops into action it becomes will, it becomes a command. One might think it is only one's wish, and indeed it is a wish as long as it is still: although it is there, it has not sprung up, it is inactive.[16]

But since we are gifted with wisdom to decide whether a wish is desirable at our stage of evolution, wisdom becomes at a certain stage the expression of our freedom to control will.

The difference between people is according to the wishes they have. One wishes for the earth, the other wishes for heaven. The desire of the one takes him to the height of spiritual progress, and the desire of the other takes him to the depths of the earth. Man is great or small, wise or foolish, on the right road or on the wrong road, according to the desire he has.[17]

One might call wisdom the ability to overcome will when one realizes that it will "deprive the heart of its freedom." There is always a battle between will power and wisdom.

Whether a wish is desirable or not depends upon our stage of evolution.

There are many things in this world which we want and which we need, and yet we do not necessarily think about them. If they come it is all right, and if they do not come we may feel uncomfortable for a time, but that feeling passes. We cannot give our mind and thought to them if we are evolved and thinking of something higher and greater than what we need in everyday life, and that slips from our grasp. This is why great poets, thinkers, and saints very often lacked the things of everyday life. With the power they had, they could command everything, even gold to come to their house, or the army to come and go—they had only to command. Yet they could not give their mind to it, they could only wish for something which was in accordance with their particular evolution.

But if he feels in his heart, "No, I really cannot wish for this, I can think of something much higher," then he must accept the consequences. And the consequences will be that he will have to go through tests and trials; and if he does not mind this, so much the better.[18]

There are many degrees of wisdom, ranging from opinion based on rational thinking to the higher wisdom that sees the cause behind the cause, and still further to the wisdom that intuits the divine intention. When man's will is illuminated by that ultimate wisdom, it becomes the divine will.

In the influence that controls a situation the hand of God is seen.[19]

No sooner do we become aware of delegating the divine power manifested throughout the whole universe in which we discover the hidden hand behind all happenings, and dedicate ourselves to fulfill that will unadulterated by the deviations or interpretations or limitations we tend to brand it with, than a strange miracle takes place—at the very thought of something, lo and behold, it happens! The secret of this idea is in the Qur'an: "Be [*Kun*] He said: and it became." The Seers and Knowers of life know this not only in theory, but by their life's experience. By setting things into motion one is delegating the divine creativity that makes dreams come true, placing one's hand on the rudder of the world, loading the mechanism of the universe with a dynamic impulse. In so doing, one applies a cosmic axiom: It is not good enough to hope that the Divine Will be done, you have to will it yourself, and do it, and take responsibility for it. That is why Murshid said, "Let Thy wish become my desire."

Murshid used to tell the typical Eastern story of the king who ordered ten slaves each to throw a glass to the floor, then asked each one, "Why did you do it?" Nine answered: "I obey your Majesty's orders," as most people do in life. But one named Ayaz said: "I apologize, I did it"; he took the responsibility upon himself. Consequently, the king in his wisdom made him his treasurer.

There is yet another story. A prince lay on his bed dying. His father, the king, asked if there was anyone in the kingdom who could cure him. After all the healers had failed, they called in the Sufi dervish Shems-i Tabriz. He said, "In God's name arise," but nothing happened. Then he said, "Rise in my name," whereupon the prince came back to life. But Shems-i Tabriz paid with his life; this apparent affront to the religious law caused him to be beaten to death. When he said "Thy will," he envisioned God as other than himself, and was therefore powerless. When he lost his individuality in God's consciousness, he could not use the word *Thy* anymore, since he embodied the divine will. That is when the miracle happened.

The ultimate freedom is implementing the overall divine will in increasingly concrete detail; and, moreover, completing it within the laws of its harmony, taking into account the divine intention which is the objective. In the same person there is the divine will unadulterated and also that fragment of the divine will that has undergone limitation and deviation. If one stays the personal vector, the overall Will comes through: but Murshid shows that even within our limitation of the Divine Will, the potentialities are inexhaustible.

Murshid distinguishes three stages in planning. At the first stage, the all-possibility is present unlimited by the free will of the person. At the second stage, it becomes obvious that only certain among all the possibilities originally present are going to materialize because the individual limits his scope to the idea that he has of himself, which determines his free will and also eliminates many of the original possibilities by the Karma of his actions. In the last phase, the final outcome, the Planner determines what is the best that can now be done with the remaining cards in the game used to the best advantage, perhaps better than could have been foreseen, because the creative resources of the divine Planner are inexhaustible. He can conjure a plethora of bounty from that which the individual had narrowed down, and even turn a fiasco into a triumph. Yes, we think that we are hampered in our freedom by circumstances, which we attribute either to an unaccountable fate or to an intelligent predestination beyond our understanding, or the karma that we ourselves have set in motion in the universe. But Murshid sees a yet further dimension—the planning adjusting itself as things develop:

And no sooner he took the colours and brush in his hand and began to paint his picture, every line he made and every colour he applied suggested to him something, and that altogether altered his plan.

This throws a new light upon the whole subject, because it enables the Planner to take our free will into account and readjust the planning accordingly.

Destiny is always at work with free will, and free will with destiny. The more one becomes conscious of one's will, the more one sees that destiny works around it and that destiny works according to it. And the less conscious one is of that will, the more one finds oneself subject to destiny. In other words, either a person is a mechanism or an engineer; but if he is a mechanism then in him there is a spark of engineer, and if he is an engineer then the mechanism is part of his being.

One has to rethink law now, no longer in terms of what was originally prefigured but accepting that new laws may arise as new developments occur, just as the mutations in a plan present one with a whole new set of possibilities. And even if the possibility of the mutations had been foreseen, if anything is gained by creation, then there must be new vistas for the divine consciousness as life gains new horizons in its inexorable advance. For example, we humans will have to draw up new laws for outer-space traffic and moral codes for communication with interplanetary beings. We are obviously talking about laws covering the causality in events and phenomena in respect to their planning, including the laws governing human action, and the effects of human action upon the causal chain of events.

It seems that one has to consider different dimensions of law, a progression of laws, instead of just Law. Similarly, our school geometry greatly indebted to Euclid applies only to terrestrial stretches of space; it does not apply to sidereal calculations as it does not account for the curvature of space posited by Einstein, spurred on by Minkowski's intuition. This accounts for the terms used by Murshid: the cause behind the effect, and the cause behind the cause, and a still further cause—the Divine Intention. At first, the universe appears as a machine. Whatever you put in comes out, perhaps with a time lag, transformed; predictably, if one understands how the machine is made. But Murshid then speaks of that "subtle machine," the computer built in the machine (one would say nowadays) which displays another set of laws, the laws of electronics instead of mechanics. One could interpose computers hierarchically; similarly, one could envisage a chain of causes superimposed in order of precedence. Clearly, the ultimate one in the series would have a privileged status; but the purpose transcends it, because it belongs to a different order, beyond the causal—the intention beyond the law. Paradoxically, while the purpose is oriented toward the future, it is prior to the cause; and while the cause is sought in the past, its chain unfolds in becoming.

The purpose seems to be in the cause, but it is finished in the effect.

The seed is the cause, the plant is the effect, and the perfume is the purpose. The purpose which is the perfume is not to be found in the seed which is the cause, but in the effect—the plan that is continually evolving. Therefore, do not seek the purpose of your life in past causes, but in what is continually and ever freshly programmed for you, with your participation, and through you. In fact, since God cannot be hampered by his past planning, which we think of as law, He is continually breaking into new dimensions of creativity, which we call evolution.

There is not always the same process, because God is not subject to law and His creation not subject to a process. And the habit He makes in one creation is called nature; and those who perceive its process recognize the process of the change of nature, His Law; this law does not hold good in every cycle of creation, though it is significant to some extent in that particular cycle of creation; and those who have insight into that law are called seers.

There comes a time that one realizes that true freedom is the affirmation of the divine spontaneous creativity, inventiveness and grace manifesting through those cells of God's being we take to be ourselves, beyond the order he had previously catalyzed in the universe which has long since been reified into causality. And man thinks he is challenging the divine order!

Of course, the ultimate freedom is the gift of one's freedom to others. In fact, that is the meaning of the Message of our time that Murshid calls the Message of spiritual liberty:

What is that religion? It is nature's religion of freedom, the religion that will liberate man. When man sees that the ideal of every soul is freedom, and that he cannot enjoy his own freedom unless he has shared his freedom with others, then and only then can troubles and unhappiness cease.[20]

Part III
SPIRITUALITY
IN ACTION

CHAPTER 17

Dare You Renounce
Renunciation Out of Love?

RENUNCIATION

Either you must pass from all things that interest you in this life, or else they will pass you.

Renounce the good of the world,
Renounce the good of heaven,
Renounce your highest ideal
And then renounce renunciation.
—Farid-ud-Din Attar, Persian Sufi poet

The bell had tolled for Murshid to step out of the cosmic dream beyond existence, into that very existence, at its most active setting, in New York.

One day a Brahmin palmist told the fortune of all present. When looking at Murshid's hand, he was visibly taken aback and apologized for being so presumptuous as to venture a forecast; he touched his feet, as a sign of respect and left. A similar incident had occurred in Baroda, when a soothsayer who was an enormous Brahmin occupying the place of four persons bade all leave the room that he might intimate to Murshid alone what he had seen. "Welcome Mahatma," he said. "Excuse my not speaking in the presence of the others, but I must tell you that you will be faring to the West on a mission beyond reckoning." Truly enough, the day soon came when chance struck at the door.

Then Murshid lost all his gold medals, coveted prizes from many musical contests and the fruit of unflinching efforts. It would have been most heartbreaking had he not seen in this test a meaning. "Of what avail the time you have spent gaining what never belonged to you," he exclaimed. Then he prayed: "Let all be lost from my imperfect vision but Thy true Self."

Later he said,

Every loss in life I consider as the throwing off of an old garment in order to put on a new one; and the new garment has always been better than the old.

That Murshid had passed the test as to whether he would cling to his laurels was an unmistakable augury; music had fulfilled its task. Now a new life was opening. His Murshid's last words had already beckoned him to fare forth and unite East and West in the music of his soul, and here the chance was coming his way—at least a chance connection seemed to bridge the gap. A fellow Barodian was in New York and offered to help open their way, which he failed to do when they actually arrived in New York.

At the Royal Academy of Music and the European School of Music of Baroda headed by Dr. Allaodin Khan, the brunt of responsibility had gradually been falling upon the shoulders of Murshid's brother Maheboob Khan, who also adopted all Allaodin's pupils. He had proven himself most conscientious, reliable, and competent. One can imagine the determination it must have required when he received Murshid's telegram to join him on the ship from Bombay, to abandon this responsibility and promising future and his uncle who depended upon him at every turn for a precarious unknown. Yet such was Maheboob Khan's faith in his brother's resolve that he left everything and joined him. For a retiring nature, too shy to sing his beautiful extemporizations in his incomparable silky voice before India's public, standing before a profane audience was a terrible trial. And to make things more difficult, his faith in his elder brother was put to a yet more painful test: He had been invited by the Maharajah of Jumnagar to become Director of Musical Education in his state. Murshid also called his cousin,

Ali Khan, who had always responded with loving docility to the call "chelo" (let's go). He followed his revered and beloved cousin blindly, disregarding the success he was having as a teacher of music, especially European, and as a healer, and the friends he had gathered by his sociable disposition, and the esteem he enjoyed of the Prince Singravo.

Ali Khan had come not asking where he was going, and what he was to do, and why he should come. He was loved and liked by all who met him, and our friends were all struck by what seemed to them his almost infantile innocence and simplicity, with his cheerful nature.

How painful it must have been for Murshid to have to sacrifice his life among the hermits, seers, and recluses, for a world that showed itself harsher, cruder, and less receptive than he would have ever believed. When he made the decision to sail for the venture of his life, could he have predicted that sixteen years later, at the closing of his life on earth, he would have said, after meeting a silent recluse sitting under a lean-to on the banks of the Jumna, "If I were to leave the world and sit here in silence, thousands would come"? Had he not given up the way of the silent renunciate to bestow treasures of wisdom upon the crowds who could not value them?

How few in the West could even understand the subtleties, the refinement, and the grandeur of the mystic insight? When he sat among his disciples in the West, eulogizing sages like the silent muni he was now seeing again, did they realize how, in describing them, he was applying their vow of silence to the secret of his own person? The one who gave up the way of the silent muni to become the mouthpiece of the Message of our time to the masses, was speaking out of the silent depths. "It was like shouting against the noise of a thousand drums and knowing solitude in the crowd."

We know how deeply the way of the recluse not only attracted Murshid but answered his own longing. This personal predilection sometimes emerges very strongly in the plays he wrote. In "The Bogeyman," he portrays a sage married to a Queen and deserting the palace for the wilderness:

Wilderness, my dearest friend, why did I leave you? When did I leave you? Though I had left you, still you were always in my heart. . . . Though I long to be in the solitude, yet I never felt I was away from you.[1]

One can well imagine how Murshid felt—the very same nostalgia that led Buddha to leave on his search for the cause of suffering. At the very end of "The Living Dead," the Maharaja offers his kingdom to his son, Puran; the latter replies, "No, father; I am going in search of another kingdom."[2]

In "The Faithful Trustee," Amin, who really represents the Prophet Mohammed, wanders in the desert of Hera, looking at the wide expanse, saying,

Home is a world, the life outside home is the underworld, but this wilderness is my Paradise. I feel myself only when I am by myself. It is then that I look at the whole world as an onlooker. There must be some reason why I am attracted to this spot. . . . There are many reasons, but how many can be explained? The heavy responsibility of home life and the continual struggle with the outside world; the smallness of human character; the everchanging nature of life; the falsehood that exists in the life of the generality; the absence of justice and the lack of wisdom; all these and many other things make life unbearable for me. Besides, the ever jarring influences coming from all around work upon my sensitive heart and sometimes make me feel lost. It is only here, away from the continual turmoil of life in the world that I find some rest. . . . And yet, I wonder if my heart is really at rest. No, my heart cannot be really rested. If I am here away from the world and my fellow men are in the midst of the turmoil, it cannot give me the peace that I want; it keeps my mind uneasy. . . . What could I do to make the condition of my people better? . . . I must seek God myself first before I speak of goodness to my fellow men. And where shall I find Him? If He is to be found anywhere, it is here in this solitude where my soul feels free.[3]

And then, having first heard the divine Beloved's gentle whisper "through the whispering of the breeze, through the cooing of the wind, through the rippling of the water, through the cracking of the thunder, through the fluttering of the leaves," he realizes that he is not to be found only in the wilderness:

Beloved God, where art Thou not present? Thou art everywhere. The solitude was his ideal, but the reality is ever-present: O Thou who wert the ideal of my belief hitherto, art now a reality to me.[4]

The ideal cannot be confined to a fixed idea.

In order to teach how to put spirituality in practice in life, which is the message of our time, Murshid had to experience in his person and in his mission the antithetical pull between his predilection for asceticism and the sense of fulfillment conferred by involvement with one's fellow men, and resolve it.

In order to arrive at spiritual attainment, two gulfs must be crossed: the sea of attachment and the ocean of detachment.[5]

Here lies the crux of the drama in the soul of every sensitive being, for so many of us are essentially, in our very deep nature, simultaneously the recluse and a conscientiously responsible member of the human family. One can find a vivid description of this situation in D. Gopal Mukerji's book, *My Brother's Face.*

Murshid's musings on the desirability of the asceticism which was so much part of his being and of his traditional background, as opposed to or superimposed upon the way of achievement he chose, run as a leitmotif throughout his life's teaching. Maybe seclusion will give insight, he thought, but is all that life offers to be discarded? Wherefore was it all created? And does not action involve interest, enthusiasm as opposed to indifference and detachment? One might well say that the whole of Hazrat Inayat Khan's message gravitated around finding the answer to this quandary in the soul of modern man. One might say that Murshid was given the experience he needed in order to teach from experience. Of course, Murshid knew what it was to give up something of value and therefore speaks to one's soul:

During my stay in the West, I longed to see the rising of the sun in my land, the full moon in the clear sky, the peace of the midsummer night, night of vigil, the sunset that calls for prayers, and the dawn that moves the soul to sing, besides the occasion that a seeker has of meeting souls who can understand, who can heal hearts and kindle souls, enfolding all that comes in to the peace of their own being.

I learned later why a darvish soul like me, indifferent to the life of the world, constantly attracted to solitude, was set in the midst of the worldly life. It was my training; I learned, as a man of the world, the responsibilities and the needs of the worldly life; which one standing apart from this life, however spiritually advanced, cannot understand; to feel in sympathy with my mureeds placed in different situations of life, and to be able to place myself in their situation and look at their life, it was necessary for me. Besides, to have to do with different natures and souls in the different grades of evolution, it was necessary to have had the experience of home life, especially with children, with their different stages of development, which gives a complete idea of human nature.

If practicing renunciation as a principle were a good thing, there would seem to be no purpose behind the whole of creation. Why are the eyes given if not to appreciate all that is beautiful? Why are the ears given if one may not enjoy the music? Why has one been sent onto the earth if one cannot look at the earth for fear of being called a materialist? Those who make spirituality out to be something like this, make a bogeyman of God, something frightening. In fact, spirituality is the fullness of life.

Yes, most of us feel this even though one part of ourself may be clamoring for the freedom of the renunciate. For the Sufi, every time one's soul leaps in response to beauty, one is participating in God's nostalgia for the fulfillment of his perfection in that expression of himself that is the universe; and, conversely, every time one yearns for silence, one experiences God's resorption of all created things into the resurrected universe of the heavens, where one finds eternal life. This is why most people are attracted to both, yet some more to one than to the other.

The Yogi says that it is better to leave the world, but the Sufi chooses a life in the world with renunciation.[6]

The Sufi has no need to run away from the world, for he has recognized and sees the face of his Beloved, the face of God, everywhere.[7]

Murshid could talk from experience. His very temperament was that of the ascetic, and he knew the value of austerity, even though his Murshid had said when he asked whether he could undergo some feat of mortification: "Whom do you torture? Yourself." Of course, some disciples were banking upon his making ascetics of them. Had he not on several occasions declined the offer of living in a Maharaja's palace, and chosen to sleep on the floor in a derelict hut exposed to snakes and mosquitos? He had even turned down an invitation by the Maharaja of Sylhet to function as a murshid at his palace.

Yet we have seen that by withdrawing from the world, yogis and fakirs were able to develop profound insight.

Such people are the ones who make experiments of life by the sacrifice of all the joy and pleasure that the earth can give.

What was happening to Murshid's soul, then, is what has been happening to the soul of humanity ever since the time of Shiva, Buddha, and Ramvira: Man, a particle of the only Consciousness, sought to look beyond; and when hoisted up high, saw the created world through the mist of vertiginous perspective, unreal and deluding; then the Only Consciousness descended more fully into human consciousness, thereby experiencing himself in the fulness of the manifestation of himself. For man the world may seem *samsaric*, illusory, when it falls out of his focus, as his capacity is not stereoscopic enough to incorporate the void and the fulness in one. But for the One of whom it is the expression, it is very real, and so it is to a person who becomes transparent to the Divine Consciousness acting through himself. Thus he realizes what God realizes of himself as he offers himself in and through the Universe. This is the difference between the point of view of a man who is alienated from the earth plane, and God, bursting the limits of man's sense of individuality to enable him to experience his vastness.

Thus when spiritually sensitive beings are called upon to give up their longed-for solitude, they are participating in a process of transformation that is taking place in humanity in our time. God is incorporating more and more concretely in more and more beings, which means right in the thick of bustling life, rather than in rare avatars, thereby increasingly experiencing his divine perfection. This is what Murshid says characterizes the Message. All the teaching of Murshid embodies a momentous challenge. If life in the world has a cosmic import, could one not bring the precious qualities and faculties developed by ascetics to bear for the purpose of improving one's own understanding of what is being enacted on the scene of life, in order to fulfill one's purpose in life?

Where does renunciation function in action? One is continually facing problems where one has to make a choice. There is an old proverb: "You cannot have your cake and eat it too." Murshid says,

There is no gain that is not a loss and there is no loss that is not a gain. There is no gain without pain.[8]

So when one is thrown onto the horns of a dilemma, one has to sacrifice one thing for another. This is where we are at. How should one turn? "If I do this, I will be missing out on something important; but if I do the alternative, there is also a loss, the way I see it." If only one could see right! The problem becomes all the more acute for the one who has a severe scruple about right and wrong. One is continually tested in one's relation with people and situations, in one's integrity, in one's intention, in one's ego, in one's degree of kindness, tolerance, and patience, in the quality of one's emotion. Sometimes there is a wrong beneath a right and a right hidden beyond what appears wrong. Yet one's discrimination is the measure of one's insight and it is one's own choice that builds one's destiny.

Is it conceivable to introduce the basic principles underlying the life of the recluse into the middle of the active life? Could one thus hope to develop in some measure the precious qualities he displays? I am convinced that this is the soul-searching question of all new age people. Would not the vastness of the realization of the sage, gained by renunciation, give one the insight into the overall purpose of one's life, thus helping one to see beyond the limitations of the immediate relative purpose one generally grasps?

Somewhere, one feels intuitively how fragile one's judgment is when confronted with something momentous. Of course, one cannot see correctly from one angle of view alone, just like the blind people of the tale, who tried to make out what an elephant was—each thought it was something different. One's awareness of the inadequacy of one's understanding spurs one to seek to intuit the higher understanding that transpires sometimes just above one's limited understanding. One thinks one's understanding is one's understanding, until one realizes it is one's sharing in the understanding of God. If one thinks that one decides things, then one's decision is arbitrary. The best decision is the expression of one's very understanding of the divine intention.

One knows that one often finds oneself at the crossroads, faced with a situation in which one is compelled to make a choice between two alternatives where one wishes for both, yet one still has to renounce something. It may be in one's job: Should I give it up? Should I persevere? Or in personal relationships, or in allegiance to a group or society. One does not know at the time that, in fact, one will feel happier later on if one chooses that which one now feels has a higher value. Murshid's teaching had grown out of his experience.

Where in order to gain silver coins, one has to lose the copper ones, one must learn to lose them.

We have seen how, after reaching the summit of his musical career, Murshid was directed by his Murshid to take the Message of Sufism to the West, whereupon he gave up that object which was nearest to his heart—music. "The sacrifice of music for me was not a small one," he has said. At first in the West he used music as a shield, although Indian music had no particular place in the professional world of the West. "Most often I had to sell my pearls at the value of pebbles," he says.

I would have been most happy sitting with my vina in my hand in some corner in the forest, in the solitude, and nothing better would I have asked for. There came a time when I could not have sufficient time to keep up my musical practice, which was too great a loss for my heart to sustain. Yet I had to bear it, for every moment of my time was absorbed in the work. I especially yearned for the music of India, the fluid with which my soul was nourished from the moment I was born on earth. But for my music, the soil of India was necessary, the juice of the soil for me to live on, the air of India to be inspired by.

It may be that one's choice seems arbitrary, but one may learn thereby the difference between that which one is attached to and that which one values even more. One may regret the loss of what one had to abandon, but one has to learn to let go and may console oneself by realizing that one is sustaining less of a loss than if one decided to sacrifice that which one has now chosen. And later, one might find, as the Master often says, that what seemed a loss at the time, reveals itself as a gain. One recalls Murshid's reflections when he had lost his medals; now they could be brought to bear in his teaching.

It was a good lesson to resist the tendency of being disappointed, and see in this, as he did, an indication that those values were now obsolete for him, and overcome, and a new phase in his life was due. If one could only assess things in their ultimate relevance, one would avoid much unnecessary suffering and bitterness.

Indecision, failure to make a choice, will block one in one's progress by the fact that one thereby loses an opportunity to unfold oneself, since the very fact of taking a decision upon oneself would make one stronger. Of course, every new asset is a gain, but also everything that one has given up frees one from a load, if done without resentment and because one clearly sees that it is the only way of reaching out to a greater fulfillment. This is where the ascetic's attitude of detachment can help in one's achievement, for one progresses by giving up something one was attached to for something more worthwhile. Imagine looking back and realizing how lucky that what one wished so much a few years ago never materialized. "Beware of what you want," said Emerson, "it might happen."

One reaches a point where one is continually practicing discrimination with regard to the greater or lesser value of things one pursues. Then one is tested.

Thus the value of all things that we consider precious or not precious is according to the way we look at them. For one person the renuciation of a penny is too much; for another that of everything he possesses is nothing. Renuciation depends upon the evolution of the soul. For those who develop spiritually, all things are easy to renounce.

There is nothing valuable except what we value in life; and a man is fully justified in renouncing all that he has, or that may be offered to him, for the sake of that which he values, even if it be that he values it only for this moment; for there will never be a thing which he will value always in the same way.

When man has to choose between his spiritual and his material profit, then he shows whether his treasure is on earth or in heaven.

If you wish to prove the depths of a man's character, test him with that which is his life's greatest need.

In the Bible it is written, "Where your treasure is, there will be your heart also."[9]

But how can one assess the comparative value of one's pursuits? The criterion used by the ascetics is whether it is transient or lasting. One has to decide whether to:

renounce momentarily precious things for everlasting things, or everlasting things for momentarily precious things.

One must train one's sense of discrimination in order to distinguish what is more valuable and what is less so. One can learn this by testing,

just as real gold is tested by imitation gold. We might ask if we should not recognize them by their beauty; but we must also recognize beauty in durability. Think of the difference in the price between a flower and a diamond.[10]

"You can't take it with you" is a popular expression. One carries upward into resurrection the realization that one has attained through action (not the object achieved). There is a basic meditation theme practiced by the Hindu rishis: Discriminate all in and around oneself that is transient *(prakriti)* from that which is imperishable, which has always been and always will be, your eternal spirit *(Purusha)*. The Sufis use the same theme with the *wazifa* (mantram) "Ya Hayyo, Ya Qayyum." If one identifies with one's eternal being unfolding in the course of time, like a plant growing out of the seed, then one has a completely different scale of values than if one thinks one is the ephemeral ego, hemmed in by the limits of personal judgment.

What determines that which one values is one's degree of realization at the time. For example, the little girl may attach so much importance to her dolls that she cannot sleep without them; when she grows up, she will give them up. A man may strive at the cost of his health or his peace of mind to buy himself a beautiful house, hoist himself up to a position of worldly power at one time, and then realize that there are things more meaningful to him, such as playing music, learning about plants or planets, healing people, or understanding the purpose of his life.

Thus, every step of progress is made by renouncing more personal values for more cosmic ones. . . . Every act of courtesy, of politeness, shows renunciation.[11]

However, the Master advises his disciples to start by first achieving something concrete, because if one has achieved an objective, one is in a better position to assess it in its real value. Now one may renounce it for a greater goal. For example, the man who longs to compose music may suffer because he is unable to earn a good enough living to own a nice, comfortable home; but if once he has experienced what sacrifice of his art he has to make to play in a night club in order to pay for a fashionable flat, he may prefer living in a hut and giving free vent to his musical inspiration. Murshid gave up music after having reached the summit most musicians in his time were craving. But he first achieved the fulfillment of his aim.

Murshid's teaching gives another dimension than the spectacle of our problems seen from our individual vantage point. Of course, ultimately one wishes to see how one's life has contributed to an overall purpose. At first, one is unable to encompass so vast a purpose with one's mind. However, in the course of working for a concrete objective, one learns to assess its relevance to the well-being of one's fellow man. Perhaps at a further stage one undertakes something one values still more and will be able to see its relevance in the context of that which is being enacted on the cosmic scene. For example, a musician becomes a good cellist in an orchestra and may be aware of the measure in which his playing contributes to the perfection of the performance, and ultimately to the elevation of the public. But suppose he gives up his cello playing and becomes a composer; then in order to contribute something worthwhile to human culture, he must express something of the victory of the human spirit over despair, or the incorporation of the cosmic mass celebrated in the heavens into the consciousness and nature of beings on earth. One's problems are part of what is happening to humanity.

Life is a fulfillment, the fulfillment of the desire of the Creator to know himself in creation and through the creature. This is the basic tenet of Sufism. If desire is experienced in man, then it must originate in God, in whom the archetypes of all things exist, at least as latencies. This is intriguing, if not paradoxically challenging, to those who have been taught desirelessness. Man appropriates desire egotistically, and that enslaves him, causing enmities and cruelty.

It is the interest of the Creator that has made this creation. The hidden desire of the Creator is the secret of the whole creation.

The Sufis recognize God in all things; to them the desires for accomplishment or attainment or fulfillment or unfoldment which one feels are expressions of the divine impulse. Such was the motivation that set the course of Murshid's voyage to the United States. Yet he knew how men misuse or betray the original inspiration by their limitation.

There is no impulse which in its beginning is wrong. It is during the process through which the impulse passes that it becomes right or wrong.

There is a saying in the Gayan, which not everbody is able to understand, "To repress desire is to suppress a divine impulse." Those who distinguish between divine and not divine certainly make the greatest error, as is the same as that between the machine and the engineer. The mind of God is working and at the same time the instrument, the machine of God is working; therefore that which arises as a desire has God as its source and is thus a divine impulse.

Thus it is oneself that deviates the purpose by appropriating it and losing touch with the original intention. It follows that murder would be the deviation of that necessary cosmic principle which is destruction. Life can only advance at the cost of the disintegration of all formations that have become fossilized. But when this divine impulse is used by someone against another for what might appear to him to be a personal advantage, then it is a clear misappropriation of a cosmic principle, and is what is meant by evil. Whereas if one welcomes one's own death as an expression of the law of dissolution of all that is transient and perishable, one is resonating in harmony with the divine impulse. Conversely, if one incorporates God's wish to unfold himself in oneself, one is fulfilling a divine impulse. An appreciation of the many-splendored aspects of life in their relative values would bring the nostalgia of the Creator into the focus of one's awareness; and then if one learns to counterbalance desire with detachment, one substitutes more cosmic desires for more personal ones. In fact, we are both divine nostalgia and divine freedom.

One may strive for a position in life that gives one a sense of power, expressing thereby the divine impulse of power; at the same time, power goes to one's head and one is oppressing other people for one's own vanity. Then one comes in contact with beings who have renounced the world and one is deeply touched by their examples. Now without oneself renouncing the world, one becomes indifferent to one's prestige and one will begin to manifest divine sovereignty— powerful yet impersonal—in one's own being and atmosphere. Here interest and indifference go hand in hand. By renouncing the object that one has achieved one makes room for a greater purpose; and when once one has accomplished one desire, one will have that something which is needed for the accomplishment of something greater.

Every desire you accomplish is one step further towards that final goal which every soul ultimately has to reach. If you tell yourself that you do not desire anything, you go back. This whole creation is the result of desire. The purpose of creation, therefore, must be the fulfillment of this desire.

Is it possible to combine both?

Mastery is greater than seership, because the master both sees and accomplishes.

Indifference to worldly things gives insight into them, because one is not emotionally involved, but interest gives motivation for accomplishment; both give one a sense of power.

Indifference gives great power. [But] the whole manifestation is a phenomenon of interest. All this world that man has made, where has it come from? It has come from the power of interest. The whole creation and all that is in it is the product of the Creator's interest. But at the same time the power of indifference is a greater one still. Why is the power of indifference greater than the power of interest? Because, although motive has a power, yet at the same time motive limits power. Yet it is the motive that gives man the power to accomplish things. But the motive reduces the power to a drop. Without a motive the power of the soul is like an ocean; but at the same time that ocean-like power cannot be used without a motive.

Indifference releases that limitation automatically. There are people who run after money, and there are people after whom money runs.

There are some who wish to wield power, what little power they can get; and there are others upon whom power is heaped though they do not want it. We also see many examples in this world of how interest often limits man's power, and how indifference makes it greater. But at the same time indifference should not be practiced unless it springs naturally from the heart. There is a saying in the Hindi language, "Interest makes kings, but indifference makes emperors."

The Master had seen as a young man how the courtiers and musicians were scrambling for power around the rajas, and later in his own movement how leaders fought for position and supremacy. Does one realize how the struggle for a power position robs one of a greater power? No one can take away what one is in one own realization, nor place one where one has not yet reached. If only one could see these outer appearances from higher up, one would be able to discern what is real from what is show and sham. One is only ready for a position if one has given up wishing for it.

Even rank and position and power do not matter very much, for all these are also false claims. In order to occupy a certain position, one has to deprive others of it. But when a position or rank no longer makes any difference, then one has reached a still higher stage.

Not only should one refrain from resting on one's laurels, that is, abandon what one has attained only after attaining it (in the *Bhagavad Gita* it is called abandoning the fruit of action), but the very thought of gain will confine one to a limited purpose as one is pursuing it. Murshid was applying the principles of both interest and indifference, each in its right place. If one has set one's mind upon achieving something, like starting a new business or enterprise, one's very motivation will give one determination to accomplish or obtain the coveted object. One would develop great power. But supposing that, after it is all built up and is in such good running condition that one can entrust it to somebody else, one gives it up for something one feels is more worthwhile? One will thus acquire a still greater power. Supposing one toiled for years to build oneself a house, just as one fancied it, and now having completed it, one donates it for a home for retarded children; or supposing one gives up piano playing in order to hold a responsible position which means a lot for many people! Supposing that pursuing a greater motive involved giving up a personal relationship dear to you? One would develop tremendous power. The one who wields the power of indifference toward personal wishes becomes a dervish king.

One feels that power at times when one has risen above a desire or an attachment that was pulling one down or weighing heavily upon one, and one feels it standing in the way of one's progress.

It is the nature of life in the world that all the things we become attracted to in time become not only ties but burdens.

This is where renunciation can be seen as:

a flight of stairs by which to rise above all things.[12]

For all things of this world that man thinks he possesses he does not really possess; in reality, he is possessed by them, be it wealth, or property, or a friend, or rank.

Paradoxically, as we saw when musing upon renunciation, it is renunciation that is the secret that leads one from one accomplishment to a still greater one, because unless one renounces one's gain for a higher accomplishment, one will stagnate. At the cost of mixing popular metaphors: The choice is between "beating one's records" or "sleeping upon one's laurels."

Hence, the first step toward accomplishment or attainment, whether it be spiritual or worldly, will be to proceed with purpose toward the goal of one's desire. But once one has realized some gain, it would keep one from striving for something greater if one rested on one's laurels.

When a person has in view an object he wants to attain, he is smaller than the object; but when a person has attained the object, he is greater than the object; and as he holds the object which he has attained, so he diminishes his strength; but when he renounces the object he has once attained, he rises above the object.

Furthermore, the tendency to doubt, the tendency to distress, the tendency to fear, suspicion, and confusion, where does it all come from? It comes from the thought of getting something in return, anxiety as to whether anyone will give one back what one has given.

Every gain a person has in view limits him to a certain extent to that gain, directs his activities into a certain channel, and forms the line of his fate. At the same time it deprives him of a still greater or a better gain and of the freedom of activity which might perhaps accomplish something still better.

But if one were to renounce a thing before achieving it, thinking it is not worth the effort, yet would still like to have it without working for it, that is laziness, not renunciation; one has not grown out of it, like the girl outgrowing her dolls' play.

When should one practice resignation, and when accomplishment?

Resignation is the attribute of the saints, and hopefulness is the attribute of the masters. We should be resigned to all that we have suffered, to all that has gone wrong, to all that we have lost, but we should not continue that resignation for the things of the present, because the present should be met with hopefulness.

There is a story of three frogs that were caught in a bowl of milk. One gave up right away. The second kept on trying to get out and finally gave up. The third kept on churning and churning the milk until it turned into butter and he got out safely.

If one has risen above certain things in life one does not attach any more importance to them; to be contented in that case is the contentment of the sages, of the wise. But if one wishes to obtain things which one considers to be of great importance to one, one should not practice contentment, but enthusiasm. One should let enthusiasm grow, so that the will-power may use the enthusiasm to produce the desired results from it.[13]

You may be in a situation where you want to accomplish something, and people laugh at you or are apt to criticize you. In that situation, you should be indifferent. But if in order to promote your business you have to see someone to get connections, all this will only succeed according to your interest. If you are indifferent about it, you will defeat your own ends.

Murshid does not advise his pupils to force the pace by giving up prematurely what they are hankering after, as these inhibited desires will fester in the form of harbored despondency. A group of Ceylonese Buddhist monks on a visit to Paris were caught up in the night life of the city. If one still has some leaning for the world, one had better first live, then renounce.

He would always remain exposed to temptation, and subject to the distracting influence of his surroundings.

Those who renounce their desires for God, for spiritual perfection, and bury their own desires in their heart, they are entombed in the heart, and there they will produce all sorts of germs and worms, and they will decay.[14]

He is only entitled to say that he does not want the sweet when he has had so much of it that he cannot eat anymore. If he is still longing, well, he may say "no" but it will only be formality; perhaps it would not be good etiquette to say "yes" but he longs for it just the same! So it is that you have to rise above everything that you renounce. You go on seeking so long as you have a desire for a thing.[15]

He alone is capable of renunciation who finds a greater satisfaction in seeing another eat his piece of bread than in eating it himself.[16]

Only those whose heart is full of happiness after an act of renunciation should make a renunciation.[17]

Yet to the advanced pupils Murshid said:

If you wish to develop mastery, should you be hungry, you don't eat for a time; should you be sleepy, you don't sleep for a time; should you wish to talk, you don't talk for a time; should you wish to move, you don't move for a time.

So, if renouncing what one has already depreciated marks the natural process of growing up, one might accelerate that growth by giving up something one has depreciated in one's higher understanding, yet to which one is still attached. Granted, one should not sacrifice should one resent doing so; yet as one progresses, one is called upon to sacrifice that which one loves most.

One always seems to be tested in that which one cares for most. How much does one know of the soul-searching of beings, forced to give up their all that they were living for, let down, betrayed, maligned, desperate, dismayed in frightful anguish of soul, facing an ordeal. Recall the fate of Abraham summoned to sacrifice his dearest son—an extreme case, but does one not see one's problem sometimes better through a magnifying glass?

All of a sudden, by a supreme effort, one reaches the point of accepting the unacceptable, and now all is changed. The miracle has happened; all is understood. The loss has been turned into a gain. How glad one is that things did not happen as one wished. When the Sufi dervish Al Hallaj heard the verdict that he was due to be tortured and then crucified, he said:

The divine host has invited me to the banquet and offered me to drink from the chalice of poison from which He Himself drinks; how could I refuse?

If one were to see the hand of the divine guidance training one through the tests that one thinks one encounters fortuitously, one would grasp how, at a certain stage of progress, one is placed before a painful choice of either sacrificing something to which one is still emotionally attached or renouncing the spiritual unfoldment or mission to which one is dedicated.

Sometimes renunciation is like death; but having once renounced one finds oneself standing above death.

It is certainly better if one recognizes oneself as the target of an intentional test by the Divine Planner incorporated in his assistant guides, watching one's destiny, than to succumb to the thought that one is the innocent victim of blind fate.

When Murshid was a little boy, he used to muster his friends to enact a play that certainly embodies one of the most extreme forms of renunciation for an ideal in order to live up to a promise. The priests who were collecting money for cremations at the ghats of Benares had a bet as to how reliable a king, Haris Chandra, was. One of them appeared before the king and asked him if he would grant him a wish. As Haris Chandra greatly revered priests and rishis, he accepted, whereupon the priest said, "I wish to be king." Haris Chandra, his wife, and child left on foot for a neighboring country. When they were about to cross the frontier, the priest appeared once more to him, telling him that as they had been traveling in his territory, they owed him a tax. As Haris Chandra had abandoned all his wealth to the priest, he told him that he had no money to pay. The priest retorted that as Haris Chandra had given his word that he recognized him as king, he had to pay the tax. Thereupon Haris Chandra sold his wife and child into slavery, and he himself engaged in the service of the priest to collect money at the ghats. Shortly afterward his little son died, and when his wife wished him to be cremated at the ghats, Haris Chandra asked for the fee. As she did not have it, he was in duty bound to refuse. At this point the priest, according to the story, brought an end to the test, and restored the prince to life and the king to his throne, and everyone lived happily ever after.

The Sufi dervish Ibrahim Ibn Adham said that he was commanded to demonstrate in his own person the condition of man as the eternal Adam. He became so oblivious of his own person that worms, insects, and vermin had settled all over his body, which was bruised from stumbling through sheer weakness.

I have to demonstrate that joy can spring in the midst of the most excruciating suffering. I have to experience the condition of man at its worst and at its best: the condition of Adam, fraught with infirmities, scorned, abused, trampled upon, despised, and simultaneously glorious in the divine consciousness. It is God in me who is experiencing the ignominies to which the creature is subjected and who is at the same time experiencing the ecstasy of overcoming. You think you are experiencing suffering—it is the condition of the whole universe; you think you are experiencing joy—it is the condition of the whole universe.

A case nearer to us is that of the priest who used to celebrate Mass every Sunday in a concentration camp, exhorting his fellow inmates to overcome despair by divine glorification. He would be dragged away and flogged, then he came back again and exhorted his hearers even more fervently than before, in an exultation that transmuted suffering into jubilation.

There comes a time in the adept's progress when he passes a further threshold of realization: He grasps that in renouncing objects, or power, or material advantage, it is actually something in himself that he is renouncing. This is a symptom of growth. One sees how, when thinking oneself to be what one thought oneself to be, one could not have not pursued the aspiration one pursued; and one observes everybody doing just that. The scene of life moves on; men are caught up in the rat-race, coveting vain objectives that seem at that time so important. How the one who has awakened from the hoax watches on with a smile, and also with much compassion for all the suffering resulting from ignorance.

This awakening starts when one wonders what one is, instead of taking oneself for granted. And then one wishes to give up oneself. It is like a deadly fight with a phantom whom one realizes is a picture of one's own limitation. A dervish once said: "I may appear to you as yourself, until you are so confused that you do not know anymore who yourself is." That is when the inner eye opens.

In order to be, one must pass through a stage of being nothing. The false self is lost, and the true self is gained.

In the play *Una* the artist, wishing to give her life so that her ideal in the form of her sculpture may live, takes a glass of poison. The external image says to her, "Now thou art living with my life."[18]

Lost in deep grief and exaltation after the brutal death of his radiant inspirer, the Sufi poet Jelal-ud-Din Rumi cried out "The Beloved is all in all, the Beloved is all that lives." And at the sheer recollection of this thought, many a dervish has burst into ecstasy. Of course, says the Master, "If you lose yourself in an object, you live as that object."

If one were attuned to the ecstasy of the realization of the Presence of the One and Only Beloved, then the sense of oneself would be completely obliterated, and to renounce the ephemeral would not seem a sacrifice. Pain is born of ignorance, and joy of understanding. This is the state of the awakened ones. Imagine that, having lost oneself, one does not entertain a wish for oneself, as one has become completely impersonal; every wish that arises in one's consciousness is the divine will. This is why "the soul which naturally rises to heaven does not need to practice renunciation."

Here it is obvious that the love of God reveals itself as the secret of awakening from the personal self. The paradox is that, finding oneself, one discoveres oneself as being completely impersonal and therefore as a part of all being(s). The difference between "mine" and "thine" and the distinction of "I" and "You" fade away in the realization of the one Beloved that is within and without, beneath and beyond; and that is the meaning of the verse in the Bible, "In Him we live, and move, and have our being."

Now everything in life assumes a different significance. If you have become conscious of being all beings, there is nothing that is yours, so there is no possession to renounce; it is no sacrifice if one sees every being as oneself. No one will sacrifice for another except when he is oneself.

If this feeling develops, it extends further, not only with the friend and the neighbor, but with the stranger, with the beast and bird and insect; one is in at-one-ment with all living beings, and it gives one as much insight into another as the other person has into himself. One knows as much about him as he knows, even more. When one is tuned to the divine will, one does not need to be resigned, for one's wish becomes the divine impulse.

One tends to conceive of an ideal objective, which then fossilizes in time into a set principle; however, "the ideal is like the horizon." Therefore, we have to know how to renounce it in order to reach further. This explains Murshid's perplexing motto, "Shatter your ideal on the rock of truth."

In fact, if one has set oneself an ideal of renunciation without losing oneself, the chances are that one is pursuing asceticism selfishly or renunciation out of weakness. And thus Murshid's whole vision of the dichotomy between renunciation and desire, which one has woven in and out of one's mind during this first contact with his thought and being, gravitates around a verse of the Sufi poet Farid-ud-Din Attar:

Renounce the good of the world; renounce the good of heaven; renounce your highest ideal; and then renounce your renunciation.

During one's spiritual ascent all this time, renunciation had lifted one above subjection to whims, attachment, bondage, conditioning, delusion in vain values; and now, at the peak, dare one renounce all that has been gained by renunciation, out of love? The secret mechanism of life is paradoxical; so is Sufism.

Sufism is *fana*, annihilation, and *baqa*, resurrecting through annihilation, transmuted and transfigured. It is knowing while one does not know, seeing while one cannot see, hearing while one cannot hear, understanding and being conscious while one has gone beyond consciousness. It is going beyond what one thought one knew; giving up one's love so that one may find it. And in God all things are restored: That is baqa.

CHAPTER 18

Fulfilling Life's Purpose

ACHIEVEMENT

"Fare forth, my child, and harmonize men in the East and West with the harmony of thy music, spreading the Message; become a musician of beings, for to this end, thou art gifted."—Khwaja Abu Hashim Madani

I will soar higher than the highest heavens,
I will dive deeper than the depths of the ocean,
I will reach further than the wiae horizon,
I will enter within my innermost being.
—Gayan, 140

Every soul is created for a certain purpose—the light of that purpose has been kindled in every soul.—Sa'adi, Persian Sufi poet

Every thing and being is placed in its own place, and each is busy carrying out the work which has to be done in the scheme of things.

When the sanyasin or dervish returns into the world, electrified by the magnetism of nature and endowed with insight, some people are intrigued to see whether knowledge of awakening can help in practical issues.

Murshid sailed out of Calcutta for New York on September 13, 1910, accompanied by his faithful brother and cousin. He left behind his whole world of classical music, the time-honored India of noble tradition and lofty ideals in which he revolved, and the holy men, sanyasins, and dervishes with whom he felt so much affinity, heading for a hard new world yet to be discovered, though quizzically anticipated—a world motivated by material values, reckless competitiveness, and heedless outspokenness. He went through momentous experience in the nature of a cosmic disclosure. From his autobiographical notes, we know that he was spurred on by an impelling sense of purpose.

I tried to think where I was going, what I was doing, what I was going to do, what was in store for me, how shall I set to work: will the people be favorable or unfavorable to the Message which I am taking from one end of the world to the other?

Now his trust in the realization obtained during his gradual awakening all those past years was being tested to the utmost, because it took an incomparable reliance on the innate divine nature which is the substratum of all beings to overcome the human sense of smallness or inadequacy, faced with a monumental task.

And at moments I felt too small and little for my ideals and inspirations, comparing my limited self with this vast world. But at moments, realizing Whose work it was, Whose service it was, Whose call it was, by the answer

288

which my heart gave, moved me to ecstasy, as if I had risen in the realization of truth above the limitations which weigh mankind down.

A Persian poet has said, "Through I see myself in the greatest and highest and most perfect Being, yet I find myself in poverty, limitation, and distress. The reason for this is just my own ignorance of myself, of my true self. It is the delusion of the limitation of life."

The Sufi strives to overcome the source of poverty hidden within the life of everyone. The source of poverty is limitation.[1]

Discover in yourself the same power that moves the planet. It takes just that moment of grappling with one's tendency to limit one's personal outlook to overcome it. A voice seemed to emerge repeatedly:

Thou art sent on Our service, and it is We who will make thy way clear.

[Man] is limited because he is conscious of his limitation.

Here we touch upon the clue to the ultimate awakening: switch the setting of consciousness.

What is meant by limitation and what by perfection? These are only conditions of the consciousness. When one is conscious of limitation, one is limited: when one is conscious of perfection, one is perfect.[2]

Murshid experienced these two settings of consciousness as he cast off on his task.

The nature of being in tune with the infinite is this: comparing our soul to a string of an instrument, it is tied at both ends: one is infinite, and the other is the finite.

The aim of the mystic is to stretch his range of consciousness as widely as possible, so that he may touch the highest pride and the deepest humility.[3]

Imagine an inverted cone or pyramid whose base is contiguous to the universe, all-encompassing: We are the totality indicated by the infinite base and also all that lies between the totality and the apex. All the bounty of that totality is concentrated, highly charged, as it piles upon itself, yet squeezed and consequently impoverished at the sharp end, although there it gains in concreteness, bringing out the richness latent in the totality. Now imagine that instead of focusing cosmic consciousness through the vantage point of the apex, which is the bottom of the inverted cone, you should spread it throughout the base at the top, which is infinite. The result would be that, being conscious of the bounty of your cosmic being, you would be able to look upon your personal being as a limitation, though a distinctive determination, of that bounty; namely, as an image of yourself. Having experienced this, you would know that it was fallacious to think that you were that image.

Man is not a footprint of God but God Himself; as if the sun had thought by looking at the sunflower, "I am the sunflower," forgetting at that moment that the sunflower was only its footprint.

One could quote further examples: Imagine the sun looking at the rainbow and discovering the spectrum that throws into perspective the colors that it cannot see in itself, and being so fascinated by this discovery of itself that it forgets what it itself is; or a vibration looking at its pattern on an oscillograph; or a component of the cosmic harmony of the universe, being a precarious balance of energy poised in unstable equilibrium, discovering itself in a snowflake and forgetting that it is pure enough and of more wonder than the snowflake could ever evidence.

This is precisely what we are doing continually. It is epitomized in the Greek myth of Zagreus, the son of God, being so amazed by his image in the mirror presented by the Titans that he was precipitated from his throne into the abyss. The meaning of the eschatological fall is our succumbing to the appearance: not only the way things look but mainly our idea of ourselves; indeed, what the Hindus mean by maya.

It is the situation we are in which makes us believe we are this or that. Whatever the soul experiences, that it believes itself to be. If the soul sees the external self as a baby it believes: I am a baby. If it sees the external self as old it believes: I am old. If it sees the external self in a palace it believes: I am rich. If it sees that self in a hut it believes: I am poor. But in reality it is only: I am. . . . When man lives in this limitation he does not know that another part of his being exists, which is much higher, more wonderful, more living and more exalted.[4]

The only way to shift this focus upward is to overcome the optical pull arising out of one's conception of the confines of what one imagines to be one's self.

How to become conscious of the spirit? Our great Sufi poetess, Zab-un Nissa, says, "Thou art a drop in the ocean. But if thou wilt hold the thought of the ocean, thou wilt be the same."

More specifically, meditation can be applied, as is done classically, with a view to discovering oneself as a finer order of reality whose frontiers are less defined than the body, or as one's magnetic auric body, as pure thought or feeling, or again as consciousness.

As he goes further in the meditative life, he then begins to see . . . that he himself is a thought, that he himself is a feeling, and that he himself is the creator of thought, even a creator of feeling. And as he goes still higher, he sees that he is happiness himself as well as the creator of happiness.[5]

One might say that the experience of pure intelligence is possible only for the only Being, for God, but no one can stand outside of the only Being, and therefore, each and everyone is in the only Being.[6]

One can further the more cosmic span of consciousness in taking over from the more personal by dwelling upon a sense of vastness, together with becoming more and more impersonal.

How did I rise above narrowness? The edges of my own walls began to hurt my elbows.[7]

In order to see life clearly the outlook should be wide. The surest proof that a person can give of his greatness is his vast outlook.

The difficulty is in maintaining the focus of the unlimited consciousness while also being aware of the limitation imposed by the location of the body in space and the viewpoint taken up by consciousness operating through the mind. This causes consciousness, in its confinement, to distinguish itself as the subject from the totality which is envisioned as the object. Otherwise, we would not be able to operate at the physical and mental levels and would find ourselves in a state of samadhi.

How then can the awakened one walk on the physical earth and move in an environment if it appears to him to be a hallucination? Consciousness operates simultaneously at several levels, at once bringing itself into a focus in that aperture of the human camera that one may call the personalized "I," fenced in by our limited notion of ourselves; and at the same time at the setting of the latent substrate of collective consciousness underlying the personal perspective. Consciousness functioning at one level may experience reality in its physical condition, while simultaneously consciousness functioning at a more transcendental level espies behind the scene that which is on its way down into the scene. It is as though one were able to see at the same time the plants blossoming above the surface of the earth and the seeds sprouting under the earth before they emerge as plants.

Compared with that person, everyone else seems to have open eyes and yet not to see.[8]

As one awakens, the operation of the impersonal consciousness is not hampered by the vision of the personal focus from affirming its wider vision. One can neutralize the normally confining effect of body consciousness by envisioning one's body as part of the whole deployment of planet Earth since the historical moment when that agglomeration of gases was exuded by the sun and cooled as it orbited. In the surge and flow of differentiated bodiness, the limits we ascribe to our body blurr in a continuum of proliferating bodies, each perpetuating all the preceding ones. The same applies to what we assume is our thinking, which is really the thinking of the planetary intelligence, and beyond, that cosmic intelligence condensed into its components, which we call our minds.

Then man becomes God-man, God-conscious; outwardly he is in the universe, inwardly the universe is in him. Outwardly he is smaller than a drop, inwardly he is larger than the ocean.[9]

There are some beings who are in themselves the universe. By expanding to the vastness of God the mystic experiences the greatness of God in every form.

One's sense of personal self undergoes a change by being continually overwhelmed by the consciousness of one's cosmic being: It is taken into orbit, as it were, by one's all-encompassing awareness. Usually, one tends to proceed the other way round; being quartered in one's individual consciousness, one tries to grasp cosmic consciousness at the horizon of one's reach, as though it were the object to be known. Here lies the fatal error. It is like looking at the top of the mountain from the bottom, rather than looking at the bottom from the top.

The higher the stratum of one's being, the less personal one is. It is like the difference between roses and rosehood, like the differences in the numbers in a logarithmic progression; and the more impersonal one is, the more one merges into all beings. This explains Jung's collective unconscious, a memory of the race, or of the planet, carried by all humans but mostly buried by the personal memories. Even the body carries the memory of the fish state, for example; and the mind, the basic elements of the legends and myths of all civilizations; and the soul, memories of the heavenly state, the processions of heavenly beings, the glory, the jubilations, the ovations, the proclamations, the victories, the overcomings, the transfigurations.

Man inherits the qualities of the entire human race. . . . One has a right to this heritage. The collective working of many minds as one single idea, and the activity of the whole world in a certain direction, are governed by the intelligence of the planet. . . . The whole planet has an effect upon all those living on the planet.[10]

What about the sun and the moon and the stars? Is there intelligence in all of these? If the planet on which we live had no intelligence it could not have intelligent beings on it. For what is nature? Nature is the development of the planet. The planet has developed into organic nature and has culminated in human beings, intelligent beings; and it still remains a planet.[11]

Yes, this is planetary intelligence. It has been relegated to the dark recesses of the unconscious because human beings are so geared to acquiring personal gain and comfort, but it is emerging more clearly now as men begin to realize the need to compose their forces to meet problems at a planetary scale. Teilhard de Chardin had already pointed this out as the next step in evolution, the convergence of the thinking of men, and he called it Point Omega. He clarified that if men are pooling their intelligence it is because something is happening to the overall intelligence which, having fanned out and focalized in Pleiades of individual ego centers, is now integrating these centers into a center of centers by the convergence and the conjugation of these. One, having become everything and everyone, becomes the All. Teilhard stresses that Omega could not have become Omega if it had not already been contained in Alpha.

A few decades before Teilhard de Chardin's *Phenomenon of Man* appeared, Murshid pronounced himself identically:

The idea of the modern scientist is rather that what we call intelligence is an outcome of matter, that matter has evolved during thousands of years through different aspects, and has culminated in man as a wonderful phenomenon in the form of intelligence. . . . It is spirit which through a gradual action has become denser and has materialized itself into what we call matter or substance; and through this substance it gradually unfolds itself, for it cannot rest in it. It is caught in this denseness, gradually making its way out through a process taking thousands of years, until in man it develops itself as intelligence.[12]

Yet something is gained by the sharing within the One.

Passing through an evolution on earth is necessary for the spirit, in order that it should arrive at its culmination.

Obviously, there is a planning behind human endeavor, although to some it seems to happen by chance. Unfortunately, most people cannot see what the planning is until they witness the result. Yet one is gifted with an intuition of the impulse that the spiritual government of the world imparts to the strivings and activities of men, mostly unknown to them. If one really cares to offer one's service, one is given to see a glimpse of where one is going. To make interplanetary connections at all possible levels, not just at the level of space probes, but to be able to dialogue with beings on other planets, we will have to increment our thinking to the dimension of the thinking of the planet.

There is a certain characteristic peculiar to this planet, for each planet has a certain degree of intelligence. For instance, the fact that at this time and at this stage of human civilization and evolution, when hardly one in a thousand individuals wants to make war, such dreadful wars should have taken place, is due to the influence of the planet working through the minds of those who live on it.[13]

What are the myths and legends of the past and the hermetic texts and cosmologies if not an anthropomorphic way of talking about a knowledge deeply rooted in the race, nay in the psyche of humanity, in Jung's collective unconscious? Such knowledge is made of the stuff of enlightened dreams, visions of apocalyptic magnitude, realization gained in higher states of meditation when one encompasses dimensions of thinking beyond that of the individual.

That knowledge is not only gained from outside but also from within. Thus one may call knowledge that one learns from outer life learning, but knowledge that one draws from within may be called revelation.

Obviously, then, if there is a further dimension of thinking behind our individual thinking, there is a more encompassing planning behind our planning, and a wider purpose than the purpose we are able to schedule; therefore, if Murshid had to go through a test regarding his faith in his purpose, as he crossed the ocean on his way to accomplishing it, it was because he had to have a first-hand knowledge of the problems that people were facing: to guard against letting oneself be confined by the purpose that one is able to envision when judging things from one's individual vantage point, to see if and in what measure this purpose contributes toward the fulfillment of a greater purpose.

In the East there are various stories told about sages and saints who have awakened someone to the purpose of his particular life; and the moment that person has awakened his whole life has changed. . . . "Every soul is meant for a certain purpose and the light of that purpose has been kindled in that soul."[14]

One need just look around one to observe people suffering often unavowed anxiety and confusion for not being able to recognize a purpose in their lives, or sense a meaning to life. Watch around you the desperate search of beings for themselves in something desirable on the planet.

Every soul is pursuing some reality, something to hold on to, trying to grasp something which will prove dependable, a beauty that cannot change, and that one can always look upon as one's own. . . . No sooner has a person found his way than all the things he wants to accomplish will come by themselves. [15]

We must be able to still ourselves, to tune our spirit to the universal consciousness in order to know the purpose of our life. And once we know the purpose, the best thing is to pursue it in spite of all difficulties. Nothing should discourage us, nothing should keep us back once we know that this is the purpose of our life. Then we must go after it at the sacrifice of everything for when the sacrifice is great, the gain in the end gives a greater power, a greater inspiration. Rise or fall, success or failure, does not matter as long as you know the purpose of your life. If ninety-nine times you fail, the hundredth time you will succeed. [16]

But how can one ascertain one's purpose? The mind boggles at entertaining the very thought of a purpose, as one seems to succeed another, and so endlessly.

No doubt the main object of life cannot be understood at once, and therefore the best thing for every person is first to pursue *his* purpose in life; for, in the accomplishment of his personal object, he will arrive some day at the accomplishment of that inner object. [17]

At this point Murshid explains that the purpose will emerge more clearly if one starts doing something within the closer range of one's understanding. One should first determine one's object for oneself, however small that object is; once it is determined, one has begun life.

No doubt the more tangible purpose is self-expression, or the unfurling of the bounty of qualities lying dormant in one; awaken the sleeping beauty. All one need do is look at nature.

Every rock is longing for the day when it will burst out as a volcano. [18]

For instance, the seed has in it the leaf and the flower and the fruit, but the fulfilment of the purpose of that seed is that it is put into the ground, that it is watered, that a seedling springs up and is reared by the sun, that it may bring forth its flowers and seeds. Every atom of the universe is working toward perfection.

One soon comes to realize that one can only unfold one's latent qualities by encountering their counterpart in the universe; in fact, this is the essence of experience. One might discover the radiance one is aware of inside in a flaming sunrise, or one's natural crystalline clarity in a waterfall, one's quest for the immaculate in a frozen landscape of snow and ice, one's bent for majesty in an elephant, one's freedom in a hawk, or oneself in an idealized person.

The world within you is reflected in the world without, and it is the action and the reaction of the two upon one another that constitute your life.

However, unquestionably one of the direct needs felt by the strong-minded or the stalwart souls is to accomplish something like climbing a mountain, braving the seas, overcoming gravity, reaching into outer space, composing or painting or modeling a masterpiece of art, building a house or a cathedral, constructing a car or a plane, rescuing the victim of a catastrophe, doing welfare for the needy, or some other great act. How does one know which of these is right for one? It is one's particular assessment of the value, maybe of the usefulness, of what one feels like accomplishing that gives one the motivation to accomplish it.

Everything has its purpose, but knowledge of the purpose makes us able to use it to its best advantage,[19] and gives man the strength with which to stand in the midst of the opposing forces of life.

Accomplishment is unfolding oneself by helping another to unfold, or an object or a situation to unfold its possibilities. It is the vision of the latent and virtual potentialities in all things and situations calling for help that spurs man to accomplishment. According to the Sufi Ibn Arabi, the Divine Compassion consists in relieving all potential beings of the solitude of unknowing.

Kabir, the great poet of India, says "Life is a field and you are born to cultivate it. . . . All that your soul yearns after and all you need is to be got from the field, if you know how to cultivate it and how to reap the fruit."[20]

Not only every person, but every object begins to reveal its nature, its character and secret. If one flashed on the need in the object or situation for unfoldment, it is because one experiences the same in oneself.

For you must ever bear in mind that the light and life that goes out from you to the object are quite as important as that light which comes to you from the object. There is nothing which is not in [your] self. The day when [a man] finds out his life's purpose, he is stronger, more successful, his life becomes easier, he feels inspired and a greater power pours out through him.

The reciprocal is also true: Just as by changing ourselves we can change the outer circumstances, so can we also change those whom we cannot trust into trustworthy people; we can change objects and individuals of whom we are afraid into great friends. Besides, there is an unwritten law:

All that comes to a person in reality he arrives at. No one will experience in life what is not meant for him.[21]

The same applies to the support or opposition that accrues to one.

How do we select our intial objectives? One person may value a modern apartment with lots of gadgets, and another a rustic hut in the woods without electricity but an enchanting view; one may strive to be the manager of a thriving business, and another a healer.

Life offers opportunity either to pick up pearls and throw away pebbles, or to pick up pebbles and throw away pearls.[22]

The greatest opportunity is to know the value of opportunity.

Of course one must first ascertain whether the object will prove good for one or not. And one must not choose an object of attainment that blinds one to what is right and just, where, for example, there is a benefit for oneself though another's loss. Incidentally, there is an unwritten law that when you gain something from another, you may have to pass it on to someone else when the time comes, willingly or unwillingly.

If we search further, we come to realize a still vaster purpose: taking charge or taking care of a domain, an area, a group of people. One does not have to look very far to find it; it is right there where one's responsibilities lie, where one's problems are, the situation which one controls or could control, one's zone of influence.

Every soul has its domain in life, consisting of all it possesses and of all who belong to it. This domain is as wide as the width of the soul's influence; it is so to speak a mechanism which works by the thought power of each individual soul.

Wherever you go, make a world of your own.

If they make a world ignorantly then that world is their captivity, if they make a world wisely then that world is their paradise.[23]

Murshid advises to determine, when setting a choice of objective, how lasting or perishable it is. Both the rose and gold are cherished for their radiance, but gold is valued higher because it is uncorruptible. But for the one who is deterred from material motivation by the transiency of material pursuits, Murshid advises: The gain is in the mastery thus acquired and the existentiation of latent qualities consolidated in the personality by meeting the challenge of a problem, or a difficulty to surmount. Therefore, do not measure the worthfulness of your objective as a function of the effort required to accomplish it.

Every desire increases the power of man to accomplish his main desire, which is the purpose of every soul.[24]

It is better to give a small thing than nothing, because it thus gives a mastery. In every gain through life a person takes a step forward. Every object has a separate path for its achievement, but in the end all must come to the same goal. Do not, therefore, look with contempt upon someone if he is in the pursuit of something that you consider inferior to your ideal.

In fact, it is not advisable to choose an objective beyond one's reach, because failure to achieve it will frustrate one and dishearten one, and cause one to doubt one's capacity.

It is the self-confidence that one acquires in accomplishing a small objective that will give one trust to undertake a greater one.

The first thing needed is to accomplish the object which is standing before one immediately; however small it is, it does not matter. It is by accomplishing it that one gains power.

It is, however, desirable that we should hold in our thought the best and highest attainment possible for us. It is not necessary for us to force ourselves to have a much higher object of attainment, which we are incapable of holding. Of course, the object chosen must be a worthy one, but one that is within our reach.

When one is pessimistic about things, one destroys the roots of desires, because by denying one casts away that which could otherwise have been attained.

The very arousal of a sense of motivation gives the divine will a chance of operating through one and gives one a chance of experiencing the overcoming, by the divine sense of all possibility, the limitation of one's private assessment of possibility.

Possibility is the nature of God, and impossibility is the nature of the art of man.

Yet the pursuit of the impossible is inherent in man's nature.

You touch upon the very power that moves the universe. The hidden desire of the creator is the secret of the whole creation.

No doubt, behind the drive to achieve there is the urge of desire. Detachment applies, in the sacrifice needed to pursue the objective, the renunciation of other motives for the purpose pursued, resignation to the inadequacy of results in function of exertion, and the relinquishing of the fruits of action. That essential desire, as Professor Louis Massignon translates the word *Ishk* (so often referred to by the Sufis), may manifest in man as nostalgia for the beyond or the desire to experience through the senses, or the desire to possess, or to attain. In fact, Murshid outlines five fundamental desires: life, knowledge, power, happiness, and peace.

The secret of life is the desire to attain something; the absence of this makes life useless. Hope is the sustenance of life; hope comes from the desire of attaining something. Therefore the desire is in itself a very great power.[25]

As we know, Murshid, like all Sufis, seeing in life a fulfillment of God's being, encourages achievement. To achieve, one has to desire, and Murshid sees in man's desire the original divine impulse toward manifestation, albeit limited, and sometimes diverted to the point of betraying its origin. Thus he saw everywhere around him the Divine Impulse being carried out willy-nilly, awkwardly and mostly unawares, by most people who think they are pursuing their wishes. Moreover, the secret of achieving is to become aware of the divine will behind one's will, manifesting through one in one's creativity.

Every thought, every impulse, every wish, every desire comes from there, and in its accomplishment there is the law of perfection.

"Thy will be done on earth as it is in heaven." This phrase is a veil which covers the mystery of attainment. On coming to earth, man, who is the instrument of God, loses connection with the divine perfection . . . thus keeping not only himself, but God from helping his will to be done.

When the dependent nature is developed it makes man a pessimist, and when hope stands alone without dependence, this develops optimism.

The very spirit of God comes to man's rescue in the form of the optimistic spirit.[26]

What we obtain is what our belief allows us to obtain.

"Hold on to the rope of hope," was Murshid's motto. Those who help others to live are those who look forward to life with hope and courage. Achievement is a matter of exercising one's free spirit creatively instead of giving in to conditioned reflexes.

Yet, however omnipotent the Overall Power is, it is crippled in its application in human affairs by the very restraint that man, owing to the limitation of his understanding, interposes upon it. Thus it is a feature of awakening to see everywhere the divine desire (Ishk), obstructed, betrayed, blasphemed, disfigured, mutilated, even reversed.

Man has two aspects to him. One aspect is his mechanical being, where he is but a machine controlled by conditions, by his impressions, by outer influences, by cosmic influences, and by his actions. The more pronounced this aspect is in man, the less evolved he is. It is the sign of a lesser evolution. But there is another aspect in man which is creative, in which he shows he is not only part of God but linked with God, because his innermost self is God.

Therefore there is a difficulty for the fulfillment of every person's wish . . . because this is the world of limitations . . . but the power of desire is unlimited. . . .

Those who are given liberty by Him to act freely, are nailed on the earth; and those who are free to act as they choose on the earth, will be nailed in the heavens.[27]

At the outset, one should clearly make up one's mind what one really wishes for.

Once the object is decided upon, there should be no change. Even things more useful, precious, and better must be considered as temptation.

Once one has settled on a project, one must guard it against second thoughts, and against the opinions of others:

For reason is a slave to all that stands before it.

Do not for one moment think how small you are before your object of attainment, or how incapable you are of achieving it, or how long it must take to reach it.

In our desire for the accomplishment of good and helpful things, we attract good helpers, and in the evil things one desires one attracts evil helpers. The satanic side of life is ever ready to help man, as is God. As soon as a person has determined an evil thought, all the means of help about one begin to manifest themselves.

The help in good thought comes more slowly upon the physical plane, whereas with a bad thing it comes more quickly. Whichever path you choose, the right or the wrong, know that there is at the back always a powerful hand to help you along it.

Besides, one should take precautions and use safeguards to protect one's budding project.

All things in their beginning must be guarded from the sweeping winds of destruction.

Moreover, talking about one's plan is a great waste of power.

The Master gives instructions on attitudes favorable or unfavorable to achievement: "One must want the object continually." And, "hold it in one's mind, but one must see at the same time the steps that one has to climb," and set aside "a certain time of the day or night to devote entirely to the concentration of one's attainment."

Create or encourage surroundings that are in harmony with your objective. The clothes you wear, the food you eat, things have an effect upon you.

When Ruth St. Denis danced to music composed by Hazrat Inayat Khan, her apartment was furnished with Indian funishings. What was his surprise when, years later, he found the apartment completely transformed Chinese style—she was dancing a Chinese ballet.

The Master warns against speaking negatively about your project, even in jest, or acting against your ideal. And of course, need one say: "Refrain from doing that which hinders you from accomplishing your purpose in your inner and your external life."

A man who has been successful in life goes on being successful, and a person who has once failed goes on failing. The first man was impressed by his success and so he continued to be successful, and the other who was impressed with his failure, continued to have failures because that impression suggested failure to him.

Nothing ventured, nothing gained. No doubt, in setting off on a venture one is undertaking a calculated risk. Even then hopefulness is helpful.

Every experience, good or bad, is a step forward in man's evolution. Failure in life does not matter, the greatest misfortune is standing still. If you are annoyed by any disagreeable experience, it is a loss; but if you have learnt by it, it is a gain.

Failure offers a wonderful opportunity of spotting what one is doing wrong. "Every failure follows a weakness somewhere."

As one grows in realization, one discovers that behind one objective that one values, another objective lurks just within sight, and another beyond one's grasp. As we have already seen.

Man's purpose is like the horizon. As the horizon appears before the eyes, so the purpose appears before the mind, and as the horizon is in fact nonexistent, so the purpose is in fact a non-reality.

There is a propensity in man to break his own record, progress ever further, launch into new horizons, reach out for the stars, grasp infinity and taste of eternity. The indomitable spirit of man is quickened by a compulsive flair for transcendence that urges him ever further and further. "Man is the spearhead of evolution," says Aldous Huxley.

It is the dimension of insight that enables one to have a panoramic view of our motivations, aspirations, problems, and behavior. As long as we assess our objective from our limited personal vantage point, we fail to see its purpose, because an individual purpose only makes sense in terms of an overall purpose. Here we see the advantage of positing a divine viewpoint and allowing it to override one's self-centeredness. To make sense of our lives, it is important for us to grasp the relevance of the part that we are playing in relation to the whole. It is for this reason that the realization of an overall purpose is important, lest people suffer from Heidegger's metaphysical anxiety.

In this fulfillment it is not that man attained, but that God Himself has fulfilled His purpose.

The sages share the bird's-eye view of men rushing about compulsively to pursue objectives hardly planned, largely unaware of their raison d'être.

Every thing and being is placed in its own place, and each is busy carrying out the work which has to be done in the scheme of nature.[28]

Each one of us is an atom of the universe, and completes the symphony, and when we do not strike our note, it means that note is lacking in the symphony of the whole. The further we advance, the more difficult and more important our part in the symphony of life becomes; and the more conscious we become of this responsibility, the more efficient we become in accomplishing our task.

What then could be the purpose of purposes? The whole bounty of the Master's teaching converges upon this target continually and inevitably:

The purpose of the whole of creation is fulfilled in the attainment of that perfection which is for a human being to attain.[29]

Hazrat Inayat Khan repeatedly quotes his favorite saying from a dearly treasured bedside book, the Bible, the saying of one with whom he was in deep communion: "Be ye perfect as your Father in heaven is perfect." "He would not have said this," Murshid says, "if it were not possible for you to be so too."

CHAPTER 19

The Principles Under Test

*We ask for nothing less
than the impossible possibility:
infinity in a finite fact, and
eternity in a temporal act.
—Prentice Mulford*

Life was now offering Murshid a priceless opportunity to observe his ideals in action, to watch the cosmic laws set in motion by the interplay between the motivation of one who was a renunciate at heart and the great machine of the universe monitored by untold competing wills.

As he landed in New York, the Statue of Liberty quickened Murshid's anticipation in the searchings of the New World for his own very ideal of freedom. Was his Message not of spiritual freedom? He soon discovered both sides of the coin; insensitive incomprehension and ruthless exploitation from some, a high social idealism and sense of responsibility among others.

What trials and hardships Murshid had to put up with for having chosen to take upon himself the task of harmonizing East and West! He experienced poverty and continual prejudice against the East. There was the difficulty of adaptation of a refined soul brought up in an aristocratic milieu and the serene atmosphere of the sages to the brashness of quite a few uncouth materialists. Life was giving him a chance of practicing what later on he was to preach: unrelenting forbearance and selfless dedication in the accomplishment of one's ideal in action. Of course, faithful friends and allies joined and assisted him as he proceeded in his task. True to his commitment, this born renunciate, who had taken immeasurable responsibility upon his shoulders, would one day teach meditation in action to the very businessmen who were at the antipodes of his being. Some of their probity and social sense of responsibility he was, in turn, to value.

I found my work in the West the most difficult task that I could have ever

304

imagined. In the first place I was not a missionary of a certain faith, delegated to the West by its adherents, nor was I sent to the West as a representative of an Eastern cult by some Maharajah. I came to the West with His Message, Whose call I had received, and there was nothing earthly to back me in my mission, except my faith in God and trust in truth. In the countries where I knew no one, had no recommendations, was without any acquaintances or friends, I found myself in a new world, a world where commercialism has become the central theme of life under the reign of materialism. In the second place there was a difficulty of language, but that difficulty was soon overcome; as I worked more so my command of language improved.

Now before me there was the question: how to set to work and in what direction? For the Message the time was not yet ripe as I was at that time rather studying the psychology of the people than teaching.

Until Murshid was able to break through with the teaching he was assigned to bring to the West, musical performances were the only, and precarious, means of survival of "the musicians of Hindustan" in foreign lands.

Many in the Western world are afraid of mystic or psychic or occult ideas, for it is something foreign to them, and especially a foreign representative of that is doubly foreign. If music had not been my shield, my task would have become much more difficult for me in the West, and my life impossible. I had to make my living by my profession of music, which has no particular place in the professional world of the West. Most often I had to sell my pearls at the value of pebbles.

To have to expose their sacred art to the crass ignorance and mockery of the uninformed fans of a fickle and whimsical vogue of phony exoticism could only have proven excruciating to the voyagers' refined souls. Inevitably, most of their musical engagements suffered from the coarse misuse and crude profanation by the contact with men of show business of an art held so sacred in its traditional setting, originating among the holy men. Ruth St. Denis' acclaimed link-up with the traditional musicians could not but prove short-lived.

It was not satisfactory to combine real and imitation. She invented Indian dances of her own for which our music became as a colour and fragrance to an imitation flower. For the public, it was only an amusement, and therefore painful to us.

She herself admitted that:

at no time have I been sufficiently the scholar or sufficiently interested to imitate or try to reproduce any oriental ritual or actual dance.[1]

It was all over when Murshid declined to grant her request for a certificate of proficiency in Indian dance, quite understandably, when one knows the standards of the training exacted in the East.

It was at the Vedanta temple in San Francisco that Murshid received his first encouragement, signalling that the way was now open for him to leave concerts behind and start lecturing. Here he found the old familiar courtesy of the East, respect for the guru, and the evaluation of the spiritual life.

At Berkeley he drew a large crowd, preceding his music with a talk. There was a woman who "seemed to be absorbing the philosophy hidden behind the address on music." When she thanked Hazrat Inayat, he felt that there was indeed a "light kindled in that soul." Unfortunately, her letter asking for guidance was received just as Hazrat Inayat was about to leave for Seattle. He therefore had to ask her to travel there, although it was a considerable distance away. The following day he was to confer upon Mrs. Ada Martin the first initiation given during his mission in the West. His autobiography says the room was filled with light. She was given the Sufi name Rabia, the name of a Sufi woman saint. She proved a wonderful pioneer in the spreading of the Sufi Message, and was later initiated as a murshida.

An identical zeal welcomed Murshid at Baba Bhartiya's Sanskrit College in New York, but the Master knew that his mission lay further afield and consisted in opening a vaster perspective to people's nostalgia for truth, rather than converting them to an already existing spiritual conformism.

It was something strikingly new and interesting to the intellectual minds of the West, something to appeal to their reasoning faculty, which had been whetted by modern progress and had been starved by the lack of a religion of intellect. A simple religion of faith was not sufficient for the minds so rapidly progressing in all directions of life.

Noting his first impression of the West, Hazrat Inayat was glad to find so many thorough good natures among the Americans, whose way of life was their religion. He discovered in America the one who was to become his life's partner: Ora Ray Baker. She was a cousin of Mrs. Baker Eddy, founder of the Christian Science Church. The Baker family, originally from Wenatchee, Washington, had settled in Des Moines, Iowa. Ora Ray, daughter of Erestus Werner Baker, a grandniece of Judge Baker of Chicago, was at the time under the guardianship of her half-brother, Dr. Pierre Bernard. Renowned for his mastery of Hatha Yoga, Dr. Bernard was a leader of the Tantric Order in America, and ran a fashionable club, the Clarkston Country Club at Nyack, New York, in which everything from elephants to theatrics or

Yoga training was in vogue. (Dr. Bernard's nephew, Theos, an adept in Yoga and Tibetan practices, is known as the author of *Land of a Thousand Buddhas* and a book on Hatha Yoga.)

Doctors attributed Ora Ray's miraculous recovery from diphtheria as a child to her strong will: She kept on repeating, "I will not die." In early youth, Ora once saw near her bed a phantom, an Eastern sage, who appeared a moment and passed across. She afterward had a dream that an Eastern sage held her in his arms and rose toward the sky, carrying her away over seas. Shortly before Inayat's visit, she had a vision of a turbaned Indian pointing to a younger turbaned face. When she described the older face to Inayat, it was obvious to him that it answered the description of his Murshid, who had evidently earmarked her for her future role; the younger face was Inayat's. Then she dreamed of a stream of water that had come between her and Inayat. He perceived in his meditation indications of his future marriage, visions which showed him the one who was meant to be his wife, and visions in which his Murshid suggested to him that the life that was to come was a necessary one toward his life's purpose.

Not long after his appearance at Dr. Bernard's club in New York, Murshid had crossed the Atlantic to begin his work in England. Dr. Bernard put every obstacle to the marriage, and cut all the correspondence between Ora Ray and Murshid, so that it was only by a chance discovery that she found the address of Moula Bakhsh House on her half-brother's desk, which gave her the opportunity to reestablish contact. It was Ora Ray's love and determination, courage and fortitude, that enabled her to take the decision of leaving everything behind to land in England and to marry Inayat. The conditions under which they lived required the greatest self-sacrifice for one brought up in comfort and ease. In New York, Murshid foresaw and told her how difficult she would find life with one born with the heart of a fakir. Her life proved indeed to be a great test, living so close to one so completely incorporating his world missions; but everything seemed tolerable through the unique love that each had for the other, bridging East and West.

The tests that my life was destined to go through were not of a usual character, and were not a small trial for her. A life such as mine, which was wholly devoted to the Cause, and which was more and more involved in the ever growing activities of the Sufi Movement, naturally kept me back from that thought and attention which was due to my home and family. Most of the time of my life I was obliged to spend out of home, and when at home, I have always been full of activities, and it naturally fell upon her always to welcome guests with a smile under all circumstances. If I had not been helped by her, my life, laden with a heavy responsibility, would have never enabled me to devote myself entirely to the Order as I have. It is by this continual sacrifice that she has shown her devotion to the Cause.

In London, the musical and literary circles of the early century offered Murshid a vivid reception and a vina. But the musicologist Fox Strangeways used the valuable information he gave in his book on Indian music, without a word of acknowledgment.

Rabindranath Tagore, in London at the time, invited Hazrat Inayat to meet his friends; among them was a lawyer, later to be known as Mahatma Gandhi. The meeting between these two was most sacred. Murshid sang. Then they sat in silence. Murshid and Tagore met several times. Some saw great resemblance between them as Murshid grew older; during the last months of his life in India, someone asked him if he was Tagore. As among dervishes, there was a chivalrous mutual recognition. Was it of him that Tagore wrote?

I know not how thou singest, my master, I ever listen in silent amazement.

Apparently he was speaking of God, but he said:

Messengers with tidings from unknown skies greet me and speed along the road.[2]

Are dervishes fated to meet like ships in the night, like Murshid's meeting with D'Annunzio and Paderewski and Debussy and Kahlil Gibran? Can they not meet like Liszt and Chopin? or Christ and St. John the Baptist?

I live in the hope of meeting with him, but this meeting is not yet.[3]

It is paradoxical that when the author of The Prophet met Murshid, the relevance of his own words escaped his notice.

When love beckons to you, follow him.[4]

Instead, Kahlil Gibran asked him "What has brought you here?" The Messenger answered "A little service."

The vogue for orientalism had also hit Paris. Consequently, a similar welcome was awaiting the musicians of Hindustan among many fin de siècle amateur intellectuals in the salons of the French capital.

The same blatant misappropriation as experienced in the U.S.A. recurred again in Europe, particularly outrageously in the buffoonery of the Parisian show put up by the at once famous and infamous Mata Hari at the instigation of Lucien Guitry.

Murshid was at the mercy of his well-intentioned friends who wished to "promote" him. Keeping his head high in the midst of the degradation of pre-War France, among the abject revellers of a decaying intellectualist society in search of outlandish mystery, must have been a feat of exhilarating overcoming, giving a sense of mastery amid great incongruity.

Murshid, so conscious of the tradition of the dervish-kings which he inherited, held his head high when put into a situation of humiliation. He never lost awareness of the ultimate purpose for which every situation was a stepping stone. It is a mark of the human spirit to cling undauntedly to one's identification with the Being of which one is a fragment and also the ambassador, while being defiled like Jesus mocked by the Romans, or some of the Jews in concentration camps. It is sometimes like experiencing God being crucified by the very persons to whom he gives the freedom to do so.

There is nothing that I feel too humiliating for me to do; and there is no position, however exalted, that can make me prouder than I am already in the pride of my Lord.

However Murshid lost nothing of his human touch and,

It is Thou who art my pride; when I realize my limited self I feel myself the humblest of all living beings.

Gabriele D'Annunzio, that defiantly genial meteor of the new Italian rennaissance of the beginning of this century, summed up the whole paradox and glory of the first impact of Murshid with rare evocative discernment.

Another song I recall to mind. It was at the house of Ilse, one wintry, eerie Paris evening. The room was full of smoke, driven back through the glowing chimney by the wind outside. And the gooseflesh-fairy forbade the opening of windows. Around a gilded wooden unicorn from the music-loving land of Burma, Alastair had been dancing one of his gothic dances, dressed in a blue tunic embroidered with gold. Amidst bronze deer and antelope and other nimble animals from the East, seemingly grazing on the carpet, a rhymer, dressed in purple like a Bishop, had been celebrating a rhyming mass, his hair cut round in the style of Fra Angelico's tonsured holy priests. Reclining on low cushions, the lady of the house looked like a wax figurine with enamelled eyes, betraying life only through a gently moving, delicately sculptured ankle, as a snake quietly beats its tail in love or fury. It was one of those artificial hours, which folly, fancy and nostalgia conspire to brew, like three witches round a suspect potion. But amidst so much hollowness and unreality were two primeval forces: the smoke, blown back by the wind, and Inayat Khan, the singer from India. The woodsmoke killed the decadent fumes. Inayat's voice stilled the pretty moths and night-owls.

In vain the unicorn looked for a virgin lap in which to rest its proud head and sleep in the sweetness of humiliation. But through its legendary secret it seemed to contribute to the perfect stillness.

The singer sat quietly, as if the smoke came to him from the pyres at the ancestral river and couldn't harm his voice. He wore a robe reddish-yellow and a large amber-coloured turban. He held his brown hands outstretched upon his knees. A short black beard completed the oval of his bronze face. The white of his eyes was purer than the shell of a dove's egg. And he sang with his mouth always open, modulating the tones in his throat. He knew more than 500 ragas.

He was a fragile man, he was a wisp of a slender man, and his singing seemed to rise from the depths of the temple, to come from beneath the rocks, from beyond the inner caverns of the earth, and it seemed to gather in its sweep the longings of all generations of men, and the labour of all beginnings.

There were no more walls, no narrow chimney; there were no more phantoms, no masquerades, no lies. There was the smoke of the wood and sweat like jewels on the brow of the holy singer.

In the interval no one dared speak or say a word.

Inayat looked at me at the beginning of every song. He wanted to let me know that he sang for me alone. For me alone he sang the chant from before the light, the song of the time before dawn, mysterious as the message of the wind sent over the sorrow of the earth by Him "Who is destined to let the Light grow."[5]

Men of noble accomplishment and realization recognize and greet each other with a glance, like the dervishes, the uncrowned kings of the world: different clothes, different settings, whether clad in the rags of the fakir, or sophisticated Parisian fashion, sitting near unswept and crumbling tombs of Sufi saints, or in gaudy salons of a dissolute society, the human spirit remains sovereign when it flares up in a great being.

Each note, each scale, and each strain expires at the appointed time; and at the end of the soul's experience here the finale comes; but the impression remains, as a concert in a dream, before the radiant vision of the consciousness.

The French composer Debussy, introduced to Inayat through the pianist Walter Rummel and the dancer Isadora Duncan, greatly enjoyed an evening he always recalled as the "evening of emotion," where Murshid revealed to him the secrets of the different ragas. He is said to have composed *L'Apresmidi d'un Faun* in memory of that evening. He no doubt gave the ragas an interpetation that did not conform to the classical one consecrated in India by the ages.

Debussy was looking all his life for something new to introduce into modern music, and Scriabin once told me personally, "Something is missing in our music, it has become so mechanical." And I have often thought that if Scriabin, with his fine character and beautiful personality, had lived longer, he could have introduced a new strain of music into the modern world.

Edmond Bailly was the first westerner they met to give way to his delight with tears! Here was one who possessed an authentic knowledge of Indian ragas. He helped organize a concert with Lady Churchill. He taught Murshid's brother Maheboob Khan European music, and he later rendered Hazrat Inayat's mystical poems into music in most moving religious songs, sung by Ustad Ali Khan.

Opera prima donna Mrs. Emma Nevada was impressed by the possibilities in Ali Khan's voice, and trained him after the Italian school in opera singing, grooming the wonderful resources of his Indian voice into that of an unusual and remarkable tenor. Later when the Aga Khan offered him the chance of playing the role of Othello at the Opera, he insisted in showing his appreciation and loyalty to his teacher by giving a chance to her daughter to partner him: when the maestro refused, he declined the offer.

Such was the uncompromising steadfastness and loyalty of this stalwart figure; Ali Khan remained equally firm throughout his life.

Musheraff Khan, the younger brother, remained throughout thoroughly puzzled and perplexed by the western way of life. By temperament religiously inclined, and simple and sociable, he was ready to make sacrifices, certainly out of his high regard for Murshid as brother, father, and teacher.

Several lectures were arranged, and Murshid's book *Message of Spiritual Liberty* was published in French. Writing about his impressions of France, Murshid was amused to see how the spirit of democracy had fomented "a rebellion against an autocratic God unacceptable because ruling without a parliament."

A period of intense and successful social activity in London followed in 1913. Murshid was invited everywhere, and at his open house every Thursday evening, the London society of the day was often to be seen, together with anglicized Indians. Often of an evening he would sink back into the quiet of playing the vina or meditating, and mornings saw him chant and sing before dawn.

His first book in English appeared: *A Sufi Message of Spiritual Liberty,* couched in traditional Sufi terms whose English equivalent is often misinterpreted by well-meaning English advisors. He had not yet found his own personal style of the later years, but was crusading for spiritual liberty amid a world of stereotyped ideas and decadent freethinking.

Mr. Bjerregaard, who helped publish Murshid's first book on Sufism, conveniently forgot to mention his name when publishing Omar Khayyam's *Rubaiyat,* in recognition of the literary debt he owed Murshid in the translation.

Now suddenly came the opportunity to go to Russia. Murshid readily accepted, but found to his great surprise that the circumstances in which he had to perform his music were uncongenial. Here was the center of high life of the upper classes in pre-Revolutionary Russia, and Hazrat Inayat had a premonition where it would lead in the end. Murshid gave a lecture at the Ethnological Museum at the invitation of the poet Ivanov, then at the Imperial Conservatory of Music, where the enthusiasm was so great that afterward the students detached the horses of the troika to draw it themselves to his home. Princess Sirtoloff Lavrowsky introduced Murshid to the musical circles of Russia; he was invited to a supper with Chaliapin. *A Sufi Message of Spiritual Liberty* was published in Russian.

I visited Moscow, and found that the opportunity which had been offered me, to display my music, was an uncongenial one. I found the place I had been told of was a place of gaiety, where people came for the whole night for their merriment; and yet for me it was a sight to observe how the different temperaments change from the everyday pitch at the moment they engage in merriment. It was somewhat troublesome for me to stay up all night, and yet it was an opportunity of studying all the different classes of Russia, all the wealthy classes, and it showed me how the dream of life had absorbed so many of them, and where it would lead Russia in the end. It was as though God wanted to show me, before the disaster came upon Russia, how even nations are led to destruction when they of their own will choose that path. Had I known beforehand what the offered engagement was, I would certainly not have accepted it. However, God's glory is everywhere to be found.

A musical evening was arranged by them which will always remain in my memory as a most remarkable occasion, where Turks, Tartars, Siberians, Bokharians, Persians, all displayed their national art of music, and the hall was crowded by people of every country of the East. It was something that is so rarely seen, and for me, who had come from far away in the East, leaving my country thousands of miles away, this was a vision of home and yet not home. It was something new and yet akin to my nature, something that I did not know and yet that my soul knew, something so far from my knowledge and yet so near to it.

Murshid found the people of Russia

religious, devoted, idealistic, hospitable, affectionate, appreciative of all beauty, gifted in art, inclined to mysticism, seekers of philosophical truths, ready to become friends and mindful to let friendship last.

One evening Murshid was invited by a Finnish philosopher, Dr. E. W. Lybeck, to a mysterious edifice. When he entered, the monumental portals were immediately closed, and in a moment Murshid found himself in the midst of priests and monks.

I have never seen such comprehensive minds in which all that is spoken as wisdom and truth so easily finds accommodation.

The only wonder to them was how this teaching could exist outside their church. Murshid said, "In their churches there is an atmosphere quite like that in the temples of India."

Russia reminded me of my country, and the warmth that came from the hearts of the people kept us warm in the cold country where snow lies in the streets for days together, where every house is a Mont Blanc.

Thanks to Count Serge Tolstoy's help, Murshid was able to leave as the great upheavals of the revolution were about to break loose. At one time in the journey, when excited crowds had formed a barricade obstructing the hasty exodus, it was the sight of his little child Noor-un-Nisa, born in Moscow on January 1, 1914, whom Murshid raised in his arms, which opened a way to safety, rather than the free pass arranged by Count Tolstoy.

Murshid returned to Paris, but his stay there was curtailed by the sudden outbreak of World War I.

In London activity was now on the increase. Hazrat Inayat spoke a few times at the Higher Thought Centre. A few mureeds joined. A series of lectures were arranged at the Royal Asiatic Society. The rudiments of the Sufi Order were being gathered together. Mary Williams, an English mureed, joined as secretary. A Sufi publishing society was formed in England and a number of books were published: *Pearls from the Ocean Unseen, Diwan, Hindustani Lyrics, Songs of India, The Confessions of Inayat Khan*, and the Sufi magazine appeared.

A very remarkable woman, remote, aristocratic, austere, now came to receive initiations: Miss Lucie Goodenough, later named Sherifa (Reverend) and afterwards initiated as murshida. She stood as a foundation stone for the building of the Order, wrote Hazrat Inayat, who found in her "that spirit of discipleship which is so little known to the world and even rarely found in the East." She brought out Pir-o-Murshid Inayat Khan's ideas in three books in the Voice of Inayat Series: *Life After Death, The Phenomenon of the Soul* and *Love, Human and Divine*. In addition, she collected, preserved, and produced the record of Hazrat Inayat Khan's teaching and guarded it from all corruption.

In my life-long work in the West I found that in the West there are no disciples; there are only teachers. Woman, being respondent by nature, shows a tendency towards discipleship, but that is not every woman. And men in the West, who try to show the disciple-spirit, somehow fail to play this role some time or the other. Among some of my man-collaborators I saw a spirit of a slight contempt toward the woman-workers, as man has always thought that woman is superfluous or too tender, too much devotional and unintelligent; and they have always sought of a man's collaboration in the work. Nevertheless, however much qualified men proved to be in the work, the valuable service that women have rendered to the Cause has been incomparably greater. The way how some of them have worked unceasingly with sincere devotion and firm faith, has been a marvel to me. If it was not for some women as my collaborators in the Cause, the Sufi Movement would never have been formed. How easily man forgets the place of woman in all walks of life. It is his self that covers his eyes from recognizing the importance of woman's collaboration in every work. However, the progress in the Western World is mostly due to the work of man and woman hand in hand, and the lack of the same is the reason of the backwardness of the East.

There is much to be said about woman in the West. She is courageous, patient, efficient, and capable, not only of home duties but of doing all work in life. Yes, she is less concerned with home, as compared to an Eastern woman, but her duties are divided, she has a part of duty to perform outside. Woman is idealized in the East, but in the West her vanity is sustained. A lover in the West knows how to woo; a lover in the East knows how to long. Woman's life in the West I found nearly as hard as in the East, perhaps harder, for in the East woman is more protected by man. In the West she stands responsible for herself, at home and outside the home, and it is that which makes her strong in every way. Nevertheless, this blunts her feminine qualities and develops male qualities. Some women are inclined to cut their hair short, and some to smoke cigarettes. Some are inclined to rough games and crude ways of recreation. Woman thinks by this she stands equal to man, ignorant of the fact that she becomes less attractive to him, who completes her life. Whereas in the East under the shelter of man, the feminine qualities of woman develop freely and her womanly charm is maintained. Woman by nature is spiritually inclined, in the East or West. But especially in the West, where the life of man is mostly absorbed in business and politics, it is woman who interests herself in religion, even in philosophy and all works pertaining to God and humanity. The spirit of the Western woman with which she fights her battle all along through life is most splendid. There is no line of work or study which woman in the West does not undertake and does not accomplish as well as man. Even in social and political activities, in religion, in spiritual ideas she indeed excels man. The charitable organizations existing in different parts of the West are mostly supported by the women, and I see as clear as daylight that the hour is coming when woman will lead humanity to a higher evolution.

Now centers started blossoming throughout England and Murshid's books appeared, thanks to Dr. Gruner, whom Murshid helped in writing his book on Avicenna. A Khanqah or Headquarters was set up at 86, Ladbroke Road, Kensington. Here were born Murshid's children, Vilayat, on June 19, 1916, Hidayat on August 6, 1917, and Khair-un-nissa on June 3, 1919. Here receptions were often the meeting place for a number of British notables interested in Indian mysticism. At a time when the colonial problems in India were so tense, queries were made in some quarters about this Indian nobleman who had so suddenly gained the esteem of Britain's exclusive circles. Eventually,

by the rising wave of enthusiasm of a mureed, the family was situated in Gordon Square, but at the falling of the wave it was ended. I always sensed suspicion from all sides, searchlights thrown on me in suspicion whether my movements were not political, which always made my work difficult, to my great sadness. When Gandhi proclaimed noncooperation I heard its silent echo in the heart of Great Britain. I felt a hidden influence coming from every corner, resenting any activity which had a sympathetic connection with the East. The prejudice against Islam that exists in the West was another difficulty for me. Many think Sufism to be a mystical side of Islam, and the thought was supported by the encyclopedias, which speak of Sufism as having sprung from Islam, and they were confirmed in this by knowing that I am Muslim by birth. Naturally, I could not tell them that it is a Universal Message of the time, for every man is not ready to understand this. My Message of peace was often interpreted as what they call pacifism, which is looked upon unfavourably by many.

I then felt that the hour had come to remove the seat of our Movement to a place such as Geneva, which has been chosen as an international centre by all. In spite of all the urging on the part of my kind mureeds to stay on in England, I left there with my bag and baggage for Switzerland.

The time had come for Murshid to seek fresh horizons on the continent, and Miss Nagis Dowland came to the rescue of the Movement in its infancy in England, giving it fresh impetus. She issued new books by Hazrat Inayat Khan: *The Bowl of Saki, The Message, The Inner Life, The Alchemy of Happiness, The Mysticism of Sound, The Notes of the Unstruck Music,* and *The Soul Whence and Whither;* and she wrote *Between the Desert and the Sown* and *At the Gate of Discipleship.* Miss Dowland recalls how Murshid was for days in the New Forest in samadhi, that is, absorbed in divine consciousness to the point of being completely oblivious of immediate surroundings. She said his whole being seemed completely illuminated.

Now Miss Sophia Saintbury-Green, an outstanding, brilliant woman and a born leader, joined the forces. She was a niece of the Archbishop of Canterbury, and was steeped in the esoteric knowledge of theosophy as the right hand of Mrs. Annie Besant. At first sight she recognized Hazrat Inayat as the Master she had been seeking, grasped instantaneously the significance of the Message, and knew how to present it. When inspired by the Message, she drew the English public like a magnet by her masterly power of speech. She helped Hazrat Inayat Khan in founding the religious activity known as The Church of All and later renamed The Universal Worship: a service including all the great world religions. She was ordained as first *cheraga* (officiant). She was given the name Sophia for her sagely character, and initiated a murshida. She edited the Sufi Magazine and was the author of *The Path to God, The Human Personality,* and *The Message As I See It.*

Murshid's family now settled in France, first in a little village, Tremblay, and then in one nearer Paris, Wissous. A Summer School for an intimate circle was held in the garden, so sacred in its peaceful rhythm tucked away in the cornfields where Murshid was so inspired. Among this small group came Baron van Tuyll van Seeroskerken, who later became a sheikh and learned teacher and remained throughout his life a staunch apostle of the Message, and Miss Willbeck le Mair, a well-known artist of children's books. These two were married a few months later.

Murshid wrote of France:

On the soil of France I always felt at home, and the sociability, politeness, and courtesy of a Frenchman I always admired, for I saw hidden under the surface of democracy some spirit of aristocracy in their nature, although I found in France a tendency against religion. At the same time in the depth of their soul there is a craving for it, but the Frenchman always fights against it, owing to the external conditions. I found in Frenchmen a profound love of music, art, and poetry, and I enjoyed speaking to my respondent French mureeds and audiences on the subject of morals and metaphysics in allegorical and symbolical forms, and always felt encouraged by their subtle perception of it. A French lady I found to be feminine in quality, refined; and what especially attracted me to France was that it is a home of art. I never felt more inclined to practice my music anywhere than in France, since I left home.

Soon Murshid found his way to Geneva, feeling a call to go there. It was a time of great illumination. He sat meditating, on a bench, amid the yachts and passers-by, facing the lake on the Quai des Eaux Vives (the Dock of Living Waters); at his back was the Maison Royale, a palatial building crowned with an imposing stone eagle (since removed). When one knows how Eastern countries suffer from the parched earth, and how rishis choose to sit near a stream or a river, feeding on the magnetism of the water of life, one could imagine what this lavish onrush and downpour of bountiful dispensation meant to the great sage, fast becoming the great reformer. During this unusual spiritual retreat, living as an ascetic in the midst of the city, he foresaw and scheduled the whole future of the Sufi Movement, planning the entire organization to its minutest detail. By a stroke of what was obviously more than chance, two English mureeds were passing in the street one day; to their great surprise there was their Murshid. It was not long before they organized a lecture before a select audience, mainly Theosophists.

If it were not for the Theosophical Society there would not be the tolerance and response to Eastern thought of every kind which is given by people thus inclined in the West. The work of this Society has broken to a great extent the bias of the Christian faith, and the idea that the people in the East are heathens and their religion barbarous, which was prevalent in the West owing to their Christian missionary propaganda.

The impact of the Murshid's presence acted traumatically upon these seekers who had heard so much of the "masters of the East," since here was a real one right in front of them!

It is the lack of personal mystical influence and the absence of a prophetic Message that necessitated the Society bringing forward the belief in Masters, that there might be something for the believers to hold on to. Not only belief, but even imaginary pictures of these Masters are given to the adherents for worship. The Theosophical Society tried to supply to the students of theosophy the conception of different Masters which gave satisfaction to some for a time and yet did not answer the continual longing of the souls to see the Master in the flesh walking on earth, sympathizing in their pain and trouble, casting upon them His glance of compassion, stretching over their heads His hands in blessing, telling them in words that may be audible to their physical ears, of the life here and in the hereafter, inspiring them with the conviction—if not all at least some—to know and to believe in something and someone who is real. This need necessitated a Movement such as "The Star in the East," to comfort the hopeful and maintain their belief; everything has been done, is being done, and will be done, and yet who can answer this demand? He alone who is sent from above, who is appointed by God to deliver His Message, who is empowered by the Almighty to stand by them in their struggles, and who is made compassionate by the most Merciful to heal their wounds. But since no religion which is not divinely inspired will take root in this world long enough, it is a question if this Movement will really meet with success.

A disciple relates how Mrs. Annie Besant had met Murshid, bowed to his feet, as is the custom in the East, and intimated that at that moment she saw in him the Master they were awaiting. But when she found that he was married and ate meat, she begged to be excused for having made a mistake.

The Christian faith for long ages has made such a deep impression upon the people in the West, that they cannot see a spiritual teacher with a family-setting, knowing Christ in his exclusive being. Even the nearness of a woman seemed strange in their eyes.

The Message of the new age pointed toward bringing spirituality into the householder's life rather than the way of the monk. Murshid wished to show that it could be done.

Celibacy being taught in Christian religion and practiced by the Catholic priests has made the ideal of celibacy a virtue in the mind of the people in the West. Even though it is not practiced by generality, still it remains, so to speak, in the subconsciousness of the Western mind as an ideal and it has caused a great confusion in the social morals of the West. Man wants something he cannot get, man wishes to believe in something he cannot understand, man wishes to touch something he cannot reach. It is the continual struggle for the unattainable that blinds man, and he forms such high ideas even of the Prophet who is only a Messenger, a human being, one like everyone else, and who is subject to death and destruction and all the limitations of life, that the Prophet does not seem to come up to man's ideal until he has left the world, leaving behind the memory which again rises as a resurrection of the Prophet, spreading the influence of all He brought to the world and pouring from above that blessing which arose as vapour and came back from above as a rainfall.

The Star of the East was made to prepare the way for the coming teacher. But he must rise only from within the horizon of this institution, introduced to the world by the high authority of the Theosophical Society, or else he must descend directly from the sky, performing miracles. Such a thing has never been possible, nor will it ever be. As the communities in the past have waited until he came and went, and they are still waiting, the same old course is followed in the present generation by the most enthusiastic followers of the Order of the Star.

Fortunately, however serious or pathetic the matter was, Murshid was able to gloss it over with his effusive humor.

Someone asked, "Murshid, do you also work for the coming of the Master?" "Yes," said Murshid. "We all work for him." "But will you tell me, when is the world teacher coming?" asked the person. Pir-o-Murshid said, "You will get that information from the Order of the Star, for they are supposed to get the telegram of his arrival."

Murshid declined an invitation to speak at the Theosophical Society on Mrs. Annie Besant's proclamation of the coming world teacher, as he felt that such a lecture "should be given by someone more competent on the subject." After hearing the Sufi Message, a woman came and said how very much she enjoyed the lecture and asked, "What have you to say about the coming of the World Messenger?" Murshid replied, "The World Message is here, but I do not know where the

Messenger has gone." Someone asked Murshid, "What difference is there between Theosophy and Sufism? Is it not one?" "Yes," said Murshid, "These are only two doors of one puzzle; one to enter and one to exit." The questioner asked, "But which is which?" The Murshid said, "It is left to you to find out for yourself." Someone from the audience asked Murshid after his lecture: "And what do you think of the second coming of Christ?" "For me, he has never left," said Murshid.

However, the Message was on its way. Centers were opening up in Geneva, Lausanne, and Vevey, and now more mureeds came to the Murshid. A temporary headquarters of the Sufi Movement was formed with Miss Lucie Goodenough as Secretary General. One day, years later, a mureed remarked:

"How strange that you should have chosen Geneva as headquarters for the Sufi Movement and that the same place should have been selected for the League of Nations." "It is so strange," Murshid said, "perhaps the same place was chosen for these activities, at the same time, and by the same thought. When I was here in the Spring of 1914, I saw them both as they would be later after the war."

Every thought and imagination of a mystic has an effect. When he thinks of something it may materialize the week after, or the next month or the next year, or perhaps after many years, but all that a mystic says or thinks is fulfilled sooner or later.

The Swiss heart proved difficult to conquer at first. Murshid wrote,

Since the Swiss lay their beauty-laden land at the feet of the travellers, they naturally guard their hearts from being caught in the nets thrown in the lakes of Switzerland by the fishers of men.

It was here that Murshid found Mrs. P. Egeling, later to become a murshida and receive the name Fazal Mai (Mother of Grace), which aptly fit her:

This saintly soul came into my life as a blessing; her hand as the hand of providence became my backbone which comforted me and raised my head upwards in thanksgiving.

Twice he had been offered a castle and once a fortune; but they would have robbed him of the independence of the dervish that he was.

Many underestimate the greatness of the Cause, seeing the limitation through which I have to work my way out. It is not true that my life was always deprived of riches. There occurred several occasions which offered me enormous wealth. Only every time an occasion like this came, it did not fit in with my principle, and I had to renounce that profit for the sake of my principle. I consider it no loss, although it was a loss outwardly. The strength that I gained by standing by my principle was much greater than any riches of this earth. Nevertheless, poverty proved to be my bitterest enemy. For it always put me in a position that gave my adversaries every facility they desired to cause me harm. With all my mistakes and failings, which I must not disown, I have always tried to avoid dishonour. I was several times in a position which I should never have chosen to be in, but I was constrained by unfortunate circumstances. My pride at the time was very much hurt, and often that has happened. If there are any pages in the book of my life which I would rather be closed than open, they are narrative of my lack of means. But in this respect my life has been that of a bird, who must descend on earth to pick up a grain, but his joy is in flying in the air.

Thanks to Fazal Mai's selfless attitude, Murshid received the where-withal to devote his time totally to the cause. For Fazal Mai meeting Murshid was meeting the Master she had always awaited. Spontane-ously she said, "May I offer you a house and every support you need; I have nothing more in life, no family, and should be privileged to share life with your family," and so she stepped into the life of the family from the outset as a much loved "grandmother" to the children. Being so completely committed to his overwhelming task, Murshid was grateful "that when going out to preach in the world, I might have the relief of knowing that my little ones are sheltered from heat and cold under a roof." Now the French soil was being kindled by the Message. The first center in Paris "flourished as a garden in spring, but in the fall, the leaves dropped." But when it was reorganized, it grew. The clue as to success or failure is clear:

They will give great help who will not only help in the work, but will adopt my way of working in the delivery of the Message.

A lecture tour was arranged in Holland. The Movement was build-ing up steadily on Dutch soil and Murshid found the Dutch people "straightforward, proud, and self-willed, open to any ideas which appealed to them and willing to spread them among their circle of friends—especially spiritual ideals—which must be put plainly before them." Activities also were started in Belgium.

However, some mysterious intrigues deliberately sabotaged Mur-shid's trip to Germany. On his arrival, it was revealed that the professor who had written enthusiastic letters about arrangements had made no arrangements at all. It was discovered that the main obstacle was due to a hesitation developed by Anthroposophists toward Eastern thought, as it seemed to undermine the ego they felt was the mainstay of the achievement of Western civilization.

Every effort has been made by its founder [Rudolph Steiner] to impress his followers with the idea that Eastern wisdom is different from the Western, and the way of the West is different from the way of the East, and what is called in Buddhism, Nirvana, annihilation, is not the thought of Christ; Christ's teaching is the eternal and ever-progressing individuality, by which he means to say that it is not God alone Who Lives forever, but every individual entity as a distinct and separate entity is eternal and is gradually progressing to the fulness of its own individuality. In this way he divides one truth into two thoughts opposing each other, the oneness of the whole being on the part of the Eastern thought. The ego is "notion," that is, a concept arising out of failing to see things from an overall point of view, and being caught by the limitation urged by body consciousness, and identification. When you stand with your back to the sun, your shadow is before you; but when you turn and face the sun, then your shadow falls behind you.

Murshid saw the Goetheanum at Dornäch as it was being built in its original form in wood under the personal supervision of Dr. Steiner. Later he told one of his disciples that he was surprised that it was still standing, "Because symbols were used in a way that challenges the divine order of things." Did he mean the unusual place assigned to Lucifer, mediating between the forces of Christ and Ahriman, whereas traditionally Lucifer had identified himself with the forces opposing God's supremacy? Not long after the building was completed, it burned to the ground.

In Frau Foerster-Nietzsche, the sister of the well-known philosopher, Murshid discovered a kindred spirit. Murshid felt the clouds of depression of the aftermath of war weighing heavily on the German people, but the young people were "most responsive to any idea tending toward the unfoldment of the soul."

However, in that land of most exquisite beauty of nature, there is always genius to be found. A nation so proud, efficient and capable as Germany would blaze up, if once blown by the word of God.

Those who came in touch with Murshid at this time for the first time seemed to have been encountered by an unforgettable emotion, that of something decisive in their lives. It was what was behind this beautiful and powerful personality that transfigured at first sight. They had the impression of having found at last the spiritual haven to which they had always belonged, of having found a master and a friend. Here was one haloed by the real spirituality for which they had always dreamt; here was one who knew and *was* what he knew. He came into their lives as a smiling downpour of sunshine with the simplicity of an old acquaintance, casting a joyous glow on the most humdrum aspects of their existence, and lifting their souls by his exalted atmosphere and his loving kindness.

The Summer Schools in 1921 and 1922 at Fazal Manzil near Paris were, according to some, perhaps among the most serene, yet pregnant with significance for the future. Murshid found his natural surroundings sitting under a tree in the lovely garden of Fazal Manzil, surrounded by a circle of the privileged few who had so far discovered him. As he mused over life before death, the experience of the soul, and the practice of God's presence, or sat rapt in silent at-one-ness, one knew that he was imparting the knowledge of his personal experience and communicating his own inner life to those who could allow themselves to be absorbed in his holy atmosphere.

After the evening classes at Fazal Manzil, Murshid would recite the prayers, standing in the middle of the circle of his mureeds, lifting his arms in praise: "Praise be to Thee, most supreme God," bowing in reverence; "Take us in Thy parental arms, and raise us from the denseness of the earth"; then holding his arms outstretched as receptive to God's grace, "Pour upon us Thy love and Thy light." Then again he would invoke all the prophets and masters of the past as the incorporation of the eternal spirit of guidance and pray for the spreading of the Message of God, bringing back to the mureeds vistas of the prophetic tradition to which the master belonged. As the mureeds left one by one, holding in their hearts as a treasure the serene atmosphere of these unforgettable evenings, the master would bless them in turn as he stood at the top of the steps of Fazal Manzil.

Shortly after the Summer School in Suresnes in 1921, Murshid held a short Summer School among the dunes by the seaside at Katwijk in Holland. Here came to the master all those who later became the principal workers and leaders of the Dutch movement. As Murshid walked from his rooms to the lecture hall, the fishermen would line up along his path and take off their caps reverently as he passed. Asked by a mureed who they thought he was, they said he was someone like St. John the Baptist must have been.

In 1922 headquarters in Geneva were removed from the Salle Centrale to Quai des Eaux Vives, in the house (Maison Royale) which Murshid had on his previous visit already earmarked as the future headquarters. Mr. Talewar Dussaq took over as General Secretary, with the help of his sister, Countess Pieri, who was made General Treasurer. "The beautiful manner in which these both offered a smiling welcome to friends and strangers won for them the love and affection of all those who came in contact with them," wrote Murshid. Now came a wonderful worker, Mr. de Cruzat Zanetti, "who answered the great need of our movement." He was given the most responsible charge of administration: He was appointed Executive Supervisor of the Sufi Movement.

On the ship sailing to the United States in 1923, the presence of the Master whose being had now grown to great stature called for an inevitable response among the passengers who, one by one, became his friends. It was a "phenomenon of the spirit of universal brotherhood" said Murshid.

In the ship through the rain and storm the Message was felt by people travelling from different countries to the States having different opinions, who became my friends one after another, up to the moment that we arrived at the point of our destination. By this time almost all had become my friends. No wonder my soul would have sought after seeing for itself this phenomenon of the spirit of universal brotherhood.

But the mureeds who came to meet Murshid upon his arrival were most shocked to find that he had been detained by the authorities on Ellis Island because the quota of Indians for that month had been reached.

And I, whose nation was all nations, whose birth place was the world, whose religion was all religions, whose occupation was search after truth, and whose work was the service of God and humanity, my answers interested them, yet did not answer the requirements of the law.

Mrs. Mary (Ihushi) Cushing's energetic intervention soon brought embarrassment upon the high-handed officials for this shameful reception of a venerated guest whose arrival had been awaited by thousands. Murshid delivered lectures in New York and Boston at numerous societies, and the over-crowded applications for interviews had to be screened and pruned for lack of time to meet the sudden overflow. Murshid traveled to California, where he met with Mr. Luther Burbank, who gave him a clue to some aspects of the American way of life, "proving that it is not only fine arts and culture, but science and work with the earth that elevates a man to that serenity and simplicity of love."

Murshida Rabia Martin's joy in meeting Murshid in San Francisco was boundless. The movement was charged with a new life. After the crowded lectures in the great cities, the more enterprising mureeds formed a galaxy of small groups. Murshid found the international ideal gaining in strength in the United States and admired the American generosity to those in need.

The broad outlook of the people in America gave me a great hope and a faith that it is this spirit which in time must bring the universal idea to the view of the world. I saw in the people of America the sum total of modern progress. I called it "the Land of the Day."

An American as a friend is very agreeable and desirable and most sociable. One feels affection, spontaneity in his feelings; although the business faculty is most pronounced in him, yet together with it he is most generous. The American readily responds to the idea of universal brotherhood. He is open to study any religion or philosophy, although it is a question if he would like to follow a certain religion long enough, because freedom, which is the goal, by many in America is taken as the way, and therefore, before starting the journey towards spiritual freedom, they want the way also to be a way of freedom, which is impossible. I found America progressing more rapidly upon the lines that it is active in than my friends in the East can ever imagine.

If there is anywhere that the international ideal finds response it is in the United States. For spiritual things their love is growing every day more and more. There are so many things to attract their attention, right and wrong both, that they cannot always make out which to accept and which to reject. Many, therefore, go from one thing to another, and get so accustomed to moving on that they do not feel contented with one thing. That is where is the contrast between the extreme East and the extreme West. The people of India have their Vedantas, the people in China have Buddhism; for ages they never can get tired of their religions. It is the evermoving life in America which keeps people so restless that one cannot find peace anywhere. And yet so many different spiritual movements seem to have been born in the United States and carried successfully to the ends of the worlds. The great difficulty I found in the United States was to make the Message audible, for I felt as though blowing a whistle in the noise of a thousand drums. Anything good or bad should be brought before the people in a grand manner, and if one cannot do it, then however valuable the Message, it will not find any response.

However, the U.S. press, which had assumed such importance in people's lives that "a man would rather go without bread than without a paper," made a profession of making light of anything serious.

Everything spiritual is treated by the press lightly in order to please the multitude. Therefore, the only source by which to reach the public seems to be almost a closed door for an earnest exponent of truth. Many reporters from the press came to me and had a conversation. My answers to their questions, if they had been put in the papers, would have had so much influence upon the mind of the people. The difficulty was that if a reporter happened to be an understanding and appreciative young man, still he had to show his report to someone else at the office before it was accepted. And if he did not spoil the report, then his chief thought it was too serious; for his readers something different must be put in. It is a kind of profession that the press has taken to distort every good thing and to make light of something which is serious. These tactics of the American press are followed more or less by the press in Europe also.

The reporters seemed so interested and deeply moved; when the report was published, it was as if the flesh of a living person had been carved off and the skeleton were presented before all. They do not feel that they are doing any harm to the spiritual truth. They only think that they are doing good to both: bringing the speaker to the knowledge of the people and amusing the mob at the same time, which is ignorant of the deeper truth. Their main object is to please the man in the street. The modern progress has an opposite goal to what the ancient people had. In the ancient times the trend of the people's thought was to reach the ideal man. Today the trend of the people's thought is to touch the ordinary man.

I was once very amused in Boston. A reporter of a newspaper came to me and his first question was which hall was it where I was going to lecture. I thought the first important question he would have asked would have been what was the subject that I was going to lecture on. But his most important point was the hall in which I was to lecture. And as unfortunately the hall was not so large as he had anticipated, all the conversation with him and every impression he had turned out to be nothing, because the hall was not large enough for the editor to admit the article.

Back in Europe in 1923, Murshid was invited one evening to a dinner given by Paderewski at his lovely villa by Lake Geneva. Paderewski was most intrigued to know something about this Oriental priest. Before being introduced, Murshid had been warned about three prohibitions in conversing with the maestro: not to speak about politics, religion, or music. To Murshid, Paderewski broached each subject one after the other, and letting everyone leave in turn, gave Murshid the unique joy of playing to him alone (he observed strictly the rule of never playing privately). The pianist became more and more exalted as he played, breaking into extemporizations as he caught the train of Murshid's meditative moods, and expressing them, thus spurring them yet further, so that both penetrated together into unexplored realms in the mystery of musical expression known only to those two. Such was the atmosphere that not a word was said as they shook hands in farewell.

While Murshid was in Rome, there was to be a pontifical high mass, officiated over by the Pope himself. Murshid asked his secretary, Sirkar van Stolk, to try to obtain tickets. None were available. Nevertheless, Murshid called for a carriage and went to St. Peter's.

Slowly he walked toward the morning-coated dignitary checking the cards at the foot of the steps. The latter, the epitome of lordly officialdom, duly asked in Italian for his card. Murshid looked at him, smiling, and firmly, with the utmost courtesy, replied, "It is quite all right. . . ." His tone was irresistible. The man moved back, overcome in the presence of this majestic stranger . . . . Murshid ascended in a completely unruffled, stately manner.[6]

Once inside, Murshid and his secretary witnessed the almost incredible spectacle of the High Mass.

Murshid was going more and more deeply into a state of ecstasy. Rapt and still, he seemed in another world. And then suddenly, as if the words had been wrung from him, he cried, "How wonderful is the power of the living Christ!"[7]

The regal splendor of the Vatican, its powerful organization, the grandeur of the churches in Rome and the troops of priests, rejoiced Murshid, seeing the importance given to a religion also here in the West.

Interviewed by Cardinal Gasperi, then Secretary of State for the Vatican, Murshid was asked what he meant by wisdom; that his answer was approved seemed to be indicated by the fact that he was granted an audience with His Holiness the Pope.

Rome made upon me a great impression. Once after having seen the Church in its glory in Russia, which I did not think I could see anymore, I witnessed in Rome that glory of the old Church still in existence. I went to see the church the likes of which I have never seen before in its form and beauty and in its grandeur. The troops of priests-to-be, fifteen, twenty, or a hundred, moving about hither and thither, gave me quite a new sight, which never in my travelling through the Western world I have seen. I attended some services at the Catholic Church, and what I learned from it was that it was all a preparation, which a service is meant to be, a perfectly organized drill by which to learn to respect man, above all a spiritual man, and in the end by bowing and bending to mankind, which represents spirituality, to arrive at worshipping man (the son of God), God's Representative. I thought it is the very sentiment that is needed to waken in man, though it is done in a narrow way, and yet in no other way can it be very well done. The present deplorable condition of religion that is to be found in the Western world is owing to the lack of the same principle which, it seemed to me, the service of the Roman Catholic Church taught: the lack of veneration for one's advanced brother. The spirit of the present generation is, "I am as good as you"; When a soul has nothing to look up to, it drops its wings, and a soul who was meant to be a bird remains a beast.

By 1923, the work was progressing increasingly. Everywhere the little seedlings sown by the Master were taking root and showing their heads, so that centers were sprouting in all the great cities of Europe and America. The work in Holland was progressing through the wonderful classes of Baron van Tuyll. From the time Mr. van Stolk took over the organization of the Summer School, it flourished wonderfully. Murshid called it an *urs*, which means pilgrimage. A press bureau was now founded by the efforts of Sheikh R. Mumtaz Armstrong, who started issuing the *Sufi Quarterly*. At Uppsala, Murshid was interested to hear Archbishop Nathan Söderblom, who was working to bring the Christian Churches together, say that "this was the first step." "That showed me that he believed in the second step also," wrote Murshid. The work was spreading in Sweden through Miss Haglund, in Norway through Miss Suzanna Kjosterud, and in Denmark through Mr. Pauls Steven. However, it was in Holland that activity was at its highest.

Murshida Goodenough, who was the first trustee of Murshid's teaching, was inspiring people in her talks in Paris. The efforts of Kismet Stam, Murshid's personal assistant and the second trustee, kept the work together. Miss Furnee, later called Nekhbat, became the third trustee of Murshid's teachings. In her, Murshid saw the spirit of the Message reflected at first glance.

Now Murshid's activity was heightened to an almost inconceivable pitch. His being, the living expression of the divine Message, vitalized every place he visited with renewed magnetism and awakened those who came into touch with him to a sudden God-realization within themselves. Wherever he went now, more and more people gathered. Pushing his physical resistance to its utmost, he seemed to be conscious of the brevity of the time accorded to him to build the foundation of the world message he was bearing.

During a hurried visit to Berlin and Munich in the spring of 1925, Murshid found Mr. Rhettich Heidyl (Sherdyl). Noticing him among a numerous audience, Murshid called for him after a lecture, saying, "I need your help for Germany." Sherdyl, who had not thought of disturbing the master for an interview, responded with true chivalry, thereafter devoting himself unswervingly to the Cause.

The Summer School in 1925 was a great success. Mureeds had gathered from all the different countries and, under the impulse of Mr. van Stolk and through the generosity of the mureeds, a plot of land was purchased to build the Universel—a temple—and the mureeds' house, intended by the donators to house mureeds attending the Summer School. Murshid was there amid his beloved mureeds, radiating light and power and ecstasy, even more so than ever before.

Murshid then made his last trip to the United States. In December 1925 in New York there was a rush of reporters to Murshid's flat at the Waldorf Astoria, and the auditorium where he spoke was crowded. The growing center in New York was placed in the hands of Sheikh Fatha Engle. Yet many had come because of the publicity or to see some phenomena, said Murshid. Many wished for an expedient and practical solution to human problems fitting into their desiderata and expected "the divine inspiration to be speeded up to their rhythm."

Dr. Carrol, the author of *Man the Unknown*, invited Murshid to the

Rockefeller Institute, wishing to enquire from the Indian mystic what he knew about supernatural power and whether it can be made manifest to view. "That power can better be used to lift the heart of man to a higher idea," answered Murshid.

While traveling in the Western countries, I was often asked by people if I had the power of clairvoyance, if I could see their auras, if I could tell them their colour or note, if I could read their thoughts, if I had any psychical powers, if I could foretell what will happen, if I was mediumistic, if I spoke under spiritualistic control, if I knew automatic writing, if I was able to magnetize, if I could psychometrize. Firstly, I was most amused with these questions, to which I could neither give an affirmative nor a negative answer. By an affirmative answer I would have been put to the test, and a negative answer would be my defeat; and yet I often preferred defeat and in some cases I avoided answering. It is something which in the East a sage does not expect. For a real sage all these powers are outward plays, little things. Some people claim them, and the theosophical influence made it more difficult even for me to answer people. The same is true of spiritualists. They think spiritual phenomena will make man believe in the soul and in the hereafter, which today is not believed in by many. But this love of phenomena gives scope to many who wish to deceive the world by a spiritualistic fad, and once a person knows its falsehood even the believer would turn into an unbeliever.

Again, at Detroit, crowds thronged the Twentieth Century Club where Murshid delivered his lectures and he was unable to see in the given time even the smallest fraction of all those who had applied for interviews. The newspaper snatched a glimpse of Murshid's interview with Henry Ford, in its headlines: "Business magnate of the West meets spiritual genius of the East." Mr. Ford was reported as saying: "What I have searched after all my life, you have found it. If you were a business man, you would certainly have made a success, but I am glad you are as you are."

CHAPTER 20

Pygmalion

THE ART OF PERSONALITY

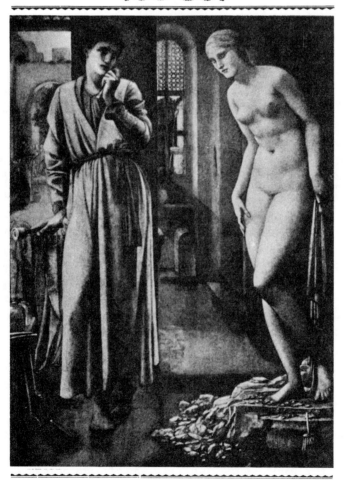

Was Du ererbt von Deinen Vätern Erwirb es, um es zu besitzen. (That which you inherit from your forefathers, you must reconquer in order to possess it.)—Goethe

When a glimpse of Our image is caught in man, when heaven and earth are sought in man, then what is there in the world that is not in man? If one only explores him, there is a lot in man.—Gayan, 5

What was it that Henry Ford, that astute and originally enterprising businessman—considered by some as the epitome of the American self-made man—had spotted in Murshid? What was it that he said Murshid had found, the very thing that he had been searching for? What was it that Murshid was teaching all the while? What was that Message that he was spreading in the course of his unrelenting travels?

We have already hinted at some of the answers; it seems like a many-sided prism: music, asceticism, intuition, mastery, saintlihood, realization, freedom, ecstasy, awakening, mysticism, religion ... But the accent was always in bringing the wisdom of the East gained in the seclusion of the recluse to bear right in the midst of the activity of the West. From the point of view of the westerner, it would make for more efficiency if an active person could develop enough detachment to find serenity and enough intuition to muster insight into people and affairs; and by building up magnetism, develop personal power in dealing with problems, and God-consciousness if it will give self-assurance, and ecstasy if it will make people contented in the middle of material strife.

For the easterner, it was gratifying to see those so involved in business being so altruistic. It was also heartening to see just how much this teaching is in demand in the West.

What exactly Mr. Ford had spotted was that Murshid, unlike what he had expected from hearsay about the Eastern temperament, had shown most explicitly and in detail how to bring this teaching, which so many idealize but consider impractical and intangible, to bear in everyday life:

330

It is in this way that self-denial is learned; not always by fasting and retiring into the wilderness.

But the one who proves trustworthy to every soul he meets, and considers his relationships and connections, small or great, as something sacred, certainly observes the spiritual law of that religion which is the religion of all religions.

That is applying realization to practical affairs. Murshid had placed the accent on achievement and shown how renunciation introduced in achievement makes for progress because, by "giving up the fruit of achievement, one can go on beating one's own records," increasing the challenge, which is precisely what Mr. Ford had been doing and what accounted for his success. Further, Murshid stressed the need to unfold one's personality rather than escape in the transpersonal, and yet further cultivate that most valuable gift, friendship in relationship.

The awakening of consciousness and the perfecting of the personality constitute the two antithetical poles of the purpose of life: to see and to be. Thus the spirit may experience bodiness without being hemmed in by the ego, and matter display the perfection latent in the spirit without being hampered by the individuality. The permutation of these two polarized purposes of life is to be found in the axiomatic dichotomy of Hermeticism: the spiritualization of matter and the materialization of spirit.

The spirit is conscious of the body, and the body is conscious of the spirit. When this is so, then man is perfect.

We know that so much of the traditional esotericism is seen in terms of liberation from existence, or from the necessity of reincarnation, or salvation from the condition of the flesh; however, Murshid stresses the meaningfulness of the human being.

We want a human spirit, and self-realization is the search for this human spirit; everything must become human in us. But how should we accomplish this?

This will be the objective of the new age, cultivating the personality instead of accumulating gadgets.

Personality is more valuable than wealth. How strange it is that there is such a large population in this world and that there are so few personalities! Think of that Greek philosopher who went about with a lighted lantern in daytime. People asked, "What are you looking for?" He said, "For a human being."

This was the perennial teaching of the great ones, since sclerosed as religion.

By seeking liberation, one tacitly devalues the personality, envisioning it as a feature of maya.

To this day the Hindus repeat early in the morning, "Ram, Ram"; the Buddhists call on the Lord Buddha and the Christians on Christ. Why? Only because of the personality of these holy ones. . . . There are many pious people sitting in the Mosques and the churches telling their rosaries. Their piety is for themselves; they cannot move the world. So if it is not spirituality and not piety, what is it, then? It is the development of humanity in us.[1]

Very often people have taken the ascetic path and have gone where they could keep away from the world, because they did not care for the personality.

Murshid, embodying the outlook of the Sufi, pinpoints the importance of incorporating the divine perfection in one's personality in a concrete, tangible way.

Make God a reality and he will make you the truth.[2]

God-realized ones bring to the world the living God. At present there exists in the world only a belief in God; God exists in imagination, in the ideal. It is such a soul which has touched divine Perfection that brings to earth a living God, who without him would remain only in the heavens.

This makes sense of creation; otherwise existence would be a useless, whimsical play of shadows. Surely creation must have a purpose; if not, it would not be.

We have already come across the Murshid's attitude toward desire, which is the motivation behind creation: the desire to achieve, to unfold, to know, to master, all manifestations of the divine impulse toward fulfillment in manifestation. And it is this divine impulse which, pressing forth in the individual, is most often limited and deviated, sometimes misused or even betrayed by man. What is the purpose of life, if not to germinate and burgeon the inexhaustible plethora of potentialities lying dormant within us—to awaken the sleeping beauty? Imagine, so many are seeking in meditation to reach the causal plane, encompass the eternal models behind all created things! But the purpose of the model is the finished product. The mold is an empty shell, maybe displaying more perfection than the exemplar, but its fulfillment is in the object created. This is the end-product.

Personality is the fruit of the tree of life.[3]

Murshid compares the eternal aspect of one's being to the seed and the transient and evolving personality to the fruit. The purpose is in the fruit and not in the seed. The seed seems to be more important than the fruit because without the seed there can be no continuation, and in the seed everything is contained, and yet if there was a purpose in the creation, it was that the seed should become the fruit. Much more went into producing it than shows, for it manages to condense a vast gamut of abstract principles into a tangible masterpiece.

The fulfilment of this whole creation is to be found in man. And this object is only fulfilled when man has awakened to this part of his being which represents the Master: in other words God Himself.

We are touching upon one of the greatest mysteries there is: that the divine perfection need not be sought in samadhi, the causal plane, but in man. Repeatedly, entreatingly, Murshid reiterates the words of Christ, which became like a motto, as a mainstay of his own teaching: "Be ye therefore perfect, as your Father which is in heaven is perfect." By saying this, Christ implied that you too could reach this perfection, not only himself. But the important thing is to detect this perfection latent in an imperfect being. This explains the words of a Sufi dervish Abd-ul-Jabbar Niffari:

Why do you look for God up there? He is here! Here!

Actually, the plant is the seed that has unfurled itself. The seed itself passes through the growth process of the plant, and appears at the end of the process inside the fruit. It was always there, though not recognizable as it deployed itself in the plant.

The same God, who was unmanifested as the seed of the plant of the creation, rises again towards fulfilment; and in that fulfilment he produces the seed.

Divinity resides in humanity, divinity is the outcome of humanity. Man, in the flowering of his personality, expresses the personality of God.

The awakening enjoined upon the Murshid consists in being able to discern the seed while looking at the plant, to espy the divine perfection in the not yet perfected personality of man.

As the seed comes last, after the life of trunk, branch, fruit, and flower; and as the seed is sufficient in itself and capable of producing another plant, such as that of which it was but a small product; so man is the product of all the planes, spiritual and material, a being small in comparison with the mountains, and rivers, and seas, or even in comparison with many beasts and birds; and yet in him alone that shines forth which caused the whole—that primal intelligence, the seed of existence—God. Therefore is man termed Ashraf-ul-Makhlukat, the ideal of the universe.

This, then, would mean spotting the divine perfection in wait in the depth of one's being.

The effect is in the cause and the cause is in the effect, as the flower is the outcome of the seed and the seed is in the heart of the flower.

The inexhaustible propensities of a rose are latent within the rose: Obviously the deploying of the seed we call the plant can only display a fraction of its bounty, since it is the function of the exposure to the sun, the temperature, the wind, the altitude, the quality and composition of the soil, even psychological factors; second, acclimatization into new surroundings or latitudes will bring out new features, unobserved so far; and third, breeding may lead to mutations undetectable in the original strands. The horticulturist may discover untapped possibilities in one strand of a species. They are present, latent, but can only be discovered in the course of the unfoldment of the plant under various conditions. Yet an expert horticulturist will have a flair for the outcome of his experiments before making them, which will definitely orient him in deciding in which direction or areas to pursue his experiments. In the same way the gardener of the personality develops a sixth sense, a hunch of the potentialities lying dormant in a human being, because the archetypes of one's being have been incorporated into the subliminal depths of our personality, even into the substructure of our cells; but are, in scientific language, recessive instead of dominant.

No doubt the personality grows as best it can in the prevailing circumstances, but if we are dissatisfied with our development, it means that we are not cultivating it, or not cultivating it effectively. It will not blossom satisfactorily without some care and thought given to it. This is the art of personality. "The personality must be developed."

One identifies oneself with one's present personality, instead of one's potentials:

"These are my tendencies, my fancies, my inclinations, and by respecting them I respect myself, by considering them I consider myself." But one forgets that what one calls mine is not oneself; it is what wills that is oneself.

Nature can achieve much, but in the course of evolution the human will takes over where nature leaves off.

As the whole of nature is made by God, so the nature of each individual is made by himself.

Murshid often distinguishes between nature that is created without the free participation of the creature, and art, where we complete the divine creativity by using our free will. Yet in any art, particularly in the art of personality, we are exercising the divine creativity, which now acts through our will.

It is God himself who through man completes the beauty of nature, and this is called art. . . . But the best of all arts is the art of personality.[3]

In the making of personality it is God who completes His divine art.[4]

There are many arts, but the art of molding and burnishing a wonderful personality is the art of arts.

The artist learns his art by his admiration of beauty. When a person gets an insight into beauty, then he learns the art of arts, which is the art of personality.[5]

It is the art of Pygmalion who molded and chiseled at the form of his ideal Galatea until, thanks to Aphrodite, the goddess of love, she sprang to life. Can there be anything more challenging and fascinating?

Murshid distinguishes between nature, character, and personality.

Nature is born, character is built, and personality is developed. . . . Sa'adi says, "The kitten in the end proves to be a kitten. Even if it were kept on the queen's sofa petted and kissed and loved and cared for, when the mouse came it would show that it was a cat."[6]

Nature then would be the raw material of our idiosyncracies, inherited either through parents and ancestors, or through the planes during the descent, or from one's causal conditioning. Any qualities that we may acquire, or cultivate in our being, come under the category of character, the second layer that builds itself upon the foundation of the nature, and maybe weaves itself into it to such an extent that the nature may hardly be distinguishable anymore though it may burst forth when one has lost control of oneself.

Character is, so to speak, a picture with lines and colours which we make within ourselves. . . . A child begins by noticing all kinds of things in grown-up people, and then it adopts whatever it likes most and whatever attracts it.[7]

This is where we see the drawback of introspection.

There is always a conflict between their character and their nature; for the character is made by a certain habit, but the nature says, "You must not make this a habit, I will fight with you about it."

The personality is the finished product. The art of personality consists in integrating all the elements entering into one's formation with all the richness culled from the confrontation with the universe; that is the blending of nature and character.

Personality is the finishing of character. Personality is like a cut diamond. Personality is a picture which the soul reflects in order to manifest according to that design.

One could conceive of Pygmalion as the master—or guru—and Galatea as the pupil whose personality he is contriving to fashion into a masterpiece. Should he prove to be a real master, he would bring the indigenous traits out while harmonizing them into an admirable pattern, as a good cabinetmaker burnishes the surface of the wood to bring out the grain, and the violinmaker blends different woods, after duly maturing them, carving them into harmonious shapes, then ordinating them together into a fascinating construction. If he is a self-styled master, he will endeavor to coerce the pupil's personality into conforming to his preconceived idea, as in Bernard Shaw's play. This can only be done by imposing an artificial veneer upon a background that has not adapted itself to the veneer, so that, under test, the fragile construction collapses.

You do not need to act in a certain way. It is the expression of your self which is the art of personality.

This points to the importance of working upon the foundation of a being. Yet the foundation seems to be the very nature which is the divine nature, and therefore unalterable. However, among the qualities in a nature, some are, as we have seen, dominant and active, and others recessive or latent, waiting to spring to life. One can enhance certain qualities in a nature that were not apparent. For example, one could bring an apparently precarious and erratic person to the awareness of a stable and reliable streak in his nature that he had not noticed before. Moreover, one can harness that very force for which one was trying to compensate by awakening the opposite tendency. For example, one could encourage the erratic person to engage in an activity where he can orient his energy in picking up ideas with verve while following them up, or apply agility and dexterity in working with hands and fingers, but coordinate these in a useful way.

On the other hand, one could conceivably think of Galatea as the very personality of Pygmalion. Since it is identification with one's personality that prevents one from being able to act upon it, Pygmalion projected it in front of himself in the aspect of what appeared to be another being: Galatea. There is much that we can do to cultivate our personality ourselves providing we awaken beyond our personality and are able to encompass all the elements that are weaving themselves into our being.

With the personality of God man has to take God's point of view.

It is an ironic reflection on our involvement in our personal image that we generally do the opposite: We identify ourselves with our personal nature, which is a limitation of our real being, and idealize the personality we would like to acquire, which is in fact precisely what we are in our real or essential being, projecting it as the coveted object, instead of realizing that we are in our real being precisely what we are seeking to become. Clearly, then, all we have to do is realize what we are, "just like an artist who tries to make a statue of his beloved ideal as beautiful, as fine as he can." This was the theme of Murshid's play *Una*, the artist who lived for her ideal and later realized that she had to die to give it life. She had to die to her image of herself and realize that she was the ideal she always idolized. We can only integrate the elements we wish to construct into a personality if we can identify them in ourselves.

What are these elements? We have to distinguish between the inherited parameters, which constitute the substructure (Murshid calls it the nature), and the characteristics acquired since one's birth on earth, which constitute the superstructure (Murshid calls it character). We have to take into account the blending, interaction, integrating of these two aspects, which is what Murshid calls the personality, the finished product. The inherited qualities are simply qualities that were acquired before, some of which constitute one's essential being, which is one's eternal archetype. Sufis consider everybody's archetype as his special share or attribution within the abundance that constitutes the divine perfection. Murshid calls this one's divine heritage.

He is a son of God who has recognized the eternal spirit as his parent, and he is a son of man who has recognized himself as the son of his parents who are as limited as he.

The difference between an acquired quality and an inherited one is that the inherited one is built into one, it is a constituent of one's being; for example, one's father continues to live in one to the extent to which his characteristics are blended with those of one's mother and other ancestors, and so back to the beginnings of time.

A child may inherit qualities of his ancestors six or seven generations back, which are not known to the family; and those may manifest in quite a concrete form.[8]

On the other hand, the acquired characteristic is like a graft that has to be incorporated over a period of time, and which the organism tends to reject under stress.

Which are the qualities within us that are inherited? First, the eternal archetype of our specific being, that is, a particular blend of the divine perfection at the fringe between the impersonal and the personal. This is our divine inheritance. We can understand when Murshid says that we are the divine perfection, because owing to the divine inheritance God continues to live in us within the limitations we impose upon him, just like the seed within the plant. So our nature is our limitation of the divine perfection, underlying that perfection that is always present potentially; conversely, the divine perfection subsumes our nature. Moreover, we must know that we have parents of each of the different bodies constituting our being. Therefore, we have to include in our inheritance qualities that were inherited in the course of our soul's descent from the parents we had at each level, endowing us with their special characteristics.

Another way of a soul's inheriting qualities, which do not belong to its parents and ancestors, is the reflection that a soul has brought with it before it has come to this physical plane.

This includes our inheritance from the vibrations that interwove into our akashic body, structuring us at that level into a melody that neither of our akashic parents constituted on his own. This becomes our contribution to the symphony of the spheres.

Now we have to include the inheritance of our light-body, or aura, from our parents: beings of light in the spheres of light; Arwah. Each of us is endowed with an aura of a unique pattern, arising out of the blending of our light-parents. Maybe we remember having been kindled as a candle, but are we conscious of the special aspect or orientation of light that is ours to radiate? Is it glowing or diaphanous, or glistening, or sparkling or incandescent or iridescent? Is the form radial or concentric or spiriform or rectiform, clearly outlined or diffused? Is it polarized, and in which chakras, and how disposed? Do we experience ourselves as beings of light?

Then we have to account for our heritage from the jinn world; specifically, from our jinn parents, which is "an accommodation for its mind, already prepared in a very negative state, from the world of the jinns."

This inheritance is sometimes more easily detectable than that of the preceding planes, particularly, for example, in a child of ordinary parents who proves to be a prodigy or genius. Do you remember engaging in creative activities prior to your birth?

From our earthly parents, we inherit not only physical characteristics, features of the body, but also mental, temperamental, and other attributes:

The mental attributes of the parents are inherited by impression on the mental plane. The thought and feeling of the parents are inherited by the child as a quality. If the father is engaged in thinking, "I should build an orphanage," the child will have a philanthropic disposition. If the father is thinking, "This person is my enemy, I should revenge myself on him," the child will have a vindictive disposition. If the mother admires something very much, for instance flowers, the child will have that love of beauty in its nature.

This means that not only the bodies of the parents and earthly ancestors continue to live as strands blended with other strands in us, but also their minds, emotional bodies and souls, which have to blend with the strands issuing from jinn parents and angelic parents, soul parents. Imagine all the profusion that we inherit! No wonder that people experience conflicts between antagonistic tendencies within themselves! Our task as the gardener of personality is to integrate these.

Sometimes the inheritance from the soul parents or jinn parents is stronger than that from the earthly parents, in which case the inheritance of the earth parents is recessive, held in abeyance. "If the impressions previously received by the soul are stronger it does not inherit them."

The composition of our being is yet more complex and yet more ingeniously devised! The whole point of creation is that the seminal characteristics cross-bred all the way down the line are continually exposed to the influence of impressions accruing from other sections of the universe, sometimes strengthening one in certain idiosyncrasies, sometimes inhibiting one:

Consciously or unconsciously we call to us that element which makes us what we are. What we experience in life, therefore, has either come from what we have already called to us in the past, or from what we call at the present moment.

One discovers oneself in every other self who reveals one to oneself, exhibiting qualities latent in one but which one had not yet noticed. In other words, the experience of the universe is a process of self-discovery: One discovers a component of oneself in the effulgence of that flamboyant dawn arrayed with the most spectacular spectrum of hues that makes one aware of one's own incandescent and radiant nature; or in the frigid hyperborean scenes at high altitudes where water trickles amid snow and ice glistening in the sun, one discovers one's own sublime aloofness, and mysteriously serene vitality; in the budding of young sprouts or the blossoming of flowers, we discover our need to express ourselves and unfold; and the strength of some people gives us confidence in our own ability to manifest strength; and so with vivacity, or kindness. These influences become incorporated in our being because we inherit all qualities, although some are more pronounced than others.

It is absurd to say, "I have not got that quality"; there is no quality in the world that man has not got, either good or bad.

Therefore, they simply call into activity recessive or dormant qualities. They come under the category of acquired characteristics, in what Murshid calls the character of a person, and it takes one's awareness of the presence of those qualities to be able to consolidate them; otherwise they remain a veneer. This means that we have to rediscover our inheritance, remember what we are.

Qualities are thus acquired at all levels on the way down: at the soul, at the angelic, or at the jinn sphere. For Murshid, the universe is a phenomenon of reflection; each fraction of the One Being reflects every other. Such is the influence of the environment upon the development of the personality, very much like the influence of the physical environment upon a plant. The soul cannot develop into a personality in isolation, just as the seed cannot blossom into a plant in a water-tight compartment, because as it grows, it draws the environment into itself, just as the plant incorporates the earth into itself. The seed incorporates certain minerals of the earth, certain gases from the air, the required amount of water, a specific range of sun rays and even cosmic rays, digesting them, as it were, and transmuting them into its own fabric, because it already possesses the nature of this environment in its own composition. But it rejects extraneous ingredients, and thrives or wilts according to whether it receives the wherewithal to unfold its innate idiosyncrasies. Just so the environment, psychological and physical, not only accrues to the inborn nature of the individual in the form of what Murshid calls the character, but interacts upon the nature, buffeting it in its foundations, resulting in the personality. Therefore, it is important to give great care to the circumstances in which one lives, the friends one frequents, the objects one selects in one's house, the books one reads, one's hobbies, etc. If one is stinted of these *essentia vitae*, one will not be able to unfold satisfactorily and will feel frustrated.

The same applies to one's need for vital space in which to deploy one's being. People living together in the family circle, husband and wife, parents and children, and at work, the boss and the worker, tend to smother one another's ego, depriving them of vital breathing space, resulting in desperate outbreaks of frustration and, if tolerated because there is no other way, often leading to despondency and grudges against the person who is thwarting one. This feeling in turn obstructs one's unfoldment even more than the outer circumstances, certainly aggravating the situation, and therefore has to be met with clear insight.

What is it that takes the part of the sun in the life of man, as the sun takes part in the growing of the rose? It is intelligence.

The place that air occupies in the growth of the soul is this: Air is symbolical of the inspiration which comes to the heart that is prepared for it. And it is not by outward learning but by what one learns through inspiration that the soul is raised towards its unfoldment.

The space which is needed around the rose bush in order to let it grow means symbolically a wide outlook on life.

Self-pity is the worst poverty. Once there is a wound in the heart the whole personality of the wounded becomes embittered. It develops in nature that weakness which in ordinary words is called touchiness, taking offence at every little thing. Everyone seems to him to be wicked, everyone's presence seems to have a jarring effect upon him. And it culminates when he dislikes himself.

How, then, can one overcome this scourge when it does not seem possible to alter the outer circumstances? First of all, there is a range within which another person cannot restrict one or even reach one; one can find an inner freedom while being captured externally. Second, it is one's intolerance of another's ego that makes one suffer; from the moment that one acquiesces to his need for his ego in his present state of development, one accommodates him instead of submitting to him, and one becomes greater for having a greater accommodation, being able to encompass him instead of abdicating to him.

It is difficult to tolerate because we do not understand them, but once we understand we can tolerate almost anything. Tolerance is the control of the impulse of resistance by the will. Tolerance practised, because one is compelled by circumstances to tolerate, is no virtue, but tolerance is the consideration through which one overlooks the faults of another and does not give way to the impulse of resistance. Depression, despair, and all manner of sorrow and sadness come from lack of generosity. Where does jealousy come from? Where does envy, aching of the heart come from? It all comes from lack of generosity. One can show generosity by a smile, by a kind glance, by a warm handshake.[9]

He who says, "I cannot tolerate," shows his smallness; he who says, "I cannot endure," shows his weakness; he who says, "I cannot associate," shows his limitation; he who says, "I cannot forgive," shows his imperfection.[10]

Perhaps the most painful form of despondency is when one pins one's frustration upon God, or fate, rather than holding a grudge against a person. Although it is obvious how well everything is programed, one fails to understand the programing of one's life. Obviously one is not being objective. Understanding of the programing is complicated by the fact that there are three factors at least: past karma, the effect of one's actions in this life-cycle, and tests programed for one in order to bring one to realization or develop certain qualities necessary for us to negotiate the next hurdle on our life's path.

Many have been resentful towards God for having sent them misery in their lives, but misery is always part of life's experience. Some may become very angry and say "This is not just," or "This is not right, for how could God who is just and good allow unjust things to happen?" But our sight is very limited, and our conception of right and wrong and good and evil is only our own, and not according to God's plan. It is true that as long as we see it as such, it is so for us and for those who look at it from our point of view; but when it comes to God the whole dimension is changed, the whole point of view is changed.

CHAPTER 21

Guard Each Man's Pride

RELATIONSHIP

I consider my action towards every man as my action towards God; and the action of every person towards me I take as an action of God.—Gayan, 70

The same bridge that connects two souls in the world, when stretched becomes the path to God.—XI, 244

Murshid was continually working with people and upon people like a gardener with his plants, improving them, unfolding them, pruning them, supporting them, and inspiring them. This meant really entering with heart and soul into their lives' patterns with genuine compassionate concern and fatherly involvement while grasping the issues behind their personal problems that they failed to see. Therefore, Murshid considered friendships sacred, because it is only in our interrelationship that we can help each other, and it is in our interrelationship with the whole universe that we unfold the potentialities in ourselves—most particularly with that section of the created realm which is the closest to us by kinship: our fellow human beings. To become what we already are, we must discover ourselves in other ourselves in whom we can witness that of ourselves which we fail to see in ourselves. Indeed, one becomes what one sees. Inevitably, therefore, one finds oneself immersed in the problem of relationship.

See yourself reflected in another. If you can attune your consciousness so that your consciousness touches the consciousness of another, then not only the thoughts of that person but his whole spirit is reflected in your spirit.

We interpenetrate each other and criss-cross as the clouds dovetail and interweave into unpredictable patterns of splendor and creativity. No being is isolated; the experimenter in an insulated box is still regurgitating past impressions, and the spaceman is connected to the planet by innumerable invisible threads as he heaves himself asunder from his earthly roots, and the deeply imbedded human ingenuity latent in Helen Keller broke through the psychophysiological curtain

344

between her and her environment. We carry numberless beings within our psyche. We take them with us as we go for a walk, or when the ship casts off, leaving the harbor behind. We may indeed be astonished to discover them inside us on the occasions when we catch ourselves thinking and feeling and speaking and acting just as they do.

It is life that entrusts us with the most precious of custodies: friendship. That there is a being to whom we can open our heart, onto whom we may unload all that is oppressing us, that we may confide ourselves into somebody's understanding, that there is someone in whose custody we may feel safe and secure—this is the greatest gift there is.

What endeared people to Murshid was that he proved to be a wonderful friend who really cared for one, standing by one in distress, supporting if one was attacked and rejoicing in one's joy. Seeing God in all beings, he naturally attached a great importance to friendship and taught how to cultivate it. He considered it the best apprenticeship to spirituality.

It is not belief in God which leads us to the goal, nor is it the analysis and the knowledge of God that brings us there. It is the friendship of God.

Friendship makes one alert to the pleasure and displeasure of others as a forerunner of the sense of the divine pleasure and displeasure. Isn't it wonderful, when you see two people together linked by silent understanding! It may be considered as spiritual schooling since it teaches one to safeguard a fellow being from one's own ego, to spare:

feeling which can be hurt by a moment's thoughtfulness. If there is any abode of God, it is in the heart of man.

As soon as a person begins to regard the pleasure and displeasure of God in the feelings of every person he meets, he can only be refined, whatever his position in life.[1]

The sheer joy of it boomerangs back, enriching the personality.

The happiness of the person to whom we wish to do good is felt by us before it is realized by him.

You will encounter it among people gifted with a particularly endearing disposition, who naturally harmonize with others.

I have seen at the head of certain factories people who have won the heart of every worker in the factory. And another head of a factory against whom every worker in the factory was speaking.

It makes for success.

Whether a person is in business, in commerce, or any other walk of life, he either repulses or attracts, and on that depends his success or failure in life.

Its genuineness can be tested by whether a person shows:

a little consideration for the aged, a little consideration for someone who is perhaps not honoured or respected.

Inevitably, it spurs one into unfolding latent qualities. Friendship stands or falls with one's honoring one's word.

No wealth of this world can be compared with one's word of honour. . . . To a real person to go back on his word is worse than death.[2]

And it is our valuation of it that will lead one to pay the price of overcoming one's selfishness by doing things for someone else.

Generosity one can show in accommodating one's fellow man, in welcoming him, in bidding farewell to one's friend. In thought, word, and deed, in every manner.

It keeps one on the alert to one's own manners, for brashness is distasteful to a friend.

Respect, consideration, reverence, kindness, compassion and sympathy, forgiveness and gratefulness, all these virtues can be best adorned by subtlety of expression.

They teach one delicacy and tact.

It is by tactfulness that we make a balance against all inharmonious influences which have a jarring effect upon our spirit.

My Murshid was very fond of hearing music, and my being a musician naturally gave him sometimes the thought of hearing some music. I was an Eastern mureed, sitting before him, but he never asked me to sing. Sometimes, if he wished it very much, he said: "What are the notes of that raga?" I thought, "He wants me to sing the raga."

Murshid was shocked by some of the bad manners he came across in the West, used as he was to the refined courtesy current in the traditional Oriental setting in which he was brought up. He felt noble behavior was a necessary feature of spirituality since it is spirituality that makes for sensitivity with regard to a fellow man's feelings. It need not be taught to a sensitive person; if he is otherwise, it is not clear how he can expect to reach sublime heights in meditation.

It is amusing sometimes to watch how good manners annoy someone who is proud of his bad manners. He will call it shallow, because his pride is hurt at the sight of something which he has not got.[3]

By what tour de force can two people endowed with different

temperaments and divergent likes and dislikes manage to get on together, if not by finding a way of accommodating each other's wishes through sensitivity and mutual respect? Does not one show one's friendship for a friend more pertinently by refraining from smoking in his presence if he dislikes smoking or from playing the type of music he is known to dislike, than by saying, "I am so glad to see you"?

There is a virtue which the Sufi calls *Muruat*. It means refraining from certain actions out of respect for someone else, whether in consideration for his age, position, knowledge, goodness, or piety. Those who practice this virtue do not do so only towards someone important or pious, for when this quality develops it manifests in one's dealings with everyone.

Muruat is the opposite of bluntness.... This virtue may even become so intense that a person, out of consideration and respect, tries to bear with the lack of the same virtue in another....

A person may show lack of muruat, if not in words, in his glance. One does not need to speak in order to be rude. In one's look, in one's intonation, in one's manner of standing or walking, in the way one closes the door on leaving the room, one can show one's feelings.[4]

Should we maintain ourselves in the focus of our higher consciousness, our relationship with people would stand out in a very different perspective from the usual. We would see what we are doing to people and what people are doing to us, what is to be achieved in our special relationship with each person, what are the karmic forces at play, what is the nature of our involvement.

To rear, nourish, and maintain a friendship is certainly one of the greatest arts there is, and the most worthwhile cultivating; but it requires a great deal of care, wisdom, and watchfulness. How many of us spoil this beautiful gift by negligence, inexperience, or sheer foolhardiness? It is nothing to trifle with!

There is a delicacy in friendship. If that delicate thread is damaged ... something goes wrong. There is no more delicate machinery than the spirit of man.... For other machinery we can get spare parts, but not for this machinery when once it is broken, when once something of it is lost.[5]

Friendship lasts only as long as that delicate thread exists. Guard carefully that thin thread that connects two souls in whatever relation or capacity.

Friendship does not sustain itself on its own, one has to continually refuel the lamp and trim the wick.

What a gamut of different sorts of ties and involvements life offers! Each one is unique in its way, and each demands a very different treatment. They offer us a valuable opportunity to penetrate into the consciousness of each being, close or distant, and to feel as they feel we ought to feel toward them. Murshid developed in his disciples a delicate sense of the special relationship they entertained with each person:

In what relation man stands to his neighbour or friend, to those who depend upon him and those who look up to him, to strangers unknown to him; how he stands with those younger than himself and with older people, with those who like him and others who dislike him and criticize him. . . .

In dealing with another we ought first to consider in what relation we stand to him, and then to consider what manner of dealing would please us on the part of another who is related to us in the same way as we are to him.

To some consideration is due, to some respect, to some service, to some tolerance, to some forgiveness, to some help. In some way or other, in every relationship . . . there is something to pay.[6]

In the despair of a friend, consolation must be given; in the poverty of a friend, support is necessary; in the shortcomings of a friend, overlooking is necessary; in the trouble of a friend, help should be given; with the joy of a friend, rejoicing is right.[7]

Relationship ranges from what we understand by a neighbor to the family, including the special case of the personal beloved, and spans the most variegated array of acquaintanceships. The bond of a parent to his child implies totally different attitudes from the relationship between teacher and pupil, between employer and employee, or colleagues, or pals. It is more fitting for a parent to admonish his child than for the child to attempt to do the same, whether justified or not. There are certain things that one will accept from a person one reveres and not from a mere acquaintance. Words may be spoken by the craftsman which should not pass the lips of the apprentice. If we overstep the bounds of propriety with regard to another, we place him in an unpleasant predicament, forcing him to restore his dignity by an action which his modesty may forbid.

Dictating on the part of parents, teachers, elderly people, or a superior in office, business, wealth, position or sense, is not so hard as when it comes from a younger person, inferior in position, or devoid of sense. Thus it is wise to act towards one's own superior with the consideration one would expect from one's inferior.

On the other hand, in a sense we are all equal, and it is unethical to take advantage of a person's dependence to hold him down.

It is not by the servility of those around him that the king is exalted; it is in the honour in which they hold him that his kingship exists.

This is one of the tenets of Islam: All stand, kneel, or prostrate on an equal basis side by side to pray, and the Imam must be corrected if he makes a mistake. There is no priesthood as such. It is not the outer position that counts, but the reality of his being.

It is said that a child of the Prophet one day called a slave by his name and the Prophet heard it. The first thing he said was, "My child, call him Uncle; he is advanced in age."[8]

Every individual is dependent upon every other. . . . This makes every person a master as well as a servant.[9]

Unfortunately, any position of dependence, whether it be the subordinate on the boss or the boss on the subordinate, may place one at the mercy of the unscrupulous, who could be offensive if crossed, placing a painful strain on the sensitive ego. Some people take advantage of another's deference toward them to exact undue service of him. This is why the wise do things for themselves if they possibly can.

It is wise to avoid putting one's own burden on another, however exalted we may be in our position in life.[10]

Sapiens omnis secum portat. (The wise man always carries all he needs on himself.)—a Latin motto

If we realized the priceless value of friendship, we would seize the opportunities that lie ahead to transform an acquaintanceship into a friendship.

He is wise who treats an acquaintance as a friend, and he is foolish who treats a friend as an acquaintance.[11]

A man should always try to develop his acquaintanceship into friendship, at least where it is possible; but where it is impossible, he should try at least to continue acquaintance, instead of going from acquaintance to estrangement. To him who considers everyone else to be a friend, even a stranger is a friend.

There are some souls who, if you do not make them your friends, will become your enemies.

Those who are closest to us by family bonds or sentimental ties qualify for pride of place, and expect special consideration.

For instance, favour shown to a neighbour and disregard to a relative in the home, sympathy shown to a foreigner while we feel bitter toward our own nation, these dealings, however unselfish or broadminded they may appear, are undesirable.

The wise thing would be to do all the good we can do to those who consider it their right to expect it from us, without even thinking whether they will return it or whether they deserve it.

Admittedly, people, particularly in the new age, are leaving their nests, tending to see themselves as citizens of the world, yet

A person cannot jump at once to universalism. There are some who have a sort of natural hatred of their relations.[12]

Yet nothing can hold back this growing sense of a greater loyalty to the larger family of mankind, or even to the heavenly father, as the soul unfolds.

All claims to love such as "I am your brother, or your sister, or your son, or your daughter," mean very little to the mature soul. No sooner has the soul matured than that person begins to know what is hidden in the human soul; in spite of all deluding appearances he will have respect, a respect for mankind, as he realizes that in the depth of every soul is He whom one worships.

Some people begrudge your kindness to others, claiming all available kindness for themselves. If you submit to this, you will fail to live up to your loyalty to the sometimes more deserving. This explains Sri Ramana Maharishi's answer to his mother when she visited him upon his father's death, years after he had left home to become a sanyasin. She beseeched him to come back home, as the family was now left without support. When he refused, she said, "But I am your mother"; to which he replied, "You are not my mother." Those words sounded very cruel; but it is a tradition that the monk or hermit severs all family ties. Years later, she came to the Ashram to help out and endeared herself to all. When she died, she was graced by him with the rare privilege of being buried as a *jiven mukta*, liberated soul. Had he acknowledged his family ties and returned, presumably he would not have come to mean what he did to people, and therefore not been able to help them in the remarkable way he did.

The experience of the matured soul is like the experience of the man who watched a play performed on the stage at night, and in the morning he saw the same stage in the sun and saw that all the palaces and gardens and the actors' costumes were unreal.[13]

Of course, one could question whether Sri Ramana would not have been able to help equally well at home. Would he not have been the same person? What part is played by circumstances and environment in the actual worth of a being?

The Eastern tradition, according to which, when a man has fulfilled his share of contribution to society, he retires to a cave, is very attractive to sensitive and idealistic beings and conjures up in India a kind of idyllic halo. The very prestige of a rishi on account of his way of life makes people inclined to listen to his advice, and even follow his precepts, thus conferring upon him a strong lever of action which he would not have if he were at home. It is true also that his environment shields him from the turmoil of daily life, and from human egotism and injustice, thus favoring the development of insight and magnetic power. However, if one were able to maintain one's peacefulness, and objectivity, and power in the midst of an angry crowd, the human drama at its worst, it would be proof of a wonderful achievement.

There is something of the idealist in all sensitive beings, alongside a sense of realism and responsibility. Can the idealist and the pragmatist be reconciled? This is our most acute problem, for unless we keep our wits about us and hold on tight to the highest motivation we experience, life will pull us down again, bit by bit and unnoticed, to a level below our ideal.

It is very difficult to evolve oneself and at the same time keep in tune with the unevolved; it is like being drawn from above and pulled from below.[14]

We develop an unconscious anxiety about having failed to fulfill our life's purpose, which might simmer into a guilt complex or at least a general dissatisfaction with ourself. When these unconscious concerns reach the conscious level, we feel moved to do something about it. But what, and how?

The earth extorts its toll.

The one who holds it is buried under it. It grows on him and swallows him. But the one who understands the purpose of the earth and of its treasures uses them to the best advantage.

It may seem at times such a waste of effort and of an opportunity to progress and fulfill your life purpose, to be involved with the petty problems by which people let themselves be entrapped. People tend to "lay their trips" on you. But so long as you see through them, yet strive to bear with them without passing judgment, even with love, there is something which you will overcome in yourself by enduring all stoically, which makes for far greater progress than does sitting in meditation of the abstract type.

When man sacrifices his time and advantage in life for the sake of another whom he loves, respects, or admires, this sacrifice raises him higher than the ordinary standard of human beings; his is then a divine nature, not human any more. He has kept alive the flame of saintliness through the continually blowing wind.

At the same time, should you attempt to force your spirituality onto someone who is not ready, you would be working against the grain and would cause conflict that could not be resolved either by coercion or by persuasion.

Spirituality comes in its time. But the preliminary purpose is what a man will contribute to the world as the first prerequisite before awakening to spiritual perfection.

Nor should you scorn people in their unquestioned observance of accepted standards.

Even if a man has outgrown his religion, still if he is walking with another on the path who has an accepted standard of morals and has not yet reached the point which he has reached, he must conform to the accepted standard of morals for the sake of the other.

It is infinitely more useful to learn how to harmonize with a person in the place where he is. This is the test of our wisdom and authority, which promises to develop our personality into a beautiful masterpiece. To rear it from its early budding and protect it from all the hazards it will encounter, up to the point of being mutually creative, is really the art of arts. It is also the greatest of challenges because, after the flourish of admiration when we first discover the beauty of a being, we inevitably come across his blemishes.

To keep up an ideal which is living on earth and which is before one's eyes is the hardest thing there is, unless one has such balance that one will never waver and such compassion that one is able at one's own expense to add to the ideal all that it lacks. No doubt this ideal is greater than all others, for in this ideal there is a miraculous power: it awakens life and gives life to dead things.

We have a responsibility toward people in avoiding disappointing them in their idealism.

We see that emotional people are apt to idealize quickly, but are also apt to cast down the object of their idealization quickly.

The converse is also true for an idealist holding high standards and expecting people to live up to them. It is all too easy to love or admire a wonderful person, but one is putting a person in a straight-jacket by exacting from him conformity to our ideal image.

But difficulty arises because everyone thinks that his friend ought to prove worthy of his ideal. . . . A person's standards may be so high that another person cannot keep to it.[15]

So many people cannot suffer fools gladly. Sometimes the clever prefer the company of the foolish to that of the semi-wise.

The wise man, with his rare thoughts of wisdom, is always disappointed in people, and when he meets someone who can perceive his ideas this gives him a joy beyond words.

The only redeeming grace is to be great enough to accommodate all beings within your fold.

The one who loves all is not unhappy. Unhappy is the one who looks with contempt at the world, who hates human beings and thinks he is superior to them.[16]

The greater a soul, the greater power it shows in getting on with everyone. The more people you can get on with, the wiser you prove to be. Tolerance is the sign of an evolved soul. A soul gives the proof of its evolution in the degree of tolerance it shows.

Simply to acquiesce in the fact that human nature is imperfect remains an unsatisfactorily negative attitude, generally referred to as tolerance, unless it is quickened by a gesture of generosity which obliges you to surrender your expectation: that is to say, what you wish to receive from the other's personality.

The perfection of friendship comes when the soul is so developed that there is no one whom it cannot bear. When it has reached this state, it has certainly passed into the ranks of those initiates whose names are written on the spiritual records. There is a tendency which gradually manifests in a person who is advancing spiritually, and that tendency is overlooking. At times this tendency may appear negligence, but negligence is not overlooking; negligence is not looking. Overlooking may be called rising above things. Overlooking is a manner of graciousness, it means to look and at the same time not to look, to see and not to take notice of being seen, not to be hurt or harmed or disturbed by something, not even minding it. It is an attribute of nobleness of nature, it is the sign of souls who are tuned to a higher key.

Faced with rudeness and crudeness and rank selfishness or duplicity, Murshid would hold his head high, remain gracious and still find room in his heart for the person. This, then, is introducing the way of saintliness into an everyday relationship.

My thoughtful self, Bear all and do nothing, Hear all and say nothing, Give all and take nothing, Serve all and be nothing.[17]

It means defending a person in your own mind against your own criticism. Instead of playing the part of Ammit, the prosecutor in the Egyptian judgment scene, you must play the part of Thoth, the advocate, the pleader. This is easier to do for the wise man because he sees the reason behind the reason, why the person is the way he is or did the thing he did.

When we see the reason behind every fault that appears to us in anyone we meet in our life, we become more tolerant, we become more forgiving.[18]

As soon as a person feels that you are going out of your way to understand him instead of imposing your standards on him, a link of sympathy is established with him.

When a man looks at every soul as a note of music and learns to recognize what note it is, flat or sharp, high or low, and to what pitch it belongs, then he becomes the knower of souls, and he knows how to deal with everybody. In his own actions, in his speech, he shows the art; he harmonizes with the rhythm of the atmosphere, with the tone of the person he meets, with the theme of the moment. To become refined is to become harmonious.[19]

For Murshid, the musician of the soul, the world was a wonderful symphony of beings, each with his particular note and contribution to the harmony of the whole.

The most serious threat to our friendship comes when somebody criticizes our friend to us. Do we realize the tremendous harm that we can do to the friends who confide in us and consign themselves trustingly to our custody? We might deliver them into the hands of the unscrupulous, or at any rate of people less committed, who might be liable to a hasty or ill-considered judgment and less merciful than we ourselves are. This is treason and betrayal; imagine! Most people are doing this all the time.

There are some people who, out of cleverness, say things to you against your friends just in fun to test you and how you feel about it; and if you responded to their influence further, to turn you against your friend.

When two people meet, criticizing those who are not there to defend themselves, they become such authorities.

If the accusation is unjustified, it is comparatively easy to spring to a friend's defense; it is most often the one who knows nothing about the background of the circumstances who is quick to pass judgment.

Of course, one cannot condone an evil action, but as one grows in insight, so one realizes to what extent the judgment of people is based upon their own limitation.

Mostly, every soul seems to be busily occupied with the lives of others. And what do they know in the end? Nothing. The moment one has lost judging, from that moment he becomes just.

Tolerance does not mean defend the wrong-doer. It means the Sufi spares himself from judging someone whom he does not know.

In view of his own limitations, at least, one should suspend judgment. Besides, one's judgment casts a slur on the divine Artist, who must have his greater purpose that we are unable to fathom.

It is a question of self-restraint or self-control. . . . When we judge others, we are certainly judging the Artist who has created them.[20]

A true worshipper of God sees His Person in all forms, and in respecting man he respects God.

But when we are faced with a substantiated criticism of our friend, we are subjected to the most decisive test of our lives. Supposing he is at fault and we have been benevolently overlooking it; now we find it difficult to adduce arguments to support him: This is where our friendship runs into the greatest danger. Just consider what has gone into that friendship! All the trust and soul-searching. It is like all the confidence, reliability, and heroism that goes into forming the links in a mountain climbing team. Your friend trusts that if he slips, you will stand firm, a trust that grows by going together through rough and smooth, hardships and celebrations, for better or for worse.

One knows that this ship has sailed perhaps a hundred times from this port to the other port and has always come back safely.

What can be done? Whichever way we turn, we are open to criticism: If we fail to spring to his defense, we are letting down, like a coward, the friend who has given himself into our trust; and if we try to condone something which in our conscience we also believe to be wrong, we are being basically dishonest.

If we have a doubt that he is a wrong-doer, the best thing is not to defend him. Why defend? We might be taken as a person who promotes wrong-doing.

Lest our friendship be used by a friend as a blank check to act with iniquity, the best thing is to do like Christ: turn the tables on the

accuser, and insist on his first assuring himself of his own blameless-
ness as a condition for throwing the first stone. This is precisely what
Murshid did when someone made an accustion about a wonderful
worker who also had a lot of defects.

Once a man has begun to judge his own actions, the fairness will develop in his
nature.[21]

We can only bring another to this realization if we have trained
ourselves to look into our own conscience as soon as, and every time, a
thought of criticism enters into our mind.

The one who has realized even one grain of the same fault of which the other
person has ninety-nine grains, that person does not speak about it.

There is a still more serious betrayal of one's secret trust with one's
friend; when, for some reason, one has been vexed with him and goes
to a third party to complain about him. This is what is called a breach
of confidence, and people are doing it all the time!

If one has an admiration for someone, or a grudge against someone, it is better
to express it directly. . . . It is better not to mix that link and connection which
is established between oneself and another with a third person. . . . Keep the
secret of your friend, your acquaintance, even of someone with whom for a
time you have been vexed.[22]

Sometimes those we love and for whom we never wish ill, under the spell of
our anger, we think of with fury and bitterness, and then, after the spell has
passed, our love for them is the same. And yet we do not know what harm we
have done to them during that spell.

He has entrusted you with his being, and at a moment of stress in the
relationship, you have given him away, you have despoiled that most
precious of all gifts, friendship. Obviously when there was pain in the
relationship, perhaps you felt desperately in need of counsel; yet this
was just the very time to prove your mettle.

---

*He who keeps no secret has no depth; his heart is like like a vessel turned upside
down.*[23]

The one who guards the interest of others even more than his own is wise.
There is an attitude which reveals a divine secret. It is the tendency to cover up
any fault that one's friend has committed from another person; and not only to
cover it from the sight of others, but even from one's own sight.

There is little pain to compare with that incurred when friendship
undergoes a strain. Heroically, to protect his friend, the wise man does
not permit people to know that he is suffering in the relationship.

He covers his wounds from the sight of others. The pain of the wise and the saintly souls is the pain they feel for others as being themselves. Spiritual life means to feel the life of another as one feels one's own life. The same life in him and in me, so his pain, his sorrow, his pleasure I share, because his life is my life.

Of course, if friendship means more complete openness on both sides, one should be able to say frankly what is in one's heart, which often means simply what one feels about his friend's faults, without hurting the relationship. This requires great sensitivity—sometimes called tact—because even one's private criticism, let alone the backbiting behind the scene, can prove to be excruciating, with all the resultant anger and bad feeling. On the other hand, if one harbors a grudge, the relationship suffers from a lack of communication.

How I can say something to someone without hurting him? If you ask someone: "Why did you do it?" you make the person firmer in his fault.

When attacked, a person will most likely get on his high horse and defend himself.

A stern and proud person, sure of his opinion and who builds a wall of his own point of view, is difficult to manage; for he shuts himself by the wall of his own point of view and covers his own eyes by his pride.

And this may well spell the end of a beautiful friendship. Naturally, one is very sensitive about what a person thinks of one, particularly a friend. This is one's most sensitive spot. "There is a tendency in man to think a great deal about what others think of him." Besides, one is exposing oneself to a judgment that may not be fair, however much one trusts one's friend. Some people feel they could only expose themselves to the scrutiny of a holy man, surrounded with a halo of great prestige. Of course, life itself is the great mentor and taskmaster.

If you let him loose, his wrong-doing will become his greater teacher. And by interfering with that teaching which a person is getting by life, a person spoils the other person's life.

On the other hand, a teacher may delegate those forces of life that are correcting him.

It is a great art to be a teacher, requiring great powers of insight and mental control, and wisdom; unfortunately, many self-styled teachers, trying their hands at counseling inexpertly, have given advice that may have spoiled the friendship of those who consulted them. What a pity! One has to spot the real issue behind the apparent ones. Therefore, sometimes just talking a matter over can make it worse.

So you think more words explain more? No, not at all. If there is no understanding between two persons, words are of no use. Arguments only increase arguments.

If a spiritual person were to bring his realizations into the marketplace, and dispute with everyone that came along about his beliefs and disbeliefs, where would he end?

Sometimes people will feel embarrassed when, through your tolerance and compassion, you spare them from criticism, and they would even prefer that you be selfish in your demands on them. It is difficult for them to understand that you really prefer their way to your own. They would like to feel sure that whatever you do for them is out of love rather than compassion; they would feel badly if they found out that you begrudged it all the while without admitting it. And how are they to know? This is why a saintly nature is often admired and revered, rarely loved in the human way. Murshid's wife, the Begum, once wrote: "It is not easy to be married to a saint." There are people who carry this virtue too far, making you feel indebted to them; those who "force upon you their kindness."

People often overdo it in the opposite direction. For the most part, whenever we are in a position to admonish a person justifiably, a sense of righteousness sticks its head up, crucifying the victim.

If we have to teach them, not to teach them as a teacher; if we help them, not to help them as a benefactor.

Generally, if a person has a defect, it is because of something he does not see clearly. Pointing it out to him will not necessarily help him to see it. His initial failure to recognize his defect was probably due to a blind spot, which almost everyone has, especially if the ego is involved. This is why to be a teacher requires such exceptional wisdom, to know just how to bring someone to see something he fails to see or does not wish to see. The primitive mind thinks he can drum sense into a person:

Someone urges another to agree with him . . . or to do as he wishes . . . by being disagreeable. Often such a person, by the strength of his will-power or by virtue of his better position in life, gets his wishes fulfilled.[24]

There are many people who are outspoken, always ready to tell the truth in a way which is like hitting another person on the head, and who proudly support their frankness by saying, "I do not mind if it makes anybody sorry or angry, I only tell the truth."[25]

Strongly opinionated people are, unfortunately, always able to brainwash underopinionated victims by sheer force of will. Usually the victim lacks the perspicacity to pin down the fallacy in the sophistry of his self-appointed judge, and his only possible retort is: "What is the use of opinion?—very relative, sometimes nil, never infallible."

They would just as well have said that, "I speak of facts," instead of "I am telling the truth." In the first place, what a difficult thing it is to know the truth, and if you do know it, then it is still more difficult to tell it. Besides that, there is the false pride that many people have of being truthful, and they are very soon titled by others, saying that they are straight-forward, whether they are bold, or whether they are outspoken, or whether they are abrupt, or whether they are insolent. Is it straight-forwardness to hurt another person's feelings? Is it straight-forwardness to insult a person?

This is certainly not the best way to ensure friendship!

The one who submits his will to another's or to what he believes to be superior argument, and is forced back upon his defenseless mind, will always be left bearing a grudge.

Besides, there are many who feel urged and obligated to say or do something because it is asked of them, and in this way they get weaker and weaker.

Even the way of the unobtrusive gentle persuasion will prove eventually to be a cause of soreness.

The other way of persuading is a gentle way, by putting pressure upon someone's kindness, goodness, and politeness, exhausting thereby his patience and testing his sympathy to the utmost. By this people achieve for the moment what they wish to achieve, but in the end it results in the annoyance of all those who are tried by this persuasive tendency.[26]

Besides, what we suppose is for the good of our friend is not always so.

Those who stand in some need of service, some help, some advice, some assistance, you give them this. And those who do not stand in need of anything, leave them alone. But if a person was standing in the garden of the summer school, and you, out of your sympathy, thought he must be brought tea: maybe this person would become ill by drinking tea. He is not standing there looking at a tree to get tea. He is standing there perhaps in his own thought. Perhaps he is meditating. Perhaps by your giving him tea you are not doing him any good.

It is a sad plight that life in the world so often seems to be a tussle of wills. Each tries to impress his self on the other. People will try you out as far as you will allow them to go. There are cases in marriage and business partnership, where a person is inextricably bound, in which the spouse or the partner will keep expanding his psychological space, suffocating the other and pushing him to the wall. Often the loser is a fine, selfless, even angelic person, while the winner is a ruthless, unscrupulous, self-opinionated indulger of likes and dislikes. This happens in friendship too; it is remarkable how often a friend will tend to push his temerity as far as it will go in imposing his will on you. He always has his way, knowing that you value his friendship too much to spoil it by a row. In doing so he forces you into a choice between open conflict that may wreck the friendship and entertaining a grudge, which may equally well spoil it. It is best to prevent a situation reaching this point by showing your spirit from the beginning. At each abdication on your part—perhaps trifling at first—he will increase in his conviction that you will not restrain him, and become more daring, pulling more and more strongly his way. That is how it gets more and more difficult for you to put your foot down.

But if a person demonstrates sovereignty over himself, people will respect him. The reason your friend has turned against you may be that he has witnessed things in you which have disappointed him. This has given him leeway to cease considering you as he used to do out of his former respect for you. When matters have reached this stage, the only way of regaining his respect, if at all, is to counter nobly, hold your own without betraying the slightest emotion of grudge or irritation. It is a great test of one's sincerity to smile upon someone who has done one harm.

On one hand he must be extremely fine and polite and delicate; and on the other hand he may not prove to his own conscience in any way insincere and externally superficial.

This is easier if one realizes that:

real kindness is that which gushes out from the heart to the worthy and to the unworthy.[27]

Murshid gives the final clue as to how to exercise an impact on another:

One must stand peacefully but firmly before all influences that disturb one's life. The natural inclination is to answer in defense to every offence that comes from outside. If you wish people to obey you, you must learn to obey yourself; if you wish people to believe you, you must learn to believe yourself; if you wish people to respect you, you must learn to respect yourself; if you wish people to trust you, you must learn to trust yourself.

It is also remarkable to see how a person who is not up to the requirements of friendship will take advantage of your familiarity or warmth while in a relaxed mood to suddenly show lack of respect when respect is due.

Another delicacy is exactly the same as it was in the ancient aristocracies, and that delicacy is that when there is a time proper to it then you talk and chum and laugh and joke. And then there is another time, then you are in that attitude which is due to that time.

Murshid outlines three standards of behavior to which people conform in their interrelationships with friends or foes. These are the bastions of ethics: the law of reciprocity, the law of benevolence, and the law of self-denial. One must assess what standard one is able to live up to, and what standard to expect of acquaintances and friends and of foes. They are convenient references to work with in everyday living.

First, the law of reciprocity, based on the old adage: an eye for an eye and a tooth for a tooth. For those who fail to turn the other cheek, at least they can be completely fair and just in relationship with their fellow beings. Sometimes people return less good for more good or more harm for less harm.

The consideration of the dealings of others with us must not be weighed against our dealings with them. . . . Therefore, in order to make a balance, we must always consider that a kind action, a good thought, a little help, some respect shown to us by another, are more than if we did the same to a friend; but an insult, a harm done to us, a disappointment caused to us by a friend, a broken promise, deceit, or anything we do not like on the part of a friend, should be taken as less blameworthy than if we did the same.[28]

Man always thinks he is just though he is often far from being so. He always overestimates his own goodness, and generosity, his kindness, his service to another person; and he blinds himself to the kindness, goodness, and generosity of the other. Thus it is seldom that people live the law of reciprocity.

Anyone applying this law rigidly will feel obliged to mete out in return to another person the same measure that he has given him. And if anybody does something irksome to him, he will return the same in like measure: They put the radio on at midnight, so I play the piano at five o'clock in the morning. Actually, there should never be a question of how much you do for your friend in terms of how much he does for you. If so, the relationship is not one of friendship anymore.

When there is a discussion between friends, and one says, "I've done so much for you, I have suffered so much for you, I have had so much pain on your account, I have such a difficult life for your sake," then he is entering into business. He wants to keep a diary of what he has given in the form of love and kindness and goodness and sacrifice.[29]

Allow a friend to enjoy giving by accepting gracefully and not giving by fair exchange, but out of the generosity of one's heart. Take all that is given to you, and give all that you have. Friendship cannot come within the purview of the law of reciprocity.

The use of friendship for a selfish motive is like mixing bitter poison with sweet rose-syrup.[30]

A person whom you would otherwise not have understood for ten years, you can understand in one day as soon as there is a question of money. . . . But if there is a question of selfishness in friendship, where would a soul go who is tired and annoyed with the selfish surroundings of the world?[31]

The second standard draws one closer to what is expected in friendship. Murshid calls it the law of benevolence: One extends more kindness to the other than that received, or is less stingy to the other than he is to one, purely out of an uncalculated generosity of one's heart. After all, one exacts a higher standard from oneself than from anyone else; the friend may also adhere to the law of benevolence himself.

The Sufi learns in the law of reciprocity to consider it a natural thing when injustice is shown by others; but he tries in every dealing with others to be just as he can.[32]

Every action of kindness we do for another, we must do for God; and then there will be no disappointment.[33]

The Sufi moral is this: love another and do not depend upon his love; and: do good to another and do not depend upon receiving good from him; serve another and do not look for service from him. All you do for another out of your love and kindness, you should think that you do not to that person, but to God. And if the person returns love for love, goodness for goodness, service for service, so much the better. If he does not return it, than pity him for what he loses; for his gain is much less than his loss. Do not look for thanks or appreciation for all the good you do to others, nor use it as a means to stimulate your vanity. Do all that you consider good for the sake of goodness, not even for the return of that from God.

Man's smile is indeed the light from the heavens. In that light many flowers grow and many fruits become ripe. The attitude of looking at everything with a smile is the sign of the saintly soul. A smile given to a friend, a smile given even to an enemy, will win him over in the end.[34]

Of course, one should do everything within one's means to avoid conflict.

It is against wisdom to allow anybody to become our enemy if we can possibly help it.

Raise not dust from the ground; it will enter into your eyes. Sprinkle some water on it that it may settle down and lie under your feet.

It may well prove to be the path of no return, irreversible, irrevocable, whatever one does.

However slight an enemy he may be, he can cause you very great pain or suffering.

However, one may be forced into a conflict by someone who takes up a course that opposes, obstructs, even avowedly or implictly aims at destroying all that one is doing for what one believes to be right. Perhaps someone is, for some personal reason, trying to harm you or push you out of your position in order to come into your place. One may even be forced into conflict with one's erstwhile friend who wishes to impose his way upon one, contrary to one's commitment. Someone perhaps tries to encroach upon one's prerogatives, in a way that amounts to obstructing one's work. In such cases, conflict reveals itself to be inevitable, however much one may have tried to avert it, which confirms what Murshid says—that both war and peace are part of life.

The more one can avoid conflict the better; at the same time we cannot always avoid a conflict. After all, life is a struggle and we must be ready to struggle; only, struggle must not make us drunk so that we lose the way of peace. Life means a continual battle; therefore one must develop the knowledge of warfare, how to fight and how to make peace. Sunshine and rain are both needed to make the fruit ripe. For instance, if a man lived through all civilizations, he would think very differently from the ordinary man of today; and so it is with God in regard to His knowledge of the entire world. We are too limited to understand.

Of course, people do not like disharmony, but if one were to give in to a will debarring one from fulfilling one's responsibility in order to maintain harmony, one would be letting one's side down and failing in one's responsibility. Indeed, by the irony inherent in the very nature of life, one will be accused of being quarrelsome, and if one gives in, one will be despised by the very one who puts one in the predicament, for not having enough backbone to fight back.

The thorns will accuse one of having trampled upon them.

Here one is faced with a dilemma: either fight like a knight for what is right, or avoid resisting evil. Supposing someone is harming another and one has the power to intervene by using coercion; if one fails to take action one carries a large share of the responsibility.

Every impression of an evil nature should be met with a combative attitude.

Should one be the victim of injustice oneself, it is more difficult to be objective. But to condone an injustice, even to oneself, is complicity.

If another person treats us badly without reason or justice, we must fight against it, and prove by doing so that the dealing was unjust.

The only issue is to battle without hatred, to stand for what one believes without judgment of the person confronted. This is what is meant by not resisting evil.

"Resist not evil" means: "do not return the inharmony that comes to you."
   As fire destroys itself, so evil is its own destruction. Why is it said: "Do not resist evil"? Because resistance gives life to evil, non-resistance lets it burn itself. In the form of anger, passion, greed, stubbornness, one sees evil, in the form of deceit, treachery; but the root of evil is one, and that is selfishness.

One can erect a barrier of firmness without acting with animosity. It is a wonderful opportunity to ascertain that one has overcome all personal feelings and can act objectively, as though it concerned a third person. That is why the best apprenticeship in the battle of life is first to learn how to do battle with one's own ego.
   Murshid tells the story of Hazrat Ali, who in battle struck an opponent to the ground, and as he raised his sword to deliver a deathblow, the man spat in his face, whereupon Hazrat Ali released him. Nonplussed, the Arab asked him why he did not kill him, especially after he added insult to injury. Hazrat Ali answered, "Because I could not kill you in anger."

Fighting with another makes war, but struggling with one's self brings peace.

The person whose face is struck, he surely will not turn the other side of his face. It is the other person who strikes who thinks that he is struck on his face, but it only falls on his shield.

Nevertheless, the quandary still persists as to whether in conflict one should apply the law of reciprocity or that of benevolence, and in which case which.
   Murshid recounts how a youth hit a dervish who, considering this as a well-deserved punishment from God, said: "This is not enough, more, more." However, when the youth, emboldened in his malevolence, tried it out on a soldier, he was taught, in no uncertain way, never to do it again. If this had not happened, he would have tried it on more people. Yet the dervish could not possibly have resorted to the admittedly more expedient method of the soldier. One's own standards may not fit in with those of the enemy. That is why a gentleman never

throws down the gauntlet before someone who does not know how to respect the rules of the game of chivalry.

Avoid conflict with a low person. If dogs bark at the elephant, it takes no notice and goes on its way. Lull the devil to sleep, rather than awaken him. Let not your reputation fall into the monkeys' hands; they will look at it curiously, will mock at it, laugh at it and snatch it from each other; in the end they will tear it to pieces. Never joke with a fool. To offend a low person is like throwing a stone in the mud and getting splashed.

Some people will take up the position as one's opponent, whatever one does, just out of a cantankerous spirit. Even if one were to take their view, they would suddenly switch over to the opposite view for the sheer joy of drawing one into a row.

A contradictory tendency in a man finally develops into a passion, until he will contradict even his own idea if it happens to be pronounced by another.

Some people will always begrudge one's being harmonious. Therefore, one cannot help them by one's harmonious approach, and they will purposely oppose one whatever one's attitude.

Partly it is the feeling of jealousy that comes to him, seeing another person harmonious with himself or with his surroundings, or he becomes proud to feel he is not the only inharmonious one, but there are others also travelling in the same boat. In time a person gets accustomed to inharmony, just as some sailors on the sea during the storm do not feel it. To him life becomes dull if it be quiet and peaceful.

Once one has ascertained that one cannot avoid a person's becoming an opponent, one should accept the situation and not persist in treating him as a friend, for by posing as a friend he is able to take advantage of one's welcome to undermine one in the center of the castle, as it were, while enjoying, in the eyes of all, one's sanction. Besides, one's friendly attitude toward him would deter one from taking necessary precautions to guard against the harm he can do to the cause that one is supposed to defend.

Trying to keep friends with the adversary in order to avoid harm coming from him is not a good policy; for your adversary gets a stronger hold on you as a friend than as an enemy. It is better that your enemy stands before your house rather than that he should live under your roof.

However, once one has taken a person into one's heart, one must never alienate oneself from him. The person may turn his back upon one, yet one must still nurture and protect his soul in the shell of one's heart, even while, if the situation requires it, one combats him nobly to defend one's ideal. But one must bear in mind that, while one's opponent is either fighting fair, following the law of reciprocity, or foul, violating that law, should one show any sign of benevolence, he would interpret it as a sign of weakness, unable to believe that one could have generosity in one's heart, while taking a stand against him. One would thus expose one's cause to his guile.

When one is sure that kindness and forgiveness will have no power whatever upon the hard heart of the enemy, but on the contrary will make him worse, weakness should never be shown to the enemy.

Before ever engaging in a wager, one must from the outset ascertain whether one has the wherewithal to take a stand; by the same token, it is foolhardy and irresponsible to involve one's cause in a gamble.

Consider whether it is possible to stand against him and his enmity or not. In the case where this is possible, with strength and courage and intelligence we should bend him down before he does so to us, for it is as unwise to underestimate the enemy's bitterness and power to do harm as it is to overestimate them.

When once one has made a resolve and launched oneself into it, one must take up the challenge and fight nobly and with all might as a knight on a crusade for a lofty idea.

Thus true aristocracy is the nobility of the soul. It is better to suppress the enemy before he can rise against us; and it is right to throw him down when he has risen against us.

And one must follow the traditional rules of strategy:

It is wise to be watchful of the movements of the enemy, and safeguard oneself against them; and it is foolish to allow oneself to be watched, and to let the enemy safeguard himself against us.

Do not entrust the devil with your secret.

This means exercising discretion also with regard to the friends of the opponent, or the opponents of a friend. "An enemy of the friend should be regarded as our enemy; a friend of the friend must be considered as our friend."

One certainly cuts a sorry figure by whining about the harm an enemy did to one.

Complaining about the harm caused by the enemy is a weakness; avoiding it by taking precautions, facing it with strength and checking it with power are the things worth doing. It is wise to take advantage of the criticism made by an enemy, for it can help to correct us.

To be true to the noble code, one should eliminate all the ugly personal traits that tend to crop up in a vulgar fight. One should refuse to allow the opponent to draw one into retaliation for his offensive behavior, and avoid any personal insult. Nor should one tolerate insults from him; this is why some walk out of a quarrel with their heads high without deigning to retort. "According to the law of reciprocity, to allow the enemy to insult or harm is a fault."

Wisdom commends one not to take one's own good faith or righteousness for granted, or to assume that all that the opponent does is wrong. He is most likely able to muster arguments himself to justify his stand, and may even be convinced of the righteousness of his cause.

When dealing with our enemies one must bear in mind that there is a possibility of exaggerated imagination; for the least little wrong done by the enemy seems to be a mountain of wrong.

One must understand that everything that one does that discredits one in the eyes of the opponent strengthens him in his allegations of being justified in opposing one; if one fights for an ideal nobly, one might even take the wind out of his sails, if he has a streak of righteousness.

Then a person thinks, "By being kind to our enemy we encourage him in his tyranny." But so long as we have kindness in our heart, instead of hardening the nature of the enemy, it will soften it, since we receive all that we give out. Our dealings with our enemy should be considered with more delicacy than our dealings with a friend.

Of course, a good fighter always keeps a door open for an eventual truce as a courtesy to his opponent, provided it does not deter him in his resolve. The opponent could maneuver one into the hope of a truce, to delay one's action, so it is better to take the initiative oneself.

It is always wise to avoid every possibility of causing enmity, and to make every effort to turn any enemy into a friend again.

If you are beginning to rise in the esteem of your opponent, that is when you should offer him the chance of a cease-fire without losing face.

It is right by every means to forgive the enemy and to take the first step in establishing friendship, instead of holding in the mind the poison of the past.

It may even be at the cost of the sacrifice of one's own face, or human pride, for the sake of the common good. Since very few knights can claim never to have made a blunder, there are always amends one can make even if one still holds that the wrongdoings of one's opponent were greater.

However great a fault may be, if one who has committed it only comes and says, "I am very sorry; I will never do it again; pray forgive me," the friendship will be restored at once. On the other hand, however trivial and slight the fault may have been, if pride prevents the man from asking forgiveness and pardon, perhaps he will lose that friendship for the rest of his life.

Murshid had tasted of the beauty of such gestures. An unforgettable moment: Murshid had just come back from a journey. Two of my uncles, having apparently done something that was disapproved, fell at his feet in Eastern fashion, tears in their eyes, asking forgiveness. The love and sincerity exchanged at that moment must have stirred the soul of the Planet.

Have you ever had the joy of seeing two friends who have quarreled asking forgiveness of one another? It is as if there were no more possibility of ill-feeling. It is the most delightful experience. It feels as if the doors of heaven were opened. Another odd thing sometimes happens, and that is when two persons are at daggers drawn for many months or years, and then suddenly throw their daggers away and become friends forever. But this is unusual. I myself have seen people who have been enemies working against one another for years, and from the day they became friends they have become the closest friends.

When the woman who had caused the Master so much harm in London, leading to his exodus to France, asked for his forgiveness, he readily gave it; having the privilege of being the instrument of God's grace seemed to move his heart to ecstasy. There had at no time been any recriminations.

Of course, the art of saving the peace is far greater than the art of warfare, requiring superior, indeed rare, qualities. Therefore it belongs to the third law: that of self-sacrifice. This does not mean withdrawing in cowardice. If strong and broad enough to face all disharmony like a bastion of strength, one will exhaust all the efforts of those trying to draw one into conflict. Here it is the strength of one's inner being rather than the strength of one's outer resources that imposes itself upon the would-be scorpions under the throne. This can only arise from a very great sovereignty attained by someone who has overcome himself. Yet it is touch-and-go whether even this force always triumphs. The inner sovereignty of Jesus did not prevent Judas from doing what he did, nor did it stay the hand of Gandhi's assassin, nor prevent hooligans from beating up Sri Ramana Maharishi; yet, when it works, it is nothing short of a miracle.

No doubt the wiser we become, the more difficulties we have to face in life, because every kind of inharmony will be directed at us for the very reason that we will not fight it. We should realize, however, that all these difficulties have helped to destroy this inharmony which would otherwise have multiplied. This is not without its advantages, for every time we stand firm where there is inharmony we increase our strength, though outwardly it may seem a defeat. But one who is conscious of the increase of his power will never admit that it is a defeat, and after a while the person against whom one has stood firm will realize that it was actually his defeat.

The victory on earth of one person over another or one group over another is not the ultimate criterion; as often as not it masks the real triumph, which is in heaven, when one who has overcome himself is given the freedom of the cities of the soul.

Those who are given liberty by Him to act freely, are nailed on the earth; and those who are free to act as they choose on the earth, will be nailed in the heavens.[35]

CHAPTER 22

Spiritual Training

The teacher has two responsibilities: to look after his fragile spirit, and to look after the spirit of the mureed, which very often is asleep.

The link between Murshid and mureed is more delicate than a thin thread and at the same time stronger than a steel wire.

The teacher lives for mureeds; his only object is to see their spiritual evolution.

Training a pupil on the spiritual path is one of the greatest arts there is. It would be difficult enough to mold a personality if it were malleable raw material. But most people have a mind of their own, and a blind spot somewhere.

Ideally, a pupil will choose to undergo training under a teacher because he holds the latter in high esteem, assumes that he knows more than the pupil does, has a large measure of confidence in him, and is prepared to give up his point of view, or even his way of doing things, for what he presumes to be a better one or a better way. Unfortunately, this ideal situation is rare, and many candidates for training come in on probation, subject to trial. They secretly debate within themselves whether they still trust the teacher's judgement, poised on the fence so that they may leave at the slightest displeasure.

His first intention is to see if his thoughts fit in with mine and if my thoughts fit in with his.

This is a contradictory situation: It is basically the student's right to vet the teacher before he can offer him his unreserved confidence. However, he has come in order to learn to see from a greater point of view than his own, so how can he judge the teacher's wisdom with the measuring rod of the point of view that he wants to change?

It is because many pride themselves on their point of view that they keep aimlessly shifting from one teacher to another, which will never lead a pupil anywhere, since he has to learn to give up his point of view.

It seems that thousands of people are every day in the spiritual pursuit. One day they go to one thing, another day to another. Just like one goes to many different theatres, everything new and sensational.

371

Among dogs, there are some who follow anyone, whoever gives them a bone is their master, and if another gives them meat, they leave the first one and follow the other. And there are some who follow only one master, who obey only one, and even sometimes sacrifice their life for him. It depends upon the breed, the heredity.

If the teacher gives the pupil the opportunity to discuss the teaching, he will be encouraging him in his point of view, which is just what is standing in the way of his understanding the new point of view.

It is better to give pupils no tendency to discuss our sacred teachings.

The pupil has to give up all preconceived ideas before starting on the spiritual path under the guidance of a teacher.

The point of view one loses is not one's own.

A child must therefore be taught from the beginning, that it is not as he sees just now, but when he will see differently, he will find the same thing different. All that one can do for another is to give him one's own experience. If a person happens to know a road, he can tell the other man that it is the road that leads to the place he wishes to find.

A teacher's main work in the West is to teach a pupil to be a pupil. Even answering questions does not always prove favorable to the work.

The one who asks a question becomes stronger than the one who is put in the position of answering the question. There are many clever people who will ask you a cross question to get out of you a certain answer which they expect to come from you. Then they hit against it, for in this way, they prepare a ground for a battle. They question in order to cover the restlessness of their minds, scratching their own hearts. Since many of them believe in themselves, they cannot believe in another, so their question remains always unanswered.

A teacher must scrupulously maintain his wakefulness in the face of the clever questions of some apparently "intellectual" people who may even join as initiates, and guard himself from being impressed with the agility of their mind, for by trying to see from their point of view, he may lose his own realization (if it is not strongly enough rooted, only appearing when he is uplifted in meditation).

If he is very intelligent and materialistic to excess, he will have an influence even on your self-confidence. An unbeliever has the power to shake the belief of the believers.

Murshid points to the types of pupils who prove difficult:

There is one of the wrong kinds who is only following the teacher for the satisfaction of his intellectual craving, and so long as the teacher has the food for his intellect he will be content; the day when the teacher's idea does not fit in with his intellectual ideas, he will have difficulties. There is no other side of the teacher that will appeal to him except one, and that is the teacher's intellectuality.

And there is another of the same kind who is curious, who wants to find out what phenomena can be traced in the doings or in the life of the teacher, if there is anything wonderful, if there is anything curious. If he can satisfy his curiosity, so long he will stay, and the day when his curiosity is not satisfied he will become discontented.

And the third kind is a victim to the teacher's influence. The teacher's influence is so strong that he is attracted to that influence as something is attracted to the magnet. He himself does not know why he is drawn to the teacher, yet he cannot help being drawn, because he is a poor victim.

And there is a fourth kind who wants to be a mureed because it is a good pastime to be able to get somebody's advice in trouble. That is all he is concerned with. Neither is he for God nor for Truth nor for evolution.

The pupils's spiritual progress is most often associated with his material problems: family relationships, job, personal hangups. And the teacher is very much like a father and mother and advisor in all respects.

Never think therefore that a spiritual teacher is too superior to interest himself in the material needs of his pupils. One may not think that by helping in a mureed's worldly affair, nothing spiritual is accomplished; for once in the spiritual path, every material and spiritual thing one does, only leads him to the spiritual goal. Wise parents pay serious attention to their children's little demands.

It is an art to know how to correct the pupil of his faults without offending him, nor giving him a guilt complex.

One should not make the pupil uncomfortable when he is at fault but allow him to notice his mistake himself. The teacher will not tell him that he is wrong, but show him what is right. The teacher will bring up the good side of the pupil's nature and deny and ignore the weak side of the pupil's nature. But the good side must not be brought before him in the form of flattery. When he realizes that there is something lacking, that is the occasion for the teacher to add that which is lacking.

The teacher has to wean the pupil from the habit of leaning on him too much, although this might flatter the teacher's ego, very much as a mother abandons a child more and more to his own will, the more capable he is of assuming responsibility, but will recall him at the slightest inclination of danger.

When the child tries to move about by its own free will, and tries to keep away, then the attention of the mother to some extent becomes released. This does not mean that the mother entirely gives up the care of the child; it only means that she allows the child to have its way to some extent, and feels sorry when the child falls and hurts itself. If the child falls, it will cry for her; but she does not prevent its falling.

The teacher must not deny help if the pupil really needs it.

If he cannot walk, then if someone gives him a hand, it is making him dependent, but it is helping him.

But the aim of the teacher should be to make the pupil a free, self-assured being, in fact independent of himself, so that he may be able to stand amid the struggle of life.

With every goodwill to help the pupil, one must not spoil him by making him too dependent.

The more man depends upon his own effort, the less God holds himself responsible for him.

If the pupil is given an opportunity to treat his teacher as a pal, he will forget at the moment of test to acquiesce to the teacher's higher wisdom, failing to detect the limitation of his vantage point, and convinced of his opinion. This is the reason that the teacher, much as he loves his pupil, has to maintain some remoteness and still at the same time be a friend. Unfortunately, some people, not understanding the delicacy of this relationship, will take advantage of the teacher's good nature to become too familiar.

Every person must answer your purpose according to the position you take before him. If you are a teacher to him, he will be your pupil, if you are his friend, he will become your chum, if you are his rival, he will become your competitor. Decide, therefore, fully well beforehand in what relation that person should be to you, and act accordingly to him. He should be closely attached, and yet detached, near and yet far.

If there be a distance, it must not be for the vanity of the initiator, it must be only if it were for the benefit of the pupil.

He may need with certain pupils to keep an outer distance, but in order make up for the outer distance, he must come inwardly close.

Nevertheless, the teacher must not expect service and reverence. Do not do anything for your spiritual guide for what you may receive from him, nor must he do anything for you as a return for what you do for him.

But if the pupil gives reverence, the teacher should not refuse it, since it is for the good of the pupil, providing that the teacher does not indulge in it. When pupils show their gratitude in volunteering to help, it is very tempting to avail oneself of that help; but sometimes pupils turn the tables on their teachers by making them feel dependent upon them. Besides, if they have a change of heart, they will resent the use the teacher made of their good will.

If you are dependent upon others, some will try to make you more dependent.

Murshid saw the danger of practical, efficient people getting:

the upper hand on a spiritual person who is kind and gentle and tolerant, enduring and forgiving, if he finds the least little opportunity of handling him.

The art of spiritual training consists in cutting a rough diamond into a polished jewel, pruning a rosebush, chiseling an amorphous piece of wood into a statue, molding an ingot of gold into a beautiful ornament, or tuning a harpsichord—cutting, pruning, chiseling, melting, molding, tuning. Prune or chisel as painlessly as possible; melt cautiously and tune gently lest the string break.

A personality is first put to melt by the initiator, and it is only after the melting of the personality that something can be made out of it.

If the pupil lends himself to this masterly operation upon him, the process becomes intensely exciting and rewarding for both the teacher and the pupil. For the training to be effective, it is not sufficient for the pupil's insight or judgment to have increased, but for him to trust himself in carrying out the action, which may require overcoming himself.

This is why the teachers in the East put their pupils through tests: For example, they observe how their pupil handles a situation, and if he has proven satisfactory, the teacher will provoke a more challenging situation with a view to trying the pupil in his resolve to carry out what he knows.

The way of the Sufi esoteric training is not only in prescribing different meditations and in giving philosophical studies, but it is in trying and testing a pupil, his sincerity, his faithfulness, his trust, his courage, his intelligence, his patience. It is weighing and measuring his sense of justice, his faculty of reasoning, probing into the depth of his heart. The confidence is tested when the mureed's patience is tried.

Once Murshid had asked a mureed if he would have the patience to take a retreat in a forest for a year; whereupon the pupil answered that he could not possibly do so. A year later, he returned to Murshid and said he had had such a terrible year that he regretted not having followed Murshid's advice. It is clear, then, that such a training can only be carried out where there is complete trust. The measure of the pupil's trust marks the extent to which the teacher is able to operate upon the pupil.

The initiator must see if the thread on the side of the initiated is thin and cannot endure the weight of the sacredness which belongs to initiation. Very often the thinness of the thread has a discouraging effect upon the initiator, and it demands a great deal of consideration and interest and sympathy on the part of the initiator to hold up something which is dropping.

On the other hand,

One must not try the patience of the pupil by asking him to do too much.

Sometimes I wait days, months, years to tell something I would have liked to tell a mureed, waiting for the time to come, waiting for the spirit of the mureed to have become ripened.

If the pupil does not have enough confidence to assume that the teacher must have his reason for what he is doing, he will naturally criticize the teacher for involving him in that situation.

Thus to the pupil the teacher may often appear to be very unreasonable, very odd, very meaningless, very unkind, very cold and unjust. And during these tests, if the faith and the trust of the pupil do not endure, he will step back. . . .[1]

He will wonder why, when Murshid has always given me a hot cup of tea, why does he give me a cold drink. It is not that Murshid's sympathy is lacking, it is because you need at that time a cold drink; it is better for you. The method of Murshid is most subtle and fine and deep. It cannot be put in gross words of explanation. It is not like the religious path where the clergy or authority says "This is wicked according to this or the other law." With Murshid there is the delicacy of conscientiousness keeping the delicate feeling alive. The delicate feeling is this, that you may not allow the teacher to tell you something in words. You must understand his pleasure before he says it.

Even if Murshid appears to be displeased, it is not so in truth. Once, after a silence, a mureed thought Murshid had looked at her harshly. "Imagine," he said, "how could I be angry at that time!" Maybe a great power was coming through.

The great teacher will always hold his pupil in his heart, however shockingly the pupil behaves. Maybe the mureed felt a bad conscience about something, because the power of truth of masters is so great sometimes that they act as a mirror, making people face themselves in truth. Obviously, if the teacher simply gives in to the will of the pupil he is not helping him; but, on the other hand, if he stands on his will, some pupils think that they are having a quarrel or a disagreement with their teacher, treating him as they would any other human being, not knowing how to behave toward their teacher.

Like children displeased with their parents,

they can come to me and talk to me, and behave in a way that they should not behave. Never for one moment do I allow myself to think that their devotion, their love, their sympathy is less. The parents never allow the relationship to be broken, even if their children happen to prove unworthy.

This link between Murshid and mureed is more delicate than a thin thread and at the same time much stronger than a steel wire. And the only way to preserve it is to keep that delicate feeling about one's teacher living in one's heart.

The teacher has two responsibilities: to look after his fragile spirit, and to look after the spirit of the mureed, which very often is asleep. And sometimes a conflict arises, so that the teacher is very often on the point of breaking his own spirit while wanting to maintain the spirit of his mureed. Very often it is that the mureed, without knowing, is holding the glass-like spirit of his teacher, and unconsciously is on the point of throwing it against the rock. And the moment the teacher says: "Please do not throw it," the teacher has lost his spirit as well as the spirit of the mureed. Why has the teacher lost his spirit? Because the moment the mureed knows that the teacher's spirit is in his hand, and he can throw it in a moment, no more the teacher is a teacher in the eyes of the mureed. The mureed thinks that the teacher's spirit is stronger than the rock. But he does not know that in spite of the strength that the teacher has, it is more fragile than the glass.

The greater the teacher, the more delicate his temperament. The more transparent the heart, the more fragile. What I mean to say, is that by hurting a fly you might hurt Murshid, and that is the thing that many cannot understand.

In the path of discipleship the whole beauty of the way is fineness of manner between the teacher and the pupil. If one does not learn delicacy with one's teacher, with whom will one learn it?

In fact, it is in his love that the teacher is tested, rather than in his will; that is the ultimate test of the human being. The pupil can hurt him all he wishes, but should the teacher have to hurt his pupil in order to help him, the pupil will not withstand it, except inasmuch as he loves his teacher. Sometimes the greatest cruelty is the greatest kindness. The proof of the authenticity of the teacher is whether when the pupil acts despicably, he can continue to love him. As before, this is the acid test of all humans.

There is never a possibility on the part of Murshid to remove a mureed from the current he receives, unless he himself turns his back to it. There is a stage where the teacher arrives at a point where not only he loves, but he becomes love, he turns into love. Then love alone can he stand.

No matter how undesirable my mureed be, no matter how opposed, I would never turn my back. I would not call myself a murshid if I would. If the connection can be separated, it is on the part of the mureed himself. And the day when the mureed will come in focus, he will find the same thing there as has always been, perhaps a little more, because the love that does not grow is dead.

It has been inconceivable to me to see to what extent some people in the western world could be outspoken. If it was honesty, I could not think for one moment it could be wisdom. What I found missing in the West is the tendency to keep veiled all that is beautiful.

Your goodwill and blessing must reach each and every one whose hand you have once held in the sacred initiation.

While the pupil wishes for help, he makes it difficult for the teacher, sometimes to the extent of preventing the teacher from helping him. His soul wants to receive, but his ego does not want to acknowledge. Consequently, it is ultimately the teacher who is tested by the pupil rather than the pupil by the teacher. And it is only the teacher's self-confidence in the wisdom he has to impart, and his love for his pupil, that makes the training at all possible.

The teacher must care: the teacher is born to care, it is his work. For the teacher lives for mureeds, his only object is to see their spiritual evolution. There must be no limit to the teacher's compassion, because that is the teacher's test. God is testing the teacher by giving him a difficult pupil. The greater the initiator, the more he will risk difficult mureeds.

Therefore, the teacher has to keep himself always in good trim, watching his condition. "There is a constant demand on the teacher's store of power, and inspiration." Throughout, the teacher has to watch over his spirit lest it become disheartened.

To be able to carry out this great task, the teacher has to prove blameless, while his human nature will sometimes revolt against being so thwarted. If the teacher is convicted by his pupils of any fault, even if it is unfounded, his pupils will not take him seriously anymore; his teaching will evoke no response. Therefore, the teacher should be so scrupulous in his actions, in his relationship with all beings, pupils or otherwise, that he leaves no one a handle with which to slander him.

The pupil must not be given a handle by which he could dispute and make the teacher commit an error, for once the pupil holds a mistake of the teacher, he loses his regard for his teacher. No word may be said that may be taken amiss by another person.

The tendency of a devilish person is to rule. He wants to get a grip on any person in whom he feels interested. And he gets control of another most frequently by taking advantage of his faults. He draws the one he wishes to control into a ditch; and when he finds that his victim is dependent, then he stretches out to him his helping hand. But instead of lifting a person from the ditch, he would rather keep him there by the strength of his helping hand. If he lifted him up from there, it would be in order to make of him a horse and ride on his back, or a donkey to bear his load.

And should criticism arise, the teacher should take good notice of it, because it is generally an indication of something untoward.

If people speak against you, take notice of it, judge it, and weigh it in yourself impartially, and correct yourself. You may not partake of their poison by returning the same to them or even by keeping some memory of it in your heart.

Someone feeling a deep spiritual link with Murshid worried whether she was being disloyal to Christ; whereupon Murshid told the story of how one day the servant of his murshid came to him with a message. No sooner did he know he had come from his Murshid than he kissed his hands (an eastern token of respect, which no easterner would ever do to a servant). In saying this, Murshid gently tells us that he comes in the name of Christ.

The spiritual path is the balance of democracy and aristocracy. The aristocratic part is that the initiator sits on the teacher's throne and the initiated one stands in his place in all humility. And the democracy of the spiritual path is that the teacher raises him also to the same throne upon which he himself is sitting, and even higher if he can; for in raising the initiated one the initiator himself is raised high. Verily the greatness of God is brought to Him by the greatness of man.

As already said, one of the greatest secrets of training in the East is for the pupil to concentrate so intensely upon the teacher that he identifies with him. Some treasure a picture of their teacher, but it is better to do without, because one would tend to become attached to the outer form, which is idolatry. Without it, the mind is put to exercise. The next stage is:

trying every moment of one's life to think as Murshid thinks, to see as Murshid sees, to feel as Murshid feels and to act as Murshid acts.
    It is hopeless when one says: "The teacher is a teacher, and I am what I am."

At an advanced state, the pupil sees what he was used to admiring and concentrating upon in his Murshid everywhere, and then at a still further stage, he finds it within. As a consequence

the pupil learns to give everything that he has so far given to the teacher: devotion, sacrifice, service, respect, to all, because he has learned to see his teacher in all.

This accounts for the murshid in Hyderabad who called everyone murshid. The reason for this is that one finds without the same as that which is within: "The real teacher is within."

Imagine what this must be like from the teacher's vantage point—to recognize himself in his pupil must be most baffling. There is a story of a pupil who left his teacher for years and then came back. During all that time he had done what his murshid would have done in each particular case and said what his murshid would have said and acted as he would have acted. After a long time he returned to his murshid disguised as a shepherd. But the murshid recognized him, since he saw himself reflected in him.

Do you know what Murshid feels: "Myself is coming before me"? His atmosphere becomes Murshid's atmosphere, his word Murshid's word, his glance Murshid's glance.

The teacher is much closer and much higher than all relations and connections in this world.

The most favorable moments when a teacher feels moved to communicate his teaching are those when the pupil says or does something or just feels in a way that touches the heart of the teacher.

The times when I received were when through my devotion the heart of my Murshid was moved, and those moments when the heart is open are like the key.

Sometimes the teaching is given without words, just by communicating a feeling of ecstasy.

A teacher can elevate a soul much more by silent than by oral teaching.
It is simply a reflection of the teacher's spirit fallen on the heart of the pupil.

As the pupil advances, the relationship with the teacher becomes more and more wonderful—it is mutual and tacit understanding beyond words.

There are two stages of advancement in the life of a mureed. One is that the mureed knows and understands what the Murshid says. Second, that the mureed knows what Murshid means.

It culminates in the most perfect conceivable friendship.

Murshidship and mureedship is a journeying of two persons, one who knows the path, the other a stranger taken through the mist by the Murshid until they arrive at a stage where neither Murshid is a Murshid nor mureed is a mureed, though the happy memory of the journey through the path remains in the consciousness of the grateful mureed.

For the mystical teacher is not the player of the instrument; he is the tuner. When he has tuned it, he gives into the hands of the Player whose instrument it is to play.[2]

CHAPTER 23

The Blossoming
of the Message

The Message for which we have been preparing so long, as the workers of the Sufi Movement, is now being born.

It is the awakening of humanity to the divinity of man.

We belong to the tradition of the Kings of Kings.

The Summer School at Suresnes in 1926 seemed to be the culmination of Murshid's mission. More mureeds than ever came from all corners of the world. One had the impression that Murshid had reached a gigantic stature and seemed to be carrying a mighty load upon his broad shoulders. Although he was overworked beyond measure, his slow majestic steps as he walked down the steps of Fazal Manzil and then up and down the winding lane among the apricot trees before entering the hall to deliver his lectures had something of the dimension of a prophet of old. "So must have been the Nazarene" said some, perceiving his holy atmosphere; while some were haunted by a fear of being disloyal to Jesus; yet it was clear that his manner of being had brought Jesus closer and that in his higher consciousness he was no doubt very close to Jesus.

During this historic Summer School, he seemed distant and unapproachable, though as courteous as ever in the simple and natural grace with which he received mureeds. It was as if he were absorbed in cosmic consciousness. Though received by him as a friend, one felt one could only approach him in awe, as if permitted to lift the veil with which he concealed the grace glorifying him in his communion with God. Paradoxically, in contrast to this aloofness, many were struck at the evidence of his uncanny awareness of the most unnoticeable things, even seemingly unimportant things, whose significance he alone could assess. It was most endearing to see him in the midst of intense activity sit down and in all simplicity write out a birthday card to a mureed he might have met once.

Sometimes the mighty impact of Murshid's radiance seemed to be almost too much to bear. Mureeds would return to their rooms and cry

382

for sheer joy, and then he would shield the mureeds by making himself appear quite jovial and amiable. It was the spell of his humor and his graceful enjoyment of simple things, and the earnest gratitude he showed for everything. Such we experienced mainly during those festive meals at Fazal Manzil when Murshid invited a few mureeds to his table; the awe some people felt was quickly dispelled by Murshid's contagious humor and friendliness. For us children, who were relegated to a small table and committed to silence, it was like living in paradise with a heavenly father.

Someone said to Murshid, "I heard them talk against you." "Did they?" said he. "Have you also heard anyone speak kindly of me?" "Yes," the person exclaimed. "Then," said Murshid, "that is what is the light and shade to life's picture, making the picture complete." Someone asked Murshid, "Are you the head of the Sufi Order?" "No, God," he said. "And you?" asked the man. "The foot," said he. "You have nicely said to us, Murshid, how Sufism is one with all religions. Now please tell us, what is the difference between Sufism and other religions." The Murshid said, "The difference is that it casts away all differences." Someone said to Murshid, "Take some of our Christian religion to the East." Murshid replied, "It has already come from the East, sir."

Another occasion where Murshid's human touch broke into delightful mirth was during the performance of his plays. These had been devised as a practical teaching for each who played a part. Sometimes Murshid wrote the role intentionally for a mureed. This was a fascinating experience for the mureeds, and it is a wonderful testimony to Murshid's grasp of human problems in everyday life, though he invariably leavened the plot by the yeast of the divine ideal. Some even remember what must surely have been a rare occurence, when, at a picnic on the dunes after the marriage of his brother, all mureeds played blind man's buff, including Murshid, who naturally took his turn in being blindfolded and caught the national leader of Holland.

The plethora of teaching coming through the Master had now become a flood, evidencing the plentitude of the Message. In between interviews, he would jot down any thought that struck him pertinently, intimating the spiritual overtones of the human problems he was meeting. And out of this real-life experience, echoing his own inner experience, emerged the aphorisms—*Gayan, Vadan,* and *Nirtan*—jewels of thought best considered singly as seed thoughts for daily meditations. Speaking to the heart of some, to the soul of the few, and even to the intellect of those who were still involved in that dimension, he was what he knew, answering the problems of his hearers by an intuitive grasp of the questions in their minds, while tuning their souls to their own spiritual pitch, so that many said, "This was meant for me." He was so conscious of the anguished needs of his hearers that these lectures which sprang spontaneously as improvisations brought a practical answer to the problems continually recurring among people.

Though there were now too many people to be able to give personal training, Murshid had a way of reaching each one, which one could observe as they blossomed like flowers under the sunshine of his presence. He put each mureed in the melting pot, and some knew they were under test. Often, mureeds were astonished to find defects which they believed they had overcome emerge forcibly risen to the surface before they could be decanted. This is because a strong spiritual pressure forces defects into the open. But Murshid would not allow an inharmonious thought to mar the beauty of the soul of a mureed, which accounts for the harmonious atmosphere of the group surrounding him.

No doubt the most sacred moments during the Summer Schools came when mureeds sat in turn before the master for a few seconds while he was in samadhi, the supreme state of consciousness. On those Saturdays Murshid started meditating uninterruptedly from five o'clock in the morning, and was brought to the hall in a state of complete absorption in the divine unity, flanked by two mureeds, in order to give the mureeds a glimpse of the sublime yonder to which all aspired. When he opened his eyes to give a blessing through his glance, they seemed as though burnt by the blinding effulgence of angelic realms and drawn into an unearthly stratum of his higher consciousness. It was a way of making people glow by igniting their soul's with the luster of the illuminated glance. A German leader, Sherdyl Rettich Heidyl, wrote, "It was as though a veil had been lifted into heaven."

The eye of the seer becomes like a sword which cuts open so to speak all things, including the hearts of men, and sees clearly through all they contain. Every soul stands before me as a world, and the light of my spirit falling upon it brings clearly to view all it contains.

One light ignited another in the web of light that the illuminated ones thread in their spiritual communion across the fabric of the world.

Wherever Thou shall cast Thy glance, a new sun will arise there.[1]

That the glance of a human being can reach such efficacy is one of the wonders of creation. The discerning glance cross-examines and disarms people, so that they cannot but open up, revealing their most guarded secrets.

Before the eyes of the spiritual person objects and people unfold themselves; they reveal their nature and character.

It not only lifts the mask most people wear and identify with, it has a creative faculty. The glance, directed from higher consciousness, is able to investigate idiosyncrasies of a being by the very fact that the subject tends to unmask defenselessly when faced with the truthfulness manifesting in the glance of the illuminated being. The curious thing is that this perceptiveness makes him creative, in that a light shone upon a situation will dissipate the block and therefore catalyze the unfoldment intended in the design of the Divine Planner.

The glance of the seer is penetrating, and in this it differs from the glance of the average man. It has three qualities. The first is that it penetrates through body, mind, and soul. The second quality of this glance is that it opens, unlocks, and unfolds things; it also possesses the power of seeking and finding. The third quality characteristic of the glance of the seer is more wonderful. It is this: as it falls upon a thing it makes that thing as it wants to make it. It is not actually creating, but it is awakening in it that particular quality, which was perhaps asleep.

It reaches the extent of making a person thinking of himself as inadequate realize his innate beauty; in fact, it unlocks the divine potential lying dormant and manifests it.

To turn what is ugly into beauty, or beauty into ugliness, this is what the vision can accomplish.

The true faces emerge out of the sun. We see the painting; do we discern the painter in the painting? Do we know how the painting looks to the painter, knowing that is Himself?

Also, he who looks at this marvel begins to see the divine evidence in every face, as a person can see the painter in his painting. For instance, a person looking at a picture may say, "This is a portrait of so and so, it is a very good picture, exactly like him." Truth is like this; and to a mystic the whole of life is the picture of the divine Beloved.

But even in the ordinary waking state, Murshid's soul seemed to have attained sometimes the high altitude of rapt exaltation, so that his atmosphere was surrounded by a halo of reverence. His being was, during the 1926 Summer School, the meeting place of the most contrasting but powerful mystical moods, where the winds of the spirit were blowing furiously, yet leaving his soul in the utmost serenity.

There was a solemnity and severity in his glance that would encounter the visitor most firmly, and at the same time such an outpouring of love and kindness that one felt infinitely happy.

I still remember my sister, Noor-un-Nisa, when I was ten years old, saying, "Have you seen Abba's eyes today? O come and look at them as he next steps out of the Oriental Room." Those eyes were flashing with light. I never thought such eyes were humanly possible.

A sparkling soul flashes out through the eyes.[2]

There was a storm blowing about Murshid, transcendentally and humanly. Fears were being harbored in the family that we would never see him again. One night I dreamt this, and Murshid, hearing the screams of my grief, comforted me. Noor-un-Nisa dreamt that the baker had left in a plane, never to return, and when she told this to Murshid, he had tears in his eyes. During the one interview I had with him, as he looked over the field from the window of his Oriental Room, I asked him childishly why he did not go to the service of the Universal Worship; he said that the time had come for the mureeds to carry on themselves. I remembered my dream; life without him seemed an impossibility. How truly he echoed the vulnerability of our human hearts in his last poem, "Before my heart is broken, will you help my soul to live?"

Things were coming to a head on the last day of the Summer School, September 13, 1926, "Hedjrat Day," the commemoration of Murshid's departure from India on September 13, 1910, and his last day with the mureeds. A ceremony for the foundation of the first temple of the Message had been arranged in its minutest details by Murshid. With great solemnity the procession moved down from the hall: the *cherags* (ordained servers at the altar) in their black robes carrying candles, preceded by incense burners, followed by the initiates in yellow robes. Murshid seemed to be glowing as though consumed by an internal fire, yet calm as an evening sky. A circle had been chalked on the grass, no doubt by a well-intended mureed, to indicate where he was to stand. Some will never forget Murshid's expression of surprise, then of acquiescent resignation, when he bowed his head and slowly moved into the circle, for he well knew the psychological and material influence of symbology. We knew that the die was cast. He stood there a cosmic figure. He placed a list of all the Murshids of the Order, including his successor (a *Shajera,* after the custom of the Sufis), beneath the stone and asked the Begum to place there a silver engraved tablet, then one of his books. Coins of each country were lowered into the urn cemented beneath the stone by each national representative, as an augury of the universal character of the temple to be called the Universel, the temple of all religions.

Discounting proposals by mureeds to build the temple in more congenial natural surroundings, Murshid insisted on the importance of the spot as a holy one: "When your Murshid was brought here, destiny settled him here, spirits were moved to take this piece of land that a temple be made here. It is not without meaning," he said. The area so dear to the Murshid was on the slopes of Mont Valerien, which has been a place of pilgrimage since time immemorial. The remains of a Druid temple were found on its summit. St. Geneviève, the patron saint of Paris, tended her sheep on its slopes and discovered the healing stream known as *la fontaine Ste. Geneviève*, which became known for miraculous cures. A hermitage was first established as early as the fifth century, and throughout subsequent centuries it has been known as a place of retirement and meditation. In the thirteenth century a monastery was built on the Mons Valeriani, and subsequently a church, Notre Dame de Bonne Nouvelle, where monks and holy men met for prayers and meditation, assisted by the pilgrims. The place was known for extraordinary penances and feats of mortification, such as anchorites walling themselves into dark chambers for years. In the fifteenth century, a great ascetic named Antoine lived there on the leaves and roots of trees and bushes and the water of the stream, and was later surrounded by a group of disciples. In 1566, a woman ascetic, Guillemette Froissard, built a cell and subsequently a chapel, St. Sauveur. Toward the end of the sixteenth century, a famous cenobite, Jean de Haussey, inhabited her deserted cell, sleeping in his coffin.

Eventually, three crosses were erected as a calvary, representing the mysteries of the Passion, and masses of pilgrims negotiated the steep slopes of the sacred hill. They followed a tortuous path, studded by seven small chapels representing the Stations of the Cross, in a pious quest for salvation. A confraternity of hermits cultivated the ground. Through the efforts of Archbishop Henri Charpentier, a sanctuary was built there containing a fragment of wood said to be a part of the cross on which Christ had been crucified.

The Revolution swept away the last vestiges of the hermitages and made the hill national property; Napoleon established a fort there. It is a sad irony that the martyrdom of the heroes of the resistance of the Second World War, who were executed on Mont Valerien, should have brought back hordes of pilgrims to the sacred hill.

The uncanny French astrologer Nostradamus foretold that in the twentieth century a great Indian spiritual prince would establish himself in the valley of gold (Val d'Or) on the flank of the sacred hill, surrounded by many disciples. He would marry and have children and would die at age 44.

Tradition confirms that every time the sacred spot has been reinstated in its role as a place of pilgrimage, the forces within it have sprung to life. As Murshid says, "It is our thoughts and our feelings which will serve in this temple as stones and bricks and tiles." Murshid drew a circle with its center on the land where the temple was to be built. The Universel was to serve as a model and precursor of temples to come, "a souvenir," as he said to his disciples, "of your devotion to the Cause, a souvenir of that struggle and fight through which you will have to go and are going in this pioneering work."

Why, of all spots, did the Master choose Suresnes? "Many might prefer a more beautiful spot," he said, "but there are some who seek beauty in the place and others who make beauty in the place." Further, he said,

Our practical head will say no, this is not the right place for this. But this place has its own virtue, its own value, and if there is to be beauty, it is to create its own beauty. The ancient mystics, sages and prophets did not try to perform miracles; if there was a phenomenon, it was themselves, their own being. Places flourished where they trod. They turned an ordinary place into a place of pilgrimage.

The ancients knew more than we do of the importance of the *locus*, the place, particularly the sacred spot. In *Cosmic Language*, Murshid tells of the voice continually vibrating in the rocks, in the forests, and in the towns, speaking of those who have sat there or lived there.

The whole manifestation in all its aspects is a record upon which the voice is reproduced; and that voice is a person's thought.

There are those who still remember the magnetism of Murshid's hands when, standing as the embodiment of the great hierarchy of murshids and prophets, he blessed us each in turn for the rest of our lives. We joined the Confraternity, an order within the Order, whose mission was to prepare the building of stones by first building the inner spiritual temple through prayer.

Murshid sat in the gilded armchair that had been presented to him by the mureeds, and everyone enjoyed for a few hours longer that feeling of security that one had when he was within sight. It was a feeling of belonging to a large spiritual family; one had not a care in the world, for his sunshine filled the atmosphere and he seemed ageless. Then suddenly, it was all over; Murshid was on his way. Our hearts were filled with the greatest misgivings.

He traveled first to Geneva to attend the yearly council meetings, which took place earlier than usual. The meetings:

were much more lively than in previous years. For those assembled at them showed intense desire for the furtherance of the Cause. I noticed more clearly the present spirit of the people and nations, knocking at our door also, which to me seemed to be a strange psychological phenomenon. In spite of differences which gave the meetings a modern tone, I felt each one taking the welfare of the Movement too much to heart with the best intentions. I marvelled at Mr. Zanetti working so wisely under all circumstances.

After the meetings, Murshid went to Marseilles, whence he embarked for India.

CHAPTER 24

Why O My Feeling Heart Do You Laugh and Cry?

JOY AND PAIN

Why O my feeling heart
Do you live and die?
What makes my feeling heart
To laugh and to cry?
Death is my life indeed,
When I live then I die,
Pain is my pleasure,
When I laugh then I cry.
—Gayan, 247

No one has entrance into the kingdom of God who has not been so crucified.

Suffering makes the heart sincere.

Many wondered why Murshid in the last years seemed to carry the signature of suffering written on his face, while one would have thought that a liberated master would radiate only joy. Obviously, one forgets that as one becomes increasingly sensitive, one cannot let oneself be carried exclusively into landscapes of joy while ignoring all the cries of pain and despair and appeals for help (past, present, and future) that one picks up if he is aware of the whole range of what is happening, has happened, and is in store. In fact, in Murshid one found joy and pain simultaneously, the way of the broken heart both agonizing and jubilant, never indifferent or low key.

However, Murshid had a heavy cross to bear.

There is an incipient suffering ingrained in the very nature of life—life's inseparable companion. You will find it in the pangs of childbirth or the wrench of death, in the heart throb of a joy too intense to bear, in unrequited love, or having failed in requited love. Again it is there in the fear of fortuitous loss as well as in the irretrievable loss of a disappointed hope. It appears in the guilt of not having given what one could or done what one should, and in regretting having given. Suffering is there in the specter of inadequacy, of failure to fully grasp significance, of lacking the strength to believe in the face of apparent proof to the contrary.

Untold millions of beings have been the victims of brutal violence and uncalled for humiliation, subjected to the most excruciating agony of body and mind. The cruelty and aggression conceived by humans on the planet exceeds all bounds, reaching preposterous dimensions in criminal passion; even nature, when its forces break loose, engulfs humans mercilessly, as if in a kind of furor that reeks of revenge for our having perversely flouted its dignity.

Can we even begin to enter into the consciousness of a miner who is trapped underground, his legs jammed by a boulder, as the water slowly and inexorably rises; or an Eastern prisoner of war through grilling days and freezing nights cooped in a bamboo cage so that he cannot stretch himself; a woman victim of shameful bodily atrocities at the hands of sadistic captors (my own sister was whipped to death by the gauleiter of Dachau); parents who have been made to watch their children butchered in front of them; racial or political deviants under totalitarian regimes subjected to sadistic experiment or treatment by a handful of unscrupulous scientists and doctors. When one hears of the ordeals that people in concentration camps went through, packed like cattle amid feces and spew, starved, sick with dysentery, without heating in severe cold, kicked and slapped and humiliated, waiting in terror while seeing their relatives being gassed, mostly dying out of a disgust with life—one cannot but feel a sickening indignation at the shocking limits of cruelty, brutality, and savagery to which some fellow human beings stooped.

According to personal accounts, despair and utter dejection were the hardest to bear. Many died out of sheer torment from the irony of their belief in the basic decency of mankind, or the horror of creation now appearing as a nightmare. The only thought that gave some the will to survive was the heroism of those who helped fellow inmates who were more ill then themselves, and especially those who sacrificed their lives to save others. Suddenly humanity was rehabilitated and hope restored.

In the list of causes of suffering, we have equally to account for men and women who day by day fight bravely for sanity against their faltering minds, and the hopeless, desperate struggle against death of many dying slowly of cancer, particularly those who do not believe in spiritual survival. Can we bear to imagine the soul searching of a person who, through negligence, passion, even the belief he was doing right, has led someone to death or moral deprivation and now discovers his culpability? Perhaps the television has done something good in bringing before us in our homes the many adults and children who die every day in the wake of war, famine, human greed, folly, and violence; but we have trained ourselves to ignore the daily experience of mental aggression where people's lives, young and old, are marred by injustice at the hands of the unscrupulous who deprive them of their rights or prejudice people against them by slander, whether willful or stupidly thoughtless. Dare we try to imagine the vast bulk of

Why O My Feeling Heart Do You Laugh and Cry?

unacknowledged but nevertheless bitter suffering caused everywhere, every day, by ruthless egos to their dependents at home and at work?

Can one spare man from human cruelty and protect him from hazards? One may hope that willful torture can be curbed in our age. But even if one tried to prevent natural catastrophes, for example, by curtailing epidemics, or building dikes against the seas in lowlands, there would be unpredictable events. However one tries to secure people, other hazards will present themselves, because there must be room for the play of the forces set off by cosmic laws in motion. The only answer is to know how to harness the force that is suffering.

When suffering reaches a certain threshold, there is a cut-out mechanism, which may manifest itself as loss of consciousness. But this threshold sometimes seems to be set cruelly high by nature. Is it possible to set this cut-off switch to a less acute level of pain? Some people who have gone through physical torture record that their only solace, if any, was to tear their attention away from the seat of their pain, while the urgency of the pain kept pulling them back into it. A heart-rending example is the one of the black youth, lynched by the crowd, who exclaimed: "You can get my body, but you cannot touch my soul!" Try it at the dentist's chair without an anaesthetic and confirm whether it really works!

The more one can bear, the more one is given to bear.[1]

Indeed, the more courageously you face physical suffering, the higher the threshold of suffering that you can endure without fainting; at a moral level the more hardships one can endure without being flustered. It is the refusal of pain—shying off fretfully from pain—that heightens the pain by concentrating all one's energy upon it. This is equally true for psychological despair, when the victim refuses to accept the unacceptable, fighting against it. One must face it, not resist it, yet on the other hand not accept that it has power over one—the secret of Christian Science.

The best way of getting over pain is by not acknowledging it.
Denying a thing is destroying a thing. And to admit a certain thing is giving it a root.

Accept the reality of the situation—do not bury your head under the sand—but do not identify yourself as its victim. In the dentist's chair the best way to immunize oneself against pain is to think: It is just my body that is experiencing pain, not me. Likewise, when dealing with a moral issue, instead of thinking, "I am the one whose well-being is affected or who is receiving the blow," think: "It is only my ego that is being battered." It is self-pity, ascribing the suffering to oneself as the victim, that is the virus of suffering; if one realizes that one is experiencing in oneself the agony of the universe, in the being of God at the cosmic scale, then suffering is sublimated.

In reality, He feels what we imagine we feel, yet at the same time His perfect Being keeps him above all earthly joys and pains; and our imperfection limits us, so that we become subject to all joys and pains, however small they may be.

Many people choose to turn a blind eye to suffering of others, feeling they already have sufficient problems of their own. Yet it is good to bear in mind those who suffer when one complains about one's own share of pain and loss. After making an earnest attempt to really enter into the inner feelings of any of the victims we have mentioned, unless a person is totally without shame, he would feel very selfish, indeed, to fret over lesser ills that are dwarfed into frivolity by comparison.

When Sa'di was travelling to Persia, footsore because he had to walk with bare feet in the hot sun, it was so painful that he was thinking there could be no one in the world as wretched and miserable as himself. But two minutes later he came across a person whose feet were both useless, so that he was crawling along the grond and only progressing with great difficulty.[2]

Some reckon that so long as extreme tragedies do not happen to them, they are not involved, certainly so long as it happens to people in geographically far-removed places or to people unknown to them personally. Should the occurrence land on our own doorstep or that of dear ones, then it is another matter; which simply indicates that we have not yet risen to the consciousness that we are all together one being. This is why, in the East, there is a custom of parading the spectacle of suffering while people are enjoying themselves at a wedding or celebration, so that they may learn to share in that suffering at the same time, for life is one in joy and pain.

How much does the distressing specter of the emaciated beggar-boy in Benares affect that woman abandoned by her husband in her despair? Only as much as she is able to creep gently into his soul, forgetting herself. This means giving up her isolation in her own small psychological environment. This is precisely what is taught in meditation when it reaches the stage of contemplation *(dhyana)*: Remove the frontier between the self and the other.

We follow Buddha as he left his palace to seek a solution to human suffering, himself enduring the most excrutiating mortifications. He recounts how he could hardly drag his racked body on all fours, covered with maggots, to the river. In spite of all, he weathered his self-imposed ordeal in a state of bliss, proving by his prowess the reality of his discovery of the path that leads to the elimination of suffering by overcoming desire.

One is never so happy as when one has no reason to be so, because circumstances can never be so good as to suffice in making one happy.

According to Murshid detachment is not the only solution; suffering can be overcome by merging with all existence. This is why the person who gives does not suffer, it is the person who expects to receive who is disappointed, and this in the measure of the importance that one attaches to things.

He wants thousands, and when he gets them they do not satisfy him and he wants millions, and still he is not satisfied. If you give him your sympathy and service he is still unhappy; even all you possess is not enough, even your love does not help him, for he is seeking it outside instead of inside.

Happiness cannot be bought or sold, nor can you give it to a person who has not got it. Happiness is one's own being, one's own self, that self that is the most precious thing in life,

As we have seen, it was giving that made the ordeals of the concentration camps more bearable.

Sadness comes from limitation in different forms, from lack of perception, from lack of power over oneself and over conditions, and from lack of that substance which is happiness itself and which is love.[3]

When one finds oneself face to face with the reality of suffering, those who have the strength to hold to their belief in a concerted intentional planning behind human affairs, which indeed we witness in all nature, feel like storming the mind of the Planner, to wrest from him his top-secret intention. Writhing in mental agony or soul-searching quandary, especially when witnessing the unjust victimization of the innocent, many a sincere and sensitive being grasps for some restraint in holding back resentment. The great question mark looming high in disconcerted minds is: "Oh, why, oh why? Is this really necessary?"

Believing is a process. By this process the God within is awakened and made living; it is the living in God which gives happiness.[4]

The only saving grace restraining metaphysical anxiety, which is a suffering of the soul, is the realization of the dire inadequacy, ineptitude, in fact total disarray, of our limited human understanding faced with the monumental dimensions and intricacies of the planning. Where nature is concerned, scientists are unveiling, unraveling more and more the staggering ingenuity of the planning which animates every event, every phenomenon, every being; but when it comes to human destinies, we have difficulty in being objective. For we are personally involved, and the principles behind the planning are incomparably more complicated, so masterfully intertwined and inter-connected as to baffle the most skillful wit. In fact, the knowledge of this planning is the highest science there is, called by the Buddha transcendental knowledge. Such is the field of competence of the masters.

Answering the cry of our crucified souls, our Lilliputian minds ascribe suffering to a karmic debt accumulated in the past. This argument has led many a sanyasin since time immemorial and still today, particularly in India, to seek the path of liberation. This de-mands abstention from all acts that might involve further mortgaging of karma and overcoming, by realization, the ignorance that permits us to incur damaging karma. Basically it is the onesidedness of this obvious conclusion that obscures the potential of joy that one can gain by outweighing pain rather than running away from it.

There are some who will say, "I am suffering because of past errors I committed." But I personally would prefer that man who would resist against suffering by realizing that his birthright is happiness alone. And pain and suffering is foreign to his soul.

Without questioning the part played by the karmic factor in our destinies, the Murshid points out that suffering is part of the training to which we are subjected at the hands of an elaborate system of carefully selected planning. This naturally leads us to try and under-stand what is aimed at by the Planner and cooperate in the planning, rather than elude the programing.

For all souls, by the right and the wrong path, either sooner or later, will arrive at that purpose which must be accomplished, a purpose for which the whole creation has been intended; but the difference between the seeking soul and the soul who blindly works toward that purpose is like that between the material and the maker of it. The clay works toward the purpose of forming a vessel and so does the potter; but it is the potter's joy and privilege to feel the happiness of the accomplishment of the purpose, not the clay's.[5]

Finding in everything its purpose, Murshid sees in pain the lever devised by nature to make a person sincere.

Pain has a great power; the truth of God is born in pain, sincerity rises out of pain.

It also quickens one with life.

The heart is not living until it has experienced pain.

It even wakens one to enhanced awareness.

A tongue of flame rises from every wound of my heart, illuminating my path through life and guiding my way to the goal.[6]

And to the transfiguring action of joy.

If it were not for pain, one would not enjoy the experience of joy. It is pain which helps one to experience joy, for everything is distinguished by its opposite. For it is by pain the heart is penetrated,[7] and the sensation of pain is a deeper joy. Without pain the great musicians and poets and dreamers and thinkers would not have reached that stage by which they reached and moved the world. If they always had joy, they would not have touched the depths of life.

On the other hand, if the ideal is too stringent a person becomes despondent and embittered.

As fire can cook food or burn it, so also does pain affect the human heart.[8]

One would like to believe the Planner or Planners always assess how great a load a person can take, but when we witness the human wreckage left by gruelling suffering, we just hope that the positive result will be for the next life. When, however, we come across a once-devastated person who has emerged from the ordeal transfigured, cleansed and bubbling with joy, suddenly suffering reveals its true significance. What a tour de force, to turn up trumps from the battle of the mind against scathing odds, or rather from the triumph of the soul over the mind!

Out of the shell of the broken heart emerges the new born soul.[9]

The bringers of joy have always been the children of sorrow.[10]

This is precisely what Murshid was doing to his pupils. It is the crucial test of spirituality, for joy is the birthright of the soul.

Happiness is our birthright; in our happiness is the happiness of God.[11]

Very often people think that sorrow or pain, that is the sign of spirituality. One must not mistake spirituality for sorrow or pain. Yes, in many cases sorrow or pain becomes a process that leads to attaining spirituality quickly, but for that one need not afflict oneself with sorrow or pain, for life has enough sorrow or pain.

In seeking happiness, man is seeking for himself.

The soul is only able to maintain its pristine joy in spite of the eclipse it undergoes in incarnation if it remembers its citizenship in its heavenly abode. Remember the processions, the jubilations, the ovations, the glorification in the heavens?

There is no place for sadness in the kingdom of God. The attitude of looking at everything with a smile is the sign of the saintly soul.

It is the wrong method adopted in the pursuit of joy which brings, instead of joy, sorrow or disappointment.

If only we knew to what extent the forces of emotion break out in the universe! What secret stirrings prompt our thoughts, and dress themselves up in charades of make-believe!

What makes a thought convincing is the power behind it; and that power consists of feeling.[12]

For, deep in our consciousness or high in our superconsciousness looms the dim (sometimes, in the case of the enlightened, clear) awareness of an overall consciousness undergoing suffering on an unimaginable scale. One finger may not suffer because of a toothache, but the entire body suffers as a whole, or rather something beyond the local organ suffers.

Suppose your hand dropped a heavy weight upon your feet and hurt them, although the feet seem to have been hurt, yet the one who feels hurt is your absolute being.[13]

Most people engrossed in their own share of suffering fail to see the total picture: It is God, the totality of all beings, who is crucified all the time, whether through this part of his body or through another part. Everyone will sooner or later pay his share in the agony of that being called humanity, that fraction of the total being, since it is the price of joy and free will.

As soon as one finds that it is as bad if suffering happens to another as to oneself, and would even prefer that it should happen to oneself, one has access to the divine consciousness of cosmic suffering. It is quite a different way of experiencing suffering. Then one undergoes the catharsis of cosmic crucifixion—the body of Christ that is continually being crucified. Having reached the depths of despair, one is lifted into the peace of knowing why it all happened and realizes that it is all the way it is intended to be, because out of the shell of the broken heart arises a new being: This is the meaning of God resurrecting like a phoenix out of the cinders of the holocaust of the act of living, and one experiences his resurrection in a victory of joy over pain. At the time of Jesus, the role of the prophet was to take upon himself the karma incurred by people and, by his act of grace, redeem them from their accumulated burden incurred by the causal chains set into motion by past actions. Since then, humanity has gained a new freedom by going so deeply into suffering; the new trend in the role of the prophet is to guide mankind into new horizons in the azimuth of the divine intention, which is future-oriented, rather than concern himself with expiation, which is past-oriented. Consequently, people are shifting from dwelling upon suffering into rejoicing at all the new prospects opening up in the new age.

CHAPTER 25

Die Before Death
and Resurrect Now

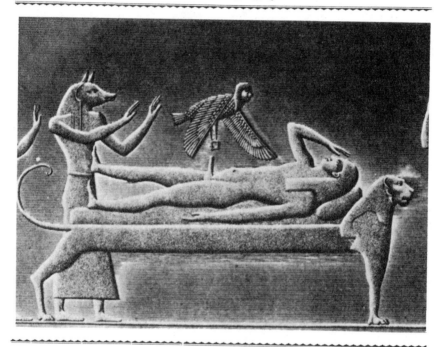

If the soul did not allow itself to be impressed with the thought of death, it would never die.—I, 167

What we call death is our impression of a change.—VI, 20

Once the soul has been able to feel itself, its own life independently of its garb, it begins to have confidence in life.—VI, 19

Is immortality to be gained—to be acquired? No, it is to be discovered.—I, 195

By myself, I become captive, and by myself I become free.—Bedil, Persian Sufi poet

Murshid had cherished memories of his beloved motherland so highly, and had so dearly looked forward to his return, that it was an unimaginable surprise and disappointment to discover how earlier ideals had been abandoned or flouted, how the philosophical attitude had given way to recklessness, detachment to neglect.

"In India one finds the best and the worst." He was distressed by the revival of internecine quarrels between Muslims and Hindus, unheard of in his youth. Had he not left his motherland all these years to convey his message of tolerance and religious unity from the Sufis of India to the West? And here he found religious bigotry in its worst form back home! Swami Shradananda, a highly revered holy man, the only one Murshid had felt thoroughly at home with after his return to India, was shot by a Muslim just a few days after Murshid had visited him. Can one imagine Murshid's pain? By some curious fate, a few days later, when he heard the news, Murshid was badly hurt as he stepped out of a cab. There are reasons to believe that Pir-O-Murshid's outspokenness rankled with some hot-headed extremists, who were infuriated at seeing a Muslim sage pay tribute to a Hindu sage. Murshid had spurned religious intolerance in a lecture in Delhi.

There was, however, a somewhat tenuous note of hopefulness; some letters were received from India: "People have caught up with me in my retreat; there is a growing demand for the Message: I cannot fail to answer the call." Mureeds were initiated. But in one of his letters to Begum, Murshid confided to her his great lassitude, his soul's longing for yonder. Although he was recharged by the Indian atmosphere, Murshid's health was failing. He had accomplished as much as the

401

human frame could stand, having undergone in sixteen years more than the fill of fifty years.

Twenty years before, his own Murshid had assembled acquaintances and servants at his deathbed to ask forgiveness for any offence; now Murshid himself sent his last Christmas message to all his mureeds, asking forgiveness of God. It is a final *cri de coeur*, a modern *miserere*, where the person speaks in the name of mankind: that grace may win over karma, love overcome law, hope overcome despair—a last reprieve for the well-intentioned to whom God has granted free will to make amends, by his own Will granted a last chance.

Before you judge my actions,
Lord, I pray, you will forgive.
Before my heart has broken,
Will you help my soul to live?
Before my eyes are covered,
Will you let me see your face?
Before my feet are tired,
May I reach your dwelling-place?
Before I wake from slumber,
You will watch me, Lord, I hold.
Before I throw my mantle,
Will you take me in your fold?
Before my work is over,
You, my Lord, will right the wrong.
Before you play your music,
Will you let me sing my song?[1]

At the sunset of his life, Murshid sat once more under the marble arches to face the earthly court of his great Sufi predecessor, Khwaja Muin-ud-Din Chishti, the "Murshid of Murshids" who had originally brought Sufism to the Indian subcontinent in the thirteenth century of our era. From him had come the instruction to his own Murshid Khwaja Abu Hashim Madani, commissioning Murshid to bring the message of Sufism to the West. Here, near the filigree screen of pure silver surrounding the mausoleum, in this atmosphere of fervor, he sat among rich pilgrims, beggars, dervishes, listening to musicians (called *qawwals*) vying with one another in singing praise to the Sultan-i-Hind, the true spiritual emperor of India, also called Gharib Nawaz, king of the poor. It was not far from here, at the outskirts of Ajmer, that sixteen years ago he had seen enraptured dervishes sigh and tear their clothes in utter abandon, heard the voice of a madhzub calling on him to awake; ever since, he too had been awakening people from the lethargy of maya. He remembered having so enjoyed the sight of dervishes in rags, yet so noble and majestic, greeting each other as "Your Majesty"; for the real king is the one who evidences the manner of God. This time, they were greeting him as "Your Majesty."

Now, himself moved by the spell of divine exultation, he mused upon his life now revolved—upon the significance of life itself, upon the perfume of life that resurrects, upon that saving grace; upon ecstasy, which is the luxury giving life its dimension, the leaven in the bread of life. All beings are born of exultation, and death is supreme exultation when it carries the promise of eternal life. At this moment in time and space, he was reporting back to the one who had sent him, and all the masters, saints, and prophets who form the hierarchies of the spiritual government of the world.

What could now be said in their secret converse? At the moment when a master is glorified in heaven, he is crucified on earth; so, as the hosts of angels welcomed him to their abode, his trustees on earth were put to severe tests before they became the foundation upon which his Message rests. To his pupils he left a briefing:

My thoughts I have sown on the soil of your mind;
My love has penetrated your heart;
My word I have put into your mouth;
My light has illuminated your whole being;
My work I have given into your hands.[2]

His last visit was to dargah of Khwaja Nizam-ud-Din Auliya in Delhi, the saint who was all love and kindness and became an example of charity, distributing food to the millions while depriving himself. Surveying an abandoned mosque in a landscape studded with the ruins of the tombs of Sufi saints from the watchtower of Pir Hasan Nizami's home, Pir-O-Murshid confided how happy he felt there. The pir responded, "You are welcome to come and stay." "Yes," answered Pir-O-Murshid, "when I come, I will stay forever." The pir understood that he meant to be buried there.

As Pir-O-Murshid descended the steps of the Jama Masjid in Delhi, a madhzub rushed at him, his eyes burning with ecstatic fire, saying: "I have been called to the court. I have been called to the court." Murshid told his disciple Kismet, who a few weeks later sat alone at his deathbed, "You will soon see what it means."

On February 5, 1927, Pir-O-Murshid Inayat Khan abandoned his body to the earth, its mother. Following is his spiritual testament:

At the moment when I shall be leaving this earth, it is not the number of followers which will make me proud. It is the thought that I have delivered His Message to some souls that will console me, and the feeling that it helped them through their life that will bring me satisfaction.[3]

At his last lecture to his mureeds, Murshid said: "And now, as we shall part outwardly I will be closer to every one of you. For the very reason that space will divide us, we are together in truth, in God, and for the service of humanity."

I am a tide in the sea of life, bearing towards the shore all who come within my enfoldment.[4]

During the last years of his life, Murshid had endured silently agony of pain in body, while going ahead, undaunted, with his mission. He had exhausted himself beyond measure, sleeping four hours a night during constant travels, austerities, and incessant interviews, and taking the sufferings of all those he came in touch with upon himself. Many entertain the theory that a holy man should never be ill, but most of those of whom we have heard have suffered dire physical ills. How can one have an idea about the suffering of people unless one has actually experienced it in one's flesh? Besides, the body must undergo disintegration that one may free oneself from its limitations.

No doubt Murshid had to undergo, because of the long protraction of his pain, that moment of truth which the great dervish Al Hallaj himself so treasured. Hallaj saw the value of going deeply into the disintegration of the body.

The one who suffers unbearable pain in body, naturally wishes for death to come as a welcome relief, but the one who knows its meaning wishes for it to come slowly that he may experience it, because it is the moment of truth.

Who will not face death one day?

Many a patient has watched his body disintegrate day by day to the point of putrefaction. Some have been panic stricken by the feeling of helplessness, faced with the advancing tide of extermination that cannot be gainsaid; others have laid their hopes upon death as a welcome release. The terrifying fear accompanying their physical suffering is obviously due to their having identified themselves with their bodies. For the one who is conscious of the significance of bodiness, death is a real thing. Quite understandably the dogmas relegating the body to the role of an extraneous garment gathered by the soul as a vehicle to function upon the planet Earth could not possibly prove convincing enough for these people, since, though the body may well be made of the fabric of the planet, still it does bear the hallmark of one's being; more so, its structure is the very architecture of one's psyche. In fact, the soul has crystallized into the flesh. Could we draw a simile from the seed that unfurls somatically as a plant, though functionally it remains unchanged throughout the process? Indeed, we do experience the way our being is processed into the flesh, and consequently the disintegration of that physical counterpart is not and cannot be perfunctory. Death therefore must be faced, gone into deeply, even enjoyed because of its free action; but it can only be experienced fully if one transfers one's hold upward where there is perpetuation, rather than hanging on to that which scatters. Death is only meaningful if one sees clearly how it eternalizes what has developed in matter. Matter is continually precariously suspended on the falling curve of becoming and can only perpetuate itself by transmuting. Here lies the meaning of resurrection. This explains Murshid's words as death was approaching:

When the unreality of life presses against my heart, its door opens to reality.[5]

Extraordinary words on the lips of one who had always prevailed upon his disciples to value life, as opposed to those who see life as maya.

This, then, would mean that if one does not accept to undergo transformation, one will really die, in the sense of closing oneself away from the experience of the new horizon, because one holds on to one's hard and fast ideas of oneself and the universe and remains encapsulated in one's own mental world. This is precisely the reason people fear death. No doubt, if they are thus stuck, their fear is justified, because the prison of the self is soul killing.

As the unfoldment of one's being is always a function of one's relationship with the environment (for relationship generates new life), without outside stimulus one's energy level drops, the nostalgia for life dwindles, and in one's lassitude one seeks the sleep of oblivion in the night of time. To allay the terror, one can beat death at its own game by keeping moving, looking forward to change. They thought they had captured Jesus, said the Muslims, but they only grabbed his body. So death loses its grip on one.

What dies? It is death that dies, not life.[6]

Before death [the soul] has realized that it is dying, yet it is really only after death that it lives. It is like a person who is alive thinking that he is dead . . . it is this state which is called purgatory. When the soul has realized itself, when it has realized that it is still living, then the clouds of confusion are dispersed and the soul finds itself, together with the atmosphere which belongs to it.[7]

Therefore, in the East meditation is devised to spare people from the illusion of death.

If the soul did not allow itself to be impressed with the thought of death it would never die, since death is nothing but an illusion which lasts for some time.[8]

People should be taught the rationale of the process of dying and be shielded from superstitions.

The soul which has become impressed by the idea it held of death, and by the impression which was created by those around the deathbed, is kept in a state of inertia which may be called fear, horror, depression or disappointment.[9]

Therefore, some masters are allotted the function of awakening people in the hereafter.

What we call death is our impression of a change. . . . Making people believe in immortality . . . should be done gradually . . . for otherwise this knowledge would frighten a person more than death itself.[10]

One may not particularly care to meditate or to rack one's brain with all those spiritual theories that some teachers pour down one's throat, but at some time, one will have to choose between being encapsulated or waking up from illusion.

Owing to its delusion, [the soul] takes upon itself all the conditions that the mind has to go through after death. . . . The earthly attachments are the string that draws the soul downwards. We see that the smoke goes up and on its way it leaves in the chimney its earth substance. All the rest of its earth substance it leaves in the air, and until it has left all behind, it cannot go up to the ether. By this simile we see how the soul cannot rise from the lower regions until it has left behind all earthly longings and attachments.[11]

One of the greatest frustrations of the human mind is its inability to grasp the phenomenon of life: It germinates here and peters out there, it lies dormant for ages then breaks through unexpectedly with staggering force, although nothing could have allowed one to foresee that every step and conjunction in its outbreak had been minutely planned from the outset. It can proliferate quantitatively by sheer multiplication and repetition of already acquired patterns, or take off by a quantum leap into new dimensions of existence. The flame that you extinguish on earth may flash in the heavens—life quickens life where it is simmering or potential, as a flame in a hearth may blaze up a weaker one or a jolt will set off a detonator. Life is communicated from one being to another as a taper may kindle a candle. Our privilege is to be the custodians of the miracle of life. That miracle coerces matter into converging atoms from different azimuths of the universe which, conforming to its own meaningfulness, then destroys any fossilizations of living patterns to ensure its own free flowing by scattering the components of all aggregations and bringing them into new life patterns. This is equally true of one's progeny, who spread the inheritance of one's being over the universe, while another part of one's being is transmuted in resurrection.

It is necessary that a precaution be taken that the door be kept open for souls who wish to enter the Kingdom of God; that they may not feel bound by the dogma that they will be dragged back after having left the earth-plane by their Karma.

This accounts for the supreme aspiration of the Hindu sanyasin, to promote resurrection while being incarnated.

The sages hold as their object in life, Mukti—liberation from the captivity caused by Karma and reincarnation.

It is all a matter of what the Sufis call maqam, the station, the stage through which one is passing in the journey of one's realization onward. At one time one realizes the importance of the flower; then one thinks one clearly sees the purpose of existence; and then, at another moment, one realizes the importance of the perfume, because the petals will fade and shrivel. Much as one might keep them in between the pages of one's book, they remain the dried-up effigies of life that is now burning somewhere else in the universe; but in that perfume the life of the rose is still active.

The rose has seeds in its heart, and so the developed souls have in their heart that seed of development which produces many roses. The rose blooms and fades away, but the essence that is taken from the rose lives and keeps the fragrance that the rose had in its full bloom. Personalities who touch that plane of consciousness may live for a limited time on the earth, but the essence which is left by them will live for thousands and thousands of years, always keeping the same fragrance and giving the same pleasure the rose once gave.[12]

It is the same with the flower and its fragrance: the flower is an illusion, but the fragrance is a reality; it stays as a spirit, it lives.[13]

On the other hand, even in that organic shroud there is still a fragmented life. Admittedly, the former integration of the whole has been dislocated, but the heart, or the retina, the kidney, the skin, may continue to live. Given the necessary nutrition, seeds and sperm may survive in a state of suspended animation. Leaves may possess medicinal properties for centuries; the grape and pollen nectar will live an extended life as wine or honey. If we study and analyze the different conditions the body has gone through, we find that it has become food for different creatures and different objects, manure for flowers and fruits and plants, and directly or indirectly it has reached the animals, the birds. The little lives that have been created from it, blown by the wind, have reached far and have been breathed by many, and have been absorbed in the breath or water by many beings. And as parents find that their children live after them, continuing their life, so every thought and feeling is also continuing its own life in the mind-sphere. By cutting the nails or the hair a part of the body is separated. That part which is separated is not lost, it is not destroyed; but one does not think about where it has gone and what has become of it.

What we call life and death are both a recognized existence within a certain degree of vibration. For instance, when a person says, "This leaf is dead," what has made it dead is the change of vibrations. It has no longer the same vibrations it had when it was on the tree; and yet it has not lost its vibrations. If that leaf were dead, then herbs would not have any effect upon a man when he takes them as medicine. In other words, there are ways of arresting and allaying the process of death at the cellular level, while it burns on at higher levels, transfigured.

Everything is so well programed in the universe. It wouldn't make sense if whatever is gained during the unfoldment of the seed by drawing earth, water, air, sunshine, cosmic rays, into itself, making it into a plant; or, at the human level, the cultivation of the personality, the enrichment that accrues through contact with one's fellow men—if all, all of this acquisition, were to be totally destroyed by a car accident or a heart attack. Obviously, it is carried upward as a thought essentialized; and then, as being moves further upward, one leaves the essentialized aggregate behind and carries the quintessence higher yet.

Man does not lose his individuality after death. That personality is making his hereafter. As the soul goes on its journey, it imparts its impressions to whichever planes it traverses. Thus while forms and names multiply upon earth, their manifold impressions are retained and absorbed by the spiritual spheres, as the souls return and pass through them. Semitic tradition has sometimes explained this by teaching that first was the world, and after the world the heavens were created.

When a soul arrives at its full bloom, it begins to show the colour and spread the fragrance of the divine Spirit of God.[14]

The real place where heavens are made is within man. And yet it doesn't add anything to the divine bounty, since it was all there in the beginning, in the seed; as Teilhard de Chardin said, the point Omega toward which we strive is already contained in Alpha. All that is gained is that the fragments of the whole become conscious of the whole and incorporate more and more the perfection of the whole.

The riches that the souls bring from the earth, by knowledge or by anything else, are no addition to God; for God it only means that something which was in the hand has come to the elbow. What difference does it make? It is all the same. Yet it is better that the thing of the hand should be in the hand rather than at the elbow. All that is known on earth and in heaven belongs to God: it already exists and is already in Him, the perfect being.[15]

We may well understand this; yet of all the struggles of the human spirit against overpowering odds, that against death is the most disconcerting and terrifying. For those who entertain an unflinching belief in life after death, this fear is somewhat allayed. It becomes, however, an impelling preoccupation among the aged and sick and those who find themselves suddenly confronted with the cold fact of the death of a dear one or friend, whether unexpected or anticipated. Most people simply avoid thinking about it, until it strikes with its inexorable, irretrievable matter-of-factness; what awes one is the thought that one will not be able ever to see that person again, at least as he or she was, or, when it happens to oneself, that one will not be the same, if at all. One's natural reaction is to question the verdict.

How is possible, that, having wished for the formation of this body, Thou should now wish that it should be tortured, crucified, burnt, scattered to the four winds?   Al Hallaj

The cry of agony of the human mind faced with the inevitability of what does not make sense is the real crucifixion of the soul of God in man. How can the dogmatic answer of the pious be meaningful for those who are eminently aware of the realness of life and existence and matter? The answer that struck Al Hallaj at the moment of truth was, "as an incense, promise of my resurrection." It suddenly became clear to him that one couldn't continue to be if one stayed what one was, so that it is one's disintegration that ensures one's continuity. The flower can continue to live in its perfume, and the very exuding of that perfume is a phenomenon of disintegration. One who knew had said this centuries before:

The one who loses his life will find it, and the one who cleaves to his life will lose it.[16]

The one who seeks life through death becomes immortal.

The Sufi therefore practices that process through which he is able to touch that part of life in himself which is not subject to death. And by finding that part of life he naturally gets the feeling of certitude of life.

Once the soul has begun to feel itself, its own life, independently of its garb (outer) it begins to have confidence in life and is no longer afraid of what is called death.

One can awake from the perspective of physical reality while still living on the planet. One realizes that physical reality is just one condition of reality and not by any means the only condition, and that one continues to exist even though one may be considerably changed. This we experience nightly in our dreams, but, as we have seen, we doubt the reality of our dreams when we return to the diurnal state; but if we could remember how the physical world appeared to us in our sleep, we would realize that it seemed like a dream that had fallen out of perspective. This is precisely what happens in death, and if one is able to retain the continuity of consciousness over the border from the physical world to the dream and vice versa, one will practice dying before death. This is taught by the Sufis as a preparation for death, rather like the *Bardo Thodol* (the *Tibetan Book of the Dead*) and the *Egyptian Book of the Dead* and other similar works. In fact, this is precisely what meditation is.

But what proof do I have that the phantasmagoria of dreams is as real as physical matter? Dreams are elusive and evanescent like cloud formations, whereas the house is still there when I wake up in the morning. Actually you can return to that dream house night after night. No doubt the most convincing answer is to be found in astral travel, because one can check whether the astral traveler saw the furniture in the places you changed it to in order to test him (although one could account for that by telepathy). But the astral traveler has a very definite experience of displacing himself in space, including sometimes a bird's-eye view of the landscape, and certainly exhibits more radical physical functional changes, like the cataleptic state. In rare cases he may perform telekinesis. The fact that one can retain a sense of one's identity, displace oneself at will, maintain unimpaired mental awareness including reasoning power, and enjoy some semblance of an experience of physical reality (albeit altered because viewed from a different vantage point) while being bereft for all intents and purposes of a body, provides man with the most tangible proof about survival. It also provides an indication that one continues to be while being different: one is buoyant, etheric to the point of passing through walls, and reaches a place by the sheer thought of it. Moreover, though physically indestructible, one knows that another death awaits one, setting off the process of transmutation to one octave higher, as it were, into an object which is a substance and yet not a substance.

In Sufi terms this object which is formed and borne out of reflection, this object which is completely like one's own physical body is called Hampta, in other words etheric double. Every one sees this in one's dreams: the thing one sees in one's dream is this object. But a developed soul does not need to dream in order to see it. He can see it in a wakeful state if he wants to.

In short, reflection may be considered as a momentary shadow fallen across the mirror of mind and then, with the moving of the object, removed. But reflection is a phenomenon whereby reality reinstates its inherent structure by proliferating.

If one knew how to hover and displace oneself at will in various spheres, starting with the one adjacent to and coextensive with the physical sphere, one would gain a sense of security that would help one overcome the fear of death. Spiritism abounds with stories of people most surprised to find themselves as alive as ever on the other side of the border, yet so different. Their whole relationship to the environment has changed, and consequently their whole *imago mundi*. However, supposing that you know that you will continue to exist if you immigrate to China, you may still prefer not to; and so, when the sun is shining and the green grass and the trees are waving in a gentle breeze and one is with the people one loves, it seems an ordeal to have to leave it all behind. We know that this is attachment; but such is life, and I am sure that one would prefer to enjoy existence and pay the price of pain for it rather than sequester oneself from it, unless one has undergone a psychological shock or has become oversaturated and blasé. But those who have dared to explore beyond the horizon bear testimony to worlds of splendor, landscapes of beauty beyond anything imaginable on the earth plane, and emotions more sublime than our rapport with the physical world can ever afford.

In comparison with the beauty of that place, the beauty of earthly creatures is *nada* (nothing).   St. John of the Cross

It just depends upon what one values. In the *Bardo Thodol* those who cannot stand the brightness or the absence of variety in the clear light are given the opportunity to experience a lesser light-scene, and if this is too boring for them they may find themselves incarnated among more tantalizing experiences. If they prefer perverse or criminal emotions, they will find themselves incarnated in the appropriate environment. So we do exercise some say in determining our post mortem location and habitat, and our selection of neighbors. Truly the concept of location or sphere is pure illusion, reflecting the conditioning of our thinking in terms of space. It would be truer to speak of a perspective or a focal setting.

The sphere of the dead and of the living is the same. They seem different, for the vehicles, such as body and mind, make them appear so. "In the other world" means in a world which is veiled from our eyes, our physical eyes; but it does not mean a world far away from us beyond our reach. Both the living and the dead inhabit the same space; we all live together. Only a veil separates us, the veil of this physical body. Separation means being unable to see one another; there is no other separation.[17]

Of course, the mureeds had beset Murshid with questions about death, especially when the death of a dear one brought the matter obsessively before their minds. Shall we ever see that being again? Will he be the same?

Is it possible for a person living on the earth to project his thought on those who are on the other side? Does one see, then, all those whom one has known while on the earth? Yes, especially those whom one has loved most, or hated most.

One would so like to know how to find one's friend in the vast universe. What are the lines of force that monitor one to the desired rendezvous? It looks as though the compulsion of an emotion, whether it is love or hate, will initiate the motivating forces that plug in a communicating link between beings, certainly between beings who are drawn by affinity (as Swedenborg affirms) or by dint of their occupation, partnership, or vocation. This communication can be established while one is still on earth, which is what is called spiritism, though one may well reach a being without the intervention of a medium.

What connection has the soul which has passed from the earth with those still on this plane? The connection of the heart still keeps intact, and it remains unbroken as long as the link of sympathy is there.

It is not only the link of love and sympathy, but also the belief in the hereafter to the extent of conviction, that lifts those on earth to know about their beloved ones who have passed over to the other side.

If this is true, it proves that those united in spirit may be thrown far apart in the world and yet be so close together that nothing stands between them. Therefore if those who have departed from this earth have a connection with someone on earth, they are close to him just the same.[18]

The dead feel the thought, the good wish of the living. Prayer and religious rites focus the mind of the living on that of the dead, so that the dead may be helped by the living, or the living may be blessed by a saintly spirit.

The custom of offering food, perfume, or incense, to the dead exists among Hindus and Muslims. If someone comes to see us and we set food before him, or whatever may please him, it is appreciated. It is so with the dead also. They enjoy by our eating, our smelling the perfume, because, although they do not enjoy the actual thing that we put upon the table, yet the impression of our mind, the joy it gives, mirrors itself upon their soul.

The dead person becomes more interested in the things that speak to the mind than in the material satisfactions. Therefore, when the food and drink and perfume are offered, the sacred names, the suras of the Qur'an, are read before them so that their intelligence may be satisfied also.[19]

One may well ask whether any attempt to contact or draw the attention of the departed does not detain them in some way from further progress.

And by making an offering one need not prevent the progress of the spirit upwards, since it is done once in a while as a religious ceremony. In order to avoid constant spirit communication the prophets have given a certain time in the year, a few days, when one could give his thought and time to the dead.

It is a custom among Sufis to consider the tomb (*mazhar*) of a murshid or pir-o-murshid as a shrine *(dargah)*. Pilgrims of all walks of life and denominations, dervishes, sanyasins, kings, and paupers flock there, especially on the day commemorating his death, called the *urs*, to receive his *baraqa*, similar to the Hindu concept of *darshan*, which could be rendered as "receiving a favorable influence through the presence." This signifies the belief either that the remnants of the body still emanate favorable vibrations or that those remnants still provide a focus for the spirit of the departed to function in some way on the planet by inspiring people or revealing something of their present celestial nature to the denizens of the earth. Furthermore, most Sufi saints were buried where they lived, and the atmosphere created by a person remains in the rocks and the earth and the trees, especially if it was a holy man, at the place where he sat meditating. This is why Sufis call Khwaja Muin-ud-Din Chishti, Sultan-i-Hind—because he still rules India spiritually, as part of the spiritual government of the world; therefore, his dargah is referred to as a king's court, whereas the tomb of Aurengzeb, who was a temporal king, is deserted though monumental. The urs is an occasion for great rejoicings: the food *langer* is served to all, rich or poor, after being ritually blessed by prayers and by the qawwals. The musicians extemporize on favorite themes by Sufi poets and the atmosphere becomes pregnant with fervor and ecstasy:

The reason for this is that the atmosphere is made of vibrations, and the life-substance in it is charged with the same rate of vibrations as that of the person who happens to be there. The atmosphere one creates and leaves in a place remains unchanged, although in time it loses its vitality. But it is difficult to believe how long an atmosphere created by someone in a certain place remains vibrating; it stays there much longer than one would think.

Not only does man create an atmosphere, but an atmosphere is also created in man.[20]

Q. Is that the magnetism?
A. Not only the magnetism, but the spirit of the saint is centered in the place where he was buried.

As reflections of one mirror can fall on another mirror so the reflections of one heart can fall on the heart of another. In other words, the one who with his faith and love makes an offering to the dead, his heart is first reflected with the offerings and their joy, and this impression is reflected again on the heart of the dead, for the very reason that it is done with that thought. To have a devotion for the immortal and holy beings who have passed away is allowable because they are more alive than the living and more than the dead.[21]

There are spirits whom we attract by our love for them, by our wish for their presence. We are surrounded in life by our friends, by those whom we like, whom by our liking we attract to us. And we attract the spirits also by our love. These are usually of a higher sort, these whom we call upon for help, for guidance, the murshids and the prophets. Sometimes there are visions of the murshids, the higher beings; these come to the initiate. They come to guide and to help in all difficulties. Someone who is quite absorbed in the thought of a prophet or murshid may be so lost in him, that if he calls upon him in any difficulty, the one upon whom he calls will always come and help him. To have devotion for a murshid or a prophet who has passed on is better than to ask for his help in whatever difficulty we may be, for God Almighty is closest to us and sufficient to help us in all our difficulties. Of course, as in life we depend upon each other's help, so also on the higher plane if the help of some holy spirit is granted to us we may accept it, but only if God's being is realized in all: from whatever source the help comes it is from God.[22]

On a smaller scale, the same principle applies to all people, and therefore Jews and Muslims are averse to cremation; but Murshid, as in all other matters, did not wish to be dogmatic.

Q. I thought you were against cremation?
A. I am against nothing. You must always know that whenever a person says, "Murshid is against this," you must say, "That is a lie. However bad the thing may be, as that everybody is against it, but if they say Murshid is against it, it is a lie, Murshid is against nothing."

He said cremation gives a shock to the soul, depriving it of what focus it might have had upon the earth; however, conceivably it may promote a release. But is not the issue that property which Murshid ascribed to a dried herb of still retaining some life value, albeit at a changed vibrational rate? The soul must follow its course, and eventually the energy is reabsorbed and converted into new energy by the earth. This does not happen with cremation in the same way, although no doubt even the cinders and the smoke carry their vibrations.

Apparently the soul, on its further course after severing from the body, may choose to linger in a kind of limbo condition (either because of its attachments or its vocation, where it is able to ascertain some kind of connection with the earth plane), or else it may divest itself further of its etheric shroud and later each of its other shrouds in order of subtlety, rising higher from plane to plane. This is what is implied in the notion of resurrection. Our prevailing upon the presence of souls may affect the delicate balance that determines their choice.

What is the condition of the soul that experiences the conditions of heaven or hell in the hereafter? The condition of the soul is that it is surrounded by what it has collected. So whatever the soul has treasured in this life, it is that which is the future of the soul. As there are different ideals of different people, so there is a particular world of every person. After the physical body has gone, the non-physical impressions are more distinct because the limitation of the physical body has fallen away.[23]

When a person after death still longs for the earthly joys, he is in a very bad state, because he has not the physical body.[24]

It is as if to be without eyes in a picture gallery and to be in a ballroom without feet. The mystic experiences this journey in life. He does not stay there. He goes there and comes back. But the person in the soul steadily progresses onward, unloading itself of all that it had on earth; or, in other words, by uncovering itself from all the fine and gross garbs that it was clad in. A soul lives in the spirit world while it is busy accomplishing the purpose of its life, which may last for thousands of years.

On its onward journey, the soul passes systematically through the same planes through which it descended, but in the reverse order. According to Murshid, the first plane that the soul encounters after it has divested itself of its etheric and astral doubles, is the jinn plane, then the angelic plane.

If one may say that the soul lives in the spheres of the jinns for thousands of years, for the sake of convenience one may use the expression millions of years in speaking of the time that the soul passes in the heavens of the angels; until at last there comes the moment when the soul is most willing to depart, even from the plane of love, harmony and beauty, in order to embrace the source and goal of life, harmony and beauty which has attracted it through all the planes.

The hereafter is the continuation of the same life in another sphere. There is no more dream after death, because the life itself is in that sphere which we now, in the physical sphere, call dream.

Death is an unveiling, the removal of a cover, after which the soul will know many things in regard to the whole world which had hitherto been hidden. The more one happens to glance into the hereafter, the more one will realize what the hereafter is, what is behind the veil of death. It is the awakening to another sphere, a sphere as real as this one or even more real.

Among the free incentives of which man can avail himself figures a supreme act of will: the ability to steer oneself or rather attune oneself to the level where one wants to be.

Life and death both are not for him conditions to which he is subject, but are conditions which he brings about upon himself. A great Persian Sufi, Bedil, says: "By myself I become captive, and by myself I become free."

The outstanding feature of one's ascent through the planes (which is what is meant by resurrection) is that as one becomes more impersonal one becomes more identified with one's real self.

The soul, drawn by the magnetic power of the divine Spirit, falls into it, with a joy inexpressible in words, as a loving heart lays itself down in the arms of its beloved. The increase of this joy is so great that nothing the soul has ever experienced has made it so unconscious of the self; but this unconsciousness of the self becomes in reality the true self-consciousness. It is then that the soul realizes fully that "I exist."

The law of gravitation is only half known to the world of science, which believes that the earth attracts all that belongs to it. It is true. But the spirit also attracts all that belongs to it, and that other side to the law of gravitation has always been known to the mystics.

Murshid sketches a most realistic picture of conditions in the spirit world: great activities in the offing.

The spirits are delighted to be among spirits, rather than among men walking on earth. Spirits are held by each other in their progress in life in the hereafter. They have their attachment and their detachment, attraction and repulsion, in the same way as among men on earth. The spirits group together, live together, like men on earth, in villages, towns, and cities. They leave their dwelling-place and journey far from home, as men do on earth. There are stories suggesting this idea, of spirits dancing together, playing together; and even there are cases when the spirits have obsessed, of many spirits obsessing one person.

A soul has a choice in its occupation and the opportunity to accomplish its ideal.

Does a soul in the spirit world continue to do the same work which it did during its life on the earth? It does in the beginning; but it is not bound to the same work because it is not subject to the same limitations as it was while on the earth. The soul eventually rises to the standard of its idea; it does that work which was its desire.

There are objects which remain unfulfilled in one's lifetime on earth; they are accomplished on the further journey in the spirit world. For nothing that the human heart has once desired remains unfulfilled.[25]

The difference between this plane and the earthplane is that one projects reality creatively:

One thinks here, but the same action there instead of a thought becomes a deed; for action which here depends upon the physical body there is the act of mind. This is the picture of the spirit world. It is the world of the optimist. The pessimist has no share in this great glory, because he refuses to accept the possibility which is the nature of life. Thus he denies to himself all he desires, and even the possibility of achieving his desires.[26]

Dedicated helpers, which might include departed relatives, await the soul as it emerges from the physical shroud, still endowed with the etheric and astral doubles.

There are experiences of the spirit world where the spirit meets with other spirits, and sometimes he is helped toward his ascent or, sometimes he is induced to descend. Elements attract their like, and so, even in the spirit world, spirits of various kinds are drawn toward their own element.[27]

Of course one is still able to think, feel, and experience, to move about and communicate with other beings, within the limitations imposed by the prevailing laws of the planes involved. For example, exactly as one living in the United States may hesitate about going to China to get something he can more easily get within the States, so there may be forces that maintain one in a given area of the spirit world or within a certain range or vital space. But exactly in the same way, supposing one is in love with a being in China, one might brave the distance even at the cost of the direct hardships, perhaps going through the most incredible detours to locate the desired person; so, if the wish is there, one can (if allowed by the prevailing laws of that plane) always find the person one is seeking.

And exactly as high-altitude flying or deep-sea diving may present a challenge to lungs and blood pressure on the physical plane, so visiting beings in lofty or nether locations may prove prohibitive, maybe risky. Visiting the king or president would require protocol unless one has privileged admission, because the members of the government of the world have to be protected against unproductive intrusion that would be too time consuming. And exactly as some may be granted a group audience, some a formal individual audience at court, and yet others may even be invited to share in the secret knowledge of the king's plans, so everyone's relationship with everyone else is naturally regulated according to cosmic laws, which we denizens of the Earth merely copy in our particular way.

So the souls who have been in the path of illumination through life dwell, in the hereafter, among the illuminated spirits, where they are helped and guided by the advanced spirits towards a higher goal. It is this association of spirits which may be called the White Brotherhood, Masters, Murshids, or Prophets.

CHAPTER 26

The Awakening
of the Soul of Humanity

That which the prophets of the past could not bring about, owing to the difficult conditions in their time, is brought about today as the fulfillment of their prayers offered for thousands of years. — IX,270

The clue to Murshid's whole achievement was, of course, making the ideal a functional reality operating among people, in their interrelationships and their rapport with practical life. So it is not suprising that the main problems manifested themselves in organization.

The work which we are doing just now is of making a building; a building in which to preserve the Message for the time when humanity will be wakened to appreciate it. And what this building is? It is the building which may be called in other words an embodiment of the illuminated souls. It is this building which is our sacred temple.

Within a matter of a few years the basic structure of the monumental edifice of the Message, the Sufi Movement, was built. It was built brick by brick, pillar by pillar, at the cost of unrelenting efforts with the efficiency of an architect—a structure made of human beings, of their goodwill, of their understanding, to serve the Cause. Each integral part of that living structure, each mureed, had to be awakened individually to his purpose in life, to his aspirations and hidden capacities, and to his purpose within the greater Purpose: the service of humanity in the cause of God. Each had to discover the wisdom of the architect in placing the different mureeds in their respective positions in this structure and find his place in his relationship with the others, with whom he may have had a great affinity or a complete absence of affinity, perhaps even antipathy.

Building the human edifice of the Message of human liberty meant that Murshid had to train each in the principles of the architectonics of the whole building, that they might awaken more and more to the

420

ultimate purpose toward which they were working, and appreciate equally the role of the others in this team work. But this could only be done according to the measure of the capacity of each to understand. It was not always easy to see why Murshid chose this form of roof or that form of window, nor to understand the reason for this disposition of the floor or of the foundations. Some aspects of the organization never fit in with the conception of some, nor was the ceremonial of the Universal Worship tolerated by all. But it was Murshid's being and Murshid's love and friendship that helped people to discover his meaning, to understand his intention.

To see the wisdom of the architect, the human components of the edifice had to be lifted to the utmost reaches of their souls. Moreover, they had to learn to love and care for human beings and their development as Murshid did, and to understand his strife with the soul of each mureed to help surmount the problems of this work performed together in the service of God's Message. It meant tuning each to the pitch his soul could stand, respecting his pride, as Murshid said, and helping each to overcome his own self-image. Murshid transformed those seeking after personal liberation into devoted workers for the Cause of God and the service of humanity. It was a gigantic task; the purpose was not the building of an edifice for itself, but the awakening of each part thereof to the highest realization through recognition of the role he had to play in the divine purpose embodied in this edifice.

Such an edifice is of course an organism rather than an organization, but that is what organization is supposed to be.

In his autobiographical notes, the Master left us his testimony.

There has been no end to my difficulties in the organization. Many I found willing to follow the Message, but not to belong to an organization, and I had constantly to answer on that question to every newcomer. It is natural that people who would be attracted to my ideas should not necessarily be attracted to the organization. Besides many organizations have failed and many have brought discredit upon the members, and many organizations are in competition with one another, ignorant of the idea for which the organization stands. It is true that in time the idea becomes lost and the organization remains as a body without a soul. But the consequence is that after seeing dead bodies, many become afraid of the living body, thinking that it also may be an apparition of the dead. I had to answer them that an organization is like a ship which is built for a purpose, to carry the people and things from one port to another. I found that without the organization it was impossible to carry the work through.

Many became interested in the idea, in the Message, most drawn to it, but in absence of organization there was nothing to keep them together, so, disappointed, many dropped away and became scattered. You cannot collect flowers without a basket; so is the organization for the ideal. For me, born with a tendency to be away from all worldly activities and growing every day more apart from all worldly things, to have an organization to make, to control, and to carry out has been a great trial. If it had not been for the Cause, which is worth every sacrifice in life, I would not for one moment have troubled about the organization.

Many who disapprove of an organization, are ready to take the benefit that comes out of it. For them to say, "We do not care for an organization," is like saying, "I like to eat, but I do not think about the kitchen." Many wished to be benefited by the Sufi teachings and my help on the path, but would not be willing to sacrifice for this what they consider their best principle, and that is to join nothing, for they were afraid they would become limited; but they did not know that they limited themselves by their own principle by not being able to join, for they were not free. Even in the search of truth they are not ready to sacrifice their little principle.

My great difficulty has been to find sufficient workers to answer the demand of the Cause. Some good ones seemed to lack the enthusiasm for going forward and standing for the Cause, and some who had the same, wanted tact and the wider point of view, that all-embracing spirit which is the key to all success. Some had not enough confidence in themselves; some did not endure sufficiently the difficulties which come as natural course of the affair; some, owing to their strong likes and dislikes, did not get on very well with their fellow-workers. Some mureeds, whose help I anticipated to further the cause, said, "My people are not yet ready for your Message," which I interpreted as meaning that they themselves were not yet ready to work for the Cause. "Murshid, you yourself are the best propaganda," they said, which did not flatter me; it only showed me that they would rather have me work than trouble themselves.

Some came to me with goodwill and every desire to help, but with their ideas and plan of working. They wanted me immediately to change the whole organization, everything I had made after the work and experience of years. It seemed to me like a person coming and seeing a new building made and offering his service to complete it, but on condition that the whole foundation must first be dug out.

On my part a continual conscientiousness to consider everybody's feeling, and on the part of my co-workers disregard of this principle, made me at times feel so sensitive as if the peeling had come off from my heart.

Some came to me, telling me, "I like your ideas, not the religious form of it." Some said, "I would like an initiation, but no discipline." Some said, "It must be all impersonal, it must not be anything personal." Some said, "The spiritual personality is the only thing that gives me the proof of the truth you have brought, though I care little for the Order." Some said, "Your ideal of brotherhood appeals to me very much, but I cannot believe in any mysticism." Some said, "In mysticism I am quite interested, but I do not care at all for the religious part of it." Some said, "It is the most beautiful thing I've heard, but I wonder if it is Christian?" Some said, "It is an Eastern idea which is foreign to the Western mind." Some said, "It is not unfamiliar to us Western people. We know all religion; what we would like to know is something of the East." Some said, "I can join only if I know that you believe in the doctrine of Karma, and Reincarnation, which has been the basis of my knowledge." Some asked if the learning of wisdom that Sufism teaches would take away their faith in their own religion. Imagine if faith, a thing which belongs to oneself, which no one in the world has power to touch, would be affected by the light of wisdom; and if the light of wisdom ever affected their faith, it would only light it up.

But I took it as a natural course of things and tried not to mind, except when I happened to have a worker whose tendency was to hold the Movement by the neck, who was thankful to have had that chance given to him, and who held the Movement back, by the power of his office, from letting it flourish. It has not happened once, but many times, and has not only showed the tyranny of human nature, but the absurdity of trying to tread a spiritual path and yet feeding that egotism as a thorn in one's soul. I pitied them more than I despaired over my affairs. I found some working in the Movement who extended their social influence among mureeds of value and importance, in order to make an impression upon me, that it was they who were holding the members, and that, if I did not agree with them, they would make all those under their influence disagree with me. The troubles which came to me from friends and helpers were sometimes harder to bear than the difficulties caused by my opponents.

It is the work of the organization that made me realize a side of human nature which I did not expect in the spiritual cause. I was amazed beyond words to find some workers who would either be my friend if I followed their advice, or otherwise they would act as my adversaries. Some workers complained about the difficulties in working, and brought before me as news something which I have always known, the solution of which difficulties could be found in themselves; nothing else would answer. Some workers said, "People say this or that against the Murshid, or workers, or the way it is worked out, or against the teachings." I found that the worker was not yet wakened to find the answer and was affected by what was said to him, and he only wanted a force to strengthen his belief against what had been said. Some critical souls put all that came through their mind as said by someone else, as something told by someone else, and in this way they got relief by giving an outlet to it. My adversaries always took advantage of a mureed's weakness of faith, a worker's feebleness of mind, and tried to do so by showing sympathy with the work or the person, and through sympathy saying, "What a great pity it is so badly done."

Many, not only strangers, but also friends, mureeds and workers, told me that they were afraid that this, our Sufi Movement, might become in time a creed; and some of them did not feel inclined to further the Cause for the same reason. I quite see their point of view, as clearly as they themselves see it, yet I dare say that a creed which holds a Divine Message freshly given, works like the heart which circulates the blood throughout the body, which is the world.

It is the creeds which have lost that magnetism after having finished their period of mission in the world, that live in this world just like dead blood cells in the body. The one who sees it rightly need not compare the heart with the dead blood cells. Besides, it is like telling the Creator God, "Make not a physical body for the soul, which is Divine; this body will be passionate, will make man material, will make him lose his way, will make him forget God, will cause him to shed blood. These bodies will fight and quarrel and create floods of blood in the world, and all sorts of sins these bodies will commit. There is so much disadvantage in creating these bodies." And the Creator would give answer, that, "You see the disadvantages, and I see the advantage beyond them all. You know not who criticize; I know, it is my affair."

There is sometimes a tendency of mureeds, especially of workers, who are capable of interesting themselves more on things of organization, of thinking that Murshid is from the East and therefore unaccustomed of Western way of organization, taking this as a good excuse for discontent. In the administration of the work I had no end of trouble and difficulty, caused by some of my helpers, who for some reason or other worked for the cause without my point of view and my outlook on life.

Then many thought they could tolerate me as a head of an organization, but not anyone else who was different. The lesson that they had to learn was tolerance.

There has always been the financial problem before me to solve. This being something that was neither in the interest of a particular creed, nor bringing success or credit to any nation in particular, but in the interests of the whole humanity, naturally no particular section of humanity took any special interest in the movement, though many admired its object; and therefore it always suffered financially. And now I am so accustomed to this condition that I feel it is natural for it to be so. But nothing in the world would discourage me. If there were not one single coin towards carrying on the work, if there was not one soul standing by my side to assist me in the work, I would still work to my last breath. For my entire strength comes from that source, whose Message it is, which I am destined to give. My only satisfaction, therefore, is in having done my best, and it does not matter under what circumstances.

May the Message of God reach far and wide, illuminating and making the whole humanity as one single Brotherhood in the Fatherhood of God.[1]

However, despite all the hardships, people from all over the globe were flocking to answer the call. The Message was spreading its wings, and the Messenger had outgrown his task. But how many realized the moment, the sheer dimension of what was happening? Such an undertaking calls for a bold front measuring up with its monumental scale; the Murshid was now coming out in the open with a proclamation and a plea.

The Message for which we have been preparing so long, as the workers of the Sufi Movement, is in reality, now being born.

That which the prophets of the past could not bring about, owing to the difficult conditions in their time, is brought about today as the fulfillment of their prayers offered for thousands of years.[2]

The mind balks at the dawning of the realization of the importance, the dimension of what is implied! A call of urgency arises in the soul of the Murshid as he foresees his departure from the planet.

And if they only knew the greatest need of serving the Cause at the moment when it has come as an answer to the cry of humanity, and if they only knew every moment that is being lost, what loss it is, they would feel in the same way as I feel very often, my heart full of anxiety and eagerness for the way that the Movement is progressing and spreading.

And now every day the time of the Message is becoming more precious, and I wish that my mureeds will remember that saying that "Life is an opportunity," and if this opportunity is lost, that which will be accomplished will be accomplished, but that privilege is lost.

The more you will think, the more you will see the importance of the humble little work we are doing. However small our number, still the Power behind is great, and trusting in that mighty Power, we are working.

The Murshid has strained his body to its limits in the service of the spiritual government of the world; it is now your turn.

Have I not gone where people have called me, whether appreciative or not, poor or rich, to spread the Message when there was no trace of our Sufi Movement, no organization, no friends except God? Even this feeling can create in your heart sympathy for your Murshid. And now the time has come that your devotion can best be expressed in serving the Cause.

Imagine, there is one Murshid and a Message to be given to the whole world, how may places will he go to, one person limited in a physical body? Do you, then, not make it easy for a person to say, "Well, I do not think that I have a gift for speaking, I cannot help it." All comes with belief. When you have the belief that you can speak you can speak.

Our hearts, which have become connected in the link of initiation in the Sufi Order, are as one heart, which may become His shrine, and the need of the living God in the world to-day may be answered.

Some asked: Why should the Message have been fostered by Sufism rather than any other group? Because it has traditionally been the cross-roads of esoteric orders, and we are living in the age of unity, of convergence of ideals and ideas.

Yet the Message far exceeds the bounds of traditional Sufism.

Yes, it happens that the Message born of this School is destined to reach far and wide. That gives us a different task of spreading the Message, which stands apart from the Sufi Order, which is an Esoteric School.

The Sufi Order is an embodiment, a body which is being composed to deliver that Message which is the Message of God. Therefore my mureeds are the particles of that body, the organs of that body; and the more they will realize that, the more they will know their responsibility.

I am neither Christian, nor Jew, nor Gaer, nor Moslem.
I am not of the East, nor of the West, nor of the Land, nor of the Sea,
I am not of nature's mint, nor of the circling heavens.
I am not of earth, nor of water, nor of air, nor of fire.
I am not of the empyrean, nor of the dust, nor of existence, nor of entity.
I am not of India, nor of China, nor of Bulgaria, nor of Saqsin.
I am not of this world nor of the next, nor of paradise nor of hell.
I am not of Adam, nor of Eve, nor of Eden and Rizwan.
My place is the placeless, my trace is the traceless; 'Tis neither body nor soul,
for I belong to the soul of the Beloved.
I have put duality away, I have seen that the two worlds are one.
One I seek, One I know, One I see, One I call.
He is the first, He is the last, He is the outward, He is the inward;
I know none other except 'Ya Hu' and 'Ya Man Hu.'[3]

A dedicated being cannot possibly sit back and receive all the bounty of this wisdom without wishing to share it.

A person who, alone, has seen something beautiful, who has heard something harmonious, who has tasted something delicious, who has smelt something fragrant, may have enjoyed it, but not completely. The complete joy is in sharing one's joy with others.

I wish that my Mureeds, those who feel in their heart this trust, shall not only receive the Sacred Message for their own unfoldment, but shall feel the privilege of being a nucleus for the reconstruction in the coming spiritual world.

As Jesus sent his disciples afield to heal the sick, Murshid beckons his mureeds to become the heralds of the Message.

No doubt it is true that the Message of God must reach all people, must reach all parts of the world, but human efforts are necessary as our part. It is necessary that some people will come out from the mureeds who will be able to take up the work in other lands, in other parts of the world, where the Message has not yet spread.

Some will have to go before the Message, and try to awaken interest and prepare the ground. And others will go in places where the Movement has started, to blow the fire and keep it going.

But when mureeds tried to pin down the Message in order to be able to convey it more definitely, they found no way by which to define it.

The sun does not teach anything, but in its light we learn to know all things. The sun does not cultivate the soil nor does it sow seed, but it helps the plants to grow, to flower, and to bear fruit.

The Message is something that grows in the consciousness of some, not something that can be taught.

It takes time for a person to grow into a thing and break the barriers of limitation; it takes time to rise above certain walls that he has built in life before him, before he can see the truth of the Message and before he can understand and be sure of its mission.

It is something which must come from themselves, a realization which must spring from their own heart, that the soul may become convinced from itself and from within, without outer teaching.

The reason is that it is an awakening, seeing from the cosmic vantage point the advancement of realization in mankind and the outlook given by the guidance that promotes this evolution. It is thinking and feeling at a cosmic scale—a further dimenstion of thinking and feeling.

The vastness of the Message is the vastness of divine understanding.
The Message of spiritual liberty is an affirmation of the freedom of God.

In the past, people knew only of a prophet or prophets who appeared in their part of the world, and it was his example that spurred them to improve themselves; now, owing to our highly technological communications network, most people are aware of the most varied teachers. But it is the reality of the impact of the teaching in people's everyday life that commands attention.

Think of the Message more than of your Murshid.
The first and greatest help mureeds can give is to make themselves the example for the Message.

People in the new age have become more real than ever before; the Message is a living reality in everyday life. It is making God a reality. What is the Message?

The Message is the awakening of humanity to the divinity of man.
Keep burning the fire I have lighted; it may seem very small to you, but one tiny flame, if kept burning, can be the means of illuminating a whole city, and some day the many lamps that shall be lighted at this small fire, will give light to thousands.
This fire of truth is now lighted, and its light will never go out; your work is to tend it, and keep it burning. The fuel needed is your every thought, your

faith, your prayers and sacrifices; you cannot see the result of this. Light can never be lost, I have kindled this small fire from which millions of lamps can be lit. Their number cannot be reckoned, and millions upon millions of other fires can now be lighted; when all have been kindled, the original fire will die out, and the place thereof be known no more. Verily the form dieth, and the spirit liveth for ever.

APPENDIX

Hazrat Inayat Khan on the New Era

The races in the coming era will mix more and more every day, developing finally into a world-wide race. The nations will develop a democratic spirit, and will overthrow every element which embitters them against one another. There will be alliances of nations until there is a world alliance of nations, so that no nation may be oppressed by another, but all will work in harmony and freedom for common peace.

Science will probe the secrets of the life unseen, and art will follow nature closely. The people of all classes will be seen everywhere. The caste system will vanish and communities will lose their exclusiveness, all mingling together, and their followers will be tolerant towards one another. The followers of one religion will be able to pray by offering the prayers of another, until the essential truth will become the religion of the whole world and diversity of religions will be no more.

Education will culminate in the study of human life, and learning will develop on that basis. Trade will become more universal, and will be arranged on the basis of a common profit. Labour will stand side by side with capital on an equal footing.

Titles will have little importance. Signs of honour will become conspicuous. Bigotry in faiths and beliefs will become obsolete. Ritual and ceremony will be a play. Women will become freer every day in all aspects of life, and married women will be called by their own names.

No work will be considered menial. No position in life will be humiliating. Everybody will mind his own business, and all will converse with one another without demanding introductions. The husband and wife will be like companions, independent and detached. The children will follow their own bent. Servant and master will be so only during working hours, and the feeling of superiority and inferiority among people will vanish.

Medicine will take away the need for surgery, and healing will take the place of medicine.

New ways of life will manifest themselves, hotel life predominating over home life. Grudges against relatives, complaints about servants, finding fault with neighbours will all cease to occur, and the world will continue to improve in all aspects of life until the day of *Gayamat*, when all vain talk will cease, and when everywhere will be heard the cry, 'Peace, peace, peace!'

Notes

Many of the quotations in this book are from unpublished writings of Hazrat Inayat Khan. These have not been referenced, as the reader would have no access to the material. Most of the notes in this book refer to the thirteen volumes of published material from Hazrat Inayat Khan, which are listed below. All references are to the volume number (in Roman numerals) and the page (in Arabic numerals):

Volume I: The Way of Illumination; The Inner Life; The Soul, Whence and Whither?; The Purpose of Life (London, 1960).

Volume II: The Mysticism of Sound; Music; The Power of the Word; Cosmic Language (London, 1962).

Volume III: Education; Rasa Shastra; Character-Building and the Art of Personality; Moral Culture (London, 1960).

Volume IV: Health; Mental Purification; The Mind World (London, 1961).

Volume V: A Sufi Message of Spiritual Liberty; Aqibat, Life After Death; The Phenomenon of the Soul; Love, Human and Divine; Pearls from the Ocean Unseen; Metaphysics (London, 1962).

Volume VI: *The Alchemy of Happiness* (London, 1962).

Volume VII: *In an Eastern Rose Garden* (London, 1962).

Volume VIII: *Sufi Teachings* (London, 1962).

Volume IX: *The Unity of Religious Ideals* (London, 1963).

Volume X: Sufi Mysticism; The Path of Initiation and Discipleship; Sufi Poetry; Art: Yesterday, Today and Tomorrow; The Problem of the Day (London, 1964).

Volume XI: Philosophy; Psychology; Mysticism; Aphorisms (London, 1964).

Volume XII: The Vision of God and Man; Confessions; Four Plays (London, 1967).

Gayan; Vadan; Nirtan (London, 1960).

Chapter 1

1. XI, 237.
2. IV, 133.
3. IX, 132.
4. IX, 134.
5. A Disciple [Murshida Saintsburg-Green], *Memories of Hazrat Inayat Khan* (London, n.d. [c.1930]), pp. 61–64.
6. IX, 134.
7. IX, 133.
8. [Saintsburg-Green], *Memories* 42–44.
9. IX, 133.
10. IX, 233 (from the *Bhagavad Gita*).
11. IX, 120.
12. VI, 186.
13. I, 34.
14. IX, 198–199.
15. I, 33.
16. VIII, 34.
17. IX, 128.
18. IX, 134.
19. IX, 130.
20. IX, 137.
21. IX, 145.
22. XI, 254.
23. IX, 146.
24. IX, 134.
25. IX, 150.
26. IX, 137.
27. *Gayan*, 101.
28. IX, 235.
29. I, 31.
30. IX, 241.
31. IX, 238.
32. I, 32.
33. XI, 166.
34. IX, 243.
35. I, 127.

Chapter 2

1. For the story of Haris Chandra, see p. 283.
2. XII, 107 (reordered).
3. XII, 113.
4. X, 94.
5. VIII, 75.
6. XII, 108–9.
7. XII, 116.
8. I, 100.
9. I, 101.
10. XII, 106–107.
11. XII, 115.
12. X, 124.
13. XII, 114.
14. Hafiz, X, 124.
15. XII, 114 (reordered).

Chapter 3

1. *Gayan*, 169.
2. X, 228.
3. XII, 136.
4. X, 223.
5. X, 256.
6. X, 227.
7. X, 225.
8. X, 229.
9. X, 223–224.
10. II, 53.
11. II, 111 (altered).
12. II, 110–111.
13. II, 92.
14. II, 52–53.
15. X, 230.
16. X, 229.
17. X, 256.
18. X, 230.
19. II, 105.
20. II, 91.
21. II, 103.
22. II, 53–54.
23. II, 103.

24. II, 104.
25. X, 223.
26. II, 111.
27. II, 57.
28. II, 115.
29. II, 117–118.
30. II, 75.
31. II, 78–79.
32. II, 50.
33. II, 73.
34. II, 79.
35. II, 50.
36. XI, 25.
37. II, 73.
38. II, 74.
39. II, 59.
40. II, 75.

Chapter 4

1. X, 93.
2. See XII, 147–8
3. X, 80–81.
4. X, 84.
5. X, 82.
6. X, 61.
7. *Minqar-i-Musiqar*

Chapter 5

1. VIII, 51.
2. VIII, 45.
3. IV, 221.
4. VIII, 50.
5. VII, 63.
6. VIII, 45–6.
7. VII, 62.
8. III, 198–199.
9. XII, 91.
10. VII, 127.
11. VIII, 47.
12. VII, 62.
13. IV, 151.
14. IV, 219.
15. VI, 99.
16. XI, 93.
17. VI, 101.

18. XI, 127.
19. VI, 99.
20. X, 112.
21. IV, 183.
22. IV, 183–184.
23. *Gayan*, 97.
24. VI, 21.
25. XII, 109.
26. VII, 159.
27. VI, 98.
28. VI, 98.
29. I, 105.
30. IV, 120.
31. I, 203.
32. VI, 21.
33. IV, 120.
34. XI, 83.
35. VI, 196.
36. IV, 121.
37. VII, 139.
38. IV, 182.

Chapter 6

1. IV, 222.
2. VI, 127.
3. IX, 28.
4. VIII, 220.
5. IV, 129.
6. XI, 164.
7. XI, 164.
8. IV, 265.
9. IV, 223.
10. VII, 84–85.
11. VII, 84.
12. XI, 205.
13. IV, 127–128.
14. IV, 217.
15. VII, 235–236.
16. IV, 125.
17. VIII, 132.
18. VII, 150.
19. XII, 62–63.
20. X, 175.
21. VI, 134.
22. IV, 215.

23. VIII, 41.
24. VI, 188.
25. X, 174.
26. XI, 24.
27. XI, 253.
28. I, 129.
29. VII, 224.
30. IV, 137.
31. IV, 106.
32. II, 194.
33. I, 139.
34. IV, 228.
35. VII, 86.
36. IV, 224.
37. IV, 222–223.
38. VII, 82–83.
39. II, 20–21.
40. XI, 212.
41. XI, 213.

Chapter 7

1. V, 126.
2. V, 128.
3. V, 123.
4. V, 125.
5. Buddha.
6. I, 67.
7. V, 108.
8. XI, 176.
9. III, 119.
10. I, 197.
11. VIII, 151.
12. X, 89.
13. I, 129.
14. I, 65.
15. I, 66.
16. I, 66.
17. I, 65.
18. VI, 163.
19. VI, 162.
20. III, 221.
21. VIII, 292.
22. I, 67.
23. VI, 87.
24. I, 87.

25. I, 97.
26. X, 136.
27. X, 17.
28. I, 79.
29. X, 32.
30. X, 14.
31. XI, 216.

Chapter 8

1. XII, 141.
2. XII, 141.
3. XII, 142.
4. II, 59.
5. II, 59–60.
6. IV, 116.
7. XI, 250.
8. IV, 116.
9. IV, 116.
10. IV, 116–117.
11. V, 148.
12. IV, 118.
13. X, 121.
14. IV, 114–115.
15. VIII, 230.
16. X, 124–125.
17. VI, 136.
18. VI, 133.
19. VI, 140–141.
20. VI, 139.
21. X, 124.
22. VI, 141–142.
23. X, 153.
24. X, 125.
25. XII, 114.
26. X, 29.
27. X, 124.
28. VIII, 328.
29. X, 123.
30. VI, 143.
31. The author, under inspiration.

Chapter 9

1. *Gayan*, 246–247.
2. VIII, 318–319.

3. VIII, 303.
4. VIII, 317.
5. XI, 18–19.
6. XI, 237.
7. IV, 187.
8. I, 78.
9. IV, 125–126.
10. VIII, 309.
11. Mevlana
    Jelal-ud-Din
    Rumi.
12. IX, 111.
13. IX, 96.
14. IX, 97.
15. I 88–90.
16. I, 99.
17. I, 90.
18. XI, 156.
19. I, 90.
20. XI, 156.
21. I, 89.
22. XI, 155.

Chapter 10

1. *Gayan,* 164.
2. *Gayan,* 166.
3. IV, 202.
4. XI, 39.
5. IV, 229.
6. IV, 211.
7. IV, 210–211.
8. IV, 212.
9. IV, 212–213.
10. IV, 210.
11. IV, 198.
12. I, 142.

Chapter 11

1. II, 221.
2. V, 88.
3. I, 162.
4. I, 163.
5. V, 17.
6. II, 13.
7. II, 62–63.

8. XI, 58.
9. II, 14.
10. II, 58.
11. II, 80.
12. II, 7 (Preface).
13. II, 14.
14. II, 18.
15. II, 13.
16. II, 17.
17. XI, 22.
18. XI, 25.
19. II, 18.
20. XI, 25.
21. XI, 31.

Chapter 12

1. XI, 55.
2. VI, 130.
3. IV, 149.
4. IV, 218.
5. I, 111.
6. XI, 240.
7. I, 181.
8. I, 122.
9. XI, 54.
10. IV, 182.
11. XI, 55.
12. XI, 55.
13. IV, 218.
14. IV, 216.
15. XI, 55.
16. XI, 15.
17. XI, 36.
18. I, 153.
19. XI, 36.
20. XI, 37.
21. IV, 218.
22. IV, 215.

Chapter 13

1. V, 100.
2. V, 104.
3. I, 129.
4. I, 122.
5. I, 119.

6. I, 120.
7. I, 122.
8. V, 100.
9. V, 102.
10. I, 119.
11. *Matthew* 26:53.
12. V, 103.
13. V, 102.
14. I, 182.
15. V, 101.
16. I, 117.
17. I, 117.
18. I, 115.
19. I, 116.
20. I, 137.
21. I, 179.
22. V, 109.
23. V, 116.
24. I, 180.

Chapter 14

1. I, 111.
2. I, 98.
3. V, 91–92.
4. XI, 154.
5. V, 83.
6. I, 172.
7. I, 122.
8. V, 83.
9. V, 119.
10. V, 236–237.
11. XI, 116.
12. V, 114.
13. XI, 116.
14. XI, 117.
15. I, 125.
16. I, 126.
17. I, 98.
18. I, 125.
19. I, 127.
20. I, 129.
21. I, 127.
22. I, 146.
23. I, 173.
24. VIII, 330.

Chapter 15

1. V, 63–65.
2. V, 75.
3. V, 78.
4. I, 174.
5. V, 107.
6. V, 70.
7. V, 76.
8. V, 75.
9. V, 74–75.
10. IV, 284.

Chapter 16

1. VIII, 130.
2. XI, 257.
3. *Gayan*, 144.
4. *Gayan*, 28.
5. X, 51.
6. X, 81.
7. *Gayan*, 101.
8. I, 161.
9. VII, 170.
10. VII, 47.
11. I, 214.
12. VIII 139.
13. VII, 46.
14. VIII 137.
15. VIII 82 (reordered).
16. VIII 80.
17. VII 82.
18. VII 82.
19. *Gayn*, 250.
20. VII 168.

Chapter 17

1. XII 191–192.
2. XII 214.
3. XII 259.
4. XII 260.
5. *Gayn*, 197.
6. VII 75.
7. VII 74.
8. III, 257.
9. VI 146.
10. VII, 78.

11. VIII, 78.
12. VIII, 75.
13. XI, 101.
14. XII, 77.
15. XII, 78.
16. VIII, 76.
17. VIII, 77.
18. XII, 230.

Chapter 18

1. XII, 80.
2. IV, 120.
3. XI, 227.
4. I, 80.
5. XI, 200.
6. XI, 69.
7. *Gayan*, 164.
8. VIII, 302.
9. XI, 164.
10. XI, 42.
11. XI, 41.
12. XI, 59.
13. XI, 42.
14. X, 145.
15. VI, 16.
16. VI, 42.
17. VI, 16.
18. X, 195.
19. XI, 237.
20. VI, 117.
21. *Gayan*, 20.
22. *Gayan*, 175.
23. XI, 199.
24. *Gayan*, 34.
25. VI, 195.
26. VIII, 246.
27. *Gayan*, 137.
28. XI, 250.
29. XI, 245.

Chapter 19

1. Ruth St. Denis, *An Unfinished Life* (New York: Harper & Brothers, 1939), p. 139.

2. Rabindranath Tagore, *Gitanjali* (London: The Macmillan Company, 1949), p. 144.
3. *Gitanjali*, p. 44.
4. Kahlil Gibran, *The Prophet* (New York: Alfred A. Knopf, 1923), p. 10.
5. Gabriele d'Annunzio, *Notturno*, 1916. Quoted in Elisabeth de Jong-Keesing, *Inayat Khan* (The Hague: East-West Publications, 1974), pp. 117–18 (paragraphing altered here).
6. Sirkar van Stolk and Daphne Dunlop, *Memories of a Sufi Sage* (The Hague: East-West Publications, 1975), pp. 65, 66.
7. van Stolk and Dunlop, p. 67.

Chapter 20

1. VIII, 235.
2. *Gayan*, 5.
3. VI, 44.
4. III, 214.
5. III, 214.
6. XI, 134.
7. VIII, 234.
8. IV, 276.
9. III, 212.
10. *Gayan*, 98.

Chapter 21

1. VIII, 200.
2. III, 222.

3. III, 226.
4. VIII, 237.
5. XI, 207.
6. I, 66.
7. III, 234.
8. III, 246.
9. III, 245.
10. III, 246.
11. III, 248.
12. III, 244.
13. VIII, 325.
14. *Gayan*, 57
15. VIII, 106.
16. I, 75.
17. *Gayan*, 139
18. VIII, 109.
19. III, 226.
20. XI, 239.
21. VIII, 200.
22. III, 202.
23. *Gayan*, 38.
24. III, 219.
25. III, 204.
26. III, 219.
27. III, 248.
28. III, 239.
29. VII, 258.
30. III, 234.
31. III, 243.
32. III, 238.
33. III, 239.
34. III, 206.
35. *Gayan*, 137.

Chapter 22

1. X, 66.
2. X, 73.

Chapter 23

1. *Gayan*, 119.
2. *Gayan*, 186.

Chapter 24

1. *Gayan*, 250.
2. IX, 41.

3. XI, 248.
4. XI, 248.
5. I, 189.
6. *Gayan*, 244.
7. XI, 229.
8. *Gayan*, 34.
9. *Gayan*, 38.
10. *Gayan*, 187.
11. XI, 230.
12. IV, 150.
13. I, 58.

Chapter 25

1. *Gayan*, 248–249.
2. *Gayan*, 118.
3. *Gayan*, 71.
4. *Gayan*, 72.
5. Kismet Dorothea Stam, *Rays* (The Hague, n.d.), p. 137; see also *Gayan*, 243.
6. I, 166.
7. V, 105.
8. I, 167.
9. V, 42.
10. VI, 20.
11. V, 43.
12. VIII, 297.
13. XI, 17.
14. XI, 233.
15. V, 126.
16. See Matthew 10:39.
17. X, 39.
18. VIII, 176.
19. V, 69.
20. XI, 34.
21. V, 70.
22. V, 71.
23. IV, 270.
24. V, 68.
25. V, 106.
26. I, 178.
27. I, 173.

Chapter 26

1. *Gayan*, 77.
2. IX, 270.
3. Jelal-ud-Din Rumi, *Mathnavi*.

Index